Straight Choices

Should I have this medical treatment or that one?
Is this computer a better buy than that one?
Should I invest in shares or keep my money under the bed?

We all face a perplexing array of decisions every day. Thoroughly revised and updated throughout, the new edition of *Straight Choices* provides an integrative account of the psychology of decision making, and shows how psychological research can help us understand our uncertain world.

Straight Choices emphasizes the relationship between learning and decision making, arguing that the best way to understand how and why decisions are made is in the context of the learning and knowledge acquisition which precedes them, and the feedback which follows. The mechanisms of learning and the structure of environments in which decisions are made are carefully examined to explore their impact on our choices. The authors then consider whether we are all constrained to fall prey to cognitive biases, or whether, with sufficient exposure, we can find optimal decision strategies and improve our decision making.

Featuring three completely new chapters, this edition also contains student-friendly overviews and recommended readings in each chapter. It will be of interest to students and researchers in cognitive psychology, behavioural economics and the decision sciences, as well as anyone interested in the nature of decision making.

Ben R. Newell is a Professor of Cognitive Psychology and an Australian Research Council Future Fellow in the School of Psychology at the University of New South Wales, Australia.

David A. Lagnado is Senior Lecturer in Cognitive and Decision Sciences in the Division of Psychology and Language Sciences at University College London, UK.

David R. Shanks is Head of the Division of Psychology and Language Sciences and Professor of Psychology at University College London, UK.

Straight Choices

The Psychology of Decision Making

Second Edition

Ben R. Newell, David A. Lagnado and David R. Shanks

Psychology Press
Taylor & Francis Group
LONDON AND NEW YORK

Second edition published 2015
by Psychology Press
27 Church Road, Hove, East Sussex BN3 2FA

and by Psychology Press
711 Third Avenue, New York, NY 10017

Psychology Press is an imprint of the Taylor & Francis Group, an informa business

First edition published by Psychology Press 2007

British Library Cataloguing in Publication Data
A catalogue record for this book is available from the British Library

Library of Congress Cataloging in Publication Data
Newell, Benjamin R., 1972–
 Straight choices : the psychology of decision making / Ben Newell,
 David Lagnado and David Shanks. — Second edition.
 pages cm
 Includes bibliographical references and index.
 1. Decision making. 2. Learning, Psychology of. I. Lagnado, David A.,
 1962– II. Shanks, David R. III. Title.
 BF448.N49 2015
 153.8′3—dc23
 2014043534

ISBN: 978-1-84872-282-8 (hbk)
ISBN: 978-1-84872-283-5 (pbk)
ISBN: 978-1-315-72708-0 (ebk)

Typeset in Bembo
by Florence Production Ltd, Stoodleigh, Devon, UK

Printed and bound by CPI Group (UK) Ltd, Croydon, CR0 4YY

Dedicated to:
Sandra, Zoila, Isabella and James
Tracy Ray
and
Ella, Will and Miranda

Contents

Preface to the second edition

In *Straight Choices* we present a scholarly yet accessible introduction to the psychology of decision making, enhanced by discussion of relevant examples of decision problems faced in everyday life. We provide an integrative account in which clear connections are made between empirical results and how these results can help us understand our uncertain world. An innovative feature of *Straight Choices* is the emphasis on an exploration of the relationship between learning and decision making. Our thesis is that the best way to understand how and why decisions are made is in the context of the learning that precedes them and the feedback that follows them. Decisions don't emerge out of thin air but rather are informed by our prior experience, and each decision yields some information (did it work out well or badly?) that we can add to our stock of experience for future benefit. This novel approach allows us to integrate findings from the decision and learning literatures to provide a unique perspective on the psychology of decision making.

In the eight years since we wrote the first edition of *Straight Choices* a lot has happened in the field of judgment and decision making. In this new edition we have tried to include a flavour of these new developments and have added three new chapters: one on *decisions from experience*, one on the *two-systems* approach, and a final chapter that ties together key findings from the book and presents a summary of our perspective. In addition to these new chapters, all the chapters have been updated with new sections and new references reflecting the advances in understanding. The book is divided into eighteen easily digestible chapters and the material is presented in as non-technical a manner as possible. Each chapter begins with a 'highlights' section and concludes with some suggestions for further reading. The book is highly appropriate and accessible for any students with an interest in decision making – be they students of psychology, economics, marketing or business. The book should also appeal to more senior scholars of decision making, or indeed any cognitive psychologists who are seeking an up-to-date review of current research and are interested in the novel learning-based perspective which we provide.

Throughout the book we have also tried to emphasize the practical applications of much of the research on decision making. We hope that by reading this book you will gain a greater understanding of the psychology of how – and how well – we make decisions and that you will apply that understanding to improve your own decision making.

Acknowledgements

It is, of course, impossible to acknowledge all the people who have influenced our thinking about the issues discussed in this book, so we will not attempt to name them for fear of missing some.

Very special thanks are due, however, to Peter Ayton and John Maule who provided insightful and very helpful criticism of a draft of the first edition and to Ken Manktelow and Linden Ball who provided very useful feedback on the proposal for this second edition. We would also like to thank the editorial team at Psychology Press for their excellent assistance throughout the publication process.

Ben Newell would like to thank his co-authors for agreeing to 'get the band back together' and write this new edition. As with the first edition it has been very educational and a pleasure to have shared the experience with two such wonderful colleagues. Thanks are also due to members of the lab over the last 8 years for many stimulating discussions. The continuing support of the Australian Research Council is gratefully acknowledged.

David Lagnado would like to acknowledge the support of the Leverhulme Trust/ESRC Research Programme 'Evidence, Inference and Enquiry', and in particular Nigel Harvey and Philip Dawid for their excellent guidance of this interdisciplinary project. Special thanks also to Aimable Jonckheere for many thought-provoking discussions, and to Fenna Poletiek for helpful comments.

David Shanks would like to thank the UK Economic and Social Research Council, who for several years have provided funding for his research, and members of his research group and in particular Maarten Speekenbrink for many enlightening discussions about aspects of decision making and learning.

Ben Newell, David Lagnado, and David Shanks,
Sydney and London, September 2014.

1 Falling off the straight and narrow

Chapter highlights

- An overview of the book
- Insights into decisions about health, wealth, and guilt versus innocence.

The cult film *Donnie Darko* begins with the hero Donnie narrowly surviving (or does he?) a bizarre accident. Donnie is lying in bed in his suburban family home when he is woken by a strange voice. The voice 'leads' him down the stairs, out of the house and into the street. Moments later a horrendous screeching noise signals the arrival of an aeroplane's jet engine crashing through the roof of the house. The engine completely destroys Donnie's bedroom.

Most of us would agree that being killed by a falling jet engine is an extremely unlikely, freak occurrence. Indeed, if we were asked the question, which is more likely: being killed by falling aeroplane parts or being killed by a shark? – the majority of us would probably think a shark attack more likely (Plous, 1993). But we would be wrong. According to *Newsweek* ('Death Odds', 1990), we are 30 times more likely to be killed by falling aeroplane parts than by sharks. The reason (or reasons) why we tend to err in answering this question is just one of the many intriguing, challenging and fundamentally important issues that are addressed in this book. Understanding the psychology of how – and how well – we make decisions can have a significant impact on how we live our lives (and how to avoid freak deaths).

Even for a decision as simple as buying a book (a decision that you may well be contemplating right now) we can engage in a series of quite complex thought processes: noting the attributes of different alternatives (cost, appearance, recommendations), comparing different alternatives by making 'trade-offs' on these attributes (e.g. this one is cheaper but it wasn't recommended), and deciding how to allocate our limited resources (e.g. money for books or beer). These processes, and many more besides, can be investigated in systematic ways to discover what leads us to make the decisions we do, how we should make decisions given the preferences we have, and why our decision making sometimes goes awry.

OUR APPROACH AND THE PLAN OF THIS BOOK

In this book we provide a novel perspective on judgment and decision making along with an accessible review and integration of many of the key research findings. Our perspective is novel in that we view judgment and decision making as often exquisitely subtle and well tuned to the world, especially in situations where we have the opportunity to respond repeatedly under similar conditions where we can learn from feedback. We argue that many of the well-documented errors or biases of judgment often occur in one-shot decision situations where we do not have the chance to learn adequately about the environment. Focusing on errors in these one-shot situations can be a very fruitful research strategy, as the 'heuristics and biases' approach which has dominated the field has demonstrated (Kahneman, Slovic & Tversky, 1982). However, the downside of this approach is that it can lead to an overly pessimistic view of human judgment and decision making (Gigerenzer, 1996). Our perspective aims to reclaim the original reason for emphasizing errors, namely that errors can be thought of as quirks akin to visual illusions. Like visual illusions, they arise in a system which is in general extremely accurate in its functioning.

Take the sharks versus falling aeroplane parts example. In a one-shot decision about the likelihood of death, we might choose sharks erroneously. One explanation for such a choice is that we base our decision on the ease with which we can recall instances of people being killed by sharks or by falling aeroplane parts. Shark attacks are likely to be easier to recall – presumably because they receive wider coverage in the media – and so we answer 'sharks'. In general, using the ease-of-recall or 'availability' heuristic will serve us well, but in certain situations, particularly when we are insensitive to the distribution of information in the environment (i.e. insensitive to the fact that shark attacks receive more media coverage than falling aeroplane parts), we make errors (cf. Tversky & Kahneman, 1974). One of the key messages of our approach is that being given the opportunity to learn about information in the environment through repetition and feedback often gives rise to exceptionally accurate judgments and decisions.

This message is pursued most directly in Chapters 7 'Associative thinking', 10 'Decisions from experience', 12 'Learning to choose, choosing to learn' and 13 'Optimality and expertise', although the theme of learning runs throughout the book. Some readers might find these chapters a little more challenging than the others, but we encourage you to persevere. Chapters 1 and 2 introduce many of the concepts that will be relevant to our exploration of judgment and decision making, through considering some practical decisions (e.g. Which medical treatment should I choose?) and by giving a brief historical overview of the field. Chapters 3 and 4 take us on a journey through the stages of judgment from the discovery of information to the role of feedback. Chapter 5 presents some formal ways of appraising our probability judgments and then in Chapter 6 we look at how people actually make judgments. In a similar fashion, Chapter 8 presents formal methods for analysing decisions and then Chapter 9 examines how people actually make decisions and choices under uncertainty. Chapter 11 extends this analysis to examine the influence of time on decisions.

Chapter 14 assesses the popular idea that there are two 'systems' for decision making, a deliberative one and an intuitive one, that operate in rather different ways. The next three chapters provide some insights into the role that emotion plays on our decisions (Chapter 15), the way groups make decisions (Chapter 16) and an investigation of some of the more practical methods for implementing what we have learned about decision making in the laboratory to the world outside (Chapter 17). Chapter 18 revisits the key questions about when, why and how to make good decisions in light of the major findings and theories discussed in the preceding chapters. The book can be read as a whole – cover to cover – or if you have particular interests, then the chapters are, for the most part, self-contained enough to enable you to dip in and choose the parts that appeal. Our aims are twofold: to introduce you to this exciting field, and to help you improve your own decision-making skills.

DECISIONS, DECISIONS . . .

We are faced by a plethora of decisions, choices and judgments every day and throughout our lives: what to have for lunch, where to go on holiday, what car to buy, whom to hire for a new faculty position, whom to marry, and so on. Such examples illustrate the abundance of decisions in our lives and thus the importance of understanding the how and why of decision making. Some of these decisions will have little impact on our lives (e.g. what to have for lunch); others will have long-lasting effects (e.g. whom to marry). To introduce many of the relevant concepts, in this first chapter we consider three important decisions that we might face in the course of our lives: (1) which medical treatment should I choose, (2) is this person guilty or innocent, and (3) how should I invest my money? For each situation we examine some of the factors that can influence the decisions we make. We cover quite a bit of ground in these three examples so don't worry if the amount of information is rather overwhelming. The aim here is simply to give a taste of the breadth of issues that can affect our decision making. There will be ample opportunity in later chapters to explore many of these issues in more depth.

Which medical treatment should I choose?

Martin and Simon have just received some devastating news: they have both been diagnosed with lung cancer. Fortunately their cancers are still at relatively early stages and should respond to treatment. Martin goes to see his doctor and is given the following information about two alternative therapies – radiation and surgery:

radiation { Of 100 people having surgery, on average, 10 will die during treatment, 32 will have died by one year and 66 will have died by five years. Of 100 people having radiation therapy, on average, none will die during treatment, 23 will die by one year and 78 will die by five years.

Simon goes to see his doctor, who is different from Martin's, and is told the following about the same two therapies:

surgery { Of 100 people having surgery, on average, 90 will survive the treatment, 68 will survive for one year and 34 will survive for five years. Of 100 people having radiation therapy, on average, all will survive the treatment, 77 will survive for one year and 22 will survive for five years.

Which treatment do you think Martin will opt for and which one will Simon opt for? If they behave in the same way as patients in a study by McNeil et al. (1982), then Martin will opt for the radiation treatment and Simon will opt for surgery. Why? You have probably noticed that the efficacy of the two treatments is equivalent in the information provided to Martin and Simon. In both cases, radiation therapy has lower long-term survival chances but no risk of dying during treatment, whereas surgery has better long-term prospects but there is a risk of dying on the operating table. The key difference between the two is the way in which the information is presented to the patients. Martin's doctor presented or *framed the information in terms of mortality*, namely how many people will *die* from the two treatments, whereas Simon's doctor framed the information in terms of how many people will *survive*. It appears that the risk of dying during treatment looms larger when it is presented in terms of mortality (in the framing adopted by Martin's doctor) than in terms of survival (in the framing chosen by Simon's doctor) – making surgery less attractive for Martin but more attractive for Simon.

This simple change in the framing of information can have a large impact on the decisions we make. McNeil et al. (1982) found that across groups of patients, students *and* doctors, on average radiation therapy was preferred to surgery 42% of the time when the negative mortality frame was used (probability of dying), but only 25% of the time when the positive survival frame (probability of living) was used (see also Tversky & Kahneman, 1981).

Positive versus negative framing is not the only type of framing that can affect decisions about medical treatments. Edwards et al. (2001), in a comprehensive review, identified nine different types of framing including those comparing verbal, numerical and graphical presentation of risk information, manipulations of the base-rate (absolute risk) of treatments, using lay versus medical terminology, and comparing the amount of information (number of factual statements) presented about choices.

The largest framing effects were evident when *relative* as opposed to *absolute* risk information was presented to patients (Edwards et al., 2001). Relative and absolute risks are two ways of conveying information about the efficacy of a treatment, but unlike the previous example they are not logically equivalent. Consider the following two statements adapted from an article about communicating the efficacy of cholesterol-reducing drugs (Skolbekken, 1998; see also Gigerenzer, 2002):

1. 'Savastatin is proven to reduce the risk of coronary mortality by 3.5%.'
2. 'Savastatin is proven to reduce the risk of coronary mortality by 42%.'

A person suffering from high cholesterol would presumably be far more willing to take the drug Savastatin when presented with statement 2 than when presented with statement 1. Moreover, a doctor is more likely to prescribe the drug if presented by a pharmaceutical company with statement 2. But is this willingness well placed?

Implicit in statement 1 is that the risk referred to is the *absolute risk reduction* – that is, the proportion of patients who die without taking the drug (those who take a placebo) minus the proportion who die having taken the drug (Gigerenzer, 2002). In the study discussed by Skolbekken (1998), the proportion of coronary mortalities for people taking the drug was 5.0% compared to 8.5% of those on a placebo (a reduction of 3.5%). In statement 2 absolute risk has been replaced by *relative risk reduction* – that is, the absolute risk reduction divided by the proportion of patients who die without taking the drug. Recall that the absolute risk reduction was 3.5% and the proportion of deaths for patients on the placebo was 8.5%, thus the 42% reduction in the statement comes from dividing 3.5 by 8.5.

Table 1.1 provides some simple examples of how the relative risk reduction can remain constant while the absolute risk reduction varies widely. Not surprisingly, several studies have found much higher percentages of patients assenting to treatment when relative as opposed to absolute risk reductions are presented. For example, Hux and Naylor (1995) reported that 88% of patients assented to lipid-lowering therapy when relative risk reduction information was provided, compared with only 42% when absolute risk reduction information was given. Similarly, Malenka et al. (1993) found that 79% of hypothetical patients preferred a treatment presented with relative risk benefits, compared to 21% who chose the absolute risk option. As Edwards et al. (2001) conclude, 'relative risk information appears much more "persuasive" than the corresponding absolute risk . . . data' (p. 74), presumably just because the numbers are larger.

So what is the best way to convey information about medical treatment? Skolbekken (1998) advocates an approach in which one avoids using 'value laden' words like risk or chance, and carefully explains the absolute rather than relative risks. Thus for a patient suffering high cholesterol who is considering taking Savastatin, a doctor should tell him or her something like: 'If 100 people like you are given no treatment for five years, 92 will live and eight will die. Whether you are one of the 92 or one of the eight, I do not know. Then, if 100 people like you take a certain drug every day for five years, 95 will live

Table 1.1 Examples of absolute and relative risk reduction.

Treatment Group		Placebo Group			
Survivals	*Mortalities*	*Survivals*	*Mortalities*	*Relative Risk Reduction (%)*	*Absolute Risk Reduction (%)*
9000	1000	8000	2000	50	10
9900	100	9800	200	50	1
9990	10	9880	20	50	0.1

Note: Adapted from Skolbekken, J. A. (1998). Communicating the risk reduction achieved by cholesterol reducing drugs. *British Medical Journal, 316*, 1956–1958.

and five will die. Again, I do not know whether you are one of the 95 or one of the five' (Skolbekken, 1998, p. 1958). The key question would be whether such a presentation format reduces errors or biases in decision making.

Is this person guilty or innocent?

At some point in your life it is quite likely that you will be called for jury duty. As a member of a jury you will be required to make a decision about the guilt or innocence of a defendant. The way in which juries and the individuals that make up a jury arrive at their decisions has been the topic of much research (e.g. Hastie, 1993). Here we focus on one aspect of this research: the impact of scientific, especially DNA, evidence on jurors' decisions about the guilt or innocence of defendants.

Faced with DNA evidence in a criminal trial many jurors are inclined to think 'science does not lie'; these jurors appear to be susceptible to 'white coat syndrome', an unquestioning belief in the power of science, which generates misplaced confidence and leads to DNA evidence being regarded as infallible (Goodman-Delahunty & Newell, 2004). Indeed, some research confirms that people often over-estimate the accuracy and reliability of scientific evidence (in comparison with other types of evidence, such as eyewitness testimony or confessions), thus assigning it undeserved probative value. For example, mock-jurors rated blood tests as significantly more reliable than testimony from an eyewitness (Goodman, 1992).

Is it simply because we have so much trust in science that DNA evidence is so compelling, or are there other reasons? Consider the 2001 trial of Wayne Edward Butler in which he was convicted of murdering Celia Douty in Brampton Island, Queensland, Australia in 1983. Police had suspected Butler for a long time but it was not until DNA profiling was used that a case was brought against him. The victim's body had been found covered by a red towel stained with semen. DNA profiling techniques unavailable in 1983 established the probability that the semen stains were Butler's, and on the basis of this evidence he was charged. At trial, a forensic expert told the jury that the probability of someone else having a DNA profile that matched the one obtained from the semen (i.e. the random match probability, RMP) was *one in 43 trillion*. Extreme probabilities such as this make it appear that there is no margin of error – the defendant must be guilty! It is not only the fact that DNA evidence is grounded in the scientific method that makes it appear more objective and indeed even foolproof, but also the manner in which DNA evidence is presented – the probabilities cited by the DNA experts – that make this evidence so influential and persuasive to jurors (Martire, Kemp & Newell, 2013).

Clearly, these numbers sound compelling, but what does an infinitesimal RMP like 1 in 43 trillion really mean? Assuming that no errors occurred in the laboratory processing and that the probability of a random match can be stated with some legitimacy, what should a conscientious juror conclude? Often people interpret the probability not simply as the likelihood that a randomly chosen other person will have the same DNA as that found on the towel (the correct interpretation), but as the probability that the *defendant was not guilty* (an incorrect interpretation). The leap from a 'match probability' to an inference about the guilt of the defendant is dubbed the 'prosecutor's fallacy' (Thompson & Schumann, 1987) and its commission has been observed in many trials (Koehler, 1993).

Perhaps the most well-known example of the prosecutor's fallacy is the case of *People v. Collins* (1968). In this case the prosecution secured a conviction by erroneously calculating a 1 in 12 million probability that a random couple would possess a series of characteristics (a female with a blonde ponytail, a man with black hair and a black beard) and then, again fallaciously, equating this probability with the probability that the accused couple did not commit the robbery. Fortunately, the original conviction was overturned in the appeals court and a stern warning was given about the dangers of 'trial by mathematics' (Koehler, 1993).

More recent work has examined the extent to which jurors understand the match probabilities that are often presented in trials. For example, Koehler, Chia and Lindsey (1995) gave students written summaries of a murder case that included evidence about a DNA match between the defendant and a blood trace recovered from the victim's fingernails. One group reviewed two items of information: (1) a random match probability of 1 in 1,000,000,000, and (2) a probability of 1 in 1000 that a human error had occurred leading to an incorrect match. A second group was told simply that the combined probability of error from random matches and laboratory mistakes was 1 in 1000. Both groups studied the evidence then provided verdicts (guilty or not guilty).

What is your intuition about the result? If you are like the students in the experiment, then you will have found the evidence about the '1 in a billion' random match probability compelling and be more likely to judge the defendant 'guilty' faced with this number. In fact, Koehler et al. (1995) found that almost

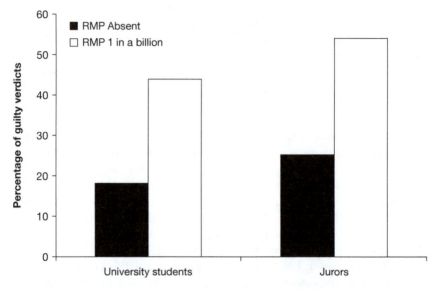

Figure 1.1 Percentage of guilty verdicts. RMP = Random Match Probability.

Drawn using data reported in Koehler, J. J, Chia, A., & Lindsey, S. (1995). The random match probability in DNA evidence: Irrelevant and prejudicial? *Jurimetrics Journal, 35,* 201–209.

three times as many guilty verdicts were recorded in the group given that figure. This pattern of results was replicated with jurors. Figure 1.1 displays the results from the two participant populations.

What is wrong with this inference? Why shouldn't we be more convinced by the 1 in a billion figure? The answer lies in how we should correctly combine both the random match probability and the human error probability. Koehler et al. (1995) use a baseball analogy to illustrate the problem: consider a baseball infielder who makes throwing errors less than one time in a million, but makes fielding errors about two times in a hundred. The chance of the player making an error on the next attempt either because he drops it or because he makes a bad throw is at least two out of a hundred. If he makes an error it will almost certainly be a fielding error – but it is still an error. The important point is that even if the player reduces his throwing error rate to one in a hundred million or one in a billion, it will have very little effect on his overall error rate. So as Koehler et al. (1995) point out, 'a baseball talent scout should be no more impressed by the infielder's throwing ability than a legal factfinder should be upon hearing the vanishingly small random match probabilities' in DNA evidence at trial (p. 211). In both cases the lower-bound threshold for error estimates is set by the greater probability – fielding errors in the case of the infielder and laboratory errors in the case of DNA evidence. (See also Chapter 5 for a more in-depth treatment of this issue.)

The example illustrates that the human error rate – the DNA laboratory error rate – is the number that really matters. Even if there is only a 1 in 43 trillion probability of a random match, if the lab conducting the analysis makes errors of the order of one in a hundred or a thousand samples, then the random match probability is essentially irrelevant. Forensic experts often know this. Koehler's experiments show that, unfortunately, jurors may not, and can as a result make flawed judgments about the probative value or weight to accord to DNA evidence.

Consistent with the medical studies discussed above, there are ways of portraying information to jurors that can improve the decisions they make. One such modification is the presentation of DNA evidence in natural frequency formats (e.g. 1 in 1,000,000 rather than probability formats, e.g. .0001%). In Chapter 6 we will discuss why such changes in format have a facilitative effect on decision making, but for now we will briefly review a study relevant to the legal domain.

Lindsey, Hertwig and Gigerenzer (2003) presented jurors and law students with a sexual assault case that included expert testimony on DNA matching linking the suspect and the crime scene. One group received all information in a probability format, while a second group received identical information presented in a frequency format. Figure 1.2 displays the percentage of guilty verdicts by the two groups of participants who received the different formats of expert numerical evidence.

The results depicted in Figure 1.2 clearly show that the *same statistical inform-ation* presented in different formats has a strong impact on the decisions made by students and jurors. When frequency formats were used, there were

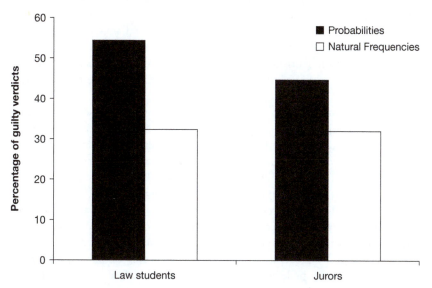

Figure 1.2 Percentage of guilty verdicts made by the two samples.

From Lindsey, S., Hertwig, R., & Gigerenzer, G. (2003). Communicating statistical evidence. *Jurimetrics Journal*, *43*, 147–163. Copyright 2003 by American Bar Association. Adapted with permission.

significantly fewer guilty verdicts. Once again, it is sobering to think that such a minor format change can have a major influence on both students' and jurors' decisions.

The results of the studies briefly reviewed here, along with many others, indicate that jurors' decisions can be influenced strongly by variations in the presentation of scientific evidence (for additional examples see Martire et al., 2013). In the light of these findings, as Koehler and Macchi (2004) conclude: 'it might be appropriate to present statistical evidence to jurors in multiple ways to minimize the influence of any particular bias' (p. 545).

How should I invest my money?

Imagine that you have just won a substantial sum of money on the lottery (if only!) and that you are faced with the enviable problem of deciding how best to invest your newfound wealth. Although you might be tempted to hide the cash under your mattress, you might also consider putting the money in the stock market – but what stocks should you invest in?

The problem you face is to work out how to 'beat' the notoriously unpredictable stock market. Unfortunately, modern theories of finance claim that players in the financial market are well informed, smart and greedy and that it is therefore impossible to make money for nothing in the long-term. This general idea is often described as the Efficient Markets Hypothesis (Batchelor, 2004). However, against the background of this rather pessimistic outlook, one extremely simple rule of thumb for investment choice might be able to help you: invest in the stocks of the companies that you recognize.

Borges et al. (1999) claim that such 'recognition-based' investment decisions can lead to much higher returns than from stocks selected by financial experts. This 'stock selection heuristic' states simply that when picking a subset of stocks from all those available for investment, one should choose those objects in the larger set that are highly recognized.

Given this formulation, it is clear that the heuristic is only useful for people who recognize some but not all of a given set of stocks. If you do not recognize any stocks, you cannot pick highly recognized ones, and similarly if you are an expert and recognize all stocks, the heuristic cannot be used. You need what Ortmann et al. (2008) describe as a 'beneficial degree of ignorance'.

How well can such a simple rule perform? Borges et al. (1999) put their recognition heuristic to the test in the following way. Germans and Americans were asked to indicate those companies that they recognized from those listed in the Standard and Poor 500 and from 298 additional stocks trading on German stock exchanges in December 1996. Four categories of participants were interviewed: Munich pedestrians, Chicago pedestrians, University of Munich finance students and University of Chicago finance students. The former two groups were described as 'laypersons', the latter two 'experts'. The recognition responses of these four groups were then used to construct stock portfolios of highly recognized companies (those recognized by 90% or more of the participants in a group) for both domestic recognition (companies from the respondent's own country) and international recognition (foreign companies). This resulted in eight recognition-based portfolios. Over a six-month period (December 1996–June 1997) these high-recognition portfolios were compared against portfolios of 'unrecognized' companies (those recognized by 10% or less of the participants in a group), market indices, mutual funds and chance portfolios (constructed by selecting companies at random).

Figure 1.3 displays the data from the two German groups (experts and laypeople) on the domestic stocks. It can be seen clearly that the portfolios of highly recognized stocks produced much higher returns over the six-month period than those of the unrecognized stocks. Even more impressively, the high-recognition companies outperformed the market index and the managed mutual funds. The data for all the groups showed similar patterns – the recognized stocks always outperformed the unrecognized ones – although recognition did not outperform the market index or mutual funds for the US domestic recognition markets.

These results appear to suggest that we can go from 'recognition to riches' (Ortmann et al., 2008) and that ignorance can indeed be beneficial (see also Alter & Oppenheimer, 2006 for a related 'trick' for beating the stock market using the pronunciation fluency of company names). And, it may not only be

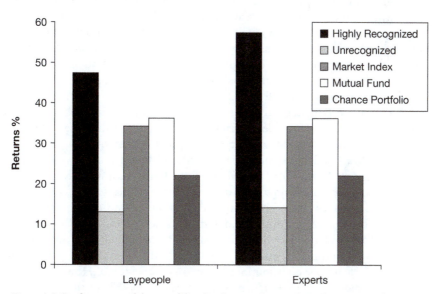

Figure 1.3 Performance of the portfolios by German laypeople and experts in the German domestic market.

From data reported in Borges, B., Goldstein, D. G., Ortmann, A., & Gigerenzer, G. (1999). Can ignorance beat the stock market? In G. Gigerenzer, P. M. Todd, & The ABC Research Group (Eds), *Simple heuristics that make us smart* (pp. 59–72). New York: Oxford University Press. Copyright 1999 by Oxford University Press. Adapted with permission.

in the financial domain that ignorance can be good for you. For example, Goldstein and Gigerenzer (2002) reported that German students made slightly more correct inferences about the relative sizes of American cities than US students – despite the US students knowing much more about and recognizing more of the cities. Goldstein and Gigerenzer suggest that this counter-intuitive 'less-is-more' effect occurs because the German students were able to rely more often on the recognition heuristic (simply inferring that a recognized city is larger than an unrecognized one) than the US students. The US students, because of their higher rate of recognition, were forced to rely on other knowledge about the cities, which in some instances appeared to lead them to incorrect inferences.

Ayton, Önkal and McReynolds (2011) report a similar less-is-more effect in the sports domain. They asked groups of Turkish and English students to predict the outcomes of English football matches and found that despite the Turkish students' low levels of recognition of the teams, their accuracy in predicting the results barely differed from the knowledgeable English students (62.5% compared to 65.5% respectively). We will return to the recognition heuristic in Chapter 3 and scrutinize the claims about the benefits of ignorance, but for now let us return to the question of what to do with your money.

Even if you are not fortunate enough to win the lottery, a financial decision that you will probably have to make at some point in your life is how to save for your retirement. As Benartzi and Thaler (2001; 2002) have noted, there is a growing worldwide trend towards giving individuals some responsibility in making their own asset allocation decisions in defined contribution saving plans. Such devolvement of responsibility raises the question of people's ability to make these decisions. For example, if you were asked to allocate your contributions among money markets, insurance contracts, bond funds and stock funds, how would you do it?

According to Benartzi and Thaler (2001), many investors simply use a '1/n strategy' in which they divide contributions evenly across the funds offered in the plan. In their first experiment Benartzi and Thaler offered participants a plan with a bond fund and a stock fund and found that the majority of participants opted for a 50:50 split between the funds – consistent with the use of a 1/n strategy. In a follow-up study, two multiple plans were compared – one with five funds comprising four stock and one bond fund, the other also with five but comprising four bond and one stock fund. The question was: do these different combinations of stock and bond funds lead to different allocations of contributions? In the plan dominated by bond funds, participants allocated 43% of their contributions to the single stock fund. However, in the plan dominated by stock funds, participants allocated 68% of their contributions to the stock funds. As the 1/n rule predicts, the total amount allocated to a particular type of fund (stocks) increases when there are more such funds in the portfolio. This result shows that a simple change in the composition of the two plans gives rise to a 25% shift in the amount allocated to the riskier stock funds. Put simply, when more stock funds were offered, more of the available resources were allocated to them. The result implies that participants' attitudes to risk (i.e. exposure to fluctuations in the stock market) are highly contingent on the way in which options are presented (cf. Hilton, 2003, and Chapter 9).

The '1/n strategy' is a special case of a more general choice heuristic described by Read and Loewenstein (1995) as the 'diversification heuristic'. The idea is that when people are asked to make several choices simultaneously they tend to diversify rather than selecting the same item several times. Simonson (1990) demonstrated the use of such a heuristic in an experiment in which he offered students the opportunity to choose three items from a selection of snack foods (chocolate bars, crisps, etc.) to be eaten during class time each week. One group was told at the start of the first class that they had to select snacks in advance for the following three weeks, while another group was given the opportunity to select a snack at the beginning of *each* class. Simonson found that 64% of the participants in the advance choice condition chose three different items, whereas only 9% did so when each choice was made shortly before being consumed. This outcome is consistent with the idea that people seek variety when asked to make advance choices (Read & Loewenstein, 1995).

This rather naïve diversification strategy might be useful in many circumstances, but is it appropriate for investment decisions? Benartzi and Thaler (2001) conclude that using a diversification heuristic 'can produce a reasonable portfolio [but] it does not assure sensible or coherent decision making' (p. 96). For example, an employee with little confidence in his or her ability to invest wisely might assume that an employer has compiled a selection of options that is sensible for his or her plan. However, the plan might offer a large number of higher risk stock options, leading the employee to invest too aggressively (i.e. too heavily in stocks), which may be inappropriate for that person (Benartzi & Thaler, 2001).

SUMMARY

These examples drawn from the medical, legal and financial arenas clearly show that our decisions can be greatly influenced by the way in which information is provided. Subtle differences in the way numbers are represented or options are displayed can affect the decisions we make – often in ways of which we are completely unaware. As we noted at the start of the chapter, our aim is to illustrate the breadth of situations in which understanding how we make decisions is relevant. The details of why some of these effects arise will be explored in the coming chapters. By investigating, systematically, these types of framing and representational issues and understanding the reasons behind the effects, you will have a better chance of keeping your decision making on the straight and narrow. But what is 'the straight and narrow' – what makes a decision correct or incorrect, good or bad? We turn to these questions in Chapter 2.

Suggested further reading

- The rest of this book!
- Goldstein, D. G., & Gigerenzer, G. (2002). Models of ecological rationality: The recognition heuristic. *Psychological Review, 109*, 75–90. A detailed examination of how and when relying on recognition can lead to good decisions.
- Tversky, A., & Kahneman, D. (1974). Judgment under uncertainty: Heuristics and biases. *Science, 185*, 1124–1131.
- Tversky, A., & Kahneman, D. (1981). The framing of decisions and the psychology of choice. *Science, 211*, 453–458.
  - Two seminal papers outlining how we are influenced by availability, among other biases, and how framing impacts choice.

2 Decision quality and a historical context

Chapter highlights

- Simple intuitions about the quality of decisions: what makes a 'good' decision?
- An introduction to expected utility and bounded rationality
- Tracing the historical development of research into the psychology of judgment and decision making.

'Choose always the way that seems best however rough it may be.' This quote, attributed to the Greek philosopher Pythagoras, implies that there is always a best course of action one should take to ensure a 'good' decision. Indeed the title of this book suggests a 'straight road' to good quality decisions. But what makes a decision 'good' or 'bad'?

INTUITIONS ABOUT DECISION QUALITY

Research by Yates, Veinott and Patalano (2003) took a very direct approach to assessing decision quality by simply asking participants to think about two good and two bad decisions that they had made in the past year. Their participants, who were university undergraduates, had to rate the decisions on scales of 'quality' (goodness/badness) and 'importance', in both cases making the judgments 'relative to all the important decisions you have ever made'. An impact score was then calculated by multiplying the importance and quality ratings, and further information was elicited about the two decisions (one bad and one good) with the highest impact scores.

Table 2.1 displays the results from the initial questioning of the participants. Two aspects of the data are worth noting: (1) good decisions were rated as higher on the quality dimension than bad ones, but were also further from the neutral point (0), suggesting that good decisions are better than bad decisions are bad; (2) participants rated their bad decisions as significantly less important than their good decisions. A further interesting finding was that it took participants less time to come up with their bad decisions (53 seconds on

Table 2.1 Ratings of the quality and importance of real-life decisions

	Good Decisions	Bad Decisions
Quality (scale: +5 extremely good, 0 neither good nor bad, −5 extremely bad)	+3.6	−2.4
Importance (scale: 0 not important at all, 10 extremely important)	7.7	5.6

Note: Adapted from data reported in Yates, J. F., Veinott, E. S., & Patalano, A. L. (2003). Hard decisions, bad decisions: On decision quality and decision aiding. In S. L. Schneider & J. Shanteau (Eds), *Emerging perspectives on judgment and decision research* (pp. 13–63). New York: Cambridge University Press.

average) than their good decisions (70 seconds). Yates et al. speculate that this pattern of data suggests that in general people think their decision making in the past was, 'for the most part, just fine' (p. 54).

In other words, the fact that the badness and importance of bad decisions are rated as less extreme than the goodness and importance of good decisions suggests a certain degree of cognitive dissonance about bad decisions. It is as if we engage in post hoc re-evaluations of such decisions along the lines of 'Well, it did not work out too bad in the end' (e.g. Festinger, 1957; Wicklund & Brehm, 1976). Such a 'rose-tinted spectacles' view of the past would lead to bad decisions being recalled more quickly, perhaps because their extreme 'badness' makes them particularly distinctive and unusual (Yates et al., 2003). This positive retrospective bias also has implications for trying to improve decision making through the use of decision-aiding techniques: if people are more or less content with the way decisions have turned out in the past, they will be less likely to seek help with current decisions (Yates et al., 2003).

In the Yates et al. study, once participants had recalled and rated their decisions they were asked for specific details about the context in which those decisions were made and why they were classified as good or bad. The resulting explanations were then coded by both the experimenters and naïve coders. This coding procedure revealed a number of 'super-categories' for goodness and badness respectively. By far the most often-cited reason for a decision being classified as good or bad was that the 'experienced outcome' was either adverse or favourable. Eighty-nine per cent of bad decisions were described as bad because they resulted in bad outcomes; correspondingly 95.4% of good decisions were described as good because they yielded good outcomes. Other super categories that received some weight were 'options' in which 44% of bad decisions were thought to be bad because they limited future options (such as a career-path), and 'affect' in which 40.4% of good decisions were justified as good because people felt good about making the decision, or felt good about themselves after making it.

The results of this coding analysis point to the conclusion that a decision maker's conception of quality is multifaceted, but is overwhelmingly dominated by outcomes: a good decision is good because it produces good outcomes, while bad decisions yield bad ones (Yates et al., 2003). How far does such an intuitive conclusion get us in understanding what makes a decision good or bad? Can an outcome really be an unambiguous determinant of the quality of the decision that preceded it?

A FORMAL APPROACH TO DECISION QUALITY

The following example (proposed by Hastie and Dawes, 2001) illustrates why we cannot rely solely on outcomes to evaluate decisions. Imagine someone asked you to make an even-money bet on rolling two ones ('snake eyes') on a pair of unloaded dice. Given that the probability of rolling two ones is actually 1 in 36, taking an even-money bet would be very foolish. That is, you would think it was a 'bad' decision to take the bet. But what would happen if you *did* take the bet and subsequently *did* roll the snake eyes? Would your decision to take the bet now be a 'good' one because the resulting outcome was positive? Clearly not; because of the probabilities involved, the decision to take the bet would be foolish regardless of the outcome. This example suggests that the quality of a decision is determined not only by its outcome but also by the probability of that outcome occurring.

What else might affect quality? Consider this version of the 'snake eyes' scenario: you have no money and have defaulted on a loan with a disreputable company. If you do not repay your debts the company will send their heavies round to rough you up. Now do you take the bet, and if you do, is it a good decision? The situation is very different: if taking the bet is the only way to avoid physical harm, it is probably in your best interest to take it. Thus not only is the quality of a decision affected by its outcome and the probability of the outcome, it is also affected by the extent to which taking a particular course of action is beneficial (has value) for a given decision maker at a given point in time (Hastie & Dawes, 2001).

With these three aspects of decision quality in mind, we are beginning to approach the classical definition of what makes a decision 'good', or more specifically, what makes it rational. The origin of the notion of a rational choice can be traced to an exchange of letters between Blaise Pascal and Pierre de Fermat, two 17th-century French mathematicians with a keen (and entirely honourable) interest in gambling. Their discussions of the gambling game 'points' (a game first proposed by the Franciscan monk Paccioli in 1494 – see Almy & Krueger, 2013) led to the development of the concept of mathematical expectation, which at the time was thought to be the essence of a rational choice (see Hacking, 1975; Hertwig et al., 2004). Put simply, a choice was thought to be rational if it maximized the *expected value* for the decision maker. Expected value is defined as the sum of the product of the probability of an outcome and the value of that outcome (typically a monetary outcome) for each possible outcome of a given alternative. In the case of the 'snake eyes' example, the expected value of an even-money gamble with a $10 stake is simply a 1 in 36 chance of winning $10 plus a 35 in 36 chance of winning nothing: $(1/36 \times \$10) + (35/36 \times \$0) = \$0.27$. Because this is less than the cost of the stake, it is clearly a poor gamble. Defined this way, expected value was thought to offer both a descriptive and prescriptive account of rationality, but it soon became clear that it was neither (Gigerenzer & Selten, 2001).

In 1713 Nicolas Bernoulli, a Swiss mathematician, proposed the following monetary gamble (known as the St Petersburg Paradox) as an example of how the notion of expected value failed to capture how people actually made choices. Imagine your friend has an unbiased coin and asks you to play a game in which (a) the coin is tossed until it lands on Tails, and (b) you win $2 if it lands on Tails on the first toss, $4 if it first lands on Tails on the second toss, $8 if Tails appears for the first time on the third toss, and so on. The question your friend asks is: how much would you be willing to pay to play the game? You, along with most people given this problem, would probably not be willing to pay more than a few dollars. However, according to the expected value theory, such behaviour is paradoxical because the expected value of the gamble is infinite. Why? Because on the first toss there is a 0.5 probability of obtaining a Head, which would give an expected payoff of $1 (i.e. $0.5 \times \$2$). On the second toss, the probability reduces to 0.25 (one Head followed by a Tail) but the payoff is still $1 (i.e. $0.25 \times \$4$), etc. The calculation is as follows:

$$\text{EV (Expected Value)} = (0.5 \times \$2) + (0.25 \times \$4) + (0.125 \times \$8) + \ldots$$

$$+ (0.5)^n (\$2)^n + \ldots$$

(where n is the number of coin tosses). So if you kept playing you could end up with an infinite amount of money (in other words, the expected value of the gamble is infinite). The fact that people do not offer large amounts of money to play therefore presents a problem for expected value theory. To accommodate this 'paradoxical' finding, Daniel Bernoulli (Nicolas's younger cousin) modified the theory by exchanging the notion of expected 'value' with expected 'utility'. The latter incorporates two important caveats that are of high psychological relevance: (1) that the utility of money declines with increasing gains and (2) that this utility is dependent on the amount of money a person already has. Bernoulli (1738/1954) suggested that the relation between utility and monetary value could be captured by the concave, logarithmic function shown in Figure 2.1.

To illustrate this idea, imagine that following the previous 'snake eyes' scenario, you failed to roll two ones and the heavies came over to rough you up. You are left with nothing, starving and living on the street. Consider the following three 'lucky breaks' that could then befall you: (1) you find an unaddressed envelope on the street containing a $10 note, (2) you find an envelope containing $1000 or (3) you find an envelope containing $1010. How would you feel in these three situations? Presumably pretty happy in all three cases, but the interesting question is how your happiness would differ as function

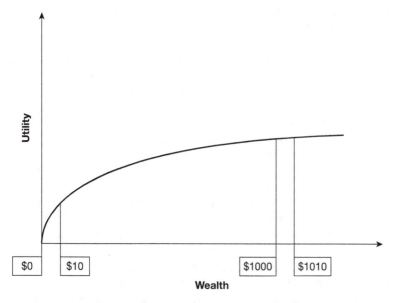

Figure 2.1 A logarithmic (concave) function showing the relation between utility (or happiness) and monetary value (or wealth).

of the numerical differences in wealth. Remember you have nothing, so finding $10 would be a real bonus (perhaps enough to stave off immediate hunger pangs); finding $1000 would be incredible, but would there be any difference to your happiness in finding $1000 or $1010? – not much. This idea is illustrated in Figure 2.1. The lower section of the curve is steep and so a small change in wealth ($10) leads to a sharp rise in utility (or 'happiness'). The curve then begins to flatten out so the increase in wealth from $10 to $1000 results in a significant rise in utility but it is not as steep as the rise from $0 to $10. Finally, by the time you have $1000, the additional $10 makes an almost imperceptible difference to your utility. The important thing to note is that this increase from $1000 to $1010 is identical in terms of wealth to the $0–$10 change, but very different in terms of utility. Although the expected value of the St Petersburg gamble is infinite, its expected utility is not because the very unlikely outcomes (a long string of Heads before the first Tail) have rapidly diminishing utility.

The discussion and analysis of these various gambling problems form an important pre-cursor to contemporary research on decision making (Almy & Krueger, 2013). They provided ways of thinking about why a choice would be good, bad, rational or irrational, but it was not until the late 1940s and early 1950s that the field began to develop into the one we recognize today. In the next section of this chapter we provide a taste of the recent history of judgment and decision-making research.

A BRIEF HISTORY OF JUDGMENT AND DECISION-MAKING RESEARCH

The treatment we offer here on the historical context of judgment and decision-making research will be necessarily rather brief. Interested readers should consult Goldstein and Hogarth (1997) for a more comprehensive coverage, or Doherty (2003) for another brief perspective. Our aim here is simply to highlight some of the historical setting for the areas of research that we consider in this book, and to indicate where topics will be covered in more depth.

Goldstein and Hogarth (1997) suggest that the recent development of judgment and decision-making research can be traced to two groups of psychologists: one group interested in 'decisions', the other in 'judgments'. A decision can be defined as a commitment to a course of action (Yates et al., 2003), thus researchers with an interest in decision making often ask questions such as, how do people choose a course of action? How do people decide what to do when they have conflicting goals and the consequences of a decision are uncertain? Do people choose rationally? A judgment, on the other hand, is often a precursor to a decision and can be defined as an assessment or belief about a given situation based on the available information. As such, psychologists with an interest in judgment want to know how people integrate multiple sources of information (many of which might be imperfect or probabilistic indicators) to arrive at an understanding of, or judgment about, a situation. Judgment researchers also want to know how accurate people's judgments are, how environmental factors such as learning and feedback affect judgment ability, and how experts and novices differ in the way they make judgments. The origin of both approaches can be traced to the late 1940s and early 1950s. First we plot the trajectory of research into decisions.

Decisions

In 1947, the second edition of von Neumann and Morgenstern's *Theory of Games and Economic Behavior* was published. Unlike the first, 1944, edition, this edition contained an appendix with a theorem for assessing decision making according to the principle of maximizing expected utility. Von Neumann and Morgenstern were interested in the mathematical rather than the behavioural implications of their theorem, but an added result of their axiomatization of expected utility was that it provided researchers with a 'set of rules' for testing the rationality of people's choices. Thus, what began with Paccioli, Pascal and Fermat's musings about how people would respond in various gambling situations grew into a fully fledged theory of rational choice.

Savage (1954) developed von Neumann and Morgenstern's work further by incorporating the notion of subjectivity into the maximization of expected utility. Savage proved that a person, whose choices satisfy all of the axioms of the theory, chooses as if she were maximizing her expected utility while assigning subjective probabilities to the possible outcomes of a choice. These ideas will be covered in much greater depth in Chapter 8, but for now, to give a flavour of these axioms or 'rules for rational choice', we will illustrate one axiom, *transitivity*, with the following simple example:

$$S > Lemon \; ; \; Lemon > Lime \; ; \; Lime > S$$

Suppose Barry prefers strawberry lollipops to lemon, and lemon to lime, *but* lime to strawberry. Assuming Barry is not indifferent in his choice between any of these alternatives, he should be willing to pay something to swap a less-preferred flavour for a more-preferred one. Barry is given a lemon lollipop. Because he prefers strawberry to lemon, he should be willing to pay something (20 cents perhaps?) to have strawberry instead. But he prefers lime to strawberry, so he should be willing to pay something to substitute these. Finally, he should also pay to substitute lime for lemon because he prefers the latter to the former.

As you can probably see, because of his 'intransitive preferences' Barry ends up back where he started (with a lemon lollipop) but he is now 60 cents out of pocket! The axiom of transitivity states quite simply that if one prefers outcome A (strawberry) to outcome B (lemon) and outcome B to outcome C (lime), then one should prefer A to C. Because Barry showed the opposite final preference – preferring C (lime) to A (strawberry), he violated the axiom of transitivity and found himself in a 'money-pump' situation which would ultimately bankrupt him.

Expected utility theory (EUT) was developed within the discipline of economics but has had a strong and lasting influence on psychological investigations of decision making. As Juslin and Montgomery (1999) note, its principal influence has been twofold: first, the subcomponents of EUT – utility functions and subjective probabilities – have been used to conceptualize how decisions are made. Second, EUT has provided the normative yardstick against which human decision behaviour is measured.

However, just as Nicholas Bernoulli had proposed the St Petersburg Paradox as a problem for expected value theory, it was not long before objections were raised to the von Neumann and Morgenstern/Savage version of EUT. Several researchers posed problems in which observed behaviour clearly violated one or more of the axioms of the theory. Many of these violations became known as 'paradoxes', like the St Petersburg Paradox we discussed earlier, but as Gigerenzer and Selten (2001) note, such findings are not *logical* paradoxes, they are labelled paradoxical purely because the theory is so 'at odds with' (Gigerenzer & Selten, 2001, p. 2) what people do when confronted with the problems. Indeed, when Daniel Ellsberg, a famous critic of rational choice theory, addressed a meeting of the Society for Judgment and Decision Making in 2002 he expressed his dismay at the fact that his work had been labelled paradoxical – it is what people do, he told the audience – where is the 'paradox' in that?

These early objections to EUT as a descriptive theory of choice were followed in subsequent decades by increasing amounts of evidence showing that people systematically violate the axioms of rational choice theory (e.g. see

Kahneman & Tversky, 2000, for a review). Broadly speaking, the evidence that human behaviour contradicted EUT had three major impacts on the development of judgment and decision-making (JDM) research. First, it inspired some researchers, most notably Herbert Simon, to raise serious doubts about the applicability of EUT to human choice. The main thrust of Simon's argument was that assessments of the rationality of human behaviour should take into account both the person and the environment in which that person operates (Simon, 1955; 1956). His famous metaphor of the two blades of a pair of scissors captures this idea: 'Human rational behavior . . . is shaped by the scissors whose two blades are the structure of the task environment and the computational capabilities of the actor' (Simon, 1990, p. 7).

Juslin, Nilsson and Winman (2009) offer the following example to give this idea some context: appreciating why a deaf person concentrates on your lips while you are talking (a behaviour) requires knowing that the person is deaf (a cognitive limitation), that your lip movements provide information about what you are saying (the structure of the environment), and that the person is trying to understand your utterance (a goal). The crucial point is that on their own none of these factors explains the behaviour or its rationality. These can only be fully appreciated by attending to the structure of the environment – this is the essence of what Simon termed *bounded rationality*. Simon's ideas have had a huge impact on JDM research, most recently in the work of Gigerenzer and colleagues (e.g. Gigerenzer, Hertwig & Pachur, 2011; Gigerenzer, Todd & The ABC Research Group, 1999) of which we will hear more in Chapter 3.

The second effect of the accumulation of evidence showing violations of EUT was to encourage researchers to examine other areas of decision-making behaviour (Goldstein & Hogarth, 1997). Ward Edwards (1968) was particularly influential in expanding the area of study to include probabilistic judgment. Rather than using EUT as the normative yardstick, Edwards compared people's judgments to those mandated by mathematical principles and the laws of probability. Edwards' early work examined questions such as whether people updated their beliefs about the probability of an outcome given some evidence in the ways dictated by Bayes' Theorem (a formal theory which specifies how beliefs *should* be updated). His finding, that people typically did not provide Bayesian estimates, laid the groundwork for subsequent investigations of probability judgment by Amos Tversky and Daniel Kahneman (e.g. Tversky & Kahneman, 1974) (although, interestingly, Edwards appeared to regret his foundational influence – see Edwards, 1983). Kahneman and Tversky's research programme, named for the *heuristic* processes that they identified (e.g. availability, representativeness, anchoring) and the characteristic *biases* evidenced through the use of these heuristics, has been perhaps the most influential programme in the history of JDM research, and its wide-spread resonance continues (e.g. Kahneman, 2011; Thaler & Sunstein, 2008). Chapters 5 and 6 provide a detailed coverage of Bayes' Theorem and the heuristics and biases approach.

The third and final impact of the observed violations of EUT was to inspire researchers to modify the theory so as to make it a better descriptive theory of choice. Perhaps the most influential of these modified theories is prospect theory, proposed by Kahneman and Tversky (1979a). As we will explore in Chapter 9, the central insight of prospect theory is in demonstrating that although our choices involve maximizing some kind of expectation, the utilities and probabilities of outcomes undergo systematic psychological or cognitive distortions when they are evaluated. These distortions have major implications for predicting choice under uncertainty.

Judgments

Research into the psychology of judgment was inspired in its early days by an analogy with visual perception (Doherty, 2003; Goldstein & Hogarth, 1997). Hammond (1955) argued that principles of perception proposed by Brunswik (1952; 1956) could be applied to the study of judgment. The main ideas in the Brunswikian approach to perception are that an object in the environment (a 'distal' stimulus) produces multiple cues through the stimulation of the perceiver's sense organs. These 'proximal' cues are necessarily fallible (due to the probabilistic nature of the relation between the cues and the environment) and therefore only imperfectly indicate the true state of the external environment. Thus perception is a constructive process, involving inferences drawn on the basis of incomplete and ambiguous sensory information.

Hammond's important contribution was to show that judgment could be viewed in the same way. Beginning with clinical judgment, Hammond and his colleagues went on to demonstrate that social judgment theory, as it became known, could be applied to a wide range of situations involving multi-attribute judgment (Doherty, 2003; Karelaia & Hogarth, 2008). The main 'tool' of the social judgment theorist is the lens model. We describe studies that have used this tool in more detail in Chapter 3 and examine the learning mechanisms underlying performance in such studies in Chapter 12. In essence the lens model is a metaphor for thinking about how a 'to-be-judged' criterion in the world (e.g. whether a patient is psychotic or neurotic) relates to the judgment made in the 'mind' of the judge. It has been used by Brunswikians to guide their research programme and, through the use of the 'lens model equation' (Tucker, 1964), aid in the analysis of data.

An important distinction between research on decisions and research on judgments is that in the former the focus is on the extent to which people's beliefs and preferences are coherent, while the latter is concerned with the correspondence between subjective and environmental states (Hammond, 1996; Juslin & Montgomery, 1999). Judgment theorists are not necessarily concerned by behaviour that does not conform to normative yardsticks like EUT or Bayes' Theorem, but instead are interested in whether a judgment is accurate in the sense that it reflects the true state of the world (see Juslin et al., 2009).

Early and highly influential work investigating the accuracy of judgment in the 'real world' was published by Paul Meehl (1954) in a book entitled *Clinical versus statistical prediction: A theoretical analysis and a review of the evidence*. In this book Meehl described how judgments made by experts – usually clinicians – were often inferior in terms of accuracy to those generated by simple statistical models provided with the same information. We describe these studies in more detail in Chapter 3; here we simply note that this controversial finding led to a surge of interest in understanding how people combine information from multiple sources to make judgments. This interest, in conjunction with the methodological and theoretical advances made by Hammond and colleagues in the application of Brunswik's principles, ensured the swift development of this important and fruitful branch of judgment research (see Hammond & Stewart, 2001, for a review).

Although not enjoying the same high profile as research into decisions and preferential choice (perhaps because of its lesser overlap with other disciplines such as Economics), research in the 'correspondence' tradition of judgment continues to be fertile and influential. Brunswik's ideas have been taken into more mainstream psychological writings through the work of the Swedish psychologists Berndt Brehmer, Mats Björkman and Peter Juslin, (e.g. Juslin & Montgomery, 1999) as well as by Gerd Gigerenzer and his group (e.g. Gigerenzer, Hoffrage & Kleinbölting, 1991). Hillel Einhorn, Robyn Dawes and Robin Hogarth, amongst others, have been instrumental in furthering our understanding of the processes underlying clinical and statistical judgment (e.g. Dawes, 1979; Einhorn & Hogarth, 1981; Karelaia & Hogarth, 2008). We will examine much of this important work in the chapters that follow.

New frontiers

Since the publication of the first edition of this book, there have been significant advances in understanding the neuroscience of decision making (e.g. Vartanian & Mandel, 2011). The aim of this work is to identify areas, pathways and biological mechanisms in the brain that underlie decision making. For example, sometimes neuroscience evidence can be used to examine whether and how the brain calculates the 'value' of different options (e.g. Vlaev et al., 2011). Alternatively, brain-imaging techniques might be used to draw inferences about the involvement of different systems in 'deliberative' as opposed to 'intuitive' judgments (e.g. De Neys, Vartanian & Goel, 2008 – see Chapter 14). Much of this work goes rather beyond the scope of our focus on judgment and decision-making *behaviour*, but where relevant we do highlight some key studies.

SUMMARY

Simple introspection can help us to understand what makes a decision good or bad ('what are some good decisions I have made, what are some bad ones?'). Such intuitive approaches tend to focus on outcomes – good decisions produce good outcomes, bad decisions bad outcomes. However, sole focus on outcomes does not provide an unambiguous index of decision quality. Researchers have found it useful to consider three main aspects of decisions: outcomes, probabilities and the value or utility of an outcome to the decision maker. From early musings about how these three aspects of quality related to preferences between monetary gambles, a theory of rational choice was developed which proposed a set of rules or 'axioms' that a person should follow in order to act in a rational manner. Research into decisions and choice followed a path of comparing human behaviour with these axioms and has produced many important insights into when and why decisions depart from normative standards. Research into judgment has taken a different approach by focusing on when and how people combine information from multiple sources to make judgments and whether these judgments correspond to the true state of the world. In the next two chapters we will explore this research by examining the stages involved in making a judgment.

Suggested further reading

- Almy, B., & Krueger, J. I. (2013). Game interrupted: The rationality of considering the future. *Judgment and Decision Making, 8,* 521–526. A contemporary investigation of Paccioli's game of points – the game from which the notion of mathematical expectation emerged.
- Hammond, K. R., & Stewart, T. R. (Eds) (2001). *The essential Brunswik: Beginnings, explications, applications.* Oxford: Oxford University Press. A comprehensive collection of papers by Brunswik and those inspired by his approach.
- Kahneman, D. (2011). *Thinking, fast and slow.* New York: Allen Lane. An accessible summary and personal reflection on the extraordinary influence of Kahneman and Tversky's work on the psychology of judgment and decision making.
- Weiss, J. W., & Weiss, D. J. (Eds) (2009). *A science of decision making: The legacy of Ward Edwards.* Oxford: Oxford University Press. An edited collection of 29 of Edwards' most important papers. The volume includes the 1983 paper (see references) in which Edwards simultaneously takes credit and apologizes for the rise of the heuristics and biases approach.

3 Stages of judgment I
Discovering, acquiring and combining information

Chapter highlights

- An introduction to Brunswik's lens model: a metaphor for judgment
- Examining multiple-cue probability learning as a means for inferring how people search for, acquire and integrate information
- Contrasting compensatory and non-compensatory methods for combining information: the adaptive decision maker
- Examining the evidence for 'fast-and-frugal' judgment heuristics: when and why should we ignore information?

Imagine that you are walking down the street with a friend and that you pass a shiny, new car parked at the side of the road. Your friend, who is interested in buying a new car, asks you how much you think the car would cost. You are faced with a judgment – how do you go about estimating the cost of the car? You might start by looking at the make – you know that a Mercedes or BMW is likely to be more expensive than a Hyundai. Then perhaps you might look at the 'trim' – does it have alloy wheels, a sunroof, chromium fittings, etc.? You might take a look through the windows – are there leather seats, a navigation system? Once you have gathered what you think is enough information, you combine it to make a global judgment about the cost. You tell your friend, 'About \$20,000.' He replies that in fact the car only costs \$15,000 (he has been doing some research in preparation for buying a car). You take this information on board, and perhaps revise your thinking about how much the various features of the car that you considered contribute to its overall value, so that next time someone asks you about the value of that car (or a similar one) you will be able to make a better judgment.

This example serves to illustrate some of the key processes involved in making judgments.

1) *Discovering information*: how do we know where to look? How do we know that the make of a car is a good indicator of cost?

2) *Acquiring and searching through information*: how much information should we acquire and in what order should we look for it? Should we look at the make first or whether the car has a navigation system?
3) *Combining information*: how should we put the information together to make a global judgment about the cost of the car?
4) *Feedback*: once we have made the judgment, how do we use information about the difference between our estimate and the actual cost of the car to revise our beliefs?

In this chapter we consider the first three of these stages in turn, and in the next chapter we will examine the role of feedback in more detail. The idea is that the processes encapsulated by these stages remain common across a vast range of situations from estimating the price of a car, to deciding whether to take up a job, or even (arguably) choosing a person to marry! Our approach focuses on the experimental analysis of these stages, so first we examine a framework for judgment that has provided the basis for the majority of the studies we consider.

CONCEPTUALIZING JUDGMENT: THE LENS MODEL

Our interaction with objects and events in the world is necessarily indirect. Our internal perceptions of external events are mediated through our sense organs – light, sound, odours are all transduced into electrical signals and interpreted by the brain. Egon Brunswik, an Austrian-American psychologist, conceptualized judgment processes as being transduced in a similar fashion through a 'lens of cues' that divides the events and objects in the real world from the psychological processes in the mind of the person making a judgment (Hammond & Stewart, 2001). Figure 3.1 is a diagrammatic representation of this relationship. The left-hand side of the diagram represents the 'real world' in which the criterion or to-be-judged event exists. The right-hand side represents the mind of the judge, and in between is the lens of cues through which the judge attempts to 'see' the true state of the world. The arrows on the left-hand side indicate that the criterion is associated (possibly causally) with the various signs or cues in the environment, which comprise the lens. The arrows on the right-hand side represent the way in which the judge utilizes information from the cues and integrates them to form a judgment. The arrows connecting the cues indicate that there are relations among the cues themselves; in other words, they are not independent. The over-arching line connecting the criterion and the judgment represents the judge's accuracy in estimating the to-be-judged criterion. Applied to our example of judging the cost of a car, the actual price is the to-be-judged criterion, the trim, make, and other features of the car are the 'cues', and the judgment is your estimate of the price.

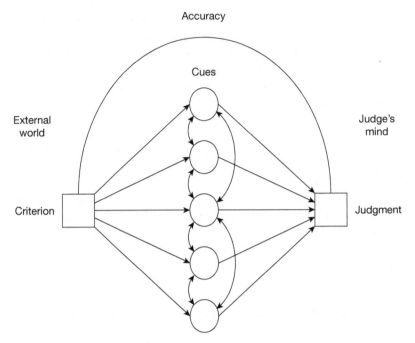

Figure 3.1 A schematic diagram of Brunswik's lens model for conceptualizing judgment.

Using this basic framework, researchers have developed ingenious methods for inferring how judges utilize information from multiple imperfect cues in the environment to make decisions about uncertain outcomes (see Karelaia & Hogarth, 2008, for a review). The framework has been used in many of the domains we examined in Chapter 1 – legal, medical and financial situations – and has sometimes been successful in influencing policy decisions in those areas (e.g. Hammond & Adelman, 1976).

As well as these applied studies, which have focused on the way existing, identifiable cues in the environment are used in judgments (e.g. Dawes & Corrigan, 1974), a wealth of experimental research which focuses on *learning* novel cue-outcome relations has also been conducted. The principal technique used in these experimental studies is multiple-cue probability learning (MCPL). As its label suggests, MCPL at its most fundamental involves learning to predict an outcome on the basis of the values of multiple cues in situations where the relation between the outcome and the cues is probabilistic. This means that cues in the environment vary in their 'validity' or their 'goodness' for predicting the outcome. (Validity is a term that is often used slightly differently by different researchers but the key idea is that it is a measure of how 'good' a cue is for predicting an outcome: a cue with a validity of 1 is perfect; a cue with a validity of 0 is useless). Most of the studies reviewed in this chapter have used this cue-learning paradigm in one form or another. The first aspect of cue learning we consider is how people discover relevant cues in the environment.

DISCOVERING INFORMATION

Dawes and Corrigan (1974) famously claimed that when making decisions involving multiple sources of information 'the whole trick is to decide what variables to look at and then know how to add' (p. 105). Later in the chapter we will consider the usefulness of 'knowing how to add', but first we will examine the intriguing 'trick' of deciding what to look at.

The majority of MCPL tasks present participants with a predetermined 'shortlist' of the cues that can be used for the required judgment or decision. For example, for predicting a person's credit rating, participants might be provided with information concerning 'average monthly debt' and 'average number of creditors' (Muchinsky & Dudycha, 1975). However, Klayman (1988a; 1984) has argued that by providing such sets of explicitly identified cues, MCPL studies are excluding a very important aspect of decision making in complex environments – namely the process of cue discovery.

Klayman (1988a) defines cue discovery as identifying a set of valid predictive cues, and uses the following example to illustrate this process:

> Suppose . . . you are a planner who wants to develop a model of patterns of usage for a certain train station. At first, you may have only base-rate information about the average number of people who pass through the station in a week. As you study the station, you may add the factor 'time of day' to your model. With further study you may incorporate more subtle factors (e.g., seasonal changes, effects of local economic conditions). As your model becomes more complete, your predictive accuracy increases.
>
> (Klayman, 1984, p. 86).

Klayman (1988a) suggests that the key process here is the discovery of new valid predictive cues and their incorporation into one's 'mental model' of the situation. To examine this process directly Klayman (1988a; 1984) used a modified MCPL task in which participants had not only to discover which cues amongst a set were valid, but also what the cues in an environment were. Participants were presented with a computer-controlled graphic display in which geometric figures appeared in various locations (see Figure 3.2). On each trial a figure appeared that could be one of three shapes (square, triangle or circle), sizes (small, medium or large) and shadings (crosshatch, narrow stripe or wide stripe). An asterisk then appeared on the screen and a straight line or trace was drawn out from that asterisk. The participants' task was to learn to predict whether a particular trace would stop before it reached the edge of the display

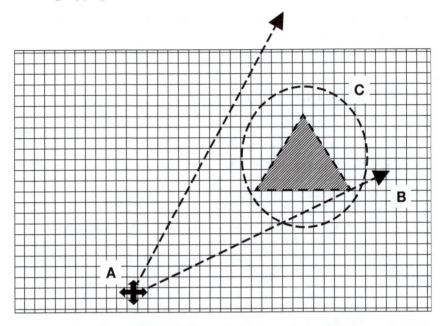

Figure 3.2 Adapted example of a display screen used to study cue discovery.

From Klayman, J. (1988). Cue discovery in probabilistic environments: Uncertainty and experimentation. *Journal of Experimental Psychology: Learning, Memory, and Cognition, 14,* 317–330. Copyright 1998 by American Psychological Association. Adapted with permission.

Note: A straight line or trace is drawn from the origin (A) in any direction. The place that the trace stops (B) is determined by, amongst other factors, how close it passes to the 'area of influence' (C). Note that in the experiments the letters did not appear on the display but grid co-ordinates not shown here were presented.

or simply go 'off the screen', and if it were to stop, where they thought it would do so (see Figure 3.2).

The element of cue discovery was introduced because participants soon learned that the explicitly identified cues (shape, size and shading) were not the only variables that were relevant to the behaviour of the trace. Over trials it became apparent that other variables such as the height of the shape on the screen and the proximity of the trace and the shape also played a role in determining where the trace would stop.

Klayman (1988a) reported two key results from these studies. First, participants were able to discover which cues were valid both among the explicit cues (e.g. size was a valid cue, shading was not) and from the inferred cues (e.g. when travelling in a more leftward direction the trace went farther). This process of discovery took a long time – an average of about 700 trials dispersed over 7 days – but by the end of this period participants had discovered about three or four of the valid cues.

Second, the experiments showed that when participants were free to design their own screens and locate the shapes and trace origins anywhere on the display, they did better than ones who just observed a random selection of trials. Within the former intervention or 'experiment' group there was wide individual variability in the degree and quality of experimentation engaged in, and there was a strong association between the quality of experimentation and success in discovering predictive cues. 'Good' experimenters only changed one variable between trials when testing a hypothesis and achieved more accurate predictions more rapidly than the 'poor' experimenters who changed a number of variables between consecutive trials.

Advances in the formal modelling of causal relations (Pearl, 2000) have stimulated renewed interest in the role of intervention and experimentation in learning (for recent reviews see Holyoak & Cheng, 2011, Rottman & Hastie, 2014). Lagnado and Sloman (2004a), for example, used a trial-by-trial-based learning paradigm in which participants obtained probabilistic data about causally related events either through observing sequences (e.g. *seeing* a high fuel temperature and a low combustion chamber pressure leading to the launch of a rocket) or through intervention (e.g. *setting* temperature or pressure to either high or low and then observing whether the rocket launched or failed). The results showed a clear advantage for interveners in terms of their ability to subsequently select the causal model likely to have generated the data (from an array of possible models).

As a result of this renewed interest in the role of experimentation, some recent work has begun to ask questions similar to those posed by Klayman (1988a). Although not examining cue discovery per se, these studies have compared intervention and observation strategies in multiple-cue judgment tasks. Thus far the evidence suggests that intervention can be beneficial (e.g. Enkvist et al., 2006), but the improvements found with intervention do not appear to be as dramatic as those seen in causal reasoning tasks. One key difference is that in the causal literature the focus has been on learning causal relations that connect events (e.g. Griffiths & Tenenbaum, 2009; Lagnado & Sloman, 2004a, 2006; Steyvers et al., 2003), but in multiple-cue judgment the task is generally to predict a criterion (see Lagnado et al., 2007, for a comparison between causal learning and multiple-cue learning). Therefore, the causal reasoning tasks may more strongly invite representation in terms of causal models, which can be tested through intervention. It seems clear that a fruitful avenue for future research will be to identify what tasks and instructions promote strategies of learning that benefit from the opportunity to intervene (e.g. see Bramley, Lagnado & Speekenbrink, in press).

ACQUIRING INFORMATION

Before making any major decision, we often attempt to gather information in the hope that it will lead to a better decision. If we are lucky, we will already know 'where to look' and will not have to go through the process of discovering relevant sources of information, but often we still have to work out how much information to look at, and in what order. For example, when you finally decide to buy a new car, do you search the Internet for information about different brands, or do you decide to trust your own experience and stick with your current brand? Once you've decided on a dealership, how many cars do you look at? How long do you test-drive a specific car before you decide to buy it? This behaviour can be described as 'pre-decisional acquisition of information' – a strategy engaged in in the hope of reducing the risk of making an erroneous or poor decision (Connolly & Thorn, 1987). But how much information should we acquire before making a decision? Acquiring too much can be extremely costly; acquiring too little can lead to excessive risk of making the wrong decision.

Many approaches to the analysis of decision behaviour characterize this problem as a trade-off between *exploration* and *exploitation* (e.g. Cohen, McClure & Yu, 2007). Remaining with an option – going to your usual supermarket – constitutes exploitation; that is, making the most of where you are. A switch to another option exemplifies exploration; going somewhere else to see if you can get better outcomes. There is a long tradition of research into how people deal with this trade-off, ranging from simple binary choice experiments (e.g. Rakow, Newell & Zougkou, 2010; Tversky & Edwards, 1966) to organizational learning (e.g. March, 1991).

Here, we keep with our focus on multiple-cue learning and review an illustrative set of studies by Connolly and colleagues (Connolly & Gilani, 1982; Connolly & Serre, 1984; Connolly & Thorn, 1987; Connolly & Wholey, 1988) that examined pre-decisional information acquisition. In a representative experiment (Connolly & Thorn, 1987), participants played the role of a manager whose task was to set a production quota for a manufacturing plant. Participants were told that if production was set too high or too low the company would incur damaging losses. To help them set their quotas, participants could buy reports of the firm's orders from the various distribution centres. On each trial participants made whatever purchases they wished and then set a production quota.

The principal finding was that the majority of participants under-purchased the reports (compared to the mathematically optimal amount). This was true regardless of whether there were two, four or six reports offered. Some learning was evident in that as the experiment progressed, participants tended to buy more 'good' reports (those which were stronger predictors of the actual quota) than 'bad' reports, but there was still considerable deviation from optimal purchasing at the end of the experiment. In general, participants purchased only about half of the good reports, and although this under-purchasing saved acquisition costs, the consequent penalties more than offset the savings. In fact, the costs incurred ranged to almost twice those incurred by an optimal policy (Connolly & Thorn, 1987).

Interestingly, in post-experimental interviews participants were able to distinguish between the good and bad sources of information, but this knowledge seemed not to prevent them under-purchasing the good reports.

What are we to make of this suboptimality in balancing the costs and benefits of information purchase? One possibility is that participants were not given enough time in the environment to develop an optimal strategy. As we will see in Chapter 12, often thousands of trials are required before optimal performance is achieved – even in simple choice games. In the Connolly experiments, typically only 40 trials were used. Given extended training perhaps participants would learn more readily about the differential validity of information sources (Connolly & Serre, 1984).

However, in the experiment described above, participants had learned to distinguish good from bad sources and yet their purchase was still suboptimal – why? One plausible explanation is that information costs are immediate and certain, whereas the payoff for making a correct decision is delayed and uncertain (Connolly & Thorn, 1987). In other words the participants were 'risk-seekers' preferring to gamble rather than methodically go through all the available information.

The observed under-purchase suggests that perhaps participants simply could not face the extra effort (and immediate cost) involved in acquiring and thinking about extra information (Connolly & Thorn, 1987). But then, if one is not going to look at everything, how does one decide on the order to look through the information that is available?

Ordering search

In many investigations of search behaviour, order is simply determined by people's preferences. To illustrate this, consider the often-used apartment-renting scenario (e.g. Payne, 1976). In this task participants are given access to information (the attributes) about a number of apartments (the alternatives, or options). The attributes might include information concerning the rent, proximity to work, shops, noise level, etc. Participants are allowed to search through the attributes and alternatives in their own preferred order. A participant who values a quiet neighbourhood highly might choose to examine this attribute for all the alternatives first, whereas a highly budget-conscious participant might choose to examine the rent first. In contrast some participants might decide to examine all the attributes for a particular apartment before looking at another apartment. What are the advantages of adopting a predominantly alternative-wise or attribute-wise search strategy?

Payne, Bettman and Johnson (1993) suggest that deciding how to decide involves a trade-off between the *accuracy* of a decision and the *effort* involved in making it. They proposed thinking of the strategies available to a decision maker as points in a two-dimensional space, with one dimension representing the relative accuracy of the strategies and the other dimension the amount of cognitive effort required to complete the strategies. Conceptualizing trade-off in this way makes it possible to see what combinations of accuracy and effort are entailed by particular strategies. The strategy ultimately selected from that set would depend on the relative weight placed by the decision maker on the goal of making an accurate decision versus saving cognitive effort.

If you have limitless time, and do not mind expending a good deal of cognitive effort, you might decide to use an *alternative-based* strategy. Such strategies consider each alternative (e.g. an apartment) one at a time and make a summary evaluation of it before considering the next one in a choice set. An example of an alternative-based strategy is the weighted additive linear rule. This rule entails placing a 'weight' or degree of importance on each attribute (e.g. cost is most important, space second most important, etc.) then examining each alternative one at a time and calculating an overall 'score' by adding up the weighted value of each attribute. Such a strategy, although prescribed by rational theories, is obviously effortful and time consuming.

As we saw in Chapter 2, Herbert Simon (1956) introduced the concept of 'bounded rationality' in acknowledgement of the need to consider the interconnectedness of the computational capabilities of the actor and the structure of the environment. Simon argued that this interconnectedness sometimes leads people to 'satisfice' – to look for 'good enough' solutions that approximate the accuracy of optimal algorithms (like the weighted additive linear rule) without incurring undue computational costs.

How would such a satisficing strategy be used to search through alternatives? A 'satisficer' searches the alternatives in a non-specified order and the first alternative examined which exceeds a predetermined aspiration level is chosen (e.g. the first apartment considered which has the combination of rent below $1000 per month and is within walking distance of work). As Payne, Bettman and Luce (1998) note, a major implication of the satisficing heuristic is that choice depends on the *order* in which alternatives are considered. If alternatives A and B both exceed the aspiration level but alternative A is considered first, it will be chosen. Such a choice would be made even if B were preferable on any or all of the choice criteria (e.g. apartment B was cheaper).

So how do people deal with this trade-off in real-world decisions? Fasolo, McClelland and Lange (2005) considered this question in a study examining pre-decisional search in a consumer choice task. They argued that difficulties arise for consumers when products available for choice have conflicting attributes such as quality and convenience; one product might be high in convenience but unattractive in price whereas another might be low in convenience but high in quality. The greater these attribute conflicts, the harder the decision for the consumer. To investigate the effect of attribute conflict on choice, Fasolo et al. gave participants a task in which they were asked to recommend to a friend one digital camera from a selection of five models. Each model was described along eight attributes (optical zoom, resolution, image capacity, etc.) and participants were able to access information about each attribute via a computer-based 'information board'. The 'friend' provided a memo indicating that all the attributes were equally important – this was to ensure participants knew they needed to consider each attribute.

Fasolo et al. (2005) found that when there was a high degree of conflict, participants tended to search more by alternatives than by attributes, whereas when conflict was low, attributes were searched predominantly. Search was also more extensive under high-conflict conditions, perhaps reflecting participants' inability to remember the conflicting implications of different attributes. Furthermore, when conflict was high, participants rated the decisions as more difficult, had lower confidence in their choice and were more dissatisfied with their decision than when conflict was low.

The results are consistent with intuitions about consumer choice – when we begin searching for a product, we can easily exclude items from our choice set that do not match our criteria – a product that is too expensive or too large. However, when we near the end of our search and have winnowed down the set to a few likely alternatives, we may find a number of conflicting attributes (one camera has a 10-megapixel resolution but poor memory capacity, another the opposite attributes) so we need to consider each alternative very carefully. As Fasolo et al. point out, the results suggest that more could be done to help decision makers in their search for information – especially in online shopping where information boards of the type used in Fasolo et al.'s experiment are often displayed.

The rise of online shopping environments highlights another dilemma facing us when we search for information and try to decide – can we have *too much* choice? Several researchers have suggested that an overabundance of options can lead to adverse consequences such as a decrease in the motivation to choose and a decrease in the satisfaction with a chosen option (e.g. Iyengar & Lepper, 2000). As Scheibehenne, Greifeneder and Todd (2010) point out, this 'paradox of choice' (Schwartz, 2000) effect has both theoretical and practical implications. From a theoretical standpoint, expanding choice sets should not – according to most psychological and economic theories of choice – make people worse off. From a practical perspective, if the drive by marketers and public policy makers to increase choice can actually lead to less-motivated and less-satisfied customers, then a rethink of such advertising campaigns and policy initiatives is in order. However, despite the intuitive appeal and resonance of this choice-overload hypothesis, a systematic meta-analysis of the empirical evidence by Scheibehenne et al. (2010) revealed an effect size of virtually zero. This means that some studies showed that increasing the number of options was bad for choice, while others showed that it facilitated choice and still others that there was no impact on choice at all. Further research is clearly needed in this area to identify when too much choice can be good, bad or make no difference.

COMBINING INFORMATION

Once the search is over and we have all the information we think we need for a decision, what should we do with it? How should we put it all together?

A decision strategy which advocates combining all information can be described as *compensatory*. This is because the acquisition of successive pieces of information can influence the judgment that is made. Consider the car example again: your estimate of the price might be high when you note that the car is a Mercedes but then lowered when you notice that the car has poor trim (no leather seats or alloy wheels – perhaps it is a bottom-of-the-range Mercedes). So your initial estimate based on the make is *compensated* by the information you subsequently acquired. In contrast, a *non-compensatory* strategy relies on less information (sometimes only one piece – perhaps the make of the car) and ignores the possible influence of other information.

In both cases, whether we have acquired many or few pieces of information, we need to know how to put what we have together to make a decision. In this section we examine methods that advocate combining all available pieces of information with those that advocate simpler and more frugal combination methods. As we shall see, some of the findings for both classes of models are counter-intuitive and remarkable.

Compensatory strategies

According to Dawes and Corrigan (1974), once we have worked out what variables to look at, simply 'knowing how to add' (p. 105) is sufficient for combining information. But what does it mean to say that we should 'add' up information – what are we adding? Back to the car example again: one strategy would be to adopt the weighted linear additive rule described above. Imagine assigning a weight (a score between 0 and 10) to each of the attributes you've identified, where 0 means 'no importance' and 10 'very important'. You might give 7 to the make, 3 to alloy wheels, 6 to a navigation system, etc. Your overall judgment about the price would then be based on the sum ('weighted additive') of these attributes – the greater the sum, the higher your estimate of the price. For example, if the car has alloy wheels, this would contribute +3 to the sum; if it does not then you would subtract 3 (–3) from the sum. This might seem rather complicated, so an alternative compensatory strategy would be to assign *equal* weights to all the attributes (e.g. now the presence of alloy wheels would add 1 (+1) and their absence would subtract 1 (–1) from the sum). How accurate would our judgments be if we adopted these types of strategies?

As we noted briefly in the section on the history of judgment research in Chapter 2, important insights into the accuracy of these types of strategies were made by Paul Meehl (1954). He described how comparisons of the judgments made by expert clinicians (psychologists and psychiatrists) and those derived from statistical models (like the weighted additive rule) that used only the empirical data (the left side of the lens model shown in Figure 3.1) revealed consistently that the statistical models either made more accurate predictions or that the two methods tied for accuracy. In other words, a rule that simply adds statistically optimal weights (derived via multiple regression analyses) in a linear fashion will in most cases outperform the considered and deliberated judgments of experts. The basic pattern of findings first reported by Meehl (1954) has been corroborated by a series of other studies in diverse contexts (e.g. Dawes, Faust & Meehl, 1989; Einhorn, 1972; Goldberg, 1968; Grove & Meehl, 1996; Werner, Rose & Yesavage, 1983). A meta-analysis of 136 studies in the areas of medicine, mental health, education and training found that on average statistical techniques were 10% more accurate than experts, and that statistical techniques were superior to experts in 47% of studies and the reverse was true in only 6% of studies. For the remaining 47% the two methods tied for accuracy (Grove et al., 2000). This consistent pattern of findings has led some researchers to conclude that 'Whenever possible, human judges should be replaced by simple linear models' (Hastie & Dawes, 2001, p. 63).

But how can a simple statistical model outperform human predictions? Dawes et al. (1989) list several factors that can contribute to this superior performance. Firstly, a statistical method will always arrive at the same judgment for a given set of data. Experts, on the other hand, are susceptible to the effects of fatigue or changes in motivation/concentration, the influence of changes in the way information is presented (as we saw in Chapter 1), and recent experience. In a well-known study of diagnostic ability, Brooks, Norman and Allen (1991) demonstrated that physicians' diagnoses of dermatological conditions were greatly affected by the similarity between current and recently experienced examples. This effect of specific similarity lasted for at least a week and reduced diagnostic accuracy by 10–20% – a reduction that was both statistically and clinically significant.

Secondly, experts are often exposed to skewed samples of evidence, making it difficult to assess the actual relation between variables and a criterion of interest. Dawes et al. (1989) give the example of a doctor attempting to ascertain the relation between juvenile delinquency and abnormal electroencephalographic (EEG) recordings. If, in a given sample of delinquents, the doctor discovers that approximately half show an abnormal EEG pattern, then she might conclude that such a pattern is a good indicator of delinquency. However, to draw this conclusion the doctor would need to know the prevalence of this EEG pattern in both delinquent *and* non-delinquent juveniles. The doctor is more likely to evaluate delinquent juveniles (as these will be the ones who are referred) and this exposure to an unrepresentative sample makes it more difficult to conduct the comparisons necessary for drawing a valid conclusion.

Dawes et al. (1989) also note that this tendency to draw invalid conclusions on the basis of skewed samples is compounded by our susceptibility to confirmation biases. Several studies have documented our propensity to seek out information that confirms our existing beliefs rather than information that might disconfirm them (e.g. Klayman & Ha, 1987; Wason, 1960). Thus once an expert has drawn an invalid conclusion, the belief in that conclusion is likely to be reinforced by a bias in the information that is subsequently attended to.

These reasons and many others (see Dawes, 1979; Dawes et al., 1989) contribute to the superiority of statistical methods over human experts and together make a strong case for adopting the statistical technique in a variety of situations. There is, however, an important distinction that needs to be made before jumping to strong conclusions about replacing humans with statistical models. Einhorn (1972), echoing an earlier review by Sawyer (1966), made the point that although 'mechanical combination' – the term used to describe the statistical mode of combining information – had been shown to be superior to 'expert combination', there is still potentially an important role to be played by the expert as the *provider* of information to be fed into the mechanical combination.

To illustrate the point, Einhorn drew a distinction between a *global* overall judgment made about a criterion and the *components* that go into that judgment. Global judgments are a combination of the components and this combination can be performed either statistically or via an expert. To explore the relation between components and global judgments Einhorn focused on an issue that had close personal significance for him – the diagnosis of Hodgkin's disease – a form of lymph cancer that he eventually died from in 1987. The global judgment in the study was the severity of the disease in a group of patients. The component judgments were ones about the relative amount of nine histological characteristics which had been identified by the three pathologists in the study as relevant for determining disease severity. Biopsy slides taken from 193 patients diagnosed with the disease were shown individually to the three expert pathologists. All of the patients used in the study had already died, making it possible for Einhorn to examine retrospectively how accurately the pathologists' analysis of the severity of the disease predicted survival time. The analysis of the global judgments conformed to the standard view that experts were poor at combining information: none of the judgments correlated significantly with survival time, and indeed for some judges the relationship was in the opposite direction – higher severity ratings associated with a longer survival time.

However, when Einhorn examined the components of the global judgment (judgments of the histological signs) he found a more encouraging picture. Ignoring the global judgments and just examining the relation between the component judgments and survival time revealed stronger correlations. For example, for one judge the amount of variance explained jumped from 0% when his global judgment was used to almost 20% when only the components were used. Although overall the correlations were not that high, they were statistically reliable and significantly more accurate than the global judgments. The findings led Einhorn to conclude that 'expert information or judgment can be a very useful method for getting input for a mechanical combination process' (p. 102). Dawes et al. (1989) echoed this conclusion, noting that only human observers may be able to recognize particular cues such as mannerisms (e.g. the 'float-like' walk of certain schizophrenic patients) as having true predictive value. However, they emphasized that 'a unique capacity to observe is not the same as a unique capacity to predict on the basis of integration of observations' (p. 1671) and thus suggested that greater accuracy might be achieved if the expert identifies the important cues through observation and then leaves it up to a statistical model to combine these observations in an optimal way.

Experts seem to be good at identifying the components necessary for accurate judgments, but are poor at combining those components. Presumably, one of the reasons for this poor performance in combination is an inability to weight the components in an optimal way – as a statistical model does (Einhorn, 1972). But which aspect of the judgment process is more important – identifying the information or combining it using an optimal weighting scheme? Dawes (1979) demonstrated convincingly that the former part of the process is the crucial one. He showed that it is not even necessary to use statistically optimal weights in linear models to outperform experts' global judgments – *any* linear model will do the job! Dawes used several data sources to construct linear models with weights determined randomly except for the sign (positive or negative), arguing that the direction in which each cue predicted the criterion would be known in advance in any prediction context of interest. Surprisingly, these *random linear models* outperformed human judges in contexts ranging from predictions of psychosis versus neurosis, to faculty ratings of graduate students on the basis of indicators of academic performance. On average the random linear models accounted for 150% more of the variance between criteria and prediction than the expert judges. For mathematical reasons, converting the random weights into *unit weights* (by standardizing and prescribing a value of +1 or −1 depending on the direction of the cue – this is the same as the *equal weight* strategy we discussed in relation to the car example earlier), led to even better performance – an average of 261% more variance explained. Models of this latter type have subsequently been described as conforming to 'Dawes Rule' (see also Einhorn & Hogarth, 1975, for a detailed discussion of unit weighting schemes).

Non-compensatory strategies

The preceding examples illustrate that models that 'mechanically' combine all the relevant information before making a decision can be very accurate. However, such an exhaustive, integrative process is not always appropriate or achievable (cf. Simon, 1956 – see Chapter 2). As we saw in the section on acquiring information, the work of Payne and colleagues (e.g. Payne et al., 1993) among others has highlighted the importance of the trade-off between the accuracy achieved by searching through and integrating all sources of information and the cost in terms of the cognitive effort and time involved in those processes. How good can our decisions be if we base them on less information?

The fast-and-frugal heuristics of Gigerenzer and colleagues (e.g. Gigerenzer et al., 1999, 2011) provide an exemplary approach to such 'ignorance-based decision making' (Goldstein & Gigerenzer, 2002). Gigerenzer et al. (1999) view the mind as containing an 'adaptive toolbox' of specialized cognitive heuristics suited to different problems (e.g. choosing between alternatives, categorizing items, estimating quantities). The heuristics contained in this adaptive toolbox capitalize on what proponents describe as the 'benefits of cognitive limitations' (e.g. Hertwig & Todd, 2004) – the observation that the bounded nature of human cognition can, in certain environments, give rise to advantages in terms of frugality and speed of the decision process *without* suffering any concurrent loss in the accuracy of judgments and decisions.

To illustrate why this somewhat counter-intuitive situation might arise, we consider one of the most prominent heuristics in the adaptive toolbox – 'Take-the-Best' (TTB). TTB is a heuristic designed for binary choice situations. Such situations are extremely common in everyday life – for example, choosing between two job candidates, choosing between two stocks, two cars, two routes to travel on and so on. TTB exemplifies non-compensatory decision making by simply using the 'best' piece of information applicable in a given situation. TTB operates according to two principles. The first – the recognition principle – states that in any given decision made under uncertainty, if only one amongst a range of alternatives is recognized, then the recognized alternative should be chosen (Goldstein & Gigerenzer, 2002). We heard about this recognition principle or heuristic in Chapter 1 when we discussed its use as an investment tool (e.g. Borges et al., 1999). The second principle is invoked when more than one of the alternatives are recognized and the recognition principle cannot provide discriminatory information. In such cases, people are assumed to have access to a reference class of cues or features. People are then thought to search the cues in descending order of feature validity until they discover a feature that discriminates one alternative from the other. Once this single discriminating feature has been found, search is terminated (the 'stopping rule') and the feature is used to make a decision (the 'decision rule'). Figure 3.3 illustrates the processing steps of the TTB algorithm.

TTB has been applied to many tasks including answering almanac questions such as 'Which has the larger population, Hamburg or Leipzig?' (e.g. Gigerenzer & Goldstein, 1996). The reference class accessed to answer such a question is assumed to include cues such as 'Is the city the capital?', 'Does it have an airport/university/football team?' and so on. Assuming both cities are recognized, as soon as a cue is discovered that has different values for the two cities (e.g. Hamburg has a soccer team in the major league – positive evidence – but Leipzig does not – negative evidence), search stops and this single cue is used to infer (correctly in this case) that Hamburg has the larger population.

TTB is a special case of a lexicographic strategy (e.g. Fishburn, 1974), so called because cues are looked up in a fixed order, like the alphabetic order used to arrange words in a dictionary. Many such strategies have been developed to explain behaviour in preference problems – most notably perhaps Tversky's (1972) Elimination by Aspects (EBA) strategy, which considers the most important cue first, retrieves a cut-off value for that cue and eliminates all alternatives with values worse than the cut-off. It continues to do this by considering the second most important attribute (and so on) until only one

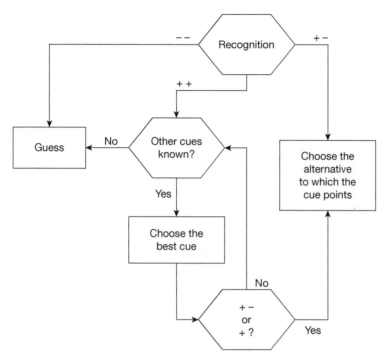

Figure 3.3 A flow chart of the processing steps of the Take-The-Best heuristic. A "+"
indicates a positive cue value; "–" indicates a negative cue value and "?"
indicates that the cue value is unknown. For example, if one knows that one
city has a football team (+) and knows either for sure that the other does not
(–) or is uncertain as to whether it has (?), then according to TTB one uses
this single piece of discriminating information to make a judgment.

From Gigerenzer, G., & Goldstein, D. G. (1996). Reasoning the fast and frugal way: Models of
bounded rationality. *Psychological Review, 103*, 650–669. Copyright 1996 by American Psychological
Association. Adapted with permission.

option remains. TTB is similar to EBA but the latter uses a probability function
to determine 'cue-importance' whereas TTB uses cue validity (see Bergert &
Nosofsky, 2007, for discussion of how TTB and EBA are related).

To test the performance of this simple decision heuristic, Gigerenzer and
Goldstein (1996) set up a competition between TTB and a range of compensatory decision rules. The task used in the competition was the German
cities task in which the aim is to determine which of a pair of cities has the
larger population. The environment comprised the 83 German cities with
a population over 100,000 and nine cues, each with its own validity (where
validity was defined as the probability that the cue will lead to the correct
choice if cue values differ between alternatives – see Newell et al., 2004,
and Rakow et al., 2005, for discussions of other ways to conceptualize cue
validity). Each decision strategy in the competition had its own method for

utilizing cue information and arriving at a decision. TTB only knows the order of the validities of the cues and simply searches down this order until it finds a cue that has different values for the two alternatives, then stops searching and chooses the alternative to which the cue points (see Figure 3.3). Importantly, if one city is recognized but the other is not, search is terminated and the recognized city is chosen without looking at any of the other nine cues. The other decision strategies in the competition were all compensatory because they look up all the cue values. Note that these strategies look up ten cues in all – the nine cues and recognition information, which is treated as 'just another cue' by the compensatory strategies. Table 3.1 presents each strategy along with a brief description of how each one combines cue information.

These six strategies were pitted against each other in a competition involving 252,000 simulated individuals. Such a large number was used to ensure that the simulation included 'people' with varying degrees of knowledge about German cities and thus enabled the simulated people to invoke the recognition heuristic. The results of the competition are summarized in Table 3.2. What is immediately surprising about the results is how well TTB does by using such a small amount of information in comparison to the strategies that use all available information. Although Weighted Tallying does as well as TTB, it uses over three times as much information on average (ten compared to three cues) and thus Gigerenzer and Goldstein (1996) judged TTB to be the overall winner of the competition.

Table 3.1 Description of the strategies used in the German Cities Task Competition in Gigerenzer & Goldstein (1996)

Strategy	Cue Combination Method
Take-the-Best *(sequential)*	Searches cues in validity order and bases choice on the first cue that discriminates between alternatives.
Tallying	Tallies up all the positive evidence, and the alternative with largest number of positive cue values is chosen.
Weighted Tallying	Weights each cue according to its validity (only looks at positive information).
Unit Weight Linear	Assigns positive and negative weights depending on cue value (same as 'Dawes Rule').
Weighted Linear	Cue values are multiplied by their respective validities (often viewed as optimal rule for preferential choice under the idealization of independent cues (Keeney & Raiffa, 1976)).
Multiple Regression	Creates weights that reflect validities of cues and covariance between cues (interdependencies). (Viewed as optimal way to integrate information – neural networks using the delta rule determine optimal weights by the same principle as multiple regression (Stone, 1986 – see Chapter 12).)

Table 3.2 Results of the competition between Take-the-Best and five compensatory strategies

Strategy	Knowledge about cues	Frugality (number of cues looked up)	Accuracy (% of correct predictions)
Take-the-Best	order	3	65.8
Tallying	direction	10	65.6
Weighted Tallying	validities	10	65.8
Unit Weight Linear	direction	10	62.1
Weighted Linear	validities	10	62.3
Multiple Regression	beta-weights	10	65.7

Note: Compiled from data reported in Gigerenzer, G., & Goldstein, D. G. (1999). Betting on one good reason: The take-the-best heuristic. In G. Gigerenzer, P. M. Todd, & The ABC Research Group (Eds), *Simple heuristics that make us smart* (pp. 75–96). New York: Oxford University Press; and Gigerenzer, G., & Goldstein, D. G. (1996). Reasoning the fast and frugal way: Models of bounded rationality. *Psychological Review, 103*, 650–669.

Why do weighted linear and unit weight linear strategies perform relatively poorly, when we know them to be highly robust in many situations (e.g. Dawes, 1979)? The answer lies in the information carried by recognition. By simply integrating recognition information along with other cues these strategies can violate the recognition heuristic by choosing the unrecognized alternative and therefore make a number of incorrect inferences. This is because in the German cities environment, most cities have more negative cue values than positive ones (for example, the answers to the 'Does it have an airport/university/soccer team?' questions are more often 'no' than 'yes'). This means that when a recognized city is compared with an unrecognized one the sum of its cue values will often be smaller than that of the unrecognized city. It follows that the overwhelming negative evidence for the recognized city will lead the unit-weight and weighted linear models to choose erroneously the unrecognized city. The tallying models do not suffer from this problem because they ignore all negative evidence and thus have the recognition heuristic 'built in' (Gigerenzer & Goldstein, 1996).

There are other mathematical reasons why TTB outperforms the more compensatory strategies. Interested readers should examine the work of Martignon and Hoffrage (1999; 2002), Hogarth and Karelaia (2005) and Katsikopoulos and Martignon (2006) for more detailed accounts of how TTB capitalizes on the nature of environments, such as whether information is structured in a compensatory or non-compensatory way, to enable its good performance. For now, though, we turn to the question of whether these 'fast' and 'frugal' heuristics are also adopted by people when making decisions.

Empirical tests of fast-and-frugal strategies

There is no doubt that the simulation data described above demonstrate the impressive speed and accuracy of fast-and-frugal strategies like TTB. The simplicity of these strategies also, according to Gigerenzer and Goldstein (1996), makes them 'plausible psychological mechanisms of inference . . . that a mind can actually carry out under limited time and knowledge' (p. 652). However, as Bröder and Schiffer (2003) eloquently pointed out, 'plausibility is a weak advisor in the scientific endeavor' (p. 278) and empirical evidence, if it is attainable, should always be preferred. The evidence that documents the formal properties and efficiency of fast-and-frugal heuristics (Czerlinski, Gigerenzer & Goldstein, 1999; Goldstein et al., 2001; Martignon & Hoffrage, 1999) needs to be complemented by empirical validation demonstrating that people do indeed use these heuristics in the environments in which they are claimed to operate (cf. Chater et al., 2003).

For example, Oppenheimer (2003) asked whether there is any evidence that recognition is indeed used in a non-compensatory manner. Recall that much of the success of TTB in the German cities competition was due to the search being stopped as soon as only one of a pair of cities was recognized – is this really what people do when faced with such a task? Oppenheimer (2003) reasoned that if knowledge other than recognition really was ignored then the recognition heuristic predicts that individuals would judge a recognized city as larger than an unrecognized city *even if the recognized city were known to be small*. Oppenheimer (2003) tested this counter-intuitive prediction in an experiment in which he paired cities that were recognizable (due to their proximity to the university where the study was conducted) but known to be small (e.g. Cupertino), with fictional cities that, by definition, could not be recognized (e.g. Rhavadran). On average, participants judged the local – recognized – city to be larger on only 37% of trials. This result, which contrasts starkly with the prediction of the recognition heuristic, led Oppenheimer to conclude that 'people clearly are using information beyond recognition when making judgments about city size' (p. B4). Subsequent investigations of the recognition heuristic in both artificial and real-world environments have found only very limited evidence for the non-compensatory use of recognition. It appears that in most inference tasks recognition is simply used as one cue among many others (Bröder & Eichler, 2006; Hilbig & Pohl, 2009; Hilbig, Erdfelder & Pohl, 2010; Newell & Fernandez, 2006; Newell & Shanks, 2004; Pleskac, 2007; Richter & Späth, 2006).

In a series of studies, Newell and colleagues (Newell & Shanks, 2003; 2004; Newell, Weston & Shanks, 2003; Newell et al., 2004; Rakow et al., 2005) sought empirical validation of fast-and-frugal heuristics using a simple MCPL-type task. The task was a share prediction task in which participants aimed to make money by investing in the company that ended up with the higher share price. Each trial consisted of a choice between two companies. To help them make their decisions participants could buy information about four cues or indicators of each company's financial status (e.g. *Is it an established company? Does the company have financial reserves?*). The cues were binary, such that the answer to each question (uncovered by clicking on a 'Buy Information' button) was either 'YES' or 'NO'. This information board set-up allowed several kinds of data to be obtained such as the order in which participants bought information, the amount of information they bought, and the final choice made. This in turn permitted examination of peoples' adherence to the search, stopping and decision rules of both the recognition heuristic and TTB.

In the experiments a number of factors were varied to examine their effects on the adoption of different decision strategies. The factors included the cost of information, the familiarity of companies, the number of cues in the environment (2, 4 or 6), the underlying structure of the task (deterministic or probabilistic) and the provision of hints concerning the validity ordering of the cues. The reason for changing these factors was to try to design environments that were strongly constrained to promote the use of TTB or recognition. Despite these attempts, in all the experiments the overall pattern of results was similar: simply stated – some of the people used the heuristics some of the time. In all experiments, a significant proportion of participants adopted strategies that violated all or some of their rules – especially the stopping rule. Indeed, in the two experiments reported in Newell et al. (2003) only a third of participants behaved in a manner completely consistent with TTB's search, stopping and decision rules.

A key finding was that a large number of participants sought more information than was predicted by the frugal stopping rules of the heuristics. That is they continued to buy information after recognizing only one of a pair of companies or after discovering a cue that discriminated between the two companies. Newell (2005) has argued that these large individual differences in the amount of evidence acquired before a decision is made are more consistent with a weighted-evidence threshold model than a fast-and-frugal heuristic. One way of explaining individual variability is to suggest that all participants use an evidence-accumulation strategy, but that some participants require greater amounts of evidence than others before making their decisions. Lee and Cummins (2004) found that such an evidence-accumulation model accounted for 84.5% of the decisions made by participants in a similar cue-learning task – more than that accounted for by either TTB or a compensatory strategy alone.

Extensions to this work on evidence accumulation models have begun to use various computational modelling and data analysis methods to investigate how people search, stop and decide in multiple cue tasks. Newell, Lee, and colleagues have argued that using such methods to characterize and explain behaviour provides a richer and more complete account than those that describe performance in terms of the operation of discrete heuristics (e.g. van Ravenzwaaij et al., 2014; Lee & Newell, 2011). This work has also explored how people adjust their search in dynamic environments (where cue structures change over time) (Lee, Newell, & Vandekerckhove, 2014) and shed light on the thorny problem of 'strategy selection' (Newell & Lee, 2011; see also Scheibehenne, Rieskamp & Wagenmakers, 2013; Söllner et al., 2014).

The picture painted by the empirical data suggests mixed support for fast-and-frugal heuristics. There is some evidence that people use 'something like' TTB some of the time (Bergert & Nosofsky, 2007; Bröder 2000; Bröder & Schiffer, 2003; Dhami & Ayton, 2001; Dhami & Harries, 2001; Reiskamp & Hoffrage, 1999; Rieskamp & Otto, 2006) but equally there is evidence suggesting wide individual differences and a poor fit with their constituent rules (Bröder & Eichler, 2006; Hilbig & Pohl, 2009; Juslin & Persson, 2002; Newell & Fernandez, 2006; Newell & Lee, 2011; Newell & Shanks, 2003; Oppenheimer, 2003; Söllner et al., 2014).

In addition to the debate about the empirical evidence, some researchers have challenged some of the key assumptions underlying fast-and-frugal heuristics. In a wide-ranging critique, Dougherty, Franco-Watkins and Thomas (2008) raised concerns about the claim that people have access to a reference-class of cues arranged in a validity hierarchy – something that is crucial for TTB and the recognition heuristic to operate frugally (see also Newell, 2005). They also question whether there are any constraints on the size of the adaptive toolbox or whether a new (potentially redundant) heuristic can be created to explain any and all observed patterns of behaviour. These are important (and hard!) questions and recent work has begun to address both the 'where do cues come from?' (e.g. Katsikopoulos, Schooler & Hertwig, 2010) and 'how is the toolbox constrained?' (e.g. Scheibehenne, Rieskamp & Wagenmakers, 2013) questions. Other researchers have advocated alternative approaches to addressing binary judgment under uncertainty that side-step the issue of cue hierarchies and toolboxes altogether (e.g. Brown & Tan, 2011; Schweickart & Brown, 2014).

Given all these developments it seems that examining the benefits and use of compensatory and non-compensatory 'fast-and-frugal' strategies in decision making will continue to be a fruitful area for research and debate.

SUMMARY

When we make judgments and decisions, we must first discover the relevant information in the environment, search through and acquire that information and then combine it in some manner. A useful metaphor for conceptualizing these processes is provided by the lens model framework of Egon Brunswik. In this framework a judge is thought to view the world through a lens of 'cues', which are probabilistically related to the true state of the environment. One experimental technique born out of this metaphor is multiple-cue probability learning (MCPL). Experiments using this technique have examined the processes underlying discovery, acquisition and combination of information.

The few studies which have examined cue discovery suggest that discovering valid cues in the environment takes many hundreds if not thousands of trials, but that the opportunity to experiment or intervene during the learning process enhances this discovery, especially in environments with causal structures. Cue search and acquisition can be guided by simple preference or objective cue-validity and is influenced by the trade-off between the cost and benefit of obtaining more information, although not always in the way specified by normative analyses.

In studies of information combination a contrast is drawn between methods which combine all relevant information (compensatory) or fewer pieces of information (non-compensatory). A wealth of evidence suggests that statistical methods for combining information outperform human judgments, but humans are useful for identifying the relevant components for combination. Some simple non-compensatory heuristics such as Take-the-Best are almost as accurate as more complex compensatory strategies such as a weighted additive rule, despite using far fewer pieces of information. However, the psychological plausibility of such simple heuristics has been questioned due to a lack of clear empirical evidence indicating that people actually employ these techniques in their judgments and decisions, and reservations about some of the underlying assumptions of the framework.

The take home message from this journey through the stages of discovery, acquisition and combination is the significance of experience in environments for improving our judgments. In keeping with our emphasis on the importance of learning, we have seen how the discovery of cues, the adoption of different strategies for information acquisition and combination are all affected by our exposure to the environment and our opportunities to learn. However, one aspect of the data we have reviewed so far that might seem inconsistent with this view is the finding that experts – who have by definition had a great deal of experience in the relevant environments – are outperformed by statistical models. We will return to this interesting issue when we cover expertise in more detail in Chapter 13, but for now we need to consider the final 'stage' in the process of making judgments and decisions – how do we use feedback to help us learn?

Suggested further reading

- Dawes, R. M. (1979). The robust beauty of improper linear models in decision making. *American Psychologist*, *34*, 571–582. A seminal paper that explains the power of linear judgment models.
- Dawes, R. M., Faust, D., & Meehl, P. E. (1989). Clinical versus actuarial judgment. *Science*, *243*, 1668–1674. An excellent summary of the work initiated by Meehl's 1954 book.
- Gigerenzer, G., Hertwig, R., & Pachur, T. (2011). *Heuristics: The foundations of adaptive behavior*. New York: Oxford University Press. A collection of papers documenting work inspired by the fast-and-frugal heuristics programme.
- Karelaia, N., & Hogarth, R. M. (2008). Determinants of linear judgment: A meta-analysis of lens model studies. *Psychological Bulletin*, *134*, 404–426. A comprehensive meta-analysis of many studies inspired by the lens model approach.

- Payne, J. W., Bettman, J. R., & Johnson, E. J. (1993). *The adaptive decision maker.* New York: Cambridge University Press. An extensive examination of how decision makers balance effort and accuracy.
- Todd, P. M., Hills, T. T., & Robbins, T. W. (Eds) (2012). *Cognitive search: Evolution, algorithms, and the brain.* Strüngmann Forum Reports, vol. 9, Cambridge, MA: MIT Press. A comprehensive summary that expands on the definitions and components of exploration and exploitation in search by humans and other organisms.

4 Stages of judgment II
Feedback effects and dynamic environments

Chapter highlights

- Understanding how feedback can vary and how different forms of feedback improve multiple-cue probability learning
- Exploring the relationship between information gained via feed*back* and information provided via feed*forward*
- Discovering how experiences of uncertainty impact on our ability to control complex dynamic systems.

'If at first you don't succeed then try, try again.' We have all been told to persevere or 'keep at it' if we get something wrong the first time. The assumption is that through repeated efforts we will improve and eventually succeed – we will learn from our experience. But what aspects of our experience do we learn from? Is it enough to simply be told that we were right or wrong or do we need to be told *why* we were right or wrong? Or at least be given the information that helps us to infer where we went wrong?

The effects of feedback have been investigated in a wide range of judgment and decision-making tasks (see Harvey & Fischer, 2005, for a discussion of the role of feedback in confidence judgment, probability estimation and advice-taking tasks), but in keeping with the focus of Chapter 3, in the first part of this chapter we will examine primarily the evidence from multiple-cue probability-learning (MCPL) tasks. In the second part of the chapter we take a more integrative view by considering how all the separate stages of judgment are combined. We note that the environments in which we make decisions are typically not controlled by 'static' rules ensuring that properties of the environment remain constant (as they are in many laboratory tasks) – but are usually dynamic and require us to anticipate and learn to control changes in those environments. Feedback is particularly important in these situations and so we consider attempts to investigate how feedback interacts with the other stages of decision making in real-time 'dynamic' tasks.

LEARNING FROM FEEDBACK

Learning from feedback is often thought of as a single process, but there are a number of different ways in which feedback may be used to improve performance on a task. First, as the section on cue discovery in Chapter 3 made clear, one needs to work out what the important variables are in the task (Klayman, 1988a; 1988b). To improve your performance, it seems essential to 'know what to look at' before you can construct any kind of 'mental model' of how your interactions with a system affect its behaviour. As Klayman has argued, though this initial process of discovery seems to be a prerequisite for understanding how feedback operates, it is perhaps the least understood aspect of learning from experience.

Once the relevant cues have been discovered, or been given to you (as is often the case in laboratory experiments), you need to work out the best way to use the information provided by the cues. Brehmer (1979) has argued that there are three components involved in ascertaining this 'best way'. First, it is necessary to learn about the functional relation between each cue and the criterion that is being predicted. Does an increase in the amount of a particular hormone always indicate an improvement in the health of a patient (a linear function) or does either too much or too little of the hormone indicate poor health (an inverted U function)? Second, the decision maker needs to learn the optimal relative weighting to ascribe to different pieces of information (is the result of Test A a stronger predictor of the presence of a disease than Test B?) Finally, if multiple cues are involved, the decision maker has to consider relations among the cues and determine the best way to integrate them, such as via a simple additive rule or some more complex interactive or multiplicative function.

Simply right or wrong: outcome feedback

Having an assignment returned with FAIL written on it tells you that you did something wrong, but will that experience help you to write a better assignment next time? Probably not: in order to improve, you need some information about *why* the assignment was poor. Did you concentrate on the wrong topics, or write too much on irrelevant details and too little on relevant ones, or perhaps fail to construct a coherent argument with the information available? Each of these failures maps onto the ways outlined above in which feedback can help learning, such as identifying the important variables (or topics), weighting them appropriately, and then integrating them correctly. Is this intuition about the ineffectiveness of simple outcome feedback for improving performance borne out by laboratory studies?

The received wisdom in answer to this question is 'yes'. Outcome feedback alone does not appear to improve performance, or as Brehmer (1980) stated in a perplexingly titled paper on the subject, 'In one word: not from experience'. As we shall see a little later, this may be overstating the case somewhat but first we will address the evidence for this rather pessimistic conclusion.

In a typical MCPL task, outcome feedback is the provision of the true value of the criterion after participants have made their estimate on each trial. For example, if the task were predicting a person's salary on the basis of their weight, age and car that they owned, a participant might predict $35,000 and then be given outcome feedback informing them that the correct answer was $50,000. Such feedback typically only leads to improvements in performance when the environment is very simple (two or three cues that are positively and linearly related to the criterion) and when feedback is combined with a long series of trials (Balzer, Doherty & O'Connor, 1989; Brehmer, 1980; Hammond, 1971; Hammond & Boyle, 1971; Klayman, 1988b; Todd & Hammond, 1965). If the functions relating the cues to the criterion are negative, or worse, non-linear, then learning can in fact be impeded by outcome feedback (Deane, Hammond & Summers, 1972; Slovic, 1974). Finally, if the cues themselves are intercorrelated, then learning is typically disrupted (Lindell & Stewart, 1974; Schmitt & Dudycha, 1975).

What is it about the paucity of outcome feedback that makes learning from it so difficult? As Harvey and Fischer (2005) note, two competing explanations have been proposed. Brehmer (1980) in the paper referred to above suggests that the difficulty arises because 'people simply do not have the cognitive schemata needed for efficient performance in probabilistic tasks' (Brehmer, 1980, p. 233). He argues that people tend to form deterministic rules about the relations between cues and criterion – assuming for example that being over 50 always leads to a salary greater than $40,000 – and that when these rules break down (because the cues and outcomes are only probabilistically related) people discard the rules rather than considering that they may be probabilistic in character. Thus, under Brehmer's interpretation it is not the paucity of the outcome feedback per se that is the problem, rather it is an inability on the part of the subject to learn *any* complex probabilistic task.

In contrast, Todd and Hammond (1965) suggested that the problem is simply that outcome feedback in most MCPL tasks does not provide the information that participants require in order to improve their performance. Specifically, it gives them no information about how to revise the weights they assign to the available cues. If their estimate of a person's salary is too high, is this because too much weight has been put on the car that the person owns, or on the person's age (cf. Harvey & Fischer, 2005)? Similarly, in writing your essay, did you fail because you concentrated on the wrong topics altogether or because you spent too long on irrelevant details of those topics?

In an effort to distinguish between Brehmer's (1980) and Todd and Hammond's (1965) competing explanations, Harries and Harvey (2000) compared performance in a typical MCPL task with that in an 'advice-taking' task. The underlying probabilistic structure of the two tasks was identical, but the cover stories given to participants differed. Both groups were required to predict sales of a consumer product. In the MCPL group, sales were predicted on the basis of four pieces of information (number of sales outlets, competitors' promotional spending, and so on), each of which varied in predictive validity.

For the advice-taking group, instead of the pieces of information, subjects were presented with sales forecasts from four 'advisors' who differed in their forecasting ability. In both conditions the actual numbers presented to participants were identical; the only difference was that in the MCPL condition the numbers were given labels corresponding to different sales indicators, whereas in the advice group *all* the numbers were labelled as sales forecasts. Thus the crucial difference between these two tasks was that in the advice-taking task the cues (forecasts) and criterion (sales) all referred to the *same* variable, whereas in the MCPL task the cues (number of outlets etc.) referred to different variables than that specified by the criterion and by the outcome feedback (sales volume). Thus in the advice-task outcome feedback informed participants not only about the error in their judgment, but also the error in each forecast provided to them. As a result, participants were given information directly about how much they should rely on each cue – the aspect of feedback that Todd and Hammond's analysis suggested was essential for improvements in performance.

Note that both the advice and MCPL tasks were relatively complex and probabilistic, so according to Brehmer's interpretation, outcome feedback should have been equally ineffective in both. Contrary to this interpretation, however, Harries and Harvey found that learning in the advice task was much faster than in the MCPL task. Even at the end of the experiment performance was poorer in the MCPL task. The results appear to lend strong support to Todd and Hammond's arguments but are inconsistent with Brehmer's (1980) pessimistic conclusion that people are just not capable of learning from experience in probabilistic tasks.

FEEDBACK OR FEEDFORWARD?

Harries and Harvey's (2000) results provide some interesting evidence about how people perform in advice and MCPL tasks, but was the difference they found really a result of the way in which people learned from their experience in the task? A surprising finding in the Harries and Harvey study was that the advantage for the advice-taking group was evident on the very first trial of the experiment. This advantage could therefore not have been the result of the more effective use of feedback, rather it must have arisen because 'the expectations about the task that people generated after reading the experimental instructions were more useful in the advice-taking task' (Harvey & Fischer, 2005, p. 122). This interpretation is consistent with the idea that people used a feedforward mechanism in which information in the environment was used to guide performance on the task – even before they began to make predictions.

Björkman (1972) made a similar point in a discussion about the interaction between feedback and feedforward mechanisms in multiple-cue probability learning. According to Bjorkman (1972), 'feedforward refers to task information transmitted to the subject by instructions, whereas feedback refers to the trial-by-trial information provided by task outcomes' (p. 153). The idea is that feedforward provides information that would otherwise have to be learned by feedback. As such, the cognitive load placed on working memory is reduced, allowing for overall better performance on the task. Information provided via feedforward is also more consistent and accurate than that provided by feedback, because it is not subject to the various sources of error and bias that affect the trial-by-trial accumulation of information.

Therefore, it is perhaps not surprising that performance in the advice-taking task was superior to that in the MCPL one. Given the framing of the task in terms of 'advice-taking', one can speculate that participants' mental models might have led them to (correctly) estimate a sales value within the range of those provided by the advisors. In contrast, in the MCPL version, their mental models may not have imposed such a constraint on their judgments (Harvey & Fischer, 2005).

Evidence from a number of MCPL studies also supports the contention that it is the structure of the learning environment, and what that structure *affords* to participants' mental models that is important for performance in MCPL tasks. For example, Muchinsky and Dudycha (1975) showed that participants' performance in an MCPL task was significantly superior when cue names were changed from the abstract 'Cue 1' and 'Cue 2' to meaningful labels such as 'average monthly debt' and 'average number of creditors'. Even greater improvements in performance are seen when the labels provided to the cues are congruent with participants' prior conceptions of how cues and outcomes are related in the 'real world'. For example, in the Muchinsky and Dudycha study, when the criterion 'credit rating' was negatively related to monthly debt (incongruent), performance was inferior compared to when the two were positively related (congruent).

Adelman (1981) found similar effects in an MCPL task which compared the level of achievement (the correlation between criterion and prediction in the lens model framework – see Figure 3.1) reached with either cognitive (detailed information about the task structure) or outcome feedback in three conditions that varied the congruence between task properties implied by the task content (or cover story) of the task and the actual task properties. When the task content was neutral (cues were presented simply as Cue 1, Cue 2, etc.) provision of cognitive feedback led to higher levels of achievement than outcome feedback alone. However, when task congruent labels were used such as 'expectations for academic achievement', and 'social success' for predicting Grade Point Averages (GPA), there was no difference between the outcome and cognitive feedback groups – both performed at a similarly high level.

Note that in the Adelman study the cognitive feedback consisted of information such as the relative weights of cues, the function forms associated with cues and levels of predictability – all forms of information that are perhaps more appropriately described as feed*forward*. Thus again, it seems that rather than *learning* from experience it is simply being able to *use* appropriate information that is responsible for higher levels of achievement.

Why is feedback sometimes (in)effective?

But does the provision of relative weights, function forms and validities that typically comprise cognitive feedback always help participants? A series of studies by Castellan (Castellan, 1973; 1974; Castellan & Edgell, 1973; Castellan & Swaine, 1977) suggests not. For instance, Castellan (1974) compared the effects of four different types of feedback on performance in a two-cue binary outcome environment. On each trial participants were shown either a square or a triangle made up of either horizontal or vertical lines and had to predict whether the event '>' or '<' would occur. Participants were given one of four types of feedback in addition to outcome feedback: simple percentage correct, cue-event validity co-efficients, cue-response utilization co-efficients, or a combination of the latter two forms. Castellan's (1974) general conclusion was that no form of feedback enhanced performance, and in fact *all types of feedback* except percentage correct led to a decrement in performance – a conclusion that was echoed in later studies (e.g. Castellan & Swaine, 1977).

How can we reconcile these findings with those of Adelman (1981) and many others showing the usefulness of cognitive feedback (e.g. Balzer et al., 1989)? The principal difference between the studies was that the Castellan ones used binary cues and binary outcomes whereas the Adelman study used continuous cues and outcomes. Why might cognitive feedback be unhelpful in the former case? Perhaps the correlation information used to convey the relations between cues and outcomes was simply not *usable* by participants in the Castellan studies. Indeed, one of the experimenters involved in running the studies recalled that even he found it impossible to understand how to *use* the feedback (Stephen Edgell, personal communication). One potential explanation for this difficulty in use is that cognitive feedback was given separately for each cue (e.g. the validity of the line orientation cue, and the validity of the shape cue) even though the cues themselves were presented as configurations (e.g. a triangle containing horizontal lines). Presenting feedback on a cue-by-cue basis when participants needed to learn about the validity of whole patterns would have made their task difficult. In contrast, in the Adelman study and many of the other studies that have examined the effects of cognitive feedback, separate cue validities may have been more usable because they apply to easily discriminable cues, such as expectations for academic achievement and social success.

Newell, Weston et al. (2009) examined the potential reasons for these different effects of feedback in binary and continuous cue MCPL tasks. Their first experiment used a design that overcame a number of the possible limitations in the Castellan experiments. Participants were given a task in which the context was meaningful (predicting a change in share price); the additional form of feedback was in a format that was directly relevant to the prescribed task (information about the probability of a change in share price); and feedback pertained to the aspect of the stimulus most useful for performing the task (patterns as opposed to individual cues). On each trial of the experiment participants had to predict whether the share price of a fictitious company would increase or decrease based on the values of four binary cues, such as *Where are the company headquarters? (1 = London, 0 = New York)* and *Which index are the shares listed on? (1 = NASDAQ, 0 = FTSE).*

Newell et al. (2009) found that those participants given the additional cognitive feedback following each prediction (i.e. 'There was a X% probability that this share price would increase given this pattern') performed more accurately across 240 learning trials than those participants only given simple outcome feedback (i.e. 'share price increased/decreased' and 'correct/incorrect'). These results suggested that poor performance in previous studies (e.g. Castellan, 1974) was not due to any inherent limitation in feedback-driven learning in binary-cue MCPL, but rather that the particular form of feedback and experimental environment used were not conducive to helping participants solve the problems they faced. In two follow-up experiments, Newell, Weston et al. (2009) demonstrated that cognitive feedback conveys its advantage by allowing participants to learn cue polarity (that is, which value of a cue is associated with which outcome). This is the first 'hurdle' that Brehmer (1979) suggested needed to be overcome in solving MCPL tasks. In other words, it allowed participants to work out whether, for example, New York or London company headquarters were predictive of share price increase.

Newell et al. also gave some consideration to the strategies participants used to solve the MCPL task. An alternative approach, connecting MCPL with extensive research on categorization, suggests that judgments about a current cue pattern (or exemplar) can be made on the basis of similarity to previously seen patterns, which are stored in memory, rather than via the abstraction and integration of individual cue weights emphasized in the MCPL tradition (e.g. Juslin, Jones et al., 2003; Juslin, Olsson & Olsson, 2003; Nosofsky, 1986). Juslin and his colleagues have noted the conceptual similarity between MCPL decision tasks and those used in the study of category learning, and have reported several studies attempting to bridge these domains both at the task level and theoretically. One conclusion of these studies is that non-linear cue-criterion relations can be exceptionally hard to learn, and that participants often find themselves 'trapped in persistent and futile attempts to abstract the cue-criterion relations' (Olsson, Enkvist & Juslin, 2006, p. 1371) (see also Juslin, Karlsson, & Olsson, 2008; Bergert & Nosofsky, 2007).

In the Newell, Weston et al. (2009) experiments, the environment was partially non-linear and feedback was provided on a pattern rather than a cue basis. These are factors that arguably should promote the adoption of an exemplar memorization strategy (cf. Edgell & Morrissey, 1992). Yet despite this, participants appeared to quickly discover the linear component of the environment and adopted a strategy that treated cues independently and additively. Evidence for this came from finding that performance failed to exceed a level predicted by simple linear cue-tallying, and that numerical estimates of the probability of an increase mapped onto those predicted by cue-tallying, rather than the veridical values. However, there was some evidence that cognitive feedback led participants to weight cues more accurately by distinguishing which ones were most predictive. Thus, under appropriate circumstances (such as elaborated feedback), participants can outperform the elementary cue-tallying (Dawes' rule) heuristic, and use a more sophisticated weighted-linear rule, akin to multiple regression (see Chapter 3). Other research has similarly highlighted people's capacity to approximate the optimal linear strategy (e.g. Lagnado, Newell et al., 2006; Speekenbrink, Channon & Shanks, 2008; White & Koehler, 2007).

The picture that emerges from this research is that the extent of learning from feedback depends on how easily the feedback can be interpreted in a way that gives judges information about how to improve their performance (Harvey & Fischer, 2005). Performance is also affected by the amount of information a participant can glean from the instructions, the framing of the task and expectations derived (presumably) from real-world experience – all elements of 'feedforward'. This notion of the interplay between feedback and feedforward is consistent with the idea that participants build a mental model of the task with which they are engaged. Development of this model is influenced both 'top-down' via feedforward information and 'bottom-up' via feedback. If feedforward information matches with the feedback gained from engaging in the task, then feedback can be used to refine the feedforward and in turn to improve performance. If there is a mismatch between expectations and experience in the task, then the feedforward information is rejected, and improvements must be sought through feedback (Harvey & Fischer, 2005; Klayman, 1988b; Newell, Weston et al., 2009).

DECISION MAKING IN DYNAMIC ENVIRONMENTS

As we noted in the opening paragraphs of this chapter, the vast majority of research in the cue-learning tradition has focused on static environments in which cue-criterion relations remain constant. These static environments contrast with the 'real world' where we often need to keep track of numerous changing variables. In such situations our ability to adapt and use both feedback and feedforward information quickly is crucial. What do we know about judgment and decision making in these dynamic environments?

A few early cue-learning studies incorporated elements of dynamic environments. Changes to environments such as a shift in the relative weights of cues in the middle of learning, or making a previously non-predictive cue valid, and vice-versa, have been employed (e.g. Dudycha, Dumoff & Dudycha, 1973; Peterson, Hammond & Summers, 1965; Sniezek, 1986; see also Speekenbrink & Shanks, 2010, for a more contemporary treatment of these issues). The findings from these tasks have in general mirrored those of the static environments (Klayman, 1988b). However, these rather minor changes to the environment do not really capture what is meant by a dynamic decision task.

Brehmer and Allard (1991) defined dynamic decision tasks as having three important characteristics: (1) they require a series of interdependent decisions;

(2) the state of the task changes over time, both autonomously and as a consequence of the decision maker's actions, and (3) decisions have to be made in real time. One class of tasks that exhibits some of these characteristics is the complex control or judgmental control tasks that were studied intensively by Donald Broadbent and colleagues in the late 1970s and '80s (e.g. Berry & Broadbent, 1984, 1988; Broadbent & Aston, 1978; Broadbent, Fitzgerald & Broadbent, 1986; Hayes & Broadbent, 1988). In these tasks participants aimed to control the interaction of several variables simultaneously to produce predictable outputs. For example, Berry and Broadbent (1984) used a 'sugar production task' in which the output variable was the volume of sugar produced by a factory and the input variable was the number of workers in the factory. Participants played the role of the manager and were required to reach and maintain the optimum sugar output level by varying the number of workers. The relationship between the number of workers and the output levels was not a simple linear one, but was determined in part by the response that participants made on the previous trial. Participants were able to perform relatively well in these tasks, despite having very little verbal knowledge of the underlying relationship of the variables governing the system. Frensch and Funke (1995) contains detailed evaluation of performance in these tasks.

However, the complex control tasks arguably only satisfy Brehmer and Allard's (1991) first and second characteristics of dynamic tasks. Interdependent decisions were required and the state of the task changed as a result of the participant's actions, but the environment did not change autonomously and the task was self-paced so no 'real-time' changes occurred.

In order to satisfy all three characteristics, Brehmer and Allard developed a dynamic environment in which participants played the role of a fire chief faced with the problem of extinguishing forest fires (see also Brehmer, 1999). The scenario was as follows: the chief receives information about the location and extent of the fires from a spotter plane. On the basis of this information he sends out fire-fighting units, which then report back on their progress in putting out the fires. Using these progress reports, the chief issues new instructions to those (and perhaps other) units, and continues to do so until the fires have been extinguished. Such an environment encapsulates all the characteristics of dynamic environments identified by Brehmer and Allard (1991): a series of decisions is required; the decisions are interdependent because sending a unit to one location precludes using it at another location; the state of the fire can change autonomously (as a result of weather conditions) or as a result of the unit's efforts; finally time is crucial because if units are sent too early they will have no fire to fight, and if too late the fire may be too severe to tackle (Brehmer, 1999).

Using this cover story Brehmer and colleagues developed a computer simulation called 'NEWFIRE' in which they monitored the performance of novice participants with no expertise in fire-fighting playing the role of the fire chief (e.g. Løvborg & Brehmer, 1991). Participants' goals were to prevent the fire from spreading and to extinguish it as quickly as possible. The simulation software allowed the experimenter to control a range of factors in the environment: the size and number of fires, the weather conditions, the location of the base (where the chief co-ordinates from), the speed at which the fire-fighting units move and so on. Importantly, the simulation is 'clock-driven' – it continues to run without waiting for the participant to respond.

The principal findings from research using the NEWFIRE environment was that although participants may not perform optimally, their behaviour is 'at least reasonable in the sense that it gets the job done' (Brehmer, 1999, p. 10). For example, Brehmer, Løvborg and Winman (1992; cited in Brehmer, 1999) set up environments in which two fires had to be tackled. One fire near the base only required one unit to extinguish it; the other required four fire-fighting teams because it was further from the base and would spread in the time it took the units to reach it. However, rather than taking this time consideration into account, participants fought both fires in roughly the same way. Although this was non-optimal because too many units were sent to the closer fire and too few to the distant one, the fires were still extinguished and the 'job was done'. Brehmer (1999) concluded that this and other similar results demonstrate that when participants cannot work out the optimal way to perform a task, they find a reasonable way instead.

In a comprehensive review of complex dynamic control tasks like NEWFIRE and the Sugar Factory task, Osman (2010) proposed a 'monitoring and control' (MC) framework in an attempt to integrate findings from this wide-ranging literature. Osman (2010) suggests that monitoring involves both processing the environment (task-monitoring) and tracking one's goals (self-monitoring). Control involves the generation and application of actions to achieve one's goals. Central to the framework is the notion that psychological uncertainty mediates both task- and self-monitoring which in turn affect control behaviours. When uncertainty is high, monitoring is continuous, and when it is low, monitoring instead becomes periodic. In keeping with our discussion of 'static' MCPL tasks, the second tenet of the framework is that there is a reciprocal relationship between monitoring and control in which *feedforward* generates appropriate control behaviours and *feedback* allows for updates about knowledge of the task and the status of desired and achieved goals.

One finding emerging from this framework is that regardless of the amount of practice one has with complex dynamic control tasks, 'if experiences of uncertainty are maintained, then no improvements in control behaviours will be observed' (p. 79). Osman thus argues that it is important to identify sources and experiences of uncertainty (i.e. whether 'low' or 'high') and methods for training in order to determine how to improve performance. Surprisingly, given their inherent difficulty, many of the standard laboratory versions of complex dynamic tasks offer only very limited opportunities for learning (e.g. between 12 and 40 trials; Berry & Broadbent, 1988; Burns & Vollmeyer, 2002; Lee, 1995; Sanderson, 1989), thereby maintaining experiences of uncertainty. Moreover, Osman points out that although extended practice alone does not necessarily lead to improved performance (e.g. Gonzalez, 2005), instructions that encourage metacognitive thinking do appear to improve task knowledge, skill-retention and resource allocation (e.g. Brehmer & Allard, 1991). Thus, in line with many of the topics we address in this book, if appropriate conditions for learning are provided, people can make good judgments and decisions even in these complex, dynamic tasks.

SUMMARY

Feedback is crucial for learning from our experience in decision problems. In many MCPL tasks the provision of outcome feedback alone is only effective if the environment is relatively simple. This may be because outcome feedback does not provide the decision maker with the information required to understand the cue-criterion relations. When cues and criterion are expressed as quantities of the same variable (as in the advice-taking task of Harries and Harvey, 2000) or when detailed information about task structure is provided (e.g. cognitive feedback), more substantial improvements are observed (e.g. Newell, Weston et al., 2009). Such improvements may be due to the interplay of trial-by-trial feedback, which accumulates throughout the course of experiencing a new environment, and feedforward information about the structure of the environment which can be provided explicitly through instruction or through intuitions derived from knowledge of the world. Experiments using dynamic environments have revealed that people do a reasonable job of making decisions and allocating resources even if the decisions are not optimal in the classical sense. Opportunities for reducing experiences of psychological uncertainty can lead to improvements in both monitoring and control of such tasks (Osman, 2010).

This brings us to the end of our journey through the stages of judgment. In the next two chapters we shift our focus to examining some formal ways for appraising our probability judgments. We ask how good are our probability judgments and to what standards should they be compared?

Suggested further reading

- Balzer, W. K., Doherty, M. E., & O'Connor, R. (1989). Effects of cognitive feedback on performance. *Psychological Bulletin, 106,* 410–433. An older but very useful review of how cognitive feedback impacts performance in multiple-cue probability learning.
- Harvey, N., & Fischer, I. (2005). Development of experience-based judgment and decision making: The role of outcome feedback. In T. Betsch & S. Haberstroh (Eds), *The routines of decision making* (pp. 119–137). Mahwah, NJ: Erlbaum. A book chapter examining how outcome feedback can lead to improved judgment and decision making.
- Osman, M. (2010). Controlling uncertainty: A review of human behavior in complex dynamic environments. *Psychological Bulletin, 136,* 65–86. An integrative review that explores the importance of controlling uncertainty for mastering complex, dynamic tasks.

5 Appraising probability judgments

Chapter highlights

- Introduces the concepts of coherence and correspondence as criteria for appraising the quality of probability judgments
- Explains how Bayes' rule can be used to update beliefs
- Provides worked examples of the use of Bayes' rule in medical and legal contexts.

CORRESPONDENCE VERSUS COHERENCE CRITERIA

A health survey was conducted in a sample of adult males in British Columbia (of all ages and occupations). Mr F. was selected at random from the sample. Which of the following statements is more probable?

1. Mr F. has had one or more heart attacks.
2. Mr F. has had one or more heart attacks and he is over 55 years old.

If you are like the majority of participants in psychological experiments (e.g. Tversky & Kahneman, 1983) you will have rated the second alternative as more probable than the first. This is the infamous 'conjunction error', because a conjunction, P(heart attack & over 55), cannot be more probable than one of its conjuncts, P(heart attack). This is illustrated in the Venn diagram in Figure 5.1. One circle (labelled H) represents the proportion of men in the sample who have had at least one heart attack, while the other circle (labelled O) represents the proportion of men in the sample who are over 55 years of age. The overlap between these two circles represents the proportion of men who have had at least one heart attack *and* are over 55 years old (labelled H&O). From the diagram it is clear that the proportion of men who have had at least one heart attack (alternative 1 above) cannot be less than the proportion who have at least one heart attack *and* are over 55 years old (alternative 2 above). In short, alternative 2 is a subset of alternative 1, and so cannot be more probable.

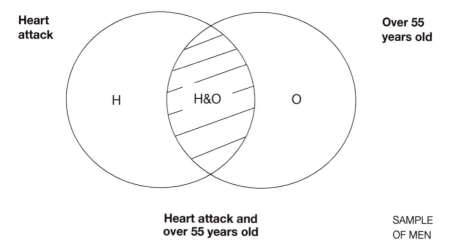

Heart
attack

Over 55
years old

H

H&O

O

**Heart attack and
over 55 years old**

SAMPLE
OF MEN

Figure 5.1 Venn diagram showing that the probability of a conjunction cannot be more
than one of its conjuncts. The area of the left circle (H) corresponds to the
proportion of men who have had at least one heart attack; the area of the
right circle (O) corresponds to the proportion of men over 55 years old.
The shaded area (H&O) corresponds to the probability of both, and cannot
be larger than either of the circles, because it is a subset of both of these sets.

The common mistake – rating alternative 2 as more probable than alternative
1 – is classified as a failure of *coherence*. It is made by many people (including
students, medical professionals and psychologists) and has been replicated using
a variety of different scenarios (see Gilovich, Griffin & Kahneman, 2002, for
a survey). The reason it is called a failure of coherence is because it violates a
basic principle of probability theory. This principle states that if A is a subset
of B, then B cannot be less probable than A. Such a principle applies irrespective
of what A and B refer to. It depends just on the formal relations between these
sets.

Consider a related question: what is more likely, that an adult male in the
USA dies from homicide or that he dies from suicide? If you share the belief
of the majority of people (Lichtenstein et al., 1978), you will have rated
homicide as more probable than suicide. This would also be an error, but of
a different kind. It is classifiable as an error of *correspondence*, because in actual
fact there are more deaths per year from suicide than from homicide. By over-
estimating the chances of homicide, your probability judgment fails to
correspond to the objective facts about homicide and suicide rates.

These two examples illustrate two different ways in which our probability
judgments can go wrong. More generally, it is possible to distinguish two
approaches to the analysis and appraisal of probability judgments, in terms of
coherence and *correspondence* (Hammond, 1996). Coherence theories focus on
structural relations between judgments or beliefs, and thus rely on formal models

of appraisal such as logic or probability theory. In contrast, correspondence theories focus on the fit between judgments and the external environment. They tend to rely on the predictive accuracy of judgments, or their correspondence to properties in the environment.

Most of the models reviewed in this book are correspondence models (e.g. the lens model in Chapter 3; associative or exemplar-based learning models in Chapters 11 and 12). Learning or judgment is mediated by mechanisms that attune in some way to the statistical structure of the environment, and the central goal of these mechanisms is predictive accuracy. In contrast, the majority of research on judgmental biases concentrates on coherence criteria, and in particular the conformity of people's judgments with the laws of probability.

One of the claims to be advanced in this chapter and the next is that both approaches are critical to understanding human judgment, and that biases often arise when correspondence-based mechanisms are assessed in terms of coherence-based standards. This is not to exonerate the judgmental inconsistencies that people fall prey to, but to fit such behaviour into a wider cognitive framework.

The laws of probability as coherence criteria

Ever since their development in the seventeenth century the laws of probability have been advocated as laws of sound reasoning (e.g. Laplace, 1812). This idea was formalized in the early twentieth century by Ramsey (1931) and de Finetti (1937). Essentially they showed that the laws of probability provide consistency constraints on judgments or beliefs. A set of probability judgments that violate the laws (termed *incoherent*) is defective because (a) it would entail that your judgments depend on the precise form in which options are presented to you, and thus (b) if you bet in accordance with these judgments, you could be made to lose money irrespective of the outcomes of the events bet upon (in other words you would be vulnerable to a 'Dutch book').

To illustrate, let us return to the earlier question about the probability that a man suffers a heart attack (H) compared with the probability that a man suffers a heart attack and is over 55 (H&O). By the laws of probability a conjunction cannot be more probable than either of its conjuncts, that is $P(H\&O) \leq P(H)$. However, suppose that you, along with the majority of respondents in the experimental studies, believe that $P(H\&O) > P(H)$, and that you are prepared to bet on these statements (don't feel guilty, insurance companies do it all the time). It can be shown that an unscrupulous person could place bets with you, on the basis of the odds implicit in your probability judgments, so that you will lose money regardless of the true outcomes (i.e. whether or not the man indeed suffers from a heart attack, and whether or not he is over 55 years old). For simplicity of exposition we will illustrate with exact figures, but the generality of the argument should be clear.

Suppose you estimate that there is a 25% chance that a randomly selected man suffers a heart attack, i.e. $P(H) = 0.25$, and a 50% chance that he suffers a heart attack and is over 55 years old, i.e. $P(H\&O) = 0.5$. This means that you accept odds of 3 to 1[1] against H, and evens odds (1:1) on H&O. Given these odds, an unscrupulous opponent just needs to (a) bet $5 on H, and (b) bet $10 against H&O, to guarantee himself a sure gain. This is shown in Table 5.1. The columns correspond to the four possible outcomes: (i) heart attack and over 55 (H&O); (ii) heart attack and not over 55 (H&~O); (iii) no heart attack and over 55 (~H&O); (iv) no heart attack and not over 55 (~H&~O). For each outcome the first row shows how much money your opponent wins, the second row shows how much money your opponent loses, and the third row shows your opponent's net gain (and hence your net loss).

For example, if the man turns out to both have a heart attack and be over 55 (outcome i), your opponent will win $15 from his bet on H, and lose $10 from his bet against H&O. This gives him a net gain of $5, and you a net loss of $5. In contrast, if the man turns out to have a heart attack and not be over 55 (outcome ii), your opponent will win $15 from his bet on H, and win $10 from his bet against H&O. His net gain is $25, and your net loss is $25. The other two alternatives (outcomes iii and iv) both result in a net gain for your opponent of $5. He loses $5 for his bet on H, but gains $10 for his bet against H&O.

Overall, then, whatever the outcome of the events, you will lose and your opponent will gain. So this is a compelling reason to avoid a Dutch book, and thus ensure that your probability estimates obey the laws of probability.

Table 5.1 An example of a Dutch book

	Possible outcomes			
	(i) H&O	*(ii) H&~O*	*(iii) ~H&O*	*(iv) ~H&~O*
Opponent wins	$15 on (a)	$25 on (a) & (b)	$10 on (b)	$10 on (b)
Opponent loses	$10 on (b)	0	$5 on (a)	$5 on (a)
Net gain	$5	$25	$5	$5

Note: H = Man suffers heart attack; O = Man is over 55 years. You offer bets of 3:1 against H, and evens odds for H&O. Your opponent (a) bets $5 on H being true, and (b) bets $10 against H&O being true. There are four possible outcomes (i–iv) and your opponent has a net gain in each. Thus your opponent wins regardless of the actual outcomes.

Are coherence criteria sufficient?

The demonstration that coherent beliefs must obey the laws of probability confirms the normative status of these laws, and serves as a basic premise in rational theories of decision making (e.g. Jeffrey, 1965; Savage, 1954). However, by itself the prescription to maintain a coherent set of probability judgments appears quite a weak constraint. So long as your judgments are coherent it seems that you can entertain any idiosyncratic probability assignment. For example, you can judge that the chance of intelligent life on Mars is 0.9, so long as you also judge that the chance of no intelligent life on Mars is 0.1.

This problem is typically dealt with in one of two ways, depending on one's theoretical persuasion. Some see it as a fundamental shortcoming of the coherentist approach, and argue that correspondence criteria are the appropriate means for appraising probability judgments (e.g. Gigerenzer, 2002). Others argue that the coherence constraint is sufficient, once we acknowledge the role played by Bayes' rule (see the section on Bayesian updating below) as a normative model of belief revision (for further discussion see Baron, 2000). A more moderate position, and the one that will be adopted in this chapter, is that these criteria are complementary rather than exclusive. The constraint of coherence serves to maintain the internal consistency of our probability judgments, whereas the requirement of correspondence (when available) serves to calibrate these judgments to the external world.

Correspondence criteria for probability judgments

Rather than concentrate on the internal coherence within a set of probability judgments, correspondence theories assess the fit between these judgments and some aspect or property of the external world. Thus frequentist theorists maintain that our judgments concern, and are assessable against, appropriate relative frequencies of events or instances. For example, responses to the question of whether a person is more likely to die through murder or suicide are assessed in the light of the actual death rates. On the face of it the claim that our probability judgments should correspond to the appropriate relative frequencies seems uncontroversial. However, under closer scrutiny the position is less clear.

For a start, how do we determine which is the appropriate relative frequency? In many real-world situations there are several different reference classes which may be relevant. For example, consider the task of estimating the probability that a particular individual X will die before 65. What is the relevant reference class here? People in general? What if X is a non-smoking female? Now the appropriate class is narrowed to deaths before 65 amongst female non-smokers. But successively refining the reference class seems to lead to a class made up of just the individual in question. A frequentist can sidestep this problem, however. They can claim that in many cases there is a privileged level at which the reference class should be set, and that the context of the problem will make this clear. Thus when assessing a judgment about the probable death of an individual, we use the reference class of people irrespective of gender. Presumably we also restrict ourselves to current death rates, and those in the geographical area for which the question is posed, and so on. This line of response re-iterates the frequentist claim that there is no such thing as *the* probability of an event, but a range of probabilities (relative frequencies) depending on the chosen reference class.

A more pernicious problem for a strict frequentist is that in many situations there seems to be no appropriate reference class on which to base a probability judgment. For example, consider the sudden introduction, in 2003, of a congestion charge for vehicles entering central London. This was an event with no precedent, and yet everyone voiced an opinion as to its likely success. Indeed many commentators made quite specific predictions about the high chances of traffic chaos just outside the charge zone and the likely overcrowding of the public transport system. These predictions were certainly meaningful and open to assessment (indeed most proved incorrect), and yet it is difficult to generate one privileged reference class against which to assess such judgments. Similar examples surely pervade much of our everyday life – we are frequently faced with novel problem situations where we cannot appeal to a specific reference class, and yet are able to make probability judgments that are open to appraisal nonetheless. This is not to argue that coherence criteria give us much guidance here – what will be argued later on is that other forms of appraisal become appropriate in such cases.

Regardless of these problems, the laws of probability apply to relative frequencies as well as they apply to coherent degrees of belief. As long as your judgments are well calibrated to the appropriate relative frequencies, they will obey the laws of probability. For example, if you base your estimate of the probability that a man has a heart attack on the frequency of heart attacks in the male population, $f(H)$, and your estimate of the probability that a man has a heart attack and is over 55 on the corresponding frequency in the same population, $f(H\&O)$, your are bound to obey the conjunction rule because $f(H) \geq f(H\&O)$.

We have seen that probability judgments permit at least two distinct forms of appraisal, coherence and correspondence, and that both can validly employ the axioms of probability as a normative model. One of the most useful theorems that can be derived from the axioms of probability is Bayes' rule.

BAYESIAN MODEL OF PROBABILITY UPDATING

Bayes' rule is a theorem derivable from the probability axioms, and is taken to provide a normative rule for updating one's probability judgments in the light of new evidence.

Informally, Bayes' rule tells us how much to adjust our prior belief in a hypothesis on the basis of a new piece of evidence. To do this we must consider how likely the evidence would be if the hypothesis in question were true and if we didn't already know about the new evidence. This factor tells us how much to adjust our prior belief (our probability judgment before the new piece of evidence is known) to yield our posterior belief (our probability judgment after the new piece of evidence is known).

To illustrate the basic idea, imagine that you are a modern-day Robinson Crusoe, stranded on an isolated tropical island. You want to know whether there are any other inhabitants on the island. You have a prior degree of belief about this based on your background information (the location of the island, the absence of any buildings, etc.). Let's assume that you think it's pretty un-likely. As you walk along the beach you encounter a set of footprints (not your own). How much should this new piece of evidence alter your prior beliefs? Bayes' rule tells you to consider (1) how likely the footprints are if there are other inhabitants, and (2) how likely the footprints are if there are no other inhabitants. You then combine these two judgments with your prior belief to yield your posterior belief (see details below). In this case the appearance of footprints is very likely under the assumption that there are other inhabitants, but very unlikely under the assumption that there are no other inhabitants. Therefore you should adjust your prior belief upwards – the appearance of footprints greatly increases the chances of there being other inhabitants (how else could they have got there?).

More formally, for a set of mutually exclusive and exhaustive hypotheses $(H_1, H_2, \ldots, H_n)$, and an item of evidence E, Bayes' rule relates the *prior* probability of H_i (in the absence of any knowledge about E) to the posterior probability of H_i given that E is true:

$$P(H_i | E) = \frac{P(E | H_i) \cdot P(H_i)}{\sum_i P(E | H_i) \cdot P(H_i)}$$

The focal idea is that once you learn E, your new estimate for the probability of H_i should be proportional to the product of your prior estimate for H_i and the probability of E if H_i is assumed true (known as the *likelihood*). The summation in the denominator of the equation serves to normalize this relative to all the other competing hypotheses. Intuitively, Bayes' rule tells us to compute $P(H_i | E)$ by considering all the different ways in which E can occur, i.e. as a result of any one of the exclusive hypotheses $H_1 \ldots H_n$. For each of these hypotheses there is a particular prior probability that it is true, and a particular likelihood that if it is true, E will also be true.

Bayesian updating in medical diagnosis

We now present a quantitative example from medical diagnosis. Imagine that you have a routine health check-up, and are tested for a rare disease. Suppose that the incidence of this disease amongst people with your profile (e.g. gender, age, race, etc.) is 1/1000. In the absence of any additional information this is the best estimate for the prior probability that you have the disease (note that this is a correspondence measure). The test for this disease, like most tests, is not perfect. In particular, suppose that the likelihood that you test positive given that you have the disease is 99%. This is known as the sensitivity of the test. Not only does the test occasionally fail to detect the presence of the disease, but it also sometimes yields a positive result when the disease is not present.

This is known as the false positive rate, and corresponds to the likelihood of a positive test given that the disease is not present. Suppose that for this particular disease and test this likelihood is 5%.

Now imagine that your test turns out positive. What is the probability that you have the disease? To calculate this posterior probability we can use Bayes' rule. Let H = you have the disease, ~H = you do not have the disease, E = test is positive. From the figures given above we have: $P(E|H) = 0.99$, $P(E|~H) = 0.05$, $P(H) = 0.001$, $P(~H) = 0.999$.

Because H and ~H are exclusive and exhaustive, we can re-formulate Bayes' rule as:

$$P(H|E) = \frac{P(E|H) \cdot P(H)}{P(E|H) \cdot P(H) + P(E|~H) \cdot P(~H)}$$

$$P(H|E) = \frac{0.99 \times 0.001}{(0.99 \times 0.001) + (0.05 \times 0.999)}$$

$$= 0.02$$

So the positive test result has raised the probability that you have the disease from 0.001 to 0.02. Although this is a huge increase, the probability that you have the disease is still relatively low (2%). As we shall see in the next chapter, many people find this kind of Bayesian reasoning difficult.

Bayesian updating in legal reasoning

Legal reasoning is another real-world context where Bayesian updating would appear crucial. For example, as we gather evidence for or against a target hypothesis (for instance that the suspect committed the crime), presumably we should update our belief in the suspect's guilt according to the probative value of the evidence. This seems particularly appropriate when presented with statistical evidence such as a DNA test result. Although there is controversy about the use of Bayesian reasoning in court (see R v T discussed below), the consensus amongst experts in forensic statistics is that the Bayesian approach is the correct normative model for evidence evaluation (e.g. Aitken, Roberts & Jackson, 2014).

The central concept used in legal and forensic science to assess the probative value of evidence is the likelihood ratio (LR). The LR compares the probability of the evidence E on the supposition that the target hypothesis H is true (the suspect committed the crime in question) to the probability of E on the supposition that H is false (the suspect did not commit the crime).

$$LR = \frac{P(E|H)}{P(E|~H)}$$

The likelihood ratio is an integral part of Bayes' rule, as can be seen if we give the 'Odds version' of Bayes' rule:

$$\frac{P(H|E)}{P(\sim H|E)} = \frac{P(E|H)}{P(E|\sim H)} \times \frac{P(H)}{P(\sim H)}$$

In other words:

Posterior Odds = Likelihood Ratio x Prior Odds

where the prior odds for H is the probability of H divided by the probability of ~H, and the posterior odds is the probability of H given E divided by the probability of ~H given E.

In short, the likelihood ratio tells us how much to change our prior belief in H given new evidence E. We simply multiply our prior odds by the LR to yield our posterior odds. If the LR > 1, then E supports H over ~H, and we should increase our belief in H. If LR < 1, then E supports ~H over H, and we should decrease our belief in H. If the LR = 1, then E is neutral between H and ~H, and we should not change our prior belief in H.

When applied in legal contexts, the likelihood ratio is often formulated in terms of a comparison between the probability of the evidence given the *prosecution* hypothesis and the probability of evidence given the *defence* hypothesis. This works fine when the prosecution and defence hypotheses are exclusive and exhaustive (but see Fenton et al., 2014, for discussion of the possible problems when the LR is applied to cases with non-exclusive or non-exhaustive hypotheses).

Reasoning with DNA evidence

To illustrate the use of Bayesian reasoning in a legal context let us consider the case of DNA evidence (as discussed in Chapter 1). Suppose that a murder has taken place in a small town. The victim was stabbed to death. Police find the murder weapon, and tests reveal DNA that does not belong to the victim on the knife handle. The police question a local man, although there is no substantial evidence against him. However, laboratory tests show that his DNA matches the profile found on the murder weapon. What's the probability that he committed the crime?

It is tempting to jump straight to the conclusion that he is guilty (or at least highly likely to be guilty) – why else would his DNA be on the murder weapon? And the likelihood ratio would seem to back up this conclusion. In court a forensic expert testifies that the chance of getting a DNA match by coincidence is one in a million. Expressed in terms of a likelihood ratio, this suggests that the DNA match is one million times more likely under the prosecution hypothesis that he is guilty compared to the defence hypothesis that he is innocent.

$$\text{LR} = \frac{P(E|H)}{P(E|{\sim}H)} = \frac{1}{1/1,000,000} = 1,000,000$$

(Note that $P(E|{\sim}H)$ is the random match probability RMP, and typically corresponds to the frequency of that DNA profile in the relevant population; $P(E|H)$ is usually assumed to be close to 1.)

But we must not move so fast. Despite the strength of the evidence, as measured by the LR, there are several inferential steps from the DNA match to the claim of guilt. One crucial step is moving from the claim that the man's DNA is on the murder weapon to the claim that he committed the crime. Perhaps he discovered the victim dead, and handled the murder weapon by mistake. There are various possibilities here – most being implausible without supportive evidence – but one must not simply ignore them and assume guilt. To address this issue we should separate out the hypothesis of guilt (let's call this G) from the hypothesis that the man is the source of the DNA on the weapon (let's call this S). The DNA evidence concerns the latter 'source' hypothesis, and only indirectly does it speak to the guilt hypothesis G, which requires a further inference.

Another crucial step is going from the likelihood ratio, which states that the DNA match evidence is far more probable if the accused is the source of the DNA rather than some other 'randomly' chosen person, to a judgment about the probability that S is true given E. This is where Bayes' rule is critical. It tells us how to update our prior belief in S by multiplying by the LR. Thus, we need some estimate for the prior probability that the man is the source (before the match evidence). This is not a trivial figure to estimate, and indeed is often considered a stumbling block in using Bayesian reasoning in legal cases.

For illustrative purposes let us assume there are 100,000 people who could have committed the crime, perhaps based on the number of people within a certain radius of the crime scene. We thus set our prior probability to 1/100,000, corresponding to an odds ratio of 1/99,999. We can now use Bayes' rule to multiply this figure by the LR, yielding posterior odds for S = 1,000,000/99,999 = 10. Thus, given the DNA evidence, S is 10 times more likely than ~S. In terms of probability, the posterior probability that the man is the source, given the DNA evidence, is 10/11 (= 0.91). Whether or not this is high enough to convict is an intriguing question (Lynch & McNally, 2003), but it is perhaps lower than you expected when told that the chance of someone else matching was 1 in 1,000,000. Moreover, this probability is clearly dependent on the prior probability. Suppose the defence proposes an estimate of 1,000,000 rather than 100,000. Based on this prior, the posterior probability for S is 0.5. Definitely not sufficient to convict!

Ignoring the prior probability, and simply assuming that a very large LR translates straight to a very high probability of guilt is the Prosecutor's Fallacy, which we introduced in Chapter 1 (Thompson & Schumann, 1987). We will encounter an analogous error in medical diagnosis in Chapter 6. Another crucial issue ignored in the above analysis is the possibility of an error in the DNA lab tests, perhaps due to contamination, or mixing up of samples, or even tampering by the police. In particular, the problem of false positives (where a lab incorrectly reports a DNA match) is often the elephant in the room in DNA testing. Such errors are very difficult to quantify, and often denied by the testing labs and investigators, and yet they do occur (Thompson, Taroni & Aitken, 2003; W.C. Thompson, 2013). As argued in Chapter 1, a proper evaluation of DNA evidence needs to take these possible errors into account.

To incorporate the possibility of false positives into our probability calculations, we must distinguish between a reported DNA match and an actual DNA match. This is a very common issue in legal, medical and everyday reasoning, where we often need to distinguish between the report of an event and the event itself. We can then include the probability of a false positive report (false positive probability, or FPP) in the likelihood ratio. Without going into the details (for full analysis see Thompson et al., 2003), the relevant likelihood ratio becomes:

$$LR = \frac{P(R \mid S)}{P(R \mid \sim S)} = \frac{1}{RMP + (FPP \cdot (1 - RMP))}$$

where R is a reported DNA match; S is the hypothesis that the suspect is the source, and RMP is the random match probability.

This shows that the strength of the DNA report is greater with lower values of RMP and FPP, and effectively it is their sum that contributes to the overall error rate. Thus, as pointed out in Chapter 1, a valid assessment of the DNA evidence requires both errors to be considered. And if the false positive probability is much higher than the RMP, then the false positive error will dominate. For example, holding the FPP constant at 1/1000, an RMP of 1/1,000,000 yields an LR = 999, whereas a much smaller RMP of 1/1,000,000,000 only increases the LR to 1000. In contrast, holding the RMP at 1/1,000,000, but increasing the FPP to 1/100, leads to an LR of 100.

These variations in error rates can prove incredibly important when integrated with the prior to give a posterior for hypothesis S. For example, suppose that our prior that the man is the source of the DNA is 1/100. If the RMP is 1/1,000,000 and the FPP is 1/1000, then the posterior probability is 0.91. However, if the FPP is larger, such as 1/100, then the posterior falls to 0.50. Hence the lab error rate can make a real difference to what inferences we should draw from DNA evidence. And note that we have not yet added the probabilistic inference from 'suspect is source' to 'suspect is guilty'. This uncertainty can only reduce the impact of the evidence even further.

To repeat the conclusions drawn in Chapter 1, the failure to take account of lab testing errors when presenting DNA evidence can lead to gross over-estimation of the value of that evidence. This is not to undermine the importance and probative value of DNA evidence, but care must be taken to incorporate the relevant uncertainties, especially when these analyses are presented to non-expert jurors. Using the Bayesian framework helps clarify the key issues, and allows us to factor in the various sources of uncertainty.

Interim summary

In summary, if you have prior beliefs about a set of exclusive and exhaustive hypotheses (possibly just one hypothesis and its complement), and then encounter a new piece of evidence, Bayes' rule tells you how to update these beliefs, given that you know, or can estimate, the likelihood that each of these hypotheses, if true, would have generated the evidence.

One reason why Bayes' rule has considerable practical application is that the likelihood of new data, given a specific hypothesis, is often an accessible and stable factor in an inference problem. This is because it is frequently determined by a stable causal mechanism, such as the propensity that a disease causes certain symptoms, that a specific personality type leads to certain behaviours, or that a particular DNA sequence appears in a specific population.

To re-iterate, by itself Bayes' rule only tells us how to pass from prior probability estimates and likelihoods to posterior estimates; it does not tell us how to set our priors in the first place. This fits with the idea that the laws of probability provide consistency relations between our beliefs – they tell us that if we hold certain probability judgments, then we ought, on pain of inconsistency, to hold certain others. It also fits with the claim that our probability estimates, in particular our priors, are sometimes appraisable in the light of their correspondence to features of the external environment, namely, observable frequencies.

Confusing coherence with correspondence

The relation between coherence and correspondence, and the potential for misunderstanding the role of Bayesian reasoning, are vividly illustrated in a recent UK legal ruling (R v T). A man was convicted of murder, and a central piece of evidence was the match between a footprint found at the crime scene and a running shoe recovered from the defendant's house. In court a forensic expert testified that the footprint match provided 'moderate scientific support' for the defendant's guilt. This was based on a likelihood ratio analysis, where the rarity of the footprint was derived from a police database of running shoes, but the expert did not present full details of this analysis to the court. The verdict was appealed on the basis that the footprint evidence was unreliable and had not been properly explained in court. (This is somewhat ironic given that the expert used conservative figures to estimate the LR, and also used a verbal reporting scale designed to make the evidential weight clearer for a lay jury.) However, the appeal rightly highlighted the difficulty with identifying the 'correct' database of shoes upon which to base the LR (running shoes in the police database; all running shoes sold in the UK between X and Y dates, and so on), and the fact that the court had not been given a full explanation of how this figure was used by the expert. The appeal court declared the conviction unsafe.

Whether or not this was a reasonable judgment goes beyond the scope of this chapter. But the judges proceeded to rule out the use of Bayes' rule or likelihood ratios in court except for DNA evidence (or something with a similarly robust statistical basis). This ruling has drawn strong criticisms from the forensic community (Berger et al., 2011), especially due to the confusions about probabilistic reasoning that it betrayed, and the precedent it set for future cases. For our purposes it highlights a confusion between the coherence and the correspondence of probability estimates. The judges might be right to question the reliability of the estimated likelihood of a coincidental match (e.g. the rarity of the running shoe), due to there being various different databases to choose from (and note that this mirrors the general problem of selecting the right reference class for a frequency-based probability judgment). However, they were wrong to conclude that Bayesian reasoning is therefore not applicable in court (except with DNA evidence). The accuracy of one's probability estimates does not undermine the validity of Bayes' rule itself, nor the likelihood ratio approach. This would be like ruling out the laws of logic, because sometimes one draws an unreliable conclusion from unreliable premises.

UPDATING BELIEFS WITH MULTIPLE VARIABLES

Most real-world inference problems involve more than a single piece of evidence and a single hypothesis. Medical diagnoses typically depend on various symptoms and numerous different tests; legal judgments require the integration of a body of evidence and often involve several interrelated hypotheses; even our everyday judgments usually recruit several pieces of evidence. Bayesian updating is readily extended to situations with multiple variables, but care must be taken to accommodate the possible interrelations between these variables. A naïve approach (aptly termed 'naïve Bayes') is to treat each piece of evidence as independent of the other pieces. This simplifies the inference problem, because the likelihoods for each item of evidence needed for Bayes' rule can be evaluated without regard to the presence of other evidence. But it also runs the risk of over-weighting the evidence when items of evidence are causally related. For example, in medical diagnosis one symptom of a disease might itself cause another symptom; or in a legal context, witnesses to a crime might share information and thus not provide independent observations.

In addition many inference problems involve more than one hypothesis of interest, and these in turn might be supported by different bodies of evidence. For example, in medical diagnosis the same symptoms can be caused by a variety of diseases, and tests might discriminate between some diseases but not others. More complicated still are situations where there is a network of related hypotheses and evidence. Thus, in a crime case there might be several alternative suspects, with different motivations and opportunities, and diverse bodies of interrelated evidence (Fenton, Neil & Lagnado, 2013; Lagnado, 2011; Lagnado, Fenton & Neil, 2013). How should we approach inference in such contexts?

Bayesian networks (Pearl, 1988) provide a general approach to represent these kinds of situation (see Fenton & Neil, 2012, and Taroni et al., 2006, for good introductions). Building upon the axioms of probability, and Bayes' rule in particular, Bayesian networks (BNs) present a normative framework for probabilistic reasoning with multiple interrelated variables. Another advantage is that even for smaller problems, BNs clarify the assumptions behind our probabilistic models and the inferences they support. This is particularly useful when there are several different sources of uncertainty in a problem. For example, Figure 5.2 presents a Bayesian network for the DNA evidence example discussed in the previous section (for more details see Thompson et al., 2003). The network clarifies the various steps in the inference from a reported match to the guilt of the suspect, each of which is probabilistic.

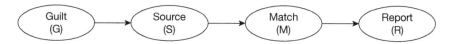

Figure 5.2 Bayesian network graph to represent the multiple variables involved in inferring guilt of a suspect from the report of a DNA match.

SUMMARY

This chapter introduces two ways of appraising probability judgments: coherence and correspondence. Coherence theories focus on structural relations between judgments or beliefs, and therefore rely on formal models of appraisal such as logic or probability theory. Correspondence theories focus on the fit between judgments and the external environment. They tend to rely on the predictive accuracy of judgments, or their correspondence to properties in the environment. The majority of research into judgmental biases has focused on coherence criteria. The chapter presents the Bayesian model of belief updating, broadly accepted as the standard normative theory. The Bayesian approach is illustrated with examples from medical and legal decision making, and extended to more complex contexts involving multiple variables.

Now that you understand some of the formal rules for how people *should* update their beliefs and make judgments, it is time, in the next chapter, to examine how people *actually* make judgments under uncertainty.

Suggested further reading

- Hammond, K. R. (1996). *Human judgment and social policy: Irreducible uncertainty, inevitable error, unavoidable injustice*. New York: Oxford University Press. A wide-ranging discussion of human judgment that explores the coherence and correspondence criteria in detail.
- Lynch, M., & McNally, R. (2003). Science, common sense and DNA evidence: A legal controversy about the public understanding of science. *Public Understanding of Science, 12*, 83–103. An intriguing discussion of how jurors should be helped to understand and combine science- and non-science-based information.
- Fenton, N., Neil, M., & Lagnado, D. A. (2013). A general structure for legal arguments about evidence using Bayesian networks. *Cognitive Science, 37*, 61–102. A detailed examination of how Bayesian networks can be used to assess the probative value of evidence.

Note

1   Odds provide an alternative way to express probabilities. In standard probability or statistics textbooks, the odds ratio for an event E is the probability of the event happening (p) divided by the probability of it not happening ($1-p$), such that Odds $= p/(1-p)$. However, in the UK bookmakers use a slightly different way of expressing betting odds. For example, they might offer odds of 3:1 against a horse winning a race, which corresponds to a probability of 1/4. More generally, odds of A:B correspond to a probability $p = B/(A+B)$. When you place a bet (of stake S) on an event with odds of A:B you will receive ($S \times A/B$) if the event occurs, plus your original stake S. But of course the odds that bookmakers offer you are biased in their favour and do not reflect their true estimate of the probability of the event: after all, they are in the business of making a profit.

6   Judgmental heuristics and biases

Chapter highlights

- Introduces the notions of attribute substitution and natural assessment
- Explains how these notions can be used to understand errors of coherence and correspondence, such as representativeness and availability biases
- Discusses the effect of frequency formats as a means for alleviating biases.

How do people actually make probability judgments? How do they process the information available to them to reach a singular estimate of what is likely to happen? The dominant approach to this question is provided by Kahneman and Tversky in their 'Heuristics and Biases' programme (e.g. Gilovich, Griffin & Kahneman, 2002; Kahneman et al., 1982; Kahneman, 2011). They claim that rather than reasoning on the basis of the formal rules of probability, people often use simplifying or shortcut heuristics to reach a probability judgment. Moreover, whilst these heuristics are well adapted to specific information-processing tasks, they can lead to systematic biases when used in inappropriate contexts.

Attribute substitution and natural assessments

At the heart of the heuristics and biases approach are the twin notions of attribute substitution and natural assessment (Kahneman & Frederick, 2002). The idea behind attribute substitution is very simple: when faced with a hard question about a particular quantity or attribute, people tend to answer a different but easier question. Thus a difficult question about a target attribute (e.g. how probable is X?) is answered by substituting a more readily accessible heuristic attribute (e.g. how easily do instances of X come to mind?). What determines the accessibility of this heuristic attribute? Two factors are critical: that it is related in some way to the target attribute, and that it is a natural assessment; that is, a relatively automatic and routinely used cognitive procedure.

In earlier expositions (Tversky & Kahneman, 1983) natural assessments were broadly characterized in terms of *representativeness* (the degree to which one thing resembles another) or *availability* (the ease with which examples come to mind). More recently, they have been couched in terms of more specific properties such as similarity, fluency (Jacoby & Dallas, 1981), causal propensity (Kahneman & Varey, 1990) and affective valence (Kahneman, Ritov & Schkade, 1999).

The basic idea remains constant – the requirement to make a target judgment about an attribute activates other related attributes, and if the target attribute is unavailable, or less accessible than a contending attribute, the agent is likely to respond with the substitute value. There is a wealth of empirical evidence in support of these claims (see the collection by Gilovich et al., 2002). This evidence is garnered through two main routes (often combined in the same experiment). First, and most dramatic, the demonstration of systematic biases, in particular the violation of basic laws of probability. Second, and more subtle, the demonstration that probability judgments correlate highly with the heuristic judgments that are alleged to replace them.

ERRORS OF COHERENCE

Judgmental heuristics can lead to errors of both coherence and correspondence. We start by reviewing some of the main violations of coherence.

Base-rate neglect

Students and staff at Harvard Medical School were presented with the following problem (Casscells, Schoenberger & Grayboys, 1978):

> If a test to detect a disease whose prevalence is 1/1000 has a false positive rate of 5%, what is the chance that a person found to have a positive result actually has the disease, assuming you know nothing about the person's symptoms or signs?

As stated, the problem was incomplete, because it did not mention the sensitivity of the test (the probability of a positive result given that the person has the disease). However, assuming that this is very high, as is the case with most tests of this nature, the correct answer to this problem is around 2%. Thus someone who tests positive for the disease is actually, under these plausible numbers, extremely unlikely actually to have it.

The striking finding in this experiment was that only 18% of the participants (including staff) got the answer correct. The modal response was 95%. How could medically educated people have got this so wrong?

An obvious explanation for the modal response of 95% is that people assume that if the test is wrong 5% of the time then it must be right 95% of the time. Although this line of thought is tempting, it is incorrect. The false positive rate tells us about one type of test error, the probability of a positive test (T) given that the disease is not present (~D), namely $P(T|\sim D)$. In the medical example this is given as 0.05. From this probability we can infer the probability of a negative test given that the disease is absent, $P(\sim T|\sim D) = 1-P(T|\sim D) = 0.95$. But this only gives us the true negative rate. What we really want to know is the probability that the person has the disease, given that they test positive, $P(D|T)$. Bayes' rule tells us that to compute this we must take into account the prior probability of the disease (i.e. the base rate), as well as the false positive rate and the sensitivity of the test. Even when people are supplied with the test sensitivity, they still tend to estimate the probability of the disease as around 80–95%, effectively ignoring the base rate of the disease.

Why do respondents neglect the base-rate information? A broad-level explanation can be given in terms of attribute substitution (Kahneman & Frederick, 2002). People are faced with a difficult probability problem – they are asked for the probability of a disease given a positive test result, and this requires a relatively complex Bayesian computation. However, there is a closely related (but incorrect) answer that is readily accessible, and so they give this. In the version of the medical problem presented above, the most accessible figure is 95%; which, as noted, is the true negative rate rather than the required posterior probability. In other versions of the problem that also supply the sensitivity of the test (typically stated as around 80–90%), people often simply report that figure. In this case they are substituting the accessible value of the probability of a positive test given the disease, $P(T|D)$, for the required posterior probability, $P(D|T)$.

This is an example of a more general bias known in psychology as the inverse fallacy (Dawes, 2001; Villejoubert & Mandel, 2002), or in legal cases as the Prosecutor's Fallacy (see Chapters 1 and 5, and Dawid, 2002).

Alert readers will notice that this diagnosis problem is very similar to the one solved in the last chapter using Bayes' rule. The false positive rate corresponds to the probability that the test is positive, given that the person does not have the disease, $P(E|\sim H)$. The sensitivity of the test is not mentioned in the problem, but it is instructive to compute the correct answers given several different possible values (e.g. 100%, 99%, 95%). The important point is that whatever the precise value for the sensitivity, the correct answer to the problem is very low (i.e. 2–5%) rather than very high (i.e. 95%).

The report of a positive test raises the probability of having the disease from 0.01% to 2%, which is a very significant rise. However, the final estimate is still relatively low. There is a chance that the test result is flawed, and this is actually higher than the initial chance that the person has the disease. Bayes' rule tells us the normatively correct way to combine these two sources of uncertainty. People, however, seem to focus just on the positive test evidence, and ignore the prior information.

Base-rate neglect has been demonstrated on innumerable occasions, and using different scenarios (Kahneman & Tversky, 1982b; Koehler, 1996; Villejoubert & Mandel, 2002). There have also been various experiments showing the conditions under which it can be alleviated (Cosmides & Tooby, 1996;

Gigerenzer & Hoffrage, 1995; Girotto & Gonzalez, 2001; Sloman et al., 2003), and heated argument as to its true reach (Gigerenzer, 1996: Kahneman & Tversky, 1996; Koehler, 1996). Some of these issues will be discussed below.

Irrespective of these debates, one robust conclusion is that people do not automatically engage in full Bayesian reasoning when solving such problems. They tend to adopt short-cut solutions, and these can lead them to give erroneous answers. But the news is not all bad. These errors tell us something about the reasoning mechanisms that people do in fact use. And, as we shall see, their reasoning can be improved when information is presented in an appropriate format.

However, the exact reason why so many people ignore base rates in these problems is still the subject of controversy (perhaps there is no single reason, but a complex interaction of factors). In the next chapter we will explore cases of base-rate neglect in experienced rather than described settings, and advance an alternative explanation for it in terms of associative learning mechanisms.

One recent attempt to explain and ameliorate base-rate neglect is provided by Krynski and Tenenbaum (2007). They argue that probabilistic inference in the medical diagnosis problem requires a prior causal model on which to map the probabilities presented in the problem. Moreover, in typical presentations of the problem it is unclear how participants should integrate the false positive information into their causal model. In particular, no mention is made of the alternative causes of a positive test other than the target disease. When this ambiguity is addressed, for example by telling participants that the positive test can also be caused by a benign cyst, then their responses conform more closely to the correct Bayesian answer (although note that the proportion of correct responses is still only around 50%). Krynski and Tenenbaum conclude that causal understanding (getting the right causal model) is often a key precursor to sound probabilistic reasoning. This conclusion chimes with other research in decision making (Hayes et al., 2014; Lagnado, 2011; Lagnado, Fenton & Neil, 2013; Sloman & Lagnado, 2015) that accentuates the role of prior causal models on probability judgment.

The conjunction fallacy

One of the most basic rules of probability is the conjunction rule – that a conjunction cannot be more probable than either of its conjuncts. We met this rule in the previous chapter when we showed that it is incoherent to judge the probability of the statement 'A man suffers a heart attack' as less probable than the conjunctive statement 'A man suffers a heart attack and is over 55 years old'. We also noted that in experimental tests the majority of participants violated this rule. These 'conjunction fallacies' have been demonstrated with a wide range of different materials. The most famous example, now part of psychology folklore, is the 'Linda' problem. Suppose you are given the following personality sketch:

Linda is 31 years old, single, outspoken and very bright. She majored in Philosophy. As a student, she was deeply concerned with issues of discrimination and social justice, and also participated in anti-nuclear demonstrations.

Which of these statements is more probable?

1. Linda is a bank teller.
2. Linda is a bank teller and active in the feminist movement.

The majority response across a range of variations (for example embedding the statements in a longer list; asking for probability ratings for each statement rather than a ranking) is to judge statement 2 as more probable than statement 1, in violation of the conjunction rule. Tversky and Kahneman (1983) accounted for this and various other examples of the conjunction fallacy in terms of the representativeness heuristic. The description of Linda is highly representative of an active feminist (F) and unrepresentative of a bank teller (B); the degree to which the description is representative of the conjunction (B&F) therefore lies somewhere in between these two extremes. This was the predominant ordering given by participants, for those asked to rank both by probability and by representativeness.

In short, the close correlation between judgments of representativeness and judgments of probability, coupled with the violation of the conjunction rule for the latter, support the claim that people are making their probability judgments on the basis of representativeness rather than a formal probability model (another example of attribute substitution). This basic finding has been replicated on many occasions and with more refined 'similarity-based' models of the representativeness heuristic (Kahneman & Frederick, 2002).

As befits a famous example, there have been numerous objections to the Linda problem, with respect to both its interpretation and its methodology. One of the main challenges is mounted by frequentists such as Gigerenzer, who claim that when the conjunction problem is asked in terms of probabilities it does not have a unique normative answer. This is because the term 'probability' is polysemous – it admits of multiple meanings. And not all of these possible meanings are bound by the laws of probability. For example, 'probability' can be interpreted non-mathematically, as referring to notions such as plausibility, credibility or typicality.

So when people give probability judgments that violate the laws of probability, they may be interpreting 'probability' in one of these non-mathematical senses. In that case, Gigerenzer and colleagues argue, they are not guilty of judgmental error. Moreover, when the mathematical reading of the term is clarified, by asking for a frequency judgment, people give judgments that conform better to the norms of probability.

We discuss the general frequentist argument in detail below. Here we focus on the argument that people interpret probability in a non-mathematical sense.

The short answer is 'too bad for them'. The normativity of the conjunction rule holds regardless. People who violate it are being inconsistent, and lay themselves open to sure loss irrespective of how things turn out. And this is not just a remote possibility. In a set of studies using realistic conjunction problems (Sides et al., 2002), people made suboptimal monetary bets that violated the conjunction rule. Furthermore, the problems intentionally avoided the use of any terms such as 'probability', so people were not misled by semantic ambiguities.

The long answer is to agree that the notion of probability admits of several possible interpretations (this is generally acknowledged in philosophical circles), and accept that people may be using a different sense to answer the conjunction problem. But this is just the first step. What is needed is a fuller account of what this concept may be, and why people systematically use it in such problems.

Are conjunction errors due to evidential support?

One of the most puzzling aspects of the conjunction error is how compelling it is, even to the initiated. Stephen Jay Gould (1992, p. 469) expresses this succinctly: 'I know that the [Bank teller & feminist] is least probable, yet a little homunculus in my head continues to jump up and down, shouting at me – "but she can't just be a bank teller; read the description."'

Is the mind really designed to make such a simple error? One way to avoid this damning conclusion is to argue that people are in fact answering a different question to that posed by the experimenter (attribute substitution). This is not to rule out the laws of probability as the correct norms (as suggested by Gigerenzer, 2002), but to propose that people are giving answers that conform to a different set of norms. People have the right answer to the wrong question.

What might this 'wrong' question be? An obvious candidate is the degree to which the evidence (e.g. Linda's profile) *supports* the conclusion (e.g. Linda is a feminist bank teller). The notion of evidential support (or confirmation) is well established in statistics and probability theory. Informally, it corresponds to the degree to which a piece of evidence changes the probability of a hypothesis. Thus evidence E is positive support for hypothesis H if it increases the probability of the hypothesis, $P(H|E) > P(H)$, and it is negative support if it decreases the probability of the hypothesis, $P(H|E) < P(H)$. There are several different proposals for how degree of support is quantified and measured (see Fitelson, 1999; Tentori et al., 2007), but this does not matter for the current argument. The crucial thing about degrees of evidential support is that they need not conform to the axioms of probability. In particular, the degree of support that evidence E gives to hypothesis H_1 can be greater than the degree of support it gives to hypothesis H_2, even if H_1 is a subset of H_2 (and thus $P(H_1) < P(H_2)$).

This line of reasoning can be applied directly to the Linda problem (Crupi, Fitelson & Tentori, 2008; Lagnado & Shanks, 2002). In this problem the evidence E is the short descriptive profile of Linda. There are three hypotheses: B = Linda is a bank teller; F = Linda is a feminist; B&F = Linda is a feminist bank teller. As shown above, according to the axioms of probability, the probability that Linda is a feminist bank teller is less than the probability that she is a bank teller, $P(B\&F) < P(B)$, because feminist bank tellers are a subset of bank tellers. However, the degree of support that the profile E gives to her being a feminist bank teller (B&F) can be greater than the degree of support it gives to her being a bank teller (B). This is because her profile raises the probability that she is a feminist bank teller, $P(B\&H|E) > P(B\&H)$, but it lowers the probability that she is a bank teller, $P(B|E) < P(B)$.

A crucial point to note is that even though the profile E raises the probability of Linda being a feminist bank teller, it can never raise it above the probability of Linda being a bank teller. However, if people are answering the original probability question with a judgment about support, they may fail to notice this, and thus violate the probability axioms. And the set-up of the problem encourages this kind of misreading. After all, it presents a strong piece of evidence (Linda's profile), and asks people to make a judgment on the basis of this profile. It is thus not surprising that many people respond by stating the degree to which that evidence supports the hypotheses in question, and therefore judge 'feminist bank teller' as more probable than 'bank teller'. They have given a sensible answer to the question, but unfortunately it is the wrong question.

This explanation of the conjunction error has received solid empirical support. In a series of experiments, Tentori and colleagues convincingly demonstrate that conjunction errors arise because people respond with judgments of evidential support rather than conditional probability (Tentori, Crupi & Russo, 2013). This account also fits well with the overarching framework of attribute substitution (Kahneman & Frederick, 2002). People are asked a question about probability, but readily substitute this with a closely related question about degree of support. Both the context of the question, and the accessibility of the substitute judgment, conspire to elicit this incorrect response.

The disjunction problem

Bar-Hillel and Neter (1993) presented students with the following kind of question:

> Danielle is sensitive and introspective. In high school she wrote poetry secretly . . . Though beautiful, she has little social life, since she prefers to spend her time reading quietly at home rather than partying. What does she study?

Participants then ranked a list of subject categories according to one of several criteria: probability, predictability, suitability or willingness to bet. The lists included nested subordinate–superordinate pairs (e.g. in the case of Danielle both 'Literature' and 'Humanities') specifically designed so that the character profile fitted the subordinate category better than the superordinate.

There were two main findings. First, people consistently ranked the subordinate category as more probable than the superordinate, in violation of the extension law of probability (whereby a subordinate category cannot be more probable than a superordinate category that contains it). Bar-Hillel and Neter termed this a *disjunction* fallacy, because the superordinate category (e.g. Humanities) is a disjunction of subordinate categories (e.g. Literature, Art, etc.). Second, probability rankings were almost perfectly correlated with suitability, predictability and willingness-to-bet rankings (and in a subsequent experiment with actual betting behaviour). This suggests that participants in the different judgment conditions used the same underlying process to reach their estimates.

This study appears to show again that intuitive judgments of probability do not respect the laws of probability. After all, the probability of a subset (Danielle studies English Literature) cannot be greater than the probability of its superset (Danielle studies one of the Humanities). What implications we draw from this depends on whether the person making the judgment is aware of the relevant subset relation. If he is unaware that English Literature is included as one of the Humanities, then he is not necessarily guilty of a violation of the disjunction rule. Perhaps he thinks that the category of Humanities excludes the category of English Literature (it does in the subject listings for certain British universities). Indeed the very fact that he has been asked both questions may encourage him to think that English Literature is not one of the Humanities. So it is possible that although the participants in the experiments violate the laws of probability according to the category structure assumed by the experimenters, they do not violate them according to their own category structures.

A clearer demonstration of a disjunction fallacy would require that people are aware of the relevant subset relations, and yet still persist in judging a subset as more probable than its superset. A set of experiments by Lagnado and Shanks (2002) comes closer to this, and will be reported in the next chapter.

SUPPORT THEORY

In addition to identifying various heuristics that people use to reach probability judgments, Tversky and colleagues advanced a more general framework for understanding subjective probability judgments: *support theory* (Rottenstreich & Tversky, 1997; Tversky & Koehler, 1994). Support theory hinges upon three central ideas: that subjective judgments of probability are description-dependent, that they derive from judgments of support, and that they lead to subadditivity (cf. Brenner, Koehler & Rottenstreich, 2002).

Description-dependence

Whereas standard theories of probability assign probabilities to events, support theory assigns probabilities to *descriptions* of events (termed hypotheses). This is motivated by the fact that people's intuitive probability judgments are sensitive to the way in which the events in question are described. Indeed alternative descriptions of the same event can lead to very different probability estimates. For example, people's estimates of the probability that someone dies from *homicide* tend to be lower than their estimates of the probability that someone dies from *homicide by an acquaintance or stranger*, even though both refer to the same event (Rottenstreich & Tversky, 1997).

More generally, the idea is that people attach probabilities to representations of events, rather than to the events themselves. This means that probability assignments are not description-invariant (as would be expected on a normative theory), and hence can change according to the representation that is provided or invoked (see also Chapter 9).

Support

How are subjective probabilities assigned to these hypotheses? According to support theory these assignments are derived from judgments of the strength of evidence (support) in favour of the hypotheses in question. In particular, the judged probability of hypothesis A is derived from the judged support for A, $s(A)$, relative to the judged support for alternative hypotheses. Thus the probability of A rather than B (where A and B are competing hypotheses) is computed via the formula:

$$P(A,B) = \frac{s(A)}{s(A) + s(B)}$$

Subadditivity

One of the central claims of support theory is that the probability assigned to a hypothesis will typically increase if it is unpacked into a disjunction of components. This is supposed to occur both when the unpacking is implicit and when it is explicit. In the implicit case, the judged support for one hypothesis (A) is assumed to be less than (or equal to) the judged support for a disjunction formed by unpacking A into exclusive subcomponents (e.g. A_1 or A_2). Thus death through 'homicide' is judged to receive less support than death through 'homicide by an acquaintance or stranger'. More formally: $s(A) \leq s(A_1 \text{ or } A_2)$.

In the explicit case, the judged support for an unpacked hypothesis is assumed to be less than (or equal to) the sum of the supports for each of the subcomponents. That is, $s(A) \leq s(A_1) + s(A_2)$. In this case death through 'homicide' is judged to receive less support than the sum of the separate supports given to 'homicide by an acquaintance' and 'homicide by a stranger'. Moreover, the latter sum is assumed to be greater than (or equal to) the support assigned to the implicit disjunction $(A_1$ or $A_2)$.

This overall pattern is summarized in the equation: $s(A) \leq s(A_1$ or $A_2) \leq s(A_1) + s(A_2)$.

In short, the sum of two separate support assignments is assumed to be greater than the single support assigned to a disjunction *(explicit subadditivity)*, which in turn is greater than the support assigned to the composite hypothesis *(implicit subadditivity)*. These patterns are termed 'subadditive' (somewhat counter-intuitively), because the composite hypotheses are assigned less support, and hence less probability, than the sum of their parts.

Evidence for and against support theory

There is a wealth of empirical evidence for explicit subadditivity across a variety of domains (e.g. with medical doctors: Redelmeier et al., 1995; options traders: Fox, Rogers & Tversky, 1996; sports experts: Fox, 1999). The evidence for implicit subadditivity is more mixed (Fox & Tversky, 1998). Moreover, some recent studies have shown an opposite pattern of superadditivity (Sloman et al., 2004).

Indeed Sloman and colleagues demonstrated that the question of whether a composite hypothesis garnered more or less support than its subcomponents depended on the typicality of these components. When the unpacked components were typical of the target hypothesis (e.g. the hypothesis 'disease' was unpacked into the most common subtypes such as heart disease, cancer, etc.) then judgments were additive (not subadditive). And when the unpacked components were atypical (e.g. 'disease' was unpacked into uncommon subtypes such as pneumonia, diabetes, etc.) then judgments were superadditive (that is, the judged support for the disjunction was less than the judged support for the composite hypothesis).

These findings are difficult to reconcile with support theory's assumption that unpacking leads to greater probability judgments. However, they do not undermine the claim that subjective probabilities attach to descriptions not events, or the claim that they involve relations of evidential support. An important project for future research is to explore the psychological models that underlie judgments of evidential support. Our hunch is that they will be closely related to the mechanisms that allow us to learn about these relations (see Chapter 12).

ERRORS OF CORRESPONDENCE

In addition to assessing probability judgments by how well they fit together (coherence), they can also be assessed by how well they fit with features in the external environment (correspondence). How good are people's probability judgments when evaluated in terms of correspondence? There are two main ways of getting at this question.

First, one can compare people's judgments with the actual frequencies of events in the world. The results of such research are mixed. An early and influential set of studies looked at people's judgments about the frequencies of lethal events (Lichtenstein et al., 1978). In one study people judged the frequency of various causes of death (e.g. heart disease, homicide, diabetes, tornado); in another they rated which of two causes of death was more frequent (e.g. the comparison between homicide and suicide used at the beginning of Chapter 5). These studies found that overall, people's judgments corresponded moderately well with the actual frequencies (on average people could distinguish between the most frequent and least frequent causes of death). However, there were some notable and systematic deviations from the actual frequencies. There was a general tendency to over-estimate rare causes of death (e.g. botulism, tornadoes) and under-estimate common causes (e.g. heart disease, diabetes). In addition there was a more specific tendency to over-estimate causes that were dramatic or sensational (see discussion of availability below).

In contrast, there is also a rich stream of research that supports the opposite conclusion – that people's judgments of frequency correspond very well to the actual frequencies (for a review see Sedlmeier & Betsch, 2002). Most of this research is conducted using trial-based paradigms, in which people are exposed to natural frequencies over the course of an experiment. One of the key claims is that people encode relative frequencies in an accurate and relatively effortless manner (Hasher & Zacks, 1979; 1984). This claim is tied in with specific theories about the cognitive mechanisms that people use to encode frequencies (Dougherty, Gettys & Ogden, 1999; Hintzman, 1988). These kinds of learning models will be explored in Chapter 12.

It should be noted, however, that even if someone encodes relative frequencies accurately, this does not guarantee that they will output a correspondent probability judgment. Lagnado and Shanks (2002) showed that people's relative frequency judgments corresponded more closely to the experienced frequencies than their probability judgments did. Indeed probability judgments were much more susceptible to systematic biases than frequency judgments.

One way to reconcile the diverse findings is to argue that people are accurate encoders of frequency information, but are sometimes exposed to biased samples (for instance, media coverage of dramatic deaths), or use biased search strategies (e.g. seeking information that favours one conclusion). Another is to accept that people sometimes encode probabilistic information in a biased fashion, and that this can depend on both the learning context and the mechanisms of learning (this alternative will be elaborated in Chapters 7 and 11).

Another correspondence-based method for evaluating probability judgments is in terms of calibration (Brier, 1950; Lichtenstein, Fischhoff & Phillips, 1982; Murphy & Winkler, 1977; Yates, 1990). Calibration applies to a series of single-case probability judgments. A person is well calibrated if, for each set of events to which they assign a specific probability *p*, the relative frequency of that event is equal to *p*. For example, imagine you are a weather forecaster. Each day you make a forecast about the probability of rain. Consider those days on which you assign a probability of 0.7 to rain. If the actual proportion of rainy days is 70%, then you are perfectly calibrated. Note that although such measures of calibration depend on there being repeatable events and judgments, the judgments themselves are single-case probabilities (i.e. what is the probability of rain today?).

The appraisal of probability judgments via calibration was developed precisely to assess weather forecasters (Murphy & Winkler, 1974; 1977). A striking finding from this research is that expert weather forecasters are almost perfectly calibrated (at least in Mid-west America). On those occasions when they state that there is a 75% chance of rain, rain indeed occurs 75% of the time. And this holds through the range of probability values. Indeed there are several bodies of evidence showing that experts in specific domains tend to be well calibrated, including bridge players (Keren, 1987), air traffic controllers (Nunes & Kirlik, 2005) and economists (Dowie, 1976). This contrasts with the calibration performances of novices, which often exhibit over-estimation (Brenner, Griffin & Koehler, 2005; Lichtenstein & Fischhoff, 1977). Perhaps this is not too surprising. Becoming an expert requires learning about the probabilistic structure of one's domain, and also knowing how to make judgments that reflect this uncertain structure.

One important extension of the notion of calibration is to the study of confidence judgments. Here, rather than making probability judgments about events in the external world (such as rainfall or aeroplane collisions), people make judgments about the accuracy of their own judgments. The main research question is whether people are well calibrated when they express their subjective confidence in categorical judgments that can either be true or false. These experiments often involve lay people's answers to general knowledge questions, but have also been extended to more real-world situations such as medical and financial forecasting. We will not explore the large literature on this subject (for reviews see Griffin & Brenner, 2004; Harvey, 1997; Juslin, Winman & Olsson, 2000; Lichtenstein et al., 1982), but just note a few of the salient findings.

Overall, people exhibit over-confidence in their responses, but this is modulated by contextual factors such as the difficulty of the test items, the nature of the response scale, the race and gender of the participants, and so on. There have been a variety of explanations offered for these effects, but no single comprehensive theory that does justice to all the empirical data.

A partial explanation for the over-confidence effect is given by Juslin and colleagues (Juslin et al., 2000; see also Gigerenzer et al., 1991). They argue that many of the experimental tests of confidence in general knowledge have a disproportionately large number of misleading or difficult questions. So although people might be well calibrated with respect to their normal performance on general knowledge questions, this can lead to over-confidence when the tests are artificially constructed by the experimenter to be difficult. Thus the crucial fault is not with their calibration per se, but with their inability to re-calibrate according to the difficulty of the items. The explanation is only partial because some over-confidence remains even when task difficulty is controlled for (Klayman et al., 2006).

Nevertheless, this focus on the environment that an individual samples from (and the possible biases introduced by non-representative samples) coheres with one central theme in this book – that we need to look at the learning environment to properly understand the judgments that people make.

Availability

In the introduction to Chapter 5 we asked which was more likely: death by homicide or death by suicide. We noted that people often judged homicide more probable than suicide, despite the fact that the latter is more prevalent (see also the sharks versus aeroplane parts example in the opening paragraphs of the book). Why do people make such estimation errors? Answers to this question often appeal to the *availability heuristic.*

Tversky and Kahneman (1973) introduced availability as a heuristic method for estimating frequencies or probabilities. People use the availability heuristic whenever they base their estimates on the ease with which instances or occurrences come to mind. Despite the simplicity of its formulation, the heuristic covers a range of cases. For one, it applies both to the recall of previous occurrences (e.g. how often you remember team X beating team Y) and to the generation of possible occurrences (e.g. how many ways you can imagine a novel plan going wrong). Second, it need not involve *actual* recall or generation, but only an assessment of the ease with which these operations *could* be performed.

Availability is an ecologically valid cue to frequency estimates because in general frequent events are easier to recall than infrequent ones. However, the main evidence that people use the availability heuristic comes from studies where it leads to biased estimates. For example, under timed conditions people generate far more words of the form _ _ _ _ *ing* than of the form _ _ _ _ _*n_*, even though the first class is a subset of the second. This shows that the first form is more available in memory than the second. Further, when one group estimates how many words in four pages of a novel have the form _ _ _ _ *ing*, and another answers the same question for the form _ _ _ _ _ *n_*, estimates are much higher for the first. This suggests that in making their frequency estimates people rely on the ease with which they can retrieve instances (Tversky & Kahneman, 1983).

The availability heuristic furnishes one method for constructing a sample of events or instances. A more general account of sampling (and possible biases) is advanced by Fiedler (2000). This extends the analysis from memory-based search to environmental search. Both kinds of search can lead to biases in the resulting set of instances. On the one hand, the environment might be sampled in a biased way. Fiedler cites an example concerning the assessment of lie detectors. Many validity studies of such devices incorporate a pernicious sampling bias: of all the people who fail the test, validity assessments only include those who subsequently confess. Those who fail the test but are telling the truth are not counted (cf. positive test strategies, Klayman & Ha, 1987). Another common route to error is when people sample from a biased environment, such as the media, that over-represents sensational and newsworthy events (Fischhoff, 2002; Slovic, Fischhoff & Lichtenstein, 1980).

Systematic biases can also arise when one generates a sample from one's own memory. This can occur due to the intrusion of associative memory processes (Kelley & Jacoby, 2000). Alternatively, it can result from the biased generation of possibilities or scenarios. For example, people tend to recruit reasons to support their own views, and neglect counter-arguments or reasons that support opposing conclusions (Koriat, Lichtenstein & Fischhoff, 1980; Kunda, 1990). Fiedler (2000) argues that many judgmental biases arise because – rather than in spite – of our ability to process sample information accurately. Samples are often biased, and we lack the meta-cognitive abilities to correct for such biases.

The availability heuristic involves the generation of a set of instances, but it does not specify how people go from this set to a probability judgment. In certain cases this will be relatively transparent, such as when more instances of horse A winning a race rather than horse B are recalled and thus A is predicted to beat B. However, many situations will be more complicated. Suppose A and B have never raced against each other, and A has only raced in easy races, B in hard ones. In this case you may need to weight their number of wins differentially, and for this, availability offers little guide.

CASCADED INFERENCE

Cascaded inference occurs when one makes a sequence of connected inferences. It is a pervasive feature of our thinking, allowing us to pursue extended paths of probabilistic reasoning. In a two-step cascaded inference you make an initial probabilistic inference on the basis of a known premise, and then make a second inference based on the output of this first stage. For example, suppose you are preparing to bet on a horse in the Grand National, and you know that rain will favour 'Silver Surfer'. You see dark clouds gathering by the race track (this is your known premise). From this you estimate the probability of rain (this is your first-stage inference). Finally you estimate the probability that 'Silver Surfer' wins given this inference (this is the second stage).

In the previous chapter we argued that the normative model for these kinds of multistep inferences is complex (involving Bayesian networks). We also hinted that people may find this kind of computation too demanding. Early research in cascaded inference confirms this. Several researchers (e.g. Gettys et al., 1973; Steiger & Gettys, 1972) have shown that people adopt a 'best guess' or 'as-if' strategy: they make their second inference *as if* the most probable outcome at the first step is true rather than probable. In our example this would involve inferring from the dark clouds that it is likely to rain (a best guess), and then basing your probability estimate that 'Silver Surfer' wins on the tacit assumption that it does rain (an as-if inference).

An independent but very similar argument has been developed in the study of how people make category inferences. Most work in this field has concentrated on the categorizations that people make when they are presented with definite information. Anderson (1991), however, proposed a rational model of categorization where people are assumed to make multiple uncertain categorizations in the service of a prediction about an object or event. More specifically, he claimed that when people make a prediction on the basis of an uncertain categorization, they follow a Bayesian rule that computes a weighted average over all potential categories.

In contrast to this *multiple category* view, Murphy and Ross (1994) have argued for a *single category* view, where just the most probable category is used to make a prediction. For example, consider the task of predicting whether the insect flying towards you on a dark night is likely to sting you. Let the potential categories in this situation be *Fly*, *Wasp* or *Bee*. According to the multiple category view, you compute a weighted average across all three categories in order to determine the probability of being stung. In contrast, on the single category view you base your prediction only on the most probable category (e.g. just one of *Fly*, *Wasp* or *Bee*) and ignore alternative categories.

Murphy and Ross (1994) demonstrate that people's default strategy is to use just the most probable category for their predictions (see also Hayes & Newell, 2009). This is consistent with the earlier research in cascaded inference, and suggests that in the face of uncertain premises people adopt strategies that simplify the computation problem. In the next chapter we will propose associative mechanisms that may underlie these strategies.

Section summary

Biases in probability judgment appear to be systematic and robust, and imply that in many contexts people do not follow the laws of probability. However, it is unclear exactly what processes *are* involved. Sometimes judgments of similarity, availability or evidential support do seem to drive judgment, but a unifying framework for understanding these biases is lacking.

THE FREQUENCY EFFECT

The conclusion that people fail to reason in accordance with the laws of probability has not gone uncontested. The most vocal challenge is provided by Gigerenzer and colleagues (e.g. Gigerenzer, 1994; Gigerenzer & Hoffrage,

1995). They maintain that the classic demonstrations of judgmental biases are flawed because the problems are couched in terms of probabilities rather than *natural frequencies*. In support of this claim they show that re-casting the problems in terms of frequencies leads to a marked reduction in biased responses. For example, when people are asked to think of 100 women like Linda, and asked for the frequencies of both bank tellers and feminist bank tellers, they are much less likely to commit a conjunction error (Fiedler, 1988; Hertwig & Gigerenzer, 1999). Similar facilitation effects have been demonstrated in the case of base-rate neglect (Cosmides & Tooby, 1996; Gigerenzer & Hoffrage, 1995; Sloman et al., 2003).

The so-called 'frequency effect', that presenting probability problems in a frequency format often reduces judgmental biases, is now well established. We met another example in the judgment made about the guilt of a defendant by mock jurors in Chapter 1 – 'Is this person guilty or innocent?' There are questions about the extent to this reduction, and situations where biases persist even with frequency judgments, but it is generally agreed that appropriate frequency representations facilitate human judgment. What remain controversial are the factors that drive this facilitation.

Let us present the frequentists' explanation first. There are several strands to their argument. First, they maintain that single-case probabilities are ambiguous and incomplete. They are ambiguous because there are numerous senses of the term 'probability', some of which are non-mathematical. They are incomplete because they do not specify a reference class. Both of these problems are avoided if uncertainty is framed in terms of frequencies. These are clearly mathematical, and they always refer to some reference class.

Second, Gigerenzer and colleagues distinguish *natural* frequencies from frequencies per se. Natural frequencies are frequencies that have not had base-rate information filtered out. They typically result from the process of natural sampling, where event frequencies are updated in a sequential fashion. In contrast, non-natural frequencies result from systematic sampling of the environment, or when frequency tallies are normalized.

Representing information in terms of natural frequencies can simplify Bayesian computations, because base rates are implicit in these counts, and do not need to be recalculated afresh. Gigerenzer illustrates this with the example of a pre-literate doctor who must assess the probability of a new disease given a fallible symptom. She simply needs to keep track of two (natural) frequencies: the number of cases where the symptom and disease co-occur, $f(S\&D)$, and the number of cases where the symptom occurs without the disease, $f(S\&\sim D)$. To reach an estimate for the probability of disease given symptom she can then apply a simplified version of Bayes' rule:

$$P(D|S) = \frac{f(S\&D)}{f(S\&D) + f(S\&\sim D)}$$

This is considerably simpler than the full Bayesian computation using probabilities or relative frequencies.

The third thread is an evolutionary argument. The idea here is that our cognitive mechanisms evolved in environments where uncertain information was experienced in terms of natural frequencies (Cosmides & Tooby, 1996). In short, the mind is adapted to process frequencies via natural sampling, and thus contains cognitive algorithms that operate over natural frequencies rather than probabilities.

The nested-sets hypothesis

In contrast to the frequentists, proponents of the nested-sets hypothesis uphold the validity of the original demonstrations of judgmental biases. They maintain that when making intuitive probability judgments people prefer to use representative or associative thinking, and are hence susceptible to judgmental biases. What facilitates judgments when problems are framed in terms of frequencies is that the critical nested-set relations are made more transparent (e.g. by using Venn diagrams, see Figure 5.1 in Chapter 5). For example, when instructed to think of 100 women just like Linda, and asked for the frequencies of both bank tellers and feminist bank tellers, people are alerted to the structural fact that the set of feminist bank tellers is included within the set of bank tellers.

On the nested-sets hypothesis, then, judgments typically improve in a frequency format because the problem structure is clarified. This is not due to the frequency representation per se, but because such a representation makes the relevant set relations transparent.

Indeed Tversky and Kahneman (1983) were the first to demonstrate the frequency effect. They attributed it to a shift from a singular 'inside' view, where people focus on properties of the individual case, to an 'outside' view, where people are sensitive to distributional features of the set to which that case belongs. It is only by taking an outside view that people can perceive the relevant structural features of a probability problem (cf. Lagnado & Sloman, 2004b).

In support of the nested-sets hypothesis there are empirical data showing that the frequency format is neither necessary nor sufficient for facilitation. Thus numerous studies show that biases remain with frequency formats, and that biases can be reduced even with probability formats (Evans et al., 2000; Girotto & Gonzalez, 2001; Sloman et al., 2003). For example, Sloman et al. (2003) showed that responses to both the conjunction and medical diagnosis problems improved in probability versions that provided cues to the relevant set structure, and declined in frequency versions that concealed this structure. There are also experiments that show a similar improvement when diagrammatic cues are given to set structure (Agnoli & Krantz, 1989; Sloman et al., 2003).

Finally, proponents of the nested-sets hypothesis question the appeal to evolutionary arguments. They argue that equally valid evolutionary stories can be spun for the primacy of single-case rather than frequency-based probabilities (see Sloman & Over, 2003, for details). After all, our ancestors back on the savannah were often required to make judgments and decisions about unique events. There would have been considerable evolutionary advantage in the ability to anticipate what might happen in novel and potentially one-off situations. (How many times can you stroll into a lion's den in order to compute the relative frequency of being eaten?) Another problem with the frequentists' evolutionary argument is that it neglects the possibility that the cognitive mechanisms that deal with uncertainty have *developed* from more primitive mechanisms (cf. Heyes, 2003).

Reconciliation

The two positions can be reconciled to some extent by noting an ambiguity in the claim that frequency formats facilitate probability judgment. There are two distinct ways in which frequency processing might aid judgment. First, it can serve as a form of natural assessment (cf. Kahneman & Frederick, 2002). That is, when asked for a probability judgment, you might base your response on a frequency estimate because it is readily accessible. And if your frequency judgments are relatively accurate then coherence comes for free, because frequencies automatically obey the laws of probability. For example, if you have an accurate memory for the number of bank tellers you have encountered, and (separately) for the number of feminist bank tellers, then the former will not be lower than the latter. Thus conformity to the probability laws is achieved without any appreciation of the necessary set relations.

The second way that frequency formats might facilitate judgment, and the focus of most of the debate, is through simplifying the computations necessary to solve a probability problem. On the nested-sets hypothesis this usually involves the clarification of the relevant set-inclusion relations. On the frequentist view this consists in the applicability of a simplified version of Bayes' rule (Gigerenzer & Hoffrage, 1995).

Cast in these terms the debate seems less pointed. Both parties can agree that frequency formulations are just one (albeit very significant) route to simplifying probabilistic computations. While this deals with the frequency effect itself, there are several general problems with the frequentist approach.

Theoretical confusion

Frequentists appear to confuse the judgments people make with the means we have of appraising them. It seems undeniable that people are able and happy to make single-case probability judgments. After all, these are the judgments most germane to our short-term decision making. You want the doctor to tell you *your* chances of surviving *this* operation; a hunter needs to act on the probability that *this* antelope is tiring; a child wants to know the probability that *he* will receive a bicycle *this* Christmas.

The frequentist maintains that such statements are incomplete, or at worst meaningless. Their main argument for this is that we have no means of appraising these singular judgments – that the event in question either happens or it does not. In contrast, they argue, a frequency judgment can be assessed in terms of its correspondence with a relative frequency in a suitably chosen reference class.

One shortcoming with this argument is that single-case probability judgments *do* admit of various means of appraisal. Aside from the coherence-based methods discussed earlier, there are correspondence-based methods such as calibration (where repeated single-case probability judgments are assessed against the relative frequencies, see above). This highlights a second shortcoming with the frequentist argument. It assumes that if a probability judgment is to be appraised in terms of frequencies, it must itself be a frequency-based judgment. But this does not follow. There is no reason why we cannot make singular probability judgments that are best appraised in terms of their correspondence to appropriate relative frequencies.

The importance of conditional probabilities and systematic sampling

Frequentists make much of the fact that natural frequencies arise from the process of natural sampling (indeed the evolutionary argument hinges upon this fact). A tacit assumption here is that it is always best to retain base-rate information in one's representation of uncertainty. But this seems to ignore the fact that (a) it may be computationally expensive to always maintain base-rate information (see the discussion in Chapter 12 about learning models), and (b) in certain circumstances base-rate information is unnecessary. For example, in the case of our own actions we are primarily concerned with the likelihood of an effect occurring given that we do something. We may be quite unconcerned with how often we in fact carry out this action. Similarly, experimentation (by scientists or lay people) seeks to establish the stable causal relations that hold between things, regardless of the base-rate occurrence of these things. Of course the latter information is often used to estimate these causal relations, but the main focus of systematic testing is on conditional relations rather than base-rate information.

This is not to deny the importance of base-rate information, but just to point out that other forms of information, such as that concerning the relations between events, is also critical to our mastery of the environment (a fact recognized by Brunswik). Sometimes the frequentist rhetoric about natural frequencies obscures this fact. We aim to redress the balance in the next chapter.

Frequentists offer no account for probability biases

Another problem specific to the frequentist account is that it offers no explanation for the systematic judgmental biases that persist when problems are framed in a probability format. The nested-sets hypothesis is a development of Kahneman and Tversky's original position, and so can avail itself of the various heuristics that they proposed to explain the biases. But, at best, the frequentist school shows us how to reduce these biases. It gives no principled explanation of why they arise.

Summary of debate about the frequency effect

The evidence marshalled in favour of the nested-sets hypothesis undermines the claim that frequency processing provides a panacea to judgmental bias. Nevertheless the frequency effect is an established phenomenon, and has triggered important applications in the communication and teaching of uncertainty (Gigerenzer, 2014; Sedlmeier, 1999). Also, the frequentists' emphasis on the fit between cognitive mechanisms and the natural environments in which they operate is well taken. Despite this, most demonstrations of the frequency effect have been with word problems using summary numerical descriptions. This is clearly not the natural environment in which frequency-processing algorithms would have evolved. A more appropriate test of their claims would be to locate people in a naturalistic environment where they are exposed to sequential information. Approaches that integrate judgment and learning into a unifying framework will be discussed in the next chapter.

SUMMARY

This chapter outlines the systematic mistakes that people make when they reason probabilistically, and discusses attempts to explain and alleviate these biases. In particular, it surveys many of the problems identified by the heuristics and biases tradition, including base-rate neglect, conjunction and disjunction problems, and mis-estimation of relative frequencies. The frequency effect – where judgments improve if the problems are formulated in terms of frequencies – is discussed and alternative interpretations of this effect critically evaluated.

In the next chapter we continue our examination of probability judgment. We propose a framework for thinking about the mechanisms that produce judgments that are usually correct but sometimes incoherent. The framework is based on the idea of 'associative thinking'.

Suggested further reading

- Gigerenzer, G. (1996). On narrow norms and vague heuristics: A reply to Tversky and Kahneman. *Psychological Review, 103*, 592–596. Provides a flavour of the debate between Gigerenzer on the one hand and Tversky and Kahneman on the other over the value of the heuristics and biases approach. The article to which this is a reply and the postscripts following each reply are also worth reading.

- Gilovich, T., Griffin, D., & Kahneman, D. (Eds) (2002). *Heuristics and biases*. New York: Cambridge University Press. A more recent collection of papers that highlights the continuing influence of the heuristics and biases approach.
- Kahneman, D., Slovic, P., & Tversky, A. (Eds) (1982). *Judgment under uncertainty: Heuristics and biases*. Cambridge, UK: Cambridge University Press. A collection of papers documenting the early work in the heuristics and biases tradition.

...iative thinking

Chapter highlights

- Proposes an associative account of how probability judgments arise
- Demonstrates the influence of category structure, or the alignment of a decision environment, on probability judgments
- Discusses the role of mental simulation and offers a brief consideration of constraint-satisfaction models of thinking and reasoning.

Judgments of probability or frequency are not conjured from thin air. They are usually made after some exposure to the domain in question. In particular, we often make judgments after learning something about the structure of the environment. It is natural to expect that the nature of this prior learning shapes the judgments we make, not just in the trivial sense that prior exposure provides us with data upon which to base our judgments, but also in the deeper sense that the mechanisms that operate during learning are active in the judgment process itself.

This leads to a more general conception of a correspondence model of judgment, one that attunes in some way to statistical features of the environment. In the case of a frequentist theory the primitives are frequencies. Judgments are based on, and appraised in terms of, their match with appropriate real-world frequencies. But this is only one possibility. In this chapter we introduce an alternative correspondence model, one where people attune to statistical relations *between* events. In particular, we argue that our learning mechanisms encode the degree of contingency or association between events, and this is often used as a basis for judgment. While this measure usually provides a good proxy for probability judgments, there are situations where it can lead to probabilistic incoherence.

Central to this approach is the idea that probability judgments are best understood in the context of the learning that precedes them. This involves both the structure of the learning environment, and the learning mechanisms that operate within it. We will discuss various learning models in Chapter 12. Here we will focus on an associative learning framework, because it seems to characterize human behaviour in a wide range of learning contexts.

ASSOCIATIVE THEORIES OF PROBABILITY JUDGMENT

Associative models of probability judgment (Gluck & Bower, 1988; Shanks, 1991) are usually applied to situations where people experience sequentially presented events. During this exposure people learn to associate cues (properties or features) with outcomes (typically another property or a category prediction), and these learned associations are supposed to form the basis for subsequent probability judgments. Analogues of several of the classic probability biases have been demonstrated within this paradigm. For example, Gluck and Bower (1988) demonstrated an analogue of base-rate neglect. In their task people learned to diagnose two fictitious diseases on the basis of symptom patterns, and then rated the probability of each of these diseases given a target symptom. The learning environment was arranged so that the conditional probability of each disease was equal, but the overall probability (base rate) of one was high and the other low. Given this structure, the target symptom was a better predictor of the rare disease than the common one, and in line with the associative model people gave higher ratings for the conditional probability of the rare disease (see Chapter 12 for more details).

Within the same associative paradigm, Cobos, Almaraz and Garcia-Madruga (2003) replicated this base-rate effect. They also demonstrated a conjunction effect, in which people rated the probability of a conjunction of symptoms higher than one of its conjuncts, and a conversion effect, where people confused the conditional probability of symptom given disease with that of disease given symptom (analogous to the inverse fallacy, see Chapter 6).

Lagnado and Shanks (2002) argued that these judgment biases arise because people attune to predictive relations between variables, and use these as a basis for their subsequent probability judgments. This can lead to error when there is a conflict between the degree to which one variable predicts another, and the conditional probability of one variable given the other. More specifically, on an associative model the degree to which one variable predicts another is measured by the contingency between these variables (known as ΔP). The contingency between outcome (O) and cue (C) is determined by the following equation:

$$\Delta P = P(O \mid C) - P(O \mid \sim C).$$

That is, the contingency between outcome O and cue C depends on the degree to which the presence of the cue raises the probability of the outcome. (Note that this is one possible measure of the degree of evidential support, cf. Chapter 6.)

The key point here is that the contingency between an outcome and a cue is not equivalent to the probability of an outcome given that cue. They will have the same value when $P(O \mid \sim C) = 0$, but they will often differ. For instance, the probability that the next prime minister of England is a male, given that you say 'abracadabra' before the next election, is very high. But, of course, this probability is just as high if you fail to say 'abracadabra'. Thus the contingency between the next prime minister being male and you saying 'abracadabra' is zero, but the probability of the next prime minister being male given that you say 'abracadabra' is high. (And this will hold true until there are more female candidates for the post.)

The learning analogues of base-rate neglect can thus be explained by the confusion between predictiveness (contingency) and probability. In these experiments people correctly learn that the contingency between the rare disease and the critical cue pattern is higher than that between the common disease and that cue pattern. Their mistake is to use this judgment to answer the question of which disease is most probable given the cue pattern.

Lagnado and Shanks (2002) extended this approach to the case of disjunction errors. They reasoned that if people use contingencies rather than conditional probability estimates, it should be possible to arrange the learning environment so that they judge a subordinate category as more probable than its superordinate category, even though this violates a basic rule of probability. This is an extreme version of the conjunction error, because a subordinate category is by definition fully contained in the superordinate category (see Chapter 6 for illustration of this point). It also mirrors the disjunction errors displayed by Bar-Hillel and Neter (1993) in one-shot verbal problems.

In Lagnado and Shanks' experiments people learned to diagnose diseases at two levels of a hierarchy, and were then asked to rate the conditional probabilities of subordinate categories (e.g. Asian 'flu) and superordinate categories (e.g. 'flu). The learning environment was arranged so that a target symptom (e.g. stomach cramps) was a better predictor of a subordinate disease than it was of that disease's superordinate category. In line with the associative account, people rated the conditional probability of the subordinate higher than its superordinate, in violation of the probability axioms. This suggests that people ignored the subset relation between the diseases, and based their conditional probability judgments on the degree of association between symptom and disease categories.

EXTENDING THE ASSOCIATIVE MODEL

So far we have argued that probability judgments are sometimes based on learned associations, and that this can lead to judgmental biases. But probabilistic reasoning often involves more than the output of a numerical or qualitative estimate. People often reach their judgments through an extended path of reasoning, or through imagining possible scenarios.

An associative account of cascaded inference

The associative account readily extends to multi-step or cascaded inferences. For example, the presence of a cue (item of evidence) can activate an associated outcome (step 1), and this in turn can serve as the input into another inference (step 2). Indeed 'as-if' reasoning is a natural consequence of associative inference, because nodes need just be activated above a threshold to count as 'assumed true'. For example, recall the deliberations from Chapter 6 about whether 'Silver Surfer' will win the horse race, given that there are dark clouds on the horizon. Presumably one has learned a strong association between dark clouds and rain. The presence of dark clouds thus activates an expectation of rain. One has also learned to associate rain on the race track with the sight of 'Silver Surfer' charging to the winning post. In short, the initial piece of evidence (dark clouds ahead) triggers a chain of association that results in a strong belief that 'Silver Surfer' wins the race.

As with the judgmental heuristics discussed in the previous chapter, this brand of 'as-if' reasoning has both a positive and negative side. On the positive side it can greatly simplify inference, allowing reasoners to focus on just the most probable inference path and ignore unlikely alternatives. If the weather is most likely to be rainy, why bother considering how well the horses are likely to perform in the sunshine? On the negative side, the neglect of alternative possibilities can sometimes lead to anomalous judgments and choices.

The influence of hierarchy on judgment and choice

The potential dangers of 'as-if' reasoning are demonstrated in a set of studies by Lagnado and Shanks (2003). They focus on situations in which information is hierarchically organized, such that objects or individuals can be categorized at different levels of a category hierarchy. For example, different treatments for cancer might be grouped in terms of either drug therapy or surgery (Ubel, 2002). Or different newspapers might be grouped as either tabloids or broadsheets. (For non-British readers: tabloids are the kind of paper that obsess about celebrities and have extensive sports coverage.)

Lagnado and Shanks (2003) argue that when reasoners are confronted with such hierarchies, they naturally assume that the most likely category at the superordinate level includes the most likely subordinate category, and vice versa, that the most likely subordinate is contained in the most likely superordinate. For example, consider the simplified newspaper hierarchy illustrated in Figure 7.1. Suppose that tabloids are the most popular kind of paper, so that if we pick someone at random they are more likely to read a tabloid than a broadsheet. It is natural to assume that the most popular paper will also be one of the tabloids (e.g. either the *Sun* or the *Mirror*). Furthermore, suppose that most tabloid readers vote for Party A, whereas most broadsheet readers vote for Party B. These two pieces of probabilistic information can be combined into a cascaded inference – someone picked at random is most likely to read a tabloid, and therefore is most likely to vote for Party B.

How good are such inferences? In many situations they will be very effective, and reduce the computational load. However, there will be situations in which they may prove problematic. Consider a sample of 100 people, each of whom

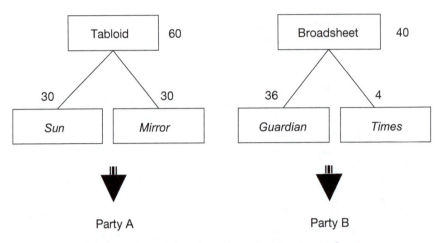

Figure 7.1 Simplified newspaper hierarchy and associated voting preferences
corresponding to the structure used in Lagnado & Shanks (2003). The
numbers denote the frequencies of people (in a sample of 100) reading each
paper. The frequencies are 'non-aligned', because although tabloids are more
popular than broadsheets (60 > 40), the *Guardian* is the most popular paper
(36 readers).

reads just one paper (see Figure 7.1). Amongst this sample, tabloids are the
most popular kind of paper, but the *Guardian* is the most popular paper. We
term this a 'non-aligned' hierarchy, because the most probable superordinate
does not align with the most probable subordinate.

Such a structure raises two problems. First, it undermines the inference from
superordinate to subordinate. The most popular superordinate (tabloid) does
not include the most popular subordinate *(Guardian)*. Second, it undermines
the cascaded inference from newspaper readership (tabloid) to voting preferences
(Party A). This is because there is an equally good (or bad) cascaded inference
to the conclusion that someone picked at random is most likely to read the
Guardian, and therefore to vote for Party B.

This highlights the possible perils of as-if reasoning. In an environment that
is non-aligned, reasoning as-if a probable categorization is true can lead to
contradictory conclusions. When categorizing an individual X at the general
level, one reasons as-if X is a tabloid reader, and thus concludes that X votes
for Party A. In contrast, when categorizing the same individual X at the specific
level, one reasons as-if X is a *Guardian* reader, and thus concludes that X votes
for Party B. But clearly the same body of information cannot support two
contradictory conclusions about X.

In their experiments Lagnado and Shanks used this kind of non-aligned
situation to show that as-if reasoning can lead to judgmental inconsistencies.
They gave participants a training phase in which they learned to predict voting
preferences on the basis of newspaper readership, using a learning environment

similar to that shown in Figure 7.1. They then asked them probability questions in three different conditions (see Figure 7.2). In the *baseline* condition, participants were simply asked for the likelihood that a randomly chosen individual would vote for Party A. In the *general level* condition, participants were first asked which kind of paper (tabloid or broadsheet) a randomly chosen individual was most likely to read. They were then asked for the likelihood that this individual voted for Party A. In the *specific level* condition, participants were first asked which specific paper (*Sun, Mirror, Guardian* or *Times*) a randomly chosen individual was most likely to read. They were then also asked for the likelihood that this individual voted for Party A.

The judgments in all three conditions were based on the same statistical information. The learning environment was arranged so that overall half the people voted for Party A and half for Party B. In line with these frequencies most participants reported a probability of around 50% in the *baseline* condition. However, in the other two conditions participants shifted their likelihood judgments depending on their answer to the question about newspaper readership. When they chose a tabloid as the most likely kind of paper, their mean judgments for Party A were raised to around 70%. When they chose the *Guardian* as the most likely paper, their mean judgments for Party A dropped to around 25%.

In sum, participants made very different probability judgments depending on whether they first categorized an individual at the general or specific level. And this pattern was not alleviated by asking participants to make frequency rather than probability judgments. These results can be explained by participants' reliance on as-if reasoning. In the *general* condition, they tend to reason as-if the randomly selected individual reads a tabloid (neglecting the probabilistic nature of their evidence), and therefore judge them most likely to vote for Party A. In the *specific* condition, they tend to reason as-if the individual reads the *Guardian* (again neglecting the probabilistic nature of their evidence), and therefore judge them most likely to vote for Party B.

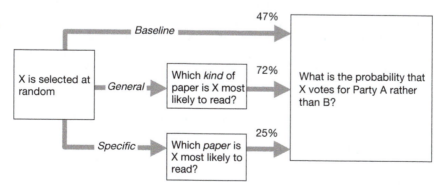

Figure 7.2 Test phase and mean probability judgments in each condition in Lagnado & Shanks (2003).

Furthermore, this use of as-if reasoning is readily explained by an associative account of probabilistic inference. During the learning phase participants build up associations between the newspapers (both at the general and specific level) and the two parties (e.g. Tabloid → Party A; Broadsheet → Party B; *Guardian* → Party B, etc.). These learned associations are then used as a basis for their responses to the probability questions. In the *baseline* condition, the balance of the learned associations does not favour one party over the other, so participants judge them equally likely. In the *general* condition, the initial judgment that tabloids are more probable than broadsheets leads to an increased activation of the representation of tabloid. This raises their subsequent judgment about the likelihood of the individual voting for Party A, because tabloids were strongly associated with Party A. In contrast, in the *specific* condition, an initial judgment that the *Guardian* is most probable leads to an increased activation of the representation of *Guardian* and this lowers their subsequent judgments about Party A (because the *Guardian* was strongly associated with Party B).

Medical choices

These experiments show that people modulate their judgments according to their initial uncertain categorizations; but what about their choices? Faced with a choice between various alternatives, do people allow the grouping of these options to influence their decisions? This is particularly pertinent when people are faced with a variety of options, all with an attendant degree of uncertainty. For instance, when faced with medical decisions people often have to choose between a variety of treatment options, each with a specific set of pros and cons. In order to help patients make better decisions in such situations some theorists recommend that similar options should be grouped together, thus reducing the complexities of the decision. For example, Ubel (2002) suggests that when presenting patients with information about different treatments for cancer, doctors should group like treatments together (that is, forming superordinate groupings such as drug therapy and surgical therapy).

Whilst the grouping of options into hierarchies is an important step in facilitating decision making, it also opens the door to the kind of flawed as-if reasoning discussed above. In particular, when grouping different medical treatments in the manner suggested by Ubel (2002), it is possible that information presented at the superordinate level has a distorting effect on judgments and choices made at the subordinate level. For example, if you tell patients that overall (at the group level) surgical therapy is better than drug therapy, this may lead them to pass over a particular drug treatment that is in fact the best option for them.

Lagnado, Moss and Shanks (2006) explored this possibility by presenting participants with either grouped or ungrouped information about the success rates of different treatments. In the *grouped* condition, four specific treatments were grouped into two superordinate categories (surgical or drug therapy). The success rates for the different treatments were arranged in a non-aligned

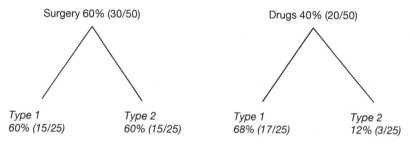

Surgery 60% (30/50)   Drugs 40% (20/50)

Type 1   Type 2   Type 1   Type 2
60% (15/25)   60% (15/25)   68% (17/25)   12% (3/25)

Figure 7.3 Success rates for treatments in Lagnado, Moss & Shanks (2006).

structure (see Figure 7.3) – the most effective particular treatment (e.g. drug X) was not a subset of the most effective group level treatment (e.g. surgery).

In the *non-grouped* condition, the four treatment options were presented without any superordinate grouping, but each treatment had the same success rate as the corresponding treatment in the grouped condition. So the only difference between the conditions lay in the superordinate grouping.

All participants learned about the success rates of the different treatments by making predictions for 100 patients on a trial-by-trial basis. For each patient, they were told which treatment the patient had been given, and then predicted whether the treatment would succeed or fail. After each prediction they received feedback as to the actual success or failure.

At the end of this training phase participants in both conditions were asked to make various choices. Those in the non-grouped condition simply had to choose the treatment that they considered most effective. In line with the success rates that they had just experienced, 75% of participants chose the most effective treatment (drug type 1). In the grouped condition, participants were first asked to choose the most effective treatment at the superordinate level, and were then asked to choose the best specific treatment. In response to the first question, most correctly chose the most effective superordinate category (surgical therapy). However, in response to the second question, only 25% chose the most effective treatment.

These results fit with the idea that people engage in as-if reasoning. In this case they expect the best treatment at the general level to include the best specific treatment. Having selected surgical therapy as the best superordinate category, they are less likely to choose drug type 1 as the best specific treatment. This contrasts with participants in the non-grouped condition, whose choices are not distorted by the superordinate grouping.

Once again it is important to re-iterate that we do not want to conclude from this study that grouping is a bad thing, nor that the strategies that people adopt are maladaptive. We have used a non-aligned structure to expose the operation of as-if reasoning, but we hypothesize that non-aligned structures are unlikely to be commonplace. In most situations as-if reasoning serves us fine; indeed it is likely that we construct hierarchies that observe alignment, and thus permit such simplifying strategies. However, these findings do suggest that probabilistic reasoning is underlain by heuristic processes rather than Bayesian computations over veridical probability representations.

ASSOCIATIVE THINKING AND MENTAL SIMULATION

The idea that people use associative processes to make inferences and reason about probabilities is not new (Dawes, 2001; Hastie & Dawes, 2001; Sloman, 1996). Indeed Hume (1748) is probably the grandfather of this claim. However, the link between associative thinking in *judgment* and associative *learning* is seldom made explicit. We have tried to build a bridge in this chapter, arguing that the associative mechanisms that learn predictive relations in the environment also direct subsequent judgments and choices. This fits with the overall aim of this book to argue for a reorientation of research on judgment and decision making to focus more on reasoners' behaviour when they can learn from feedback and less on what they do on one-shot, verbally described and often ambiguous, judgment problems.

This link between mechanisms of learning and judgment also bears on the question of *mental simulation*. This is another cognitive heuristic proposed by Kahneman and Tversky (1982a) to explain how people arrive at probability judgments. They argue that people construct a suitable causal model of the situation under question, and then 'run' a mental simulation of this model using certain parameter settings. The success or ease of achieving the target outcome is then used as a proxy for the probability of that outcome, conditional on the initial parameter settings. (We will meet this heuristic again in Chapter 13 in the discussion of how fire chiefs simulate strategies in dynamic environments.)

The simulation heuristic is particularly applicable to situations where people make plans or predictions about the future (Kahneman & Lovallo, 1993; Ross & Buehler, 2001). A robust empirical finding, termed the *planning fallacy*, is that people tend to underestimate the amount of time that it will take to complete a task or project (Buehler, Griffin & Ross, 1994; 2002; Kahneman & Tversky, 1979b), even when they have knowledge about the frequency of past failures. An example is the tendency of students to underestimate how long it will take them to finish an academic assignment. Buehler et al. (1994) found that students nearing the end of a one-year honours thesis underestimated their completion time by an average of 22 days.

The standard explanation for the planning fallacy is that people focus on their mental simulations of the project or task, generating a plausible set of steps from initiation to completion (Kahneman & Tversky, 1979b; Buehler et al., 2002). This focus on plausible scenarios over-rides the consideration of other factors, such as the past frequencies with which completion was delayed. (See Chapter 17 for further discussion of how to overcome the planning fallacy.)

Simulating an associative model

Discussions of mental simulation often neglect the influence of prior learning on how people 'run' these simulations. But just as learned associations can fuel our predictions about future states of the world, so they can drive our mental simulations. In predictive or associative learning, learning is driven by the error-correction of predictions or expectations about the environment (see Chapter 12 for details). On the basis of a set of cues and their associations with possible outcomes, a predicted state of the world is generated. This is then compared against reality (the actual outcomes), and the cue–outcome associations are updated.

Thus a mental simulation can be construed as the generation of a prediction or expectation about the world, but one that does not receive immediate corrective feedback. And the previously learned associative links between concepts (cues and outcomes) serve as the tramlines along which these simulations are run.

This can be illustrated with the Linda problem discussed in Chapter 6. Recall that people were asked to read a short profile of Linda, and then separately to judge the probability that she is a bank teller, and the probability that she is a feminist bank teller. On an associative account of this problem, the profile of Linda activates specific cues and concepts in the mind of the participant (perhaps female, philosophy student, cares about discrimination and social justice, and so on). These serve as the initial settings upon which mental simulations can be run. As the simulations are run, they are directed by previously learned associations (women concerned with discrimination tend to be feminists; philosophy students tend not to care about money, and so on). The ease with which these simulations arrive at the target category (i.e. bank teller, feminist or feminist bank teller) is then used as a proxy for the probability of that category (given the initial profile).

In the case of Linda's profile and the associations it is likely to prime, it is not surprising that people rate a feminist as the most probable category, and feminist bank teller as more probable than bank teller. It would be very easy to move from Linda's profile (via the implied associations) to the category feminist, and very hard to move from Linda's profile to the bank teller category. The activation of the feminist bank teller would be intermediate between these two extremes. The information in the profile activates the feminist part, but inhibits the bank teller part.

This associative account can be combined with the higher-level analysis of the Linda problem given in Chapter 6. In that chapter we suggested that instead of judging the probability of the various categories (bank teller, feminist, etc.), people judge the evidential support that Linda's profile gives to those categories. And they rate 'feminist bank teller' as more probable than 'bank teller' because Linda's profile supports 'feminist bank teller' more than it supports 'bank teller'. It seems plausible to see the associative account offered in this chapter as an implementation of such inductive reasoning. On this view, associative links between variables represent relations of evidential support in a complex network. Thus the overall effect of Linda's profile (and the implied associative links) is to raise the activation of 'feminist bank teller' but to lower the activation of 'bank teller'.

As mentioned previously, this associative account naturally extends to cascaded inference. Indeed in the Linda problem people are likely to engage in various cascaded inferences. From the information that Linda is a philosophy student they might infer that she is not interested in money, and from this infer that she is unlikely to work in a bank, and so on.

One special feature of cascaded inference is that it can be iterated without intermediate feedback from the environment. A sequence of these mental simulations can then be constructed, corresponding to the pursuance of a path of inference. The longer these inferences are spun out without external correction, the more they might deviate from reality.

This is just a sketch of how mental simulation and associative thinking might tie together. Much more needs to be said about the representations and mechanisms involved. For example, the role of causal models over and above associative models might prove crucial, especially when dealing with the simulation of possible actions (Lagnado, 2011; Pearl, 2000; Sloman, 2005; Sloman & Lagnado, 2004, 2005, 2015). But whatever the computational machinery that underlies our learning, it is also likely to subserve our mental simulations, and hence our probability judgments too.

Larger-scale networks and coherence-based models

So far we have considered relatively constrained inference problems, with just a few variables. But many real-world problems involve a much larger number of variables, possibly interrelated in complex ways. For example, as noted in Chapter 5, medical diagnosis often involves numerous symptoms and tests, various background factors, and multiple possible causes. Similarly, jurors in legal trials are presented with a vast amount of evidence, often ambiguous and potentially contradictory, with numerous intermediate hypotheses in addition to the key issues of guilt or innocence.

Somehow both experts and laypeople manage to make decisions in such contexts. How do they achieve this? A key factor here seems to be people's ability to encode large bodies of knowledge in an efficient way, so that they can focus on relevant pieces of information, and simplify the inference problem. Associative or semantic networks are one classic approach to this problem and there is strong evidence that semantic knowledge is encoded in network-like structures (Rogers & McClelland, 2004). However, the ability to combine generic knowledge (such as smoking causes bronchitis; bronchitis causes shortness of breath) with case-specific information (Joe smokes and is short of breath) is non-trivial, and yet an essential task in diagnostic reasoning (does Joe have bronchitis?).

Building on an associative view of human reasoning, coherence-based models address this challenge, with a focus on complex and knowledge-rich domains such as legal, medical, scientific and social reasoning (Simon & Holyoak, 2002; Simon, Snow & Read, 2004; Thagard, 2002). According to coherence-based models, people represent complex tasks using large associative networks that encode either positive (excitatory) or negative (inhibitory) relations between variables of interest. For example, in a legal case the variables might represent evidence and hypotheses about the perpetrator of a crime, with evidence either positively or negatively linked to a suspect. Reasoning or decision making is then modelled as parallel constraint satisfaction: people strive for a maximally coherent representation of the elements in this network, leading to inferences (or verdicts) that best satisfy the myriad associative constraints. This dynamic process can lead to the distortion of evidence to fit an emerging hypothesis, and the polarization of people's final decisions, even on the same evidence base. Thus, both acquitters and convictors in a legal case hold their respective conclusions with high confidence (Simon et al., 2004).

Coherence models typically concentrate on the dynamics of the decision process itself, and the construction or acquisition of these associative networks is usually left unexplained. However, it is natural to assume that they are built up in line with connectionist models of learning (see Chapter 12).

The coherence-based approach has garnered substantial empirical support, with proponents often emphasizing the dangers of coherence reasoning, insofar as it can distort evidence and deliver biased final judgments (Glöckner & Engel, 2013; Lagnado & Harvey, 2008; Simon et al., 2004). The strength of this approach is its parsimony and generality – appealing to associative networks where variables simply bear excitatory or inhibitory relations, and computationally tractable processes to capture the decision process. However, this simplicity also suggests a few limitations in the approach.

One shortcoming is that there is no explicit role for causal representations or reasoning, and yet the centrality of causality in legal and medical decision making is well documented (Norman et al., 2006). Indeed the story model of legal reasoning (Pennington & Hastie, 1986; 1992), typically cited as a precursor to coherence-based models of legal decision making, places causal networks at the heart of its theoretical model, and provides extensive empirical support for the role of causal thinking in juror reasoning.

Another shortcoming is that little is said about how the relevant associative networks are generated. How do people go from a set of facts about a case, and their background knowledge, to a suitable associative network? In the case of legal decisions or medical diagnosis this will be a specific network tailored to the case at hand, rather than a general-level semantic network. This step is as crucial as the subsequent process of inference and decision making (see Chapter 3). Tying these two issues together, it seems that the step of generating a suitable network will also require prior causal knowledge, for example knowing which variables to connect and whether these connections are excitatory or inhibitory.

Addressing these issues lies outside the scope of this book, but we will mention some ongoing research focused on these questions. As mentioned above, there is increasing use of causal models in cognition (for reviews see Rottman & Hastie 2014; Sloman & Lagnado, 2015) and the use of 'causalized' networks addresses the first shortcoming, and potentially unifies the strengths of the story model and coherence-based approaches (Lagnado, 2011). With regard to the second issue, more general models of categorization and learning are being developed that include a higher-level 'grammar' for generating structures and networks relevant to specific domains (Tenenbaum et al., 2011). For example, theory-based approaches to causal learning assume that people store high-level domain knowledge that allows them to generate possible causal models as they encounter experiential data (Griffiths & Tenenbaum, 2009). Similarly, Lagnado and colleagues (Fenton et al., 2013; Lagnado et al., 2013) propose that in legal reasoning, people use a small set of causal schemas (legal idioms), which they can combine and reuse to generate larger-scale networks to capture the complexities of a specific legal case.

Allowing that people use richer knowledge structures does not automatically solve the question of how they reason and make decisions based on this knowledge. Given that people use heuristic 'as-if' reasoning even for a few variables, it seems likely that this will be even more prevalent with large-scale problems. Indeed the story structures that seem to lie at the heart of people's reasoning in legal cases are effectively extended chains of 'as-if' reasoning. Once again any such simplifications cut both ways – greatly enhancing our capacity for reasoning in the face of large bodies of information, but also potentially exposing us to biases. Both coherence-based and story models of legal decision making highlight these strengths and weaknesses of human inference.

SUMMARY

We have argued that the way in which people learn about the statistical structure of their environment determines how they arrive at probability judgments, whether accurate or biased. Building on this idea, we proposed a unified account of probabilistic learning and judgment based on associative thinking. In particular, we suggested that our learning mechanisms encode the degree of contingency or association between events, and this is often used as a basis for judgment. In situations where contingency and probability conflict, people will make systematic errors because they attune to the contingencies rather than the conditional probabilities. Many of these errors have direct analogues in the one-shot verbal problems studied in the heuristics and biases programme. We extended this model to the more complex case of multi-step inference, where people pursue chains of probabilistic reasoning. We also highlighted a new type of judgment and choice anomaly that arises when people confront 'non-aligned' environments. Finally, we proposed a sketch of how associative models might underpin mental simulation, and be extended to larger-scale problems.

The last three chapters have covered various aspects of probability judgment, from basic appraisal methods, to the characteristic biases and errors people make in their judgments, to finally a sketched proposal for a unified account of probabilistic learning and judgment. In the following four chapters we move away from the world of probability judgment to the world of choices and decisions. First we present a framework for analysing decisions, then we ask how decisions are actually made and finally we examine the influence of time on our decision making.

Suggested further reading

- Kahneman, D., & Tversky, A. (1982a). The simulation heuristic. In D. Kahneman, P. Slovic, & A. Tversky (Eds), *Judgment under uncertainty: Heuristics and biases* (pp. 201–208). Cambridge, UK: Cambridge University Press. An account of how mental simulations 'run' over plausible causal models yield probability judgments.
- Lagnado, D. A., & Shanks, D. R. (2003). The influence of hierarchy on probability judgment. *Cognition*, *89*, 157–178. An illustration of how the alignment of a decision environment influences probability judgment.
- Simon, D., Snow, C., & Read, S. J. (2004). The redux of cognitive consistency theories: Evidence judgments by constraint satisfaction. *Journal of Personality and Social Psychology*, *86*, 814–837. Shows how coherence-based models capture biases in evidential reasoning.

8 Analysing decisions I

A general framework

Chapter highlights

- Introduces the expected utility framework
- Illustrates some classic examples of violations of expected utility such as the Allais and Ellsberg Paradoxes.

Every day we are faced with decisions. Some small – should you take your umbrella to work? Should you have salmon or steak for dinner? Some larger – should you take out travel insurance? Should you buy a laptop or a desktop computer? And some monumental – should you believe in God? Which football team should you support? Despite their diversity these decisions all share a common structure. They involve choices between several options, they concern future states of the world that are uncertain or unknown, and they have varying degrees of importance to you.

One of the major intellectual achievements in the 20th century was the development of a general decision-theoretic framework to address such questions (Ramsey, 1931; Savage, 1954; von Neumann & Morgenstern, 1947). This work itself built on pioneering work by mathematicians through the centuries (Bernoulli, 1738/1954; Pascal, 1670). In this chapter we present a simplified version of this framework, and several of its key assumptions. In the subsequent chapter we see how well people conform to these axioms, and outline a model of actual human choice behaviour.

A FRAMEWORK FOR ANALYSING DECISIONS

Acts, states and outcomes

The core ingredients for any decision problem are acts, states and outcomes. The set of acts $\{A_i\}$ are the options that the decision maker must choose between; the set of states $\{S_j\}$ correspond to various possible ways in which the world might turn out; the set of outcomes $\{O_{ij}\}$ are the different possible consequences of each act, given each possible state.

To illustrate, consider a decision problem faced by many inhabitants of the UK when summer finally arrives. Should they have a barbecue? In this case they must choose between two acts: to have a barbecue (A_1) or to eat indoors (A_2). There are two possible states of nature relevant to the outcomes: sun (S_1) or rain (S_2). And there are four possible outcomes, depending on the action taken and the state of nature that obtains: a sunny barbecue (O_{11}), a wet barbecue (O_{12}), a meal indoors while it is sunny (O_{21}) and a meal indoors while it rains (O_{22}). A decision matrix for this problem is shown in Table 8.1.

Table 8.1 Decision matrix for a barbecue

	Sunny		*Rainy*	
Barbecue outside	*100*	O_{11}	*0*	O_{12}
Meal indoors	*30*	O_{21}	*50*	O_{22}

Utilities

The next step in the decision problem is to assign utilities to the different outcomes. Ignoring various complications and subtleties (to be discussed later), the utility of an outcome corresponds to how much the decision maker values that outcome. Although it is convenient to work with exact figures here, it is not essential to the decision-theoretic approach that people themselves can assign precise numerical values to each outcome. What is crucial is that people can order the outcomes in terms of which they most prefer (with ties being allowed), and can express preferences (or indifference) between gambles involving these outcomes.

One method to infer a person's utility scale from their preferences is as follows: assign 100 to the most preferred outcome (O_1), 0 to the least preferred outcome (O_2), then find the probability p such that the decision maker is indifferent between outcome O_3 for certain or a gamble with probability p of O_1 (gain 100) and probability $1 - p$ of O_2 (gain 0). The utility for O_3, $u(O_3)$, is then equal to $p \times u(O_1) = 100p$. For example, if the decision maker is indifferent when $p = 0.5$, then their utility for O_3 equals 50. This process can be repeated for all outcomes in the decision problem. (Note that this method requires establishing a prior subjective probability scale; see Ramsey (1931) and Savage (1954) for a method that allows both probability and utility scales to be established simultaneously.)

Returning to our barbecue example, suppose that the decision maker values the four outcomes using a scale from 100 (most satisfactory) to 0 (least satisfactory). He values a sunny barbecue highest, and assigns this outcome a value of 100. He values a wet barbecue lowest (O_{12}), and assigns this a value of 0. He also prefers a meal indoors listening to the rain (O_{22}) to a meal indoors looking at the sun (O_{21}), and values these outcomes 50 and 30 respectively. These assignments are shown in the decision matrix in Table 8.1.

Probabilities

To complete the decision matrix, the decision maker needs to assign probabilities to the possible states of the world. Sometimes objective figures for these probabilities might be available, otherwise the decision maker must use his own subjective estimates. The literature on subjective probability estimates is vast and divisive, and is explored in detail in Chapters 5 and 6. What is generally agreed is that the decision maker should assign probabilities bounded by 0 (= definitely will not happen) and 1 (= definitely will happen), with the value of ½ reserved for a state that is equally likely to happen as not. In addition, the probabilities assigned to mutually exclusive and exhaustive sets of states should sum to one (see Chapter 5 for more details about constraints on probability estimates).

For the purposes of the barbecue example we will assume that the probability of rain is 0.5. Note that in this situation the probability of rain remains the same regardless of which act we actually take. This will not always be the case: sometimes one's actions themselves influence the probability of the relevant states of nature. And indeed, as far as those living in England are concerned, it often appears as if the probability of rain jumps as soon as a barbecue is decided upon. (This is not so much of a problem for those living in Australia.)

Maximizing expected utility

At this point we have a representation of the decision problem faced by the decision maker, including their assignments of probabilities and utilities. The elements that make up this specification are subjective, and may differ from individual to individual. However, the rules that take us from this specification to the 'correct' decision are generally considered to be 'objective', and thus not subject to the whims of the decision maker. Indeed there is only one central rule – the principle of maximizing expected utility (MEU).

This principle requires the computation of the *expected utility* of each act. As we described in Chapter 2, the notion of expected utility has a long pedigree in mathematics and economics (Bernoulli, 1738/1954; Pascal, 1670). The basic idea is that when deciding between options, the value of each possible outcome should be weighted by the probability of it occurring. This can be justified in several ways: in terms of what one can expect to win or lose if a gamble is repeated many times, or through constraints of coherence (Baron, 2000; Lindley, 1985; see also Chapter 5).

Applied to the general decision problem the expected utility of each act is computed by the weighted sum of the utilities of all possible outcomes of that act. Thus the utility of each outcome, $U(O_{ij})$, is multiplied by the probability of the corresponding state of nature $P(S_j)$, and the sum of all these products gives the expected utility.

$$EU(A_i) = \sum U(O_{ij}) \cdot P(S_j)$$

Once the expected utility of each possible act is computed, the principle of MEU recommends that the act with the highest value is chosen.

In our example the expected utility of having a barbecue is a weighted sum over the two possible states of nature (rain or sun).

$$EU(A_1) = U(O_{11}) \cdot P(S_1) + U(O_{12}) \cdot P(S_2)$$
$$= 100 \cdot 0.5 + 0 \cdot 0.5$$
$$= 50$$

This tells us the expected utility of having a barbecue (A_1), while the expected utility of not having a barbecue (A_2) is:

$$EU(A_2) = U(O_{21}) \cdot P(S_1) + U(O_{22}) \cdot P(S_2)$$
$$= 30 \cdot 0.5 + 50 \cdot 0.5$$
$$= 40$$

Finally, the principle of MEU recommends that we select the act with the highest expected utility, in this case to have a barbecue.

Why maximize?

So far we have simply presented the decision framework, and shown how to compute the expected utility of acts. We have not said why the principle of MEU is the appropriate rule to follow (although the fact that it would give us the best return in the long run is not too bad a reason to adopt it). One of the major achievements in the theory of decision making is that this principle can be shown to follow from a few basic postulates, each of which seems intuitively plausible. What theorists have shown is that if you accept these postulates, then you accept (on pain of inconsistency) the principle of MEU. We will discuss these axioms in later sections.

Status of the decision framework

The framework presented above is standard in most analyses of decision making. However, the status of this framework and its relevance to human decision making can be construed in several different ways. First, there is the distinction between *normative* and *descriptive* models. A normative model of decision making tells us how people ought to make decisions; a descriptive model tells us how people actually do make decisions.

Second, there is the distinction between 'as-if' and 'process' models. An 'as-if' model states that the choice behaviour of an agent can be represented *as-if* they have certain utility and probability functions, and maximize expected utility, but does not claim that they actually do this. Essentially as-if models predict the outputs of an agent in terms of the inputs it receives, but don't specify exactly how this is achieved. In contrast, a process model tells us how the agent actually carries out these computations. A process model of decision making claims that the agent does have actual utility and probability functions (prior to making a choice), and makes expected utility computations in order to decide what actions to take.

Note that this distinction applies to both normative and descriptive models. In the case of normative models the classic position is that the principle of MEU is an 'as-if' model (e.g. Harsanyi, 1977; Luce & Raiffa, 1957; Raiffa, 1968). That is, if an agent's choices are consistent with some basic axioms (see below), then their behaviour can be represented as-if they are maximizing expected utility. But on this view it is the preferences that are primary, not the utilities or probabilities. We should not say that someone prefers A to B because they assign A higher expected value; rather, we assign them a higher expected utility to A because they prefer A to B. So the validity of the model reduces to the validity of some basic axioms about preferences.

In contrast, it is also possible to construe the standard decision framework as a process model (for ideal agents). In order to make a good choice the decision maker should assign utilities and probabilities to the alternatives, and then select the option that maximizes expected utility. This approach is explicitly advanced in numerous texts on decision analysis (e.g. Hammond, Keeney & Raiffa, 1999), and is implicit in most presentations of the decision-theoretic framework.

In cognitive psychology, as-if models are often referred to as computational or rational models (Anderson, 1991; Marr, 1982). They seek to establish what an agent is trying to compute, rather than how the agent is actually computing it. In the case of decision making, then, an 'as-if' model succeeds in modelling human behaviour to the extent that it captures the macro-level choice behaviour.

On the other hand, process models strive to describe the actual cognitive mechanisms that underpin this behaviour. In the case of decision making, proponents of MEU as a process model must not only show that people's choice behaviour conforms to this principle, but also that people's assessments of probability and utility *cause* their choices via this principle.

In the rest of this chapter we will look at the descriptive adequacy of both as-if and process models. Note that if the principle of MEU fails as an 'as-if' model, then it seems to automatically fail as a process model (indeed most empirical critiques of MEU proceed in this way). However, it is important not to move too quickly here. A principle such as MEU may fail to apply to some cases of choice behaviour (especially those specifically devised to refute it), and yet still serve as an appropriate framework within which to develop good process models (cf. Busemeyer & Johnson, 2004; Usher & McClelland, 2001).

THE AXIOMS OF EXPECTED UTILITY THEORY

As noted above, a fundamental insight of decision theory is that the question of whether an agent's choice behaviour can be represented in terms of the principle of MEU is reducible to the question of whether the agent obeys certain basic choice axioms. There are several different axiomatic systems, but it is possible to extract a core set of substantive principles: cancellation, transitivity, dominance and invariance. For notational convenience we will refer to the general overarching framework of expected utility theory by the label EUT.

The first of these postulates, *cancellation* or the *sure-thing principle*, holds that states of the world that give the same outcome regardless of one's choice can be eliminated (cancelled) from the choice problem. This principle is fundamental to EUT, but has been questioned as both a normative and a descriptive rule. It will be discussed in detail in the next section. The second principle, *transitivity*, states that if option A is preferred to option B, and option B preferred to option C, then option A is preferred to option C. Although generally accepted as a normative rule, people sometimes violate this principle (remember Barry and his lollipops in Chapter 2). However, violations of transitivity seem to be the exception rather than the rule.

The principle of *dominance* states that if option A is better than option B in at least one respect, and at least as good as option B in all other respects, then option A should always be preferred to B. It has strong normative appeal – why prefer option B if it can never deliver more than option A, and will sometimes deliver less? However, people sometimes violate this axiom, especially in its weaker 'stochastic' version. This happens when people are presented with repeated choices between two options, one of which delivers a prize (e.g. money) with a higher probability than the other. People often 'probability match' in these circumstances; that is, they distribute their choices between the two options according to the probabilities that the options deliver the prize. For example, if option A gives a prize 70% of the time, and option B gives the same prize 30% of the time, then people choose option A 70% of the time and option B 30% of the time. This is a violation of stochastic dominance, because the person can expect to win the highest sum if they choose option A all the time (we discuss this phenomenon in more depth in Chapters 10 and 12).

The principle of *invariance* states that someone's preferences should not depend on how the options are described or on how they are elicited. This also has strong normative appeal, but appears to be violated in many cases of actual choice behaviour (see sections on framing and preference reversals in the next chapter, and the medical treatment example in Chapter 1).

The sure-thing principle

One of the central principles in Savage's (1954) decision model is the 'sure-thing' principle: if someone would prefer option A to option B if event X occurs, and would also prefer option A to option B if event X does not occur, then they should prefer A to B when they are ignorant of whether or not X occurs.

Savage illustrates this principle with the following example:

> Imagine that a businessman is considering whether or not to buy a property. The businessman thinks that the attractiveness of this purchase will depend in part on the result of the upcoming presidential election. To clarify things he asks himself whether he would buy if he knew that the Republican candidate would win, and decides that he would. He then asks himself whether he would buy if he knew that the Democratic candidate would win, and again decides that he would. Given that he would buy the property in either event, this is the appropriate action even though he does not know what the result of the election will be.

On the face of it this seems like a compelling principle. Why should your choice between options be affected by events that have no impact on the outcomes of interest? However, Allais (1953) and Ellsberg (1961) both presented situations in which people's intuitive choices appear to violate this principle.

The Allais Paradox

Imagine that you are faced with two choice problems:

Problem 1

You must choose between:

    A: $500,000 for sure
    B: $2,500,000 with probability 0.1, $500,000 with probability 0.89, nothing with probability 0.01

Problem 2

You must choose between:

    C: $500,000 with probability 0.11, nothing with probability 0.89
    D: $2,500,000 with probability 0.1, nothing with probability 0.9

Most people choose A rather than B in Problem 1, and D over C in Problem 2. But this pattern of choices is inconsistent, and violates the sure-thing principle.

To show that it is inconsistent, let us denote $U(x)$ as the utility that you assign to x. Then a preference for A over B implies (according to the principle of MEU) that:

$$U(\$500,000) > 0.1 \ U(\$2,500,000) + 0.89 \ U(\$500,000) \tag{1}$$

In other words, you prefer a sure gain of $500,000 to the combination gamble with a 0.1 chance of $2,500,000 and a 0.89 chance of $500,000.

But equation (1) can be re-arranged by subtracting 0.89 $U(\$500,000)$ from both sides, so that:

$$U(\$500,000) - 0.89\ U(\$500,000) > 0.1\ U(\$2,500,000)$$

which reduces to:

$$0.11\ U(\$500,000) > 0.1\ U(\$2,500,000) \tag{2}$$

Therefore your preference for A over B implies that you prefer a 0.11 chance of $500,000 to a 0.1 chance of $2,500,000.

However, in Problem 2 you preferred D over C. This implies (via MEU) that:

$$0.1\ U(\$2,500,000) > 0.11\ U(\$500,000) \tag{3}$$

In other words, you prefer a 0.1 chance of $2,500,000 to a 0.11 chance of $500,000. Clearly (2) and (3) are inconsistent, and yet both are direct implications of your pattern of preferences according to the principle of MEU.

Why is this a violation of the sure-thing principle? This is best shown by re-representing the problem (Savage, 1954). The Allais problem can be represented as a 100-ticket lottery with payoffs as shown in Table 8.2. Presented in this manner the application of the sure-thing principle becomes clear. It states that if a ticket from 12 to 100 is drawn, it should have no impact on one's pattern of preferences. This is because these tickets do not discriminate between either pair of gambles (they have the same values for each pair). According to the sure-thing (or cancellation) principle, this allows us to reduce the problem to the cases of tickets 1–11. And from inspection of the table it is clear that these are identical in both problems. This should persuade you (does it?) that if you prefer A to B, you should also prefer C to D, on pain of inconsistency.

Of course you may still persist in the 'inconsistent' pair of choices, and argue that it is the sure-thing principle (and cancellation) that is incorrect. In fact you would be in good company here, as many prominent thinkers, including

Table 8.2 Savage's representation of the Allais Paradox

Ticket number				
		1	*2–11*	*12–100*
Problem 1	A	500,000	500,000	500,000
	B	0	2,500,000	500,000
Problem 2	C	500,000	500,000	0
	D	0	2,500,000	0

the Nobel laureate Maurice Allais, maintain that the sure-thing principle is inadequate in such cases. In opposition to this, theorists such as Savage have argued that once the Allais problem is re-represented to make the sure-thing principle transparent (as in Table 8.2), it is your 'inconsistent' pattern of choices that should be abandoned, not the sure-thing principle. An interesting footnote to this debate is that when people are shown the re-represented Allais problem, they are indeed more likely to obey the sure-thing principle (Keller, 1985; for more recent work on the effects of re-representing decision problems, see Lan & Harvey, 2006).

Let us return to the original formulation of the Allais problem. Why do people prefer A to B in Problem 1, but prefer D to C in Problem 2? Savage himself had a plausible psychological explanation for such findings. He argued that people prefer A to B because the extra chance of winning a very large amount in B does not compensate for the slight chance of winning nothing. In contrast, the same people might prefer D to C because while the chance of winning something is pretty much the same for both options, they prefer the option with the much larger prize. This explanation has been developed more fully by various psychologists, and will be explored in the next chapter.

Extensions of the Allais problem

Whatever your position on the normative status of the sure-thing principle, its status as a descriptive model does seem to be undermined by people's responses to the Allais problem. Indeed over the past decades numerous versions of this problem have been presented to people, and violations of the principle are regularly observed. Kahneman and Tversky (1979a) presented people with a range of Allais-like problems, and demonstrated systematic violations of the principle of MEU. For example, they gave participants the following pair of problems:

Problem 1

You must choose between:

    E: $4000 with probability 0.8
    F: $3000 for sure

Problem 2

You must choose between:

    G: $4000 with probability 0.2
    H: $3000 with probability 0.25

In this experiment 80% of participants preferred F to E, and 65% preferred G to H. But this pattern of preferences violates the principle of MEU because a preference for F over E implies:

$U(\$3000) > 0.8\ U(\$4000)$ (1)

whereas a preference for G over H implies:

$0.2\ U(\$4000) > 0.25\ U(\$3000)$ (2)

which (if both sides are multiplied by 4) is equivalent to:

$0.8\ U(\$4000) > U(\$3000)$

So (1) and (2) are inconsistent.

Kahneman and Tversky also demonstrated violations of the principle of MEU with non-monetary gambles. For example, they presented participants with the following two problems:

Problem 3

    I: A 50% chance to win a three-week tour of England, France and Italy
    J: A one-week tour of England for sure

Problem 4

    K: A 5% chance to win a three-week tour of England, France and Italy
    L: A 10% chance to win a one-week tour of England

Most participants preferred J to I (demonstrating questionable taste), but also preferred K to L. Here again this pattern violates the principle of MEU.

Ellsberg's problems

Another choice paradox, devised by Ellsberg (1961), also challenges the status of the sure-thing principle. Imagine you are presented with two urns each containing 100 balls. Urn 1 contains an unknown number of red and black balls – there could be any number of red balls from zero to 100. Urn 2 contains exactly 50 red balls and 50 black balls. You are asked four questions, in each of which you must stake $100 on one of two bets (with the option of expressing indifference):

1.   Given a draw from Urn 1, would you rather bet on Red or Black?
2.   Given a draw from Urn 2, would you rather bet on Red or Black?
3.   If you have to bet on Red, would you rather it be on a draw from Urn 1 or Urn 2?
4.   If you have to bet on Black, would you rather it be on a draw from Urn 1 or Urn 2?

How did you choose? Overall, people tend to be indifferent between Red and Black in questions 1 and 2, but prefer to bet on a draw from Urn 2 in both questions 3 and 4. But this is problematic for the principle of MEU, because it appears to demonstrate an inconsistent pair of probability judgments. On the one hand, your preference for Urn 2 in question 3 suggests that you think that a Red ball from Urn 2 is more probable than a Red ball from Urn 1. On the other hand, your preference for Urn 2 in question 4 suggests that you think that a Black ball from Urn 2 is more probable than a Black ball from Urn 1.

According to Ellsberg (1961), this example shows that people reason differently when they know the exact probabilities (Urn 2) than when they are ignorant of the exact probabilities (Urn 1), and this difference is not captured given the standard MEU principle.

Ellsberg presented another case, which has become the standard example in the literature. Imagine an urn that contains 30 red balls, and 60 black or yellow balls in an unknown proportion. One ball is to be drawn at random. Would you bet on Red or Black? The payoff matrix is shown in Table 8.3.

Table 8.3 Payoff matrix for Ellsberg's Problem 1

Number of balls	30	60	
Colour of ball	Red	Black	Yellow
1: bet on Red	$100	$0	$0
2: bet on Black	$0	$100	$0

Most people prefer to bet on Red in this case (option 1). However, now consider a choice problem with a different payoff matrix (see Table 8.4). Here the choice is between (3) betting on 'Red or Yellow', or (4) betting on 'Black or Yellow'. Which would you choose?

Table 8.4 Payoff matrix for Ellsberg's Problem 2

Number of balls	30	60	
Colour of ball	Red	Black	Yellow
3: bet on Red or Yellow	$100	$0	$100
4: bet on Black or Yellow	$0	$100	$100

With this payoff matrix, most respondents prefer to bet on Black or Yellow (option 4). But this is a clear violation of the sure-thing principle (and thus MEU), because the two pairs of options differ only in their third column, and this is constant for either pair. If you prefer to bet on Red in the first problem, why should you prefer to bet on 'Black or Yellow' in the second problem?

Ambiguity aversion

Ellsberg concluded that people prefer to bet on outcomes with known probabilities rather than on outcomes with unknown probabilities. This is problematic for most versions of EUT, because the theory assumes that there is no substantial difference between a definite (known) probability judgment and an uncertain probability judgment with the same numerical value. Ellsberg termed this 'ambiguity aversion': people are less willing to bet on ambiguous outcomes than on unambiguous outcomes, even if they both have equivalent probabilities.

There have been numerous studies confirming people's preference for known over unknown probabilities (e.g. MacCrimmon & Larsson, 1979; Slovic & Tversky, 1974). As noted above, this finding does not fit with standard EUT; however, nor is it explained by the main model of human choice (prospect theory). We will return to the issue of ambiguity aversion once we have presented this theory in the next chapter.

SUMMARY

In this chapter we have introduced the dominant framework for modelling choices (EUT), and its central maxim of maximizing expected utility (MEU). The status of this framework has been discussed in terms of the distinction between normative and descriptive models, and the distinction between process and 'as-if' models. We have shown how representing someone's choices in terms of MEU depends on their preferences satisfying certain basic axioms, and discussed two of the classic demonstrations that people's intuitive preferences violate these axioms (Allais' and Ellsberg's problems). In the next chapter we turn to the issue of how people *actually* make choices, and present one of the most successful models of human choice – prospect theory.

Suggested further reading

- Ellsberg, D. (1961). Risk, ambiguity and the Savage axioms. *Quarterly Journal of Economics*, 75, 643–679. A seminal paper in which Ellsberg introduces the thought experiment which subsequently became known as Ellsberg's Paradox.
- Kahneman, D., & Tversky, A. (1979). Prospect theory: An analysis of decision under risk. *Econometrica*, 47, 263–291. The paper which presents a highly influential alternative theory of decision under risk.
- Savage, L. J. (1954). *The foundations of statistics*. New York: Wiley. The book in which Savage sets out the axioms of his subjective expected utility theory.

9 Analysing decisions II

Prospect theory and preference reversals

Chapter highlights

- An explanation of prospect theory and the four-fold pattern
- A discussion of framing effects and the idea that losses loom larger than gains
- An examination of preference reversals and their potential explanation via compatibility and evaluability.

How do people actually make choices? The dominant account of human choice is prospect theory (Kahneman & Tversky, 1979a, 1984; Tversky & Kahneman, 1992). Prospect theory preserves the idea that our choices involve maximizing some kind of expectation. However, the utilities and probabilities of outcomes both undergo systematic cognitive distortions (non-linear transformations) when they are evaluated. Moreover, prior to this evaluation the decision maker must construct a mental representation of the choice problem. This invokes several cognitive operations not captured by the standard EUT, such as the framing of options relative to some reference point and the editing of gambles to simplify the choice problem. In this chapter we outline the theoretical model that explains these cognitive operations and distortions, and the empirical evidence that supports it.

REFERENCE-DEPENDENCE

Before a decision maker can evaluate their options, they must represent the problem in a meaningful way. One of the key insights in prospect theory is that the mental representations that people use in choice situations have features that reach beyond anything given in economic theory. This is exemplified by Kahneman and Tversky's claim that people usually perceive outcomes as gains or losses relative to a neutral reference point. This simple observation leads to a substantial re-working of the traditional notion of utility, and its role in choice behaviour.

The value function

A milestone in the development of classical EUT was the distinction between money and its utility, and the idea that in general money has diminishing marginal utility (see Chapter 2). This is illustrated by the fact that the same amount of money, say $100, has more value for a pauper than a prince. Applied to a single individual, it amounts to the claim that one values the move from $100 to $200 more than the move from $1100 to $1200. In technical terms, the subjective value of money is a concave function of money (see Figure 2.1 for a graphical illustration). A direct consequence of this relation between utility and money is that people will in general be *risk-averse*. That is, they will prefer a sure amount $X to a gamble with the same expected value (e.g. a 50% chance of winning $2X).

Traditional theories of EUT also assumed that people evaluate gambles in terms of the overall states of wealth that they lead to. So a pauper with $1 to his name evaluates a win of $10 as a transition from $1 to $11, whereas a prince with $1 million to his name evaluates the same win as a transition from $1 million to $1,000,010. And thus a potential gain of $10 means more (is more valuable) for the pauper than the prince. The radical proposal made in prospect theory (and beforehand by Markowitz, 1952) is that people do not evaluate the outcomes of gambles in terms of the overall states of wealth to which they lead, but as gains (or losses) relative to a neutral reference point. So the pauper and prince, despite their different starting points, can show similar behaviour when faced with the same choices between gambles. (This explains why rich people are still mean.)

Furthermore, this neutral reference point is malleable, and open to manipulation. This means that the same underlying choice problem can be given different reference points, and consequently lead to divergent choices (see framing effects below). So two princes (or the same prince at different times) might make very different choices (e.g. about whom to marry) depending on their reference frame.

The flipside to risk-aversion in the domain of gains is risk-seeking in the domain of losses. Just as the difference between a gain of $10 versus $20 appears greater than the difference between $110 and $120, so a loss of $20 versus $10 will appear greater than that between losses of $120 and $110. This diminishing function for losses (now reflected by a convex function) implies risk-seeking. One prefers a probable loss to a sure loss with the same expectation. For example, people typically prefer an 80% chance of losing $1000 to a sure loss of $800.

This overall pattern of preferences is summarized by the S-shaped value function shown in Figure 9.1. It has a concave shape in the domain of gains (upper right quadrant) and a convex shape in the domain of losses (lower left quadrant). It captures several key claims of prospect theory: that people tend to evaluate gambles in terms of gains or losses relative to a neutral point, and that they are often risk-averse for gains but risk-seeking for losses.

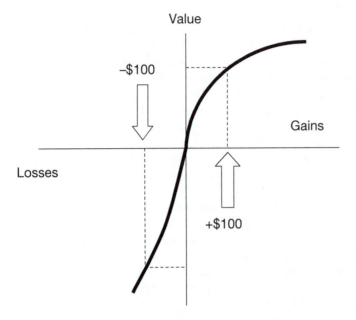

Figure 9.1 The value function of prospect theory.

As well as fitting a range of empirical studies (see below), the idea that people evaluate outcomes in terms of changes of wealth rather than final states of wealth has strong parallels in psychophysics. Our responses to sensory and perceptual stimuli often track relative rather than absolute changes, and exhibit a similar relation of diminishing sensitivity to such changes (e.g. habituation).

The isolation effect

A vivid demonstration that people evaluate outcomes in terms of changes of wealth rather than final states of wealth is given in the *isolation effect* (Kahneman & Tversky, 1979a).

Consider *Problem 1*:

In addition to whatever you own, you have been given $1000. You are now asked to choose between:

    A: a 50% chance of $1000
    B: $500 for sure.

The majority of participants (84%) in Kahneman and Tversky's experiment chose option B, demonstrating risk-aversion in the domain of gains.

Now consider *Problem 2*:

In addition to whatever you own, you have been given $2000. You are now asked to choose between:

C: a 50% chance of losing $1000
D: a sure loss of $500.

In this case the majority of participants (69%) prefer C. This demonstrates risk-seeking in the domain of losses, and fits with the predictions of prospect theory noted above. However, these two choice problems are identical if construed in terms of final states of wealth:

A = $1000 + 50% chance of $1000

  = $2000 − 50% chance of $1000

  = C

B = $1500 for sure

  = D

These choices conflict with the prescriptions of EUT, which requires that the same pattern of choices be made in both problems (e.g. either A and C, or B and D). Moreover, it also contradicts the simple assumption of risk-aversion, because in Problem 2 the risky option is preferred to the sure loss. At heart the observed choices reflect people's failure to integrate the initial bonus (either $1000 or $2000) into their evaluations of the gambles. They focus on the changes in wealth that the different options entail rather than their final states (which are equivalent).

Losses loom larger than gains

Another crucial feature of the value function is that it is much steeper in the domain of losses than the domain of gains (see Figure 9.1). This implies that the displeasure of a loss of $100 is larger than the pleasure of a gain of $100, and hence that people are more averse to losses than they are attracted by corresponding gains. There is a wealth of empirical data in support of such *loss-aversion*, and it has been extended to many real-world situations (see the collection by Kahneman & Tversky, 2000).

The simplest example of loss-aversion is the fact that people dislike gambles that offer an equal probability of winning or losing the same amount of money. That is, they tend to reject gambles that offer a 50% chance of winning $X and a 50% chance of losing $X (especially when X is a large amount). More realistic demonstrations of loss-aversion are given by the *endowment effect* and *status quo bias*.

The endowment effect was introduced by Thaler (1980). It hinges on a simple principle of behaviour that many of us learned in the school playground – once you acquire something, you are often reluctant to give it up, even if offered a price (or inducement) that is more than you yourself would have paid for the object in the first place. The sharing of different-colour sweets amongst children comes to mind here.

The endowment effect has been demonstrated in numerous experiments. One of the best known was conducted by Kahneman, Knetsch and Thaler (1990). They randomly distributed university mugs (worth about $5) to some of their students. All students were then given questionnaires. The students who had received mugs (the 'sellers') were effectively asked how much they would be prepared to sell their mugs for. The students who had not received mugs (the 'choosers') were asked about their preferences between receiving the mug or various amounts of money.

From a normative point of view both the sellers and the choosers face the same decision problem: mug versus money. However, if we factor in loss-aversion, then their situations are quite different. The sellers are contemplating how much money they would accept to *give up* their mug, whilst the choosers are contemplating how much they would pay to *acquire* the same mug. In other words, sellers are evaluating a potential loss (of a mug), while choosers are evaluating a potential gain.

In line with the predictions of loss-aversion, the median value of the mug for the sellers was about $7, while for the choosers it was about $3. Simply by endowing some students with the mug in the first place, their evaluations of its worth had shifted markedly relative to other non-endowed students. This effect has been replicated and extended in many studies (see several papers in the collection by Kahneman & Tversky, 2000).

Closely related to the endowment effect is the *status quo bias*. This amounts to the preference to remain in the same state (the status quo) rather than take a risk and move to another state, and is explained by the potential losses incurred by shifting from the status quo looming larger than the potential gains. Samuelson and Zeckhauser (1988) demonstrated this effect in the context of a hypothetical investment task. One group of participants were told that they had inherited a sum of money, and had to choose from various investment options (moderate-risk, high-risk, etc.). The other group were told that they had inherited a portfolio of investments, most of which were concentrated in one specific option (e.g. moderate-risk). They then had to choose from the same array of investment options as the other group (and were told that transaction costs were minimal). Across a range of scenario manipulations participants in the latter condition showed a strong status quo bias. They preferred to stick with the previously invested option, and this tendency increased with the number of available options.

The phenomenon of loss-aversion, and its correlative effects of endowment and status quo biases, is firmly established in experimental studies and indeed the economic world beyond the laboratory (Camerer, 2000). Although seemingly irrational in the context of business and market transactions, it has roots in lower-level psychological laws that seem adaptive to basic environmental demands. Thus the asymmetry of people's reactions to pain versus pleasure is eminently sensible in a world that punishes those who ignore danger signs more than it rewards those who pursue signs of pleasure.

THE FOUR-FOLD PATTERN

Prospect theory was constructed to fit a wide range of choice behaviour. Much of this is summarized by the 'four-fold' pattern shown in Table 9.1. The value function alone, however, only explains a 'two-fold' pattern of risk-aversion for gains and risk-seeking for losses. It does not account for the opposite pattern observed when the probabilities involved are small. To capture the whole pattern Kahneman and Tversky introduced the notion of decision weights.

Table 9.1 The four-fold pattern of choice behaviour for simple gambles

	Gains	*Losses*
Small probabilities	Risk-seeking	Risk-aversion
Medium and large probabilities	Risk-aversion	Risk-seeking

Decision weights

Just as the decision maker transforms the 'objective' utility of a gain or loss into a subjective value (via the value function), so they transform the 'objective' probability of an outcome into a decision weight. The decision weight function (see Figure 9.2) is also non-linear. Its central features are the over-weighting of small probabilities, the under-weighting of moderate and large probabilities, and extreme behaviour close to 0 or 1.

This function can explain risk-seeking with gambles that offer small probabilities of positive outcomes (e.g. the widespread purchase of lottery tickets), and risk-aversion with those that offer small probabilities of negative outcomes (e.g. the widespread purchase of insurance). This is demonstrated in the following two problems:

Problem 1:

Choose between:

    A: a 0.001 chance of winning $5000
    B: $5 for sure.

The majority of participants (72%) chose option A, indicating risk-seeking (and replicating the behaviour of thousands of lottery players world-wide).

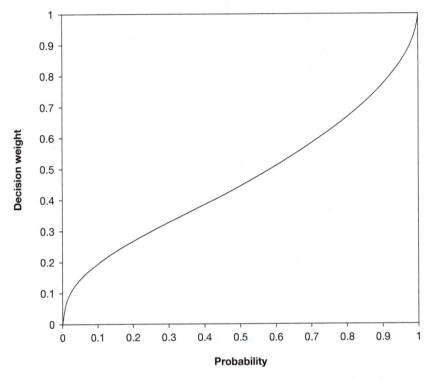

Figure 9.2 The decision weight function of prospect theory.

Problem 2:

Choose between:

    C: a 0.001 chance of losing $5000
    D: losing $5 for sure.

In this case the majority (83%) went for the sure loss D, exhibiting the risk-averse behaviour that insurers world-wide know and love.

It is important to distinguish the over- or under-*weighting* of probabilities introduced by the decision weight function from the over- or under-*estimation* of probabilities discussed in the previous chapters. The latter concerns how people estimate a probability on the basis of information such as its availability to memory, whereas the former concerns how people weight this estimate when they make a decision or choice. Someone can judge that an outcome has a specific probability (e.g. that their chances of winning the national lottery jackpot is 1 in 13 million), and yet over-weight this probability when they choose to buy a ticket. More worryingly, people can both over-estimate a probability (due to a cognitive bias), and over-weight it when making a decision. For example, media scare stories might make us over-estimate a very small probability (e.g. death by the flesh-eating Ebola virus), and then we might also over-weight this estimate in our choice behaviour (e.g. whether to purchase travel insurance).

There are now numerous empirical studies showing how people's decision weights approximate the non-linear function in Figure 9.2, both when precise probabilities are given in the problem, and when they must be estimated by the decision maker. There are also several variations on the precise shape and parameters of the curve (e.g. Wu & Gonzalez, 1996). We will spare the reader the gory details. The important take-home message is that when people evaluate decision options they often seem to distort the stated or experienced probabilities. Thus far, however, we lack a deep psychological explanation for why people do so. A relatively new proposal to address this question – decision-by-sampling (Stewart, Chater, & Brown, 2006; Stewart, Reimers & Harris, in press) – is discussed below.

The certainty effect

The non-linearity of decision weights, and their extreme behaviour near to zero and one, also accounts for the *certainty* effect. This is essentially a generalization of the findings in Allais problems (discussed in Chapter 8): that people place a special emphasis on outcomes that are guaranteed to occur (or guaranteed not to occur). For a striking illustration of this (not as yet empirically tested, due to difficulties getting ethical approval) consider a game of Russian roulette. Imagine that it is your turn to place the gun to your temple. How much would you pay to reduce the number of bullets from 1 to zero? Presumably more than you would pay to reduce the number of bullets from 4 to 3. This suggests that a shift from uncertainty to certainty (e.g. increasing the chances of survival from 5/6 to 1) is weighted more than an equivalent shift from one uncertain state to another (e.g. an increase from 2/6 to 3/6).

This emphasis on certainty cuts two ways. When people are considering possible gains, they often prefer a certain win to a probable win with greater expected monetary value. For example, they prefer a certain option of $3000 to an 80% chance of $4000 (see Problem 1, Table 9.2). In contrast, when considering possible losses, people often prefer a probable loss of a greater amount to a definite loss of a smaller amount, even when the latter has less expected monetary value. For example, they prefer an 80% chance of losing $4000 to a certain loss of $3000 (see Problem 1', Table 9.2).

This relationship between positive and negative gambles, along with the four-fold pattern noted above, is summarized in the *reflection effect* (Kahneman & Tversky, 1979a). This has effectively become an empirical law of choice behaviour, and states that the preference ordering for any pair of gambles in the domain of gains is reversed when the pair of gambles is transformed so that losses replace gains. This effect is displayed in Table 9.2, which shows the patterns of responses elicited in experimental studies (Kahneman & Tversky,

Table 9.2 Preferences between positive and negative prospects

Positive prospects				Negative prospects			
1	(4000, .80) 20%	<	(3000) 80%	1'	(−4000, .80) 92%	>	(−3000) 8%
2	(4000, .20) 65%	>	(3000, .25) 35%	2'	(−4000, .20) 42%	<	(−3000, .25) 58%
3	(3000, .90) 86%	>	(6000, .45) 14%	3'	(−3000, .90) 8%	<	(−6000, .45) 92%
4	(3000, .002) 27%	<	(6000, .001) 73%	4'	(−3000, .002) 70%	>	(−6000, .001) 30%

Note: Adapted from Kahneman, D., & Tversky, A. (1979) Prospect theory: An analysis of decision under risk. *Econometrica, 47,* 263–291.

1979a). Note that the preference orderings for gambles with positive outcomes (first column) are reversed in the corresponding gambles with negative outcomes (second column).

FRAMING

As mentioned above, one of prospect theory's main insights is that the choices people make are determined by their mental representations of the decision problem, and that this often involves encoding the outcomes in terms of gains or losses relative to a specific reference point. The classic demonstration of this is the Asian disease problem.

Problem 1

Imagine that the US is preparing for the outbreak of an unusual Asian disease, which is expected to kill 600 people. Two alternative programmes to combat the disease have been proposed. Assume that the exact scientific estimates of the consequences of the programme are as follows:

If Programme A is adopted, 200 people will be saved.
If Programme B is adopted, there is a 1/3 probability that 600 people will be saved and a 2/3 probability that no people will be saved.

Which of the two programmes would you favour?

When participants are presented with Problem 1, the majority (72%) prefer option A. This reflects risk-aversion – people prefer the sure gain of 200 lives to the 1/3 chance of saving 600 lives. Now consider a second version of this problem, identical except for the way in which the gambles involved in the two programmes are described.

Problem 2

Same background scenario.

> If Programme C is adopted, 200 people will die.
>
> If Programme D is adopted, there is a 1/3 probability that nobody will die and a 2/3 probability that 600 people will die.

Which of the two programmes would you favour?

When presented with Problem 2, the majority of people (78%) select option D (even if they have already answered Problem 1). This reflects risk-seeking – they prefer the gamble over the sure loss.

Of course the two problems are identical except for the framing of the outcomes. In Problem 1, outcomes are framed as possible gains relative to a reference point of 600 people dying. In Problem 2 they are framed as possible losses relative to a reference point of no one dying. As predicted by prospect theory, respondents shift their choices according to the reference frame that they adopt. When the reference state is 600 deaths, they evaluate the outcomes as gains, and are risk-averse; when it is zero deaths, they evaluate the outcomes as losses, and are risk-seeking.

This demonstration is compelling for various reasons. It simultaneously highlights people's susceptibility to reference frames, and their risk-aversion in the domain of gains but risk-seeking in the domain of losses. It also shows a clear violation of the principle of invariance, which lies at the heart of standard EUT.

The Asian 'flu problem has proved robust across a wide variety of domains, including politics, business, finance, management and medicine (you might recall that we met a version of the problem back in Chapter 1 in the discussion of which medical treatment to adopt; for a review of all these domains see Maule & Villejoubert, 2007). The framing effect is also demonstrated in the real world by innumerable marketing and advertising ploys. Examples include the labels that inform us that products are 95% fat free rather than 5% fat (which confuses those of us who prefer our dairy products with lots of fat).

Ironically, the ease with which framing effects can be exhibited has deflected researchers from uncovering the psychological processes that underlie these effects. This seems to be an area ripe for future research, and one that could benefit from ongoing work in mainstream cognitive psychology (Rettinger & Hastie, 2001; 2003). In particular, although Kahneman and Tversky (1979a) did introduce several editing operations in their original model, these have not been elaborated in subsequent developments (e.g. Tversky & Kahneman, 1992). Maule and Villejoubert (2007) have introduced a simple information-processing model that is a step in this direction. Their framework accentuates both the editing phase – how people construct internal representations of the decision problem, and the evaluation phase – how these internal representations generate actual choices.

Ambiguity aversion or ignorance aversion?

At the end of the last chapter we discussed Ellsberg's problem, and noted his proposal that decision makers have a basic aversion to uncertainty or ambiguity. This is not captured by standard EUT, but neither is it accommodated within the standard formulations of prospect theory. However, the claim that people are averse to uncertainty is not borne out by their choice behaviour in the domain of losses, where they often prefer an uncertain gamble over a sure loss (e.g. see Problem 1' in Table 9.2).

An alternative to ambiguity aversion is the idea that people are reluctant to choose options that they are ignorant about (Heath & Tversky, 1991). This can explain the patterns of choices in Ellsberg's problems, but also has the potential to generalize to a wider range of situations. Indeed this position argues that ignorance and uncertainty are often confounded, but if they can be teased apart people will show an aversion to ignorance rather than uncertainty per se.

To demonstrate this 'ignorance aversion', Heath and Tversky asked participants for their willingness to bet on uncertain events in various situations, including those in which they thought they had good knowledge, those in which they thought they had poor knowledge, and chance events. For example, participants gave their preferences between gambles on sporting events, results of political elections, and random games of chance. The main finding was that people preferred to bet in situations where they thought they had some competence rather than on chance events that were matched in terms of probabilities. Conversely, they preferred to bet on chance events rather than on probability-matched events in situations where they thought they had little competence.

In short, people prefer to bet on uncertain events that they are knowledgeable about (or think they are), to matched uncertain events of which they are ignorant. This may explain why betting shops are very happy to provide their punters with information about the events upon which they can bet, and why gambling houses encourage those who think they have a special system to beat the roulette wheel. This notion of ignorance aversion has been tested in various domains, and extended in several directions (Fox & Tversky, 1995; Tversky & Fox, 1995). It has also been incorporated into an extended version of prospect theory (the two-stage model, see Fox & See, 2003, for an overview).

How good a descriptive model is prospect theory?

The empirical data reviewed through the course of this chapter are largely consistent with prospect theory, especially when it is extended in certain natural ways (Fox & See, 2003; Kahneman & Tversky, 2000). Of course this should not be too surprising, as prospect theory was conceived precisely to accommodate many of these findings. However, it has also done a good job of predicting a range of novel empirical data, in areas as diverse as medicine, sports and finance. There are, however, a few shortcomings that deserve mention.

First, even though prospect theory is a descriptive theory of actual choice behaviour, it does not give deep psychological explanations for many of the processes it proposes. For example, there are no detailed accounts of how people frame decision problems, select reference points, or edit their options. Neither is there a clear cognitive account of how people integrate decision weights and values to yield a final decision. In such areas the theory operates more at the as-if level than the process level.

Second, there are certain factors that prospect theory does not include, but which seem to have a strong influence on people's decision making. Some of these will be discussed in a later chapter (15) on decisions and emotion (e.g. Rottenstreich & Hsee, 2001). One prominent factor that has received attention from decision theorists is the notion of regret (see Loomes & Sugden, 1982; Baron, 2000, for discussion). If we make a decision that turns out badly (compared to other possible outcomes), we seem to suffer something over and above the disutility of the actual outcome. We regret our decision. Similarly, if our decision leads to a much better outcome than the other alternatives, we gain something over and above the actual gain. We 'rejoice' in our decision. Thus it is argued that when making a decision, people take these possibilities of regret or rejoicing into account. They anticipate how much they might regret or rejoice in a particular decision (by comparing its outcome with other possibilities). But prospect theory does not incorporate these factors in the decision-making process.

However, it seems unlikely that a full account of choice behaviour can be built upon the notion of regret (Baron, 2000; Starmer & Sugden, 1993, 1998). Discussion of these issues lies outside the scope of this book, but interested readers should refer to work by Loomes, Sugden and Starmer (e.g. Loomes, Starmer & Sugden, 1992; Starmer, 2000). For now, we conclude that while the notion of regret has a role to play in a psychological theory of decision making, the most fruitful direction might be to supplement prospect theory rather than replace it.

Decision-by-sampling

As noted above, although prospect theory provides a description of people's choice behaviour, it does not give a model of the decision process itself. It also lacks a full explanation for the observed shape of people's value and decision weighting functions. Decision-by-sampling theory (Stewart et al., 2006) seeks to address both issues. It builds upon Parducci's (1965; 1995) range-frequency model, applying his ideas to choice behaviour rather than psychophysical judgments. Decision-by-sampling (DbS) claims that people do not possess stable internal scales to represent subjective value or probability. Instead, the subjective value of an attribute (such as money) corresponds to its rank position in a sample of attributes. This sample is drawn from memory and includes recently experienced events of that type (such as routine financial transactions). For example, \$10 will have a higher subjective value when it belongs to set A = {2, 5, 8, 10, 15} than to set B = {2, 10, 15, 19, 25}. This is because it is ranked second in set A, but fourth in set B. To assess the rank of an attribute, people make a set of binary comparisons between items in their sample, registering the proportion of favourable comparisons. In the above example, \$10 compares favourably in 3 out of 4 binary comparisons in set A, whereas the same amount only compares favourably in 1 out of 4 comparisons in set B (see Stewart et al., in press, for details).

Based on these simple principles, DbS can capture the value function described by prospect theory (shown in Figure 9.1). The key idea is that if a sample is positively skewed (e.g. there are many more small amounts than large amounts), then a concave function emerges from the process of sampling and binary comparison. This is because the same fixed-magnitude increase (e.g. gaining \$10) will correspond to a larger rise in rank position amongst smaller amounts (e.g. moving from \$10 to \$20) than amongst larger amounts (e.g. moving from \$100 to \$110).

To illustrate this point Stewart et al. (2006) used real-world data on the frequency and amount of bank credits (and debits) to derive the typical prospect theory functions. For example, in data from real-world bank transfers, credits were positively skewed: there were many more small credits than large credits. Assuming that people have a roughly accurate representation of this real-world distribution in memory, and thus their memory samples are positively skewed, one would predict a concave function for gains. A similar argument captures the convex function for losses.

More generally, DbS predicts that people's valuations of attributes will depend on the samples used to generate their rank orderings. Thus by manipulating the samples that people are exposed to, one can alter their valuations of the same fixed-magnitude attribute. This has been demonstrated for money, probability and temporal delay in several empirical studies (see Stewart, 2009; Stewart et al., in press) and extended to more diverse attributes such as pain (Vlaev et al., 2011; Watkinson et al., 2013) and well-being (Melrose, Brown & Wood, 2013).

Decision-by-sampling presents a novel approach to understanding choice behaviour. It fares well when people are evaluating simple attributes (e.g. monetary amounts), but it is unclear how well it scales to more complex decisions, especially when people draw on richer background knowledge and diverse evidence.

Interim summary

So far in this chapter we have introduced the main psychological theory of choice behaviour, prospect theory. On this theory people base their choices on their mental representations of the decision problem, and thus objectively given (or experienced) utilities and probabilities undergo cognitive distortions prior to choice. This leads to a variety of departures from EUT, including framing effects, loss–aversion, the endowment effect, the certainty effect, ambiguity aversion, etc.

As discussed above, the principle of invariance (which is critical to EUT) states that people's preferences should not depend on the way in which the choice options are described or the way in which their actual preferences are elicited. We have already seen situations where the framing of a problem drastically alters their choices. In the next section we visit situations where the means of eliciting someone's preferences radically changes the preferences themselves.

PREFERENCE REVERSALS

The idea that human choice might conform to rational principles was seriously shaken by the discovery in the 1970s of reversals of preference between a pair of choice alternatives as a result of changes in the method of eliciting the preference. How can it be rational to prefer option A to option B when one's preference is evaluated by one method and to prefer B to A with a different method? If someone prefers a burger to pasta at a particular moment, then surely this is a reflection of some underlying fact about their nervous system and bodily state. How can their preference *in the same situation* suddenly switch in a seemingly random way, merely as a result of varying the method of ascertaining that preference?

The classic demonstration was reported by Lichtenstein and Slovic (1971), who asked their participants to choose between the following pair of gambles:

A: Win $2.50 with probability 0.95, lose $0.75 with probability 0.05
B: Win $8.50 with probability 0.40, lose $1.50 with probability 0.60

Gamble A gives a high probability (0.95) of winning a small amount ($2.50) and a very small probability (0.05) of losing an even smaller amount ($0.75), while gamble B gives a medium probability of winning a large amount and a slightly larger probability of losing a modest amount. The expected value of gamble A is $2.34 and that of gamble B is $2.50, so a risk-neutral person (someone who neither seeks nor avoids risk per se) would choose B. Participants were asked either to pick the gamble they would prefer to play or to put a price on each gamble. In this latter case, they stated the monetary amount they would be prepared to accept to sell the gamble. The striking outcome was that Lichtenstein and Slovic's participants (and thousands of people tested in subsequent experiments) chose gamble A but put a higher price on gamble B. It thus seems that the ordering of preference between alternatives is not independent of the method of eliciting that preference, a clear violation of rational behaviour. Lichtenstein and Slovic (1973) showed, moreover, that gamblers in the more naturalistic setting of a Las Vegas casino were prone to the same tendency.

Another striking example of preference reversal can be observed when choice is compared to matching. Matching refers to generating a value for an attribute so as to make a pair of alternatives equally attractive. Consider this pair of candidates for an engineering job, who differ (on a scale from 0 to 100) in their technical expertise and interpersonal skills (Tversky, Sattath & Slovic, 1988):

	Technical knowledge	*Human relations*
C:	86	76
D:	78	91

When participants had to choose between the candidates, they tended to opt for candidate C who had better technical knowledge. Participants in the matching condition were given a missing value for one of the four pieces of data and asked to fill in the value that would make the candidates equally attractive. Suppose the missing datum was the human relations score of candidate D. If people's preferences are stable and in the order elicited in the choice test, then they should suggest a value greater than 91, as such a value would be needed to boost candidate D's attractiveness to that of candidate C. However, they tended to do the opposite, suggesting that in the matching test they preferred candidate D. Again their preferences seem to be reversed by a simple change in the elicitation method.

COMPATIBILITY AND EVALUABILITY

Why might such reversals occur? Although several hypotheses have been proposed, there seems to be good support for the idea that different forms of elicitation draw emphasis to different features or dimensions of the problem (the so-called *compatibility* hypothesis). Applied to the original version (choice between gambles A and B), the idea is that more weight is put on the monetary values associated with the gambles in the pricing than in the choice condition. Since setting a price for something focuses attention on money values, these values receive more attention or become more salient in pricing. Conversely, in choice the probabilities become relatively more salient. These proposals are supported by evidence from Wedell and Böckenholt (1990), whose participants reported relying more on monetary values in pricing and more on probabilities in choice. An extension of the compatibility hypothesis to the matching problem (as in the example with candidates C and D) has been proposed by Tversky et al. (1988).

With these examples (apart from the Las Vegas gamblers), one can of course argue that people's behaviour in hypothetical laboratory decisions may not tell us very much about how they behave in more realistic cases where significant amounts of their own money or utility are at stake. Economists have therefore expended considerable effort in looking for preference reversals in real markets. A study by List (2002) provides very clear evidence that this type of non-normative behaviour does indeed span both the laboratory and the 'real' world, and also demonstrated reversals in a third context in addition to the two varieties mentioned above (choice versus pricing and choice versus matching). List studied people buying sports cards at a specialist show. In one condition, collectors entered separate bids for two sets of 1982 baseball cards, worth about $4, which they viewed alongside each other. These are sought after by baseball fans. One set comprised 10 mint-condition cards, while the other bundle included these same 10 cards together with 3 additional cards in very poor condition. The collectors who were the participants in this study ·submitted higher bids, as one would expect, for the 13-card than for the 10-card bundle. In a second condition, collectors evaluated each bundle in isolation. That is to say, they made a bid either for the 10- or for the 13-card bundle. The striking finding was that in this second case, the collectors stated a higher value for the 10-card bundle. Hence a preference for the 13-card bundle in the condition where they were evaluated side by side (called joint evaluation) was reversed when participants evaluated the bundles individually (called separate evaluation). In some way, the presence of 3 poor-quality cards led to a reduction in the perceived value of the set when that set was evaluated on its own, but when it was directly comparable with another set that did not contain these inferior cards, their influence on decision making was downplayed. Why should this be?

A plausible possibility suggested by Hsee (1996), called the *evaluability hypothesis*, is that some attributes of a choice option may be harder to evaluate in isolation than others. Whether a bundle of baseball cards containing 10 mint cards is good value or not is difficult to judge. Other attributes are easier to gauge: the quality of the cards, for instance. Collectors may have no difficulty appreciating that a bundle with 3 out of 13 inferior cards is a poor purchase. Hence when judged separately, the 10-item bundle is valued higher than the 13-item one as the latter suffers from having an easily evaluated attribute: low quality. In joint evaluation, by contrast, seeing the bundles side by side makes it easier to give appropriate weight to the quality dimension. As the 13-card bundle includes everything that's in the 10-card one, the collectors could see readily that the poor quality of the 3 additional cards was insignificant.

These reversals have very considerable policy implications as they imply that the method of eliciting the public's preferences for environmental, legal, healthcare and other programmes may matter in ways that are often ignored. Examples abound of apparently incomprehensible judgments or decisions in these applied fields. People in a study by Desvousges et al. (1992) were willing to pay $80, $78 and $88 towards a scheme described (to different groups) as saving 2000, 20,000, or 200,000 birds, respectively. The scale of outcomes was plainly extremely hard to place on any objective mental scale. Yet, if they had seen the options simultaneously, people would of course have realized that amount contributed should be more closely related to number of birds saved. Similarly, Jones-Lee, Loomes and Phillips (1995) found that the amount people were willing to pay for a programme designed to reduce road accidents increased by only about 30% when the number of projected accidents avoided was increased by 200%. Again, people would of course appropriately scale these amounts if shown their judgments side by side.

Other instances of preference reversal may require a rather different explanatory approach than that offered by the evaluability hypothesis. In a striking example, Redelmeier and Shafir (1995) asked family practitioners to consider the following problem:

> The patient is a 67-year-old farmer with chronic right hip pain. The diagnosis is osteoarthritis. You have tried several nonsteroidal anti-inflammatory agents (e.g. aspirin, naproxen and ketoprofen) and have stopped them because of either adverse effects or lack of efficacy. You decide to refer him to an orthopaedic consultant for consideration for hip replacement surgery. The patient agrees to this plan. Before sending him away, however, you check the drug formulary and find that there is one nonsteroidal medication that this patient has not tried (ibuprofen). What do you do?

The family practitioners' task was to choose between

E: refer to orthopaedics and also start ibuprofen, and
F: refer to orthopaedics and do not start any new medication.

In this case, 53% chose option F with no investigation of additional medications.

Another group of family practitioners was given exactly the same scenario except that two rather than one alternative medications were mentioned. The paragraph ended with the sentences 'Before sending him away, however, you check the drug formulary and find that there are two nonsteroidal medications that this patient has not tried (ibuprofen and piroxicam). What do you do?' and in this case there were three options:

G: refer to orthopaedics and also start ibuprofen
H: refer to orthopaedics and also start piroxicam, and
I: refer to orthopaedics and do not start any new medication.

In this case, the option proposing no further investigation of medications was chosen by 72% of the sample. If anything, one would imagine that the possibility of exploring two medicines would tend to reduce, not increase, the likelihood of opting straight away for the surgery option. Yet, instead, about 19% of practitioners who would otherwise have preferred experimenting with another medication in the first scenario reversed their preference under the second scenario and selected the no-medication option.

How can it be that adding one more option to a set of alternatives can change people's preference between two other options? It may be that the added option simply adds confusion to an already complex decision. This is particularly likely when the added option has both advantages and disadvantages as this simply increases the number of conflicting reasons. Another possibility is that decision makers anticipate having to justify their decisions and that an additional option can make this harder to do. Whereas justifying option A in the first scenario is straightforward ('it seemed worth trying one last medication') this becomes harder in the second scenario where the justification would have to be developed further to account for choosing one drug over another.

Such an explanation has also been proffered for a related choice anomaly. Imagine that you are faced with a choice between two objects, A and B, which differ on two dimensions. A is better than B on one dimension but worse on the other. For example, A and B might be two people you are considering inviting out on a date, with A being more attractive than B but less intelligent. Let us suppose this is a difficult choice and you are roughly equally inclined to choose A and B. Now we introduce a third person, C, into the equation. Although this superficially makes your decision harder, the good news is that C is 'dominated' by A – which is to say, C is worse than A on at least one dimension and not better on the other (C is less attractive than A and equally intelligent). It would seem straightforward to reject C in comparison with A, and simply focus on the comparison of A with B as before. However, studies have shown that in this sort of 'asymmetric dominance' situation, C's presence is often not neutral: instead, it can increase preference for A.

Sedikides, Ariely and Olsen (1999) demonstrated this in the context of dating decisions. Participants were presented with descriptions of potential dating partners. Thus person A would be described as scoring 80 for attractiveness, 56 for sense of humour and 61 for intelligence, while person B might score 60, 61 and 82 on these dimensions, respectively. Choosing between A and B depends, obviously, on how much the participant values the different attributes which will, naturally, vary from one individual to the next. In Sedikides et al.'s study, 50% of participants preferred person A and 50% person B. When person C, who scored 80, 56 and 51 on the three attributes, was brought into the set, choice of person A increased to 62%. This is despite that fact that C must be inferior to A as they score equally on two dimensions but A is more intelligent.

This effect has occasionally been exploited by marketing experts to increase the market share of their products. A toothpaste manufacturer, for instance, might introduce a new product alongside their existing one in order to boost the latter's attractiveness to customers. Provided that this new product is clearly inferior to the existing one (more expensive and in cheaper packaging), competitors' products would be harmed in the marketplace. The need to form justifications for one's decisions (even if this is only an internal justification to oneself) may help to explain such asymmetric dominance effects. When it clearly dominates another choice alternative, an object's selection is much easier to justify than when no such dominance is evident.

EFFECT OF EXPERIENCE ON PREFERENCE REVERSALS

We have mentioned several explanations of preference reversals (including the compatibility and evaluability hypotheses) in addition to those suggested by Redelmeier and Shafir's experiment. Whatever the merits of these accounts, a key question is what happens to preference reversals when people have the opportunity to make repeated decisions? Our approach in this book assumes that to the extent that decisions are grounded in learning, feedback and experience, they tend to be optimal and hence we would expect preference reversals to be eliminated or at least reduced when choices are made or prices set for 10 or for 100 pairs rather than just one. This is exactly what is observed. In List's (2002) study, for example, professional dealers in baseball cards did not show a statistically significant tendency to value the 10-card bundle higher than the 13-card one in separate evaluation and hence did not make preference reversals to the extent that less experienced collectors did. Presumably their extensive experience with bundles of cards allowed them to develop better weightings of the dimensions on which the bundles varied.

Similarly, Wedell and Böckenholt (1990) found that choice of the option with the higher probability (equivalent to gamble A above) declined when participants were told that the gamble would be played 10 or 100 times, while the tendency to place a higher price on the alternative with a large potential payoff (equivalent to gamble B) also declined. These two effects combined to dramatically reduce the prevalence of preference reversals. Cox and Grether (1996) and Chu and Chu (1990) furnish evidence of reduction (but perhaps not elimination) of reversals in real-world economic settings where experience and expertise play a greater role than in the one-shot tasks often undertaken in the psychology laboratory.

Preference reversals tell us that the axioms of decision theory are inadequate in that preferences are not always stable. Instead, they often seem to be constructed on the fly, are highly context-dependent, and influenced by the individual's goals and expectations. As with many other examples of the 'fluidity' of mental processes, they force us to think of judgments, preferences and decision making as much more contextually embedded than is traditionally assumed in decision theory. A graphic example was described by Ariely, Loewenstein and Prelec (2003). They asked their (American) business school participants to study everyday commodities such as bottles of wine, computer accessories and luxury chocolates and to decide whether they would choose to purchase each item for a dollar amount equal to the last two digits of their social security number. Next, they stated how much they were willing to pay for each item. Remarkably, focusing attention on the individuals' social security numbers caused a dramatic change in the amounts they were willing to pay, despite the fact that they should have been able to realize that this number is random and cannot possibly have any bearing on the value of the objects. Participants whose social security numbers were in the top quintile (in the population this would be 80–99) made offers that were typically three times greater than those of participants with numbers in the lowest quintile (00–19). It seems that the initial focus on the social security number acted as an 'anchor', which was still active in working memory when the later judgment had to be constructed.

All sorts of judgments are susceptible to anchoring effects. Strack and Mussweiler (1997) found that people estimated Aristotle's birth date to be about 140 BC if they first judged whether he was born before or after AD 1825, but over 1000 BC if they first judged whether he was born before or after 25,000 BC (some further examples are given in Chapter 17). Judgments and decisions, such bizarre findings tell us, are based on highly fluid mental states and not on fixed preferences or beliefs.

SUMMARY

This chapter built on the framework for analysing decisions presented in Chapter 8 and introduced the main psychological theory of choice behaviour, prospect theory. The main contribution of prospect theory is in explaining why we observe a variety of departures from EUT when people make choices. The explanation for these characteristic violations – framing, the certainty effect, loss-aversion, the endowment effect – is built on the idea that people base decisions on their mental representations of decision problems. That is, objectively given (or experienced) utilities and probabilities undergo cognitive distortions prior to choice. The second part of the chapter reviewed extensive evidence showing that the preferences on which we act are not fixed but subject to numerous external influences. Such influences can lead to preference reversals, historically one of the most compelling violations of the normative theory of decision making.

Suggested further reading

- Kahneman, D., & Tversky, A. (1979a). Prospect theory: An analysis of decision under risk. *Econometrica, 47,* 263–291. The paper which presents the highly influential alternative theory of decision under risk.
- Kahneman, D., & Tversky, A. (2000). *Choices, values, and frames.* Cambridge, UK: Cambridge University Press. A collection of papers documenting research inspired, in large part, by prospect theory.
- Lichtenstein, S., & Slovic, P. (1971). Reversals of preference between bids and choices in gambling decisions. *Journal of Experimental Psychology, 89,* 46–55. A classic paper demonstrating how preferences can be changed by altering the method of elicitation.
- Stewart, N., Reimers, S., & Harris, A. J. L. (in press). On the origin of utility, weighting, and discounting functions: How they get their shapes and how to change their shapes. *Management Science.* An examination of how the decision-by-sampling theory can account for patterns of risky and inter-temporal choice.

10 Decisions from experience

Chapter highlights

- A discussion of under-weighting, over-weighting and the reasons for the 'description–experience gap': why do preferences reverse?
- An introduction to the four versions of the 'computerized money-machine' task
- A brief consideration of additional insights from the study of decisions from experience: search, choice-models and learning from feedback.

In June of 2013 Nik Wallenda stepped out on to a 426-metre-long wire suspended almost half a kilometre above the rocky abyss of the Grand Canyon. He had no safety harness and no safety net. Twenty-two minutes and 54 seconds later, after a wind-affected and wobbly crossing, he reached the security of the other side. When asked about his amazing feat Nik said that his faith allowed him to overcome any fear of dying: 'I know where I'm going to go when I die . . . what I do is risky, and if I die, I have peace.' But how did Nik calculate this risk and make his decision to step out on to the wire? In decision-analytic terms we might think of him as going through a process of assessing the likelihood and value of success (the 'happiness' that achieving the walk would bring him) against the likelihood and (ultimate) cost of failure. However, unlike many of the simple gamble problems discussed in Chapters 8 and 9, the probability of success was something Nik needed to determine based on his *experience* in similar situations. Just like many of the more mundane decisions we commonly face, Nik did not have a convenient look-up table of relevant probabilities and unambiguous outcomes (cf. Knight, 1921). We have to learn via experience about such outcomes and the probabilities with which they occur.

In the last 10 years or so there has been a resurgence of interest into experimental analogues of such 'decisions from experience' (see Hertwig & Erev, 2009, and Rakow & Newell, 2010, for reviews). As we will see, one of the reasons why this work has garnered so much attention is that when people are forced to learn about probabilities and outcomes from experience, their choices often diverge markedly from the predictions of prospect theory (see Chapter 9).

The 'money-machine'

The standard 'decision from experience' experiment is very simple. Participants are presented with a computerized 'money-machine' comprising two unlabelled buttons on a computer screen and are asked to click on either one on each trial of a multi-trial experiment. A click on the button reveals an outcome which the participant then receives; the probability of the outcome occurring is pre-programmed by the experimenter but the participant does not know what the probability or the potential outcomes are – she has to learn from experience.

Consider the examples in Figure 10.1. Panel A shows a typical 'decision from description' in which the outcomes and their probabilities are clearly stated. We discovered in Chapter 9 (see Problem 1, Table 9.2) that when this type of gamble is presented in a described format the overwhelming preference is for the certain reward (3) (indicated by the shaded (i.e. chosen) box). An experienced version of the same problem is depicted in Panel B. Here, a participant would see two unlabelled buttons, one paying out 3 every time it is clicked and the other 4 on 80% of clicks and 0 on 20%. In the figure, the participant has clicked the left button on trial 1 and received '4', the right button on trial 2 and received '3', then returned to the left button and received a '0' payout. The running total of payouts is shown to the participant below the buttons (i.e. 3 + 4 = 7).

Of interest is which button participants end up preferring when they are invited to play the clicking game for hundreds of trials. Contrary to the dictates of the *certainty effect* (see Chapter 9), participants now come to prefer the '4' button (Barron & Erev, 2003). Furthermore, if the prospects are converted into losses, so now one button offers –3 on every click and the other –4 on 80% of clicks, participants learn to prefer the certain loss of 3. In other words, in decisions from experience there is a striking reversal of the certainty effect and participants appear to be risk-seeking in the domain of gains and risk-averse in the domain of losses – the opposite of what prospect theory predicts. One way to explain this pattern is by assuming that people tend to under-weight the smaller (i.e. 20%) probability of getting nothing in the gain frame – leading to a choice of the 4, .80 button – and similarly under-weight the smaller possibility (20%) of losing nothing in the loss frame – leading to a choice of the –3 option. In essence, where prospect theory predicts over-weighting we see under-weighting.

A DESCRIPTION–EXPERIENCE GAP?

Several researchers have examined the reasons why decisions from experience and description diverge – the so-called 'description–experience gap' (Hertwig & Erev, 2009). One way of doing so is to disentangle the choice and information acquisition aspects inherent in an experience-based choice. In a task like the

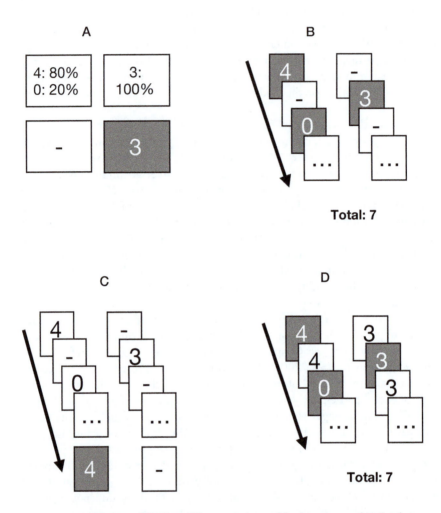

Figure 10.1 Depiction of the four different versions of the 'money-machine' task. Shaded rectangles represent consequential trials; that is, trials in which the outcome of the choice affected earnings. (A) Description: explicitly stated outcomes and their probabilities followed by a one-shot choice. (B) Partial Feedback: all trials are consequential and the total earnings for the problem are displayed. (C) Sampling: initial sampling period followed by a one-shot choice. (D) Full Feedback: identical to Partial Feedback with the addition of feedback for the foregone, or unselected, alternative.

Adapted from Camilleri & Newell, 2011a.

one shown in panel B, the only way to learn about an option is to choose it, even if one fears this choice is suboptimal. Therefore, the description–experience gap may emerge because description permits a 'pure' choice, whereas experience requires a different pattern of 'choice' in order to learn about the options.

In an effort to overcome this issue Hertwig et al. (2004) divided experiments into a sampling and a choice phase. This set-up is depicted in Panel C of Figure 10.1. In the sampling phase participants can click on either button as many times as they like in order to discover what each option offers, but these samples are non-consequential (and thus not shaded in the figure). Payment is determined in the subsequent choice phase in which participants click on their preferred option to play 'for real' and now actually receive the payoff. The participant in Panel C has sampled twice from the left button, seeing a 4 and a 0, and once from the right button, seeing a 3. She ends up choosing left and receives a payoff of 4. This sampling paradigm dissociates exploration (finding out about options) from exploitation (choosing an option for reward), the two aspects which are intertwined in the Panel B version of the task. Intriguingly, even under these sampling conditions a large 'gap' between experience and description is observed. For example, only 12% of participants in a sampling version of the money-machine chose the certain reward (3) compared to 64% when given the described version of the gamble (Panel A) (Hertwig et al., 2004). This pattern of preferences mirrors those seen in the consequential choice version (Panel B) and reinforces the idea that people under-weight the probability of rare events occurring (i.e. the 20% chance of getting nothing) when making choices on the basis of experience.

An alternative way to dissociate exploration from exploitation is shown in Panel D of Figure 10.1. In this 'full-feedback' version of the task, all choices are again consequential (as in Panel B), but now participants not only receive feedback about their chosen option but also about the foregone option (the one they did not choose). This is like playing the stock market, where we not only see the change in value of the stocks we buy but also of the ones we decide not to buy. Thus on trial 1, the participant in this example chose the left button and received '4' but in addition discovered that had she chosen the right button she would have received '3'. Perhaps surprisingly, provision of this foregone feedback appears to increase the under-weighting of rare events (Yechiam & Busemeyer, 2006; Yechiam, Rakow & Newell, 2015). These findings are consistent with the idea that seeing 'what works best' most of the time increases temptation for a risky alternative that only occasionally delivers a very poor outcome. In other words, people seem to prefer the option with the best median payout.

Taken together the findings from across these different versions of the 'money-machine' task have led some researchers to call for a new theory of risky choice because prospect theory is unable to explain the observed pattern of preferences (e.g. Hertwig et al., 2004).

Biased samples or mode of presentation?

Early objections to this call for a new theory of risky choice came from Fox and Hadar (2006), who suggested that the apparent violations of prospect theory in decisions from experience were almost entirely due to sampling error. Fox and Hadar argued that because the probabilities of outcomes that people actually *experienced* were different from the intended objective probabilities, it was problematic to compare decisions from experience with decisions from description. To make this idea concrete, imagine a situation in which a participant only samples once from each of the buttons displayed in Panel C and then makes a choice. To the participant it appears that it is a choice between a certain outcome of 4 and a certain outcome of 3 – easy decision! This is quite unlike the choice in the described version (Panel A). This is an extreme example, but it illustrates that any inferred 'under-weighting' of rare events (and thus the reversal of prospect theory predictions) may be driven in part because participants simply did not experience the event. In support of this idea, Fox and Hadar's re-analysis of the Hertwig et al. data found that prospect theory could account satisfactorily for both description and experience-based choices when its predictions were based on the outcome probabilities actually experienced by the participants (as opposed to the objective, underlying outcome probabilities).

Rakow, Demes and Newell (2008) pursued this 'biased sample' idea one stage further by yoking the description-based problems faced by one group of participants to the actual outcome distributions observed by another group of participants facing experience-based problems. For example, if a participant in the experience-sampling group sampled three times from one button and saw [4,4,0] and three times from the other and saw [3,3,3], then the yoked participant in the description group would be given a choice between a gamble offering a 66% chance of 4, otherwise nothing and 100% chance of 3. Consistent with Fox and Hadar's conclusion, Rakow et al. found that elimination of misleading samples also eliminated the description–experience choice gap. The information contained within the samples and not the mode in which it was presented was the primary driver of choice.

Other researchers have argued, however, that the gap cannot wholly be driven by unrepresentative samples. Hau, Pleskac and Hertwig (2010) argued that the null effect found in the yoked design used by Rakow et al. (2008) was carried primarily by cases in which samples had been particularly frugal and had rendered the choice trivial (e.g. 100% chance of 4 versus 100% chance of 3). When participants were obliged to take larger samples (e.g. 50 draws from the risky option), Hau et al. found that a choice gap consistent with under-weighting of rare events remained. Ungemach, Chater and Stewart (2009) removed the impact of sampling bias by obliging participants to sample 40 times from each option while ensuring that all samples were representative of the underlying outcome distribution. For example, a participant faced with the problem described in Panel A would eventually select the risky option 40 times and observe '4' exactly 32 times and '0' exactly 8 times. Participants were free to sample the options in any order, and the order of the outcomes was random. They found that although the size of the gap was reduced when compared to those in a free sampling condition, it was not eliminated. This finding is supported by three other studies in which participants observed a large number of samples either because they were incentivized (Hau et al., 2008) or simply instructed (Camilleri & Newell, 2011a) to do so. Under such conditions the choice gap often diminishes in size, but does not always completely disappear.

In a final twist of the tale, Camilleri and Newell (2011b) argued that although large samples might be representative, it does not necessarily follow that participants rely on the entire sequence of samples when making a choice. For example, participants might forget earlier sampled outcomes or weight them less (cf. Hertwig et al., 2004; Rakow et al., 2008). In an attempt to address both the representativeness and the overall size of samples, Camilleri and Newell (2011b) used an algorithm that allowed participants to choose as many (or as few) samples as they desired but ensured that however many samples were taken, a set of outcomes that perfectly represented the underlying probabilities was observed. Under these conditions, the choice gap was all but eliminated.

Together, these results suggest that the jury is still out with regard to the extent, and reason for, a 'gap' between decisions from description and those based on the sampling version of the money-machine task (Figure 10.1, Panel C). However, in the other versions, involving partial (Panel B) or full (Panel D) feedback, behaviour consistent with under-weighting rare events is much more reliable. Why does this occur?

WHY UNDER-WEIGHTING IN REPEATED CONSEQUENTIAL DECISIONS?

Camilleri and Newell (2011a) set out to answer this question in an experiment which compared all four versions of the money-machine task – description, sampling, partial feedback and full feedback (see Figure 10.1) – using the same set of gambles. Choices made in the sampling and description versions were broadly similar, but both conditions differed markedly from the two feedback versions. For example, when faced with Problem 1 (below), 45% and 48% of participants in the sampling and description versions, respectively, preferred the risky option, compared to 65% and 80% selecting it on the final (100th) trial in the partial- and full-feedback conditions, respectively.

Problem 1

You must choose between:

    A: Losing 3 points for sure
    B: Losing 32 points with probability .10, else nothing with probability .90.

In other words, participants in the feedback conditions displayed preferences consistent with under-weighting the possibility of the rare event (a 10% chance of losing 32 points). This interpretation was supported when Camilleri and Newell fit a version of prospect theory to their data and found values of the weighting parameter (see Chapter 9) consistent with under-weighting in the two feedback conditions, over-weighting in the description condition, and no clear best fit in the sampling condition.

This persistent under-weighting of rare events has been explained through a variety of psychological 'mechanisms'. First let's consider the full-feedback task where the provision of information about both the obtained and the foregone outcome obviate the need for exploration; in other words you don't have to choose an option to find out what it delivers. Erev and Haruvy (in press) suggest that the tendency to under-weight rare events in this situation is driven by the reliance on small samples of experiences. Note that this is somewhat different from the 'biased-samples' explanation discussed earlier – reliance on small samples in the feedback paradigms does not imply that participants have *never* experienced a rare outcome, which is highly unlikely because these experiments often involve hundreds of trials – rather it implies that the sample *in memory* that a participant relies on when making a choice on each trial is rather small. The implication of such reliance on small samples is that rare events will be under-represented (Hertwig & Pleskac, 2010) and thus under-weighted.

A second mechanism invoked by Erev and Haruvy is *inertia*, the tendency for people to repeat their last choice. Erev and Haruvy suggest that inertia can take two forms, *state* and *action*. State refers to an assumption on the part of the decision maker that the payoff structure is deterministic and that the state of the world is not likely to change between the current trial and the next. This often leads to more choices of options containing rare events because the most likely outcome for such options is positive (for example, not losing anything on 90% of trials in option B of Problem 1). *Action inertia* has a similar effect whereby decision makers are assumed to simply repeat their last choice unless the perceived benefit of switching outweighs the 'cognitive cost' of having to make another decision. Erev and Haruvy argue that this benefit will only outweigh the cost when recent feedback is sufficiently surprising to warrant a change in choice, such as after experiencing the rare event. (See Chapter 12 for more extensive discussion of the role played by surprise and error-correction in learning to choose.)

Turning now to the partial-feedback task, the need to *explore* in order to find out what each option offers brings an additional mechanism into play, the so-called 'hot stove' effect. Mark Twain once noted, 'We should be careful to get out of an experience only the wisdom that is in it and stop there lest we be like the cat that sits down on a hot stove lid. She will never sit down on a hot stove lid again and that is well but also she will never sit down on a cold one anymore.' The relevance of Twain's insight to situations in which people acquire feedback only from an obtained and not from a foregone 'payoff' has been examined in a variety of contexts (e.g. Denrell & March, 2001; Einhorn & Hogarth, 1978). The key point is that the effect of good and bad experiences is asymmetrical. Good outcomes (cold stove lids) increase the likelihood of repeating a choice and therefore increase knowledge about the option that yielded that outcome. Bad outcomes (hot stove lids) will decrease the probability of repeating a choice and thus decrease knowledge about the option associated with that outcome.

This hot-stove effect can lead to risk-aversion in the money-machine task because risky options are more likely to produce bad outcomes and thus subsequent avoidance. Camilleri and Newell (2011a) found some support for this pattern: participants facing Problem 1 in the partial-feedback condition chose the risky option (B) fewer times across trials than those in the full-feedback condition. This is consistent with the idea that 'getting burned' by the −32 loss drives some participants away from the risky option. Those in the full-feedback condition persist with the risky option, however, presumably because they can 'see' that most of the time it provides the better outcome (no loss), a preference pattern that has been described as 'super-under-weighting' (Yechiam et al., 2015).

Modelling experience-based choice

Many of the insights into the mechanisms underlying experience-based choice have come from attempts to develop computational models that capture key regularities in observed behaviour. Erev et al. (2010) report a large-scale model competition in which several different research groups submitted models aimed at describing and explaining behaviour in versions of the money-machine task. The most successful model in the partial-feedback condition of the competition was the 'explorative-sampler-with recency' model, and its best fit was obtained under the assumption that participants relied on only eight samples drawn from memory of past experiences with each alternative. Crucially, the first sample drawn was *the most recent experience* with each alternative. This built-in recency feature of the model allows it to capture the hot-stove effect discussed above (Erev & Haruvy, in press).

Following the model competition reported by Erev et al. (2010), several other candidate models have been proposed for explaining behaviour in the various different versions of the money-machine task. One successful class of models is based on the Instance-Based-Learning architecture (Gonzalez, Lerch, and Lebiere, 2003), a memory-based decision model which uses a combination of exemplar memory and 'blended' calculation of the expected value of different options to predict choice. Models based on this framework have proven highly effective in describing choices in the feedback and sampling versions of the money-machine task (e.g. Gonzalez & Dutt, 2011; though see Hills & Hertwig, 2012, for an alternative interpretation). More recently some researchers have attempted to model both the choices people make *and* their estimates of the probabilities with which outcomes occur in an effort to develop a comprehensive account of how people make decisions from experience (Hawkins et al., 2014).

BEYOND THE DESCRIPTION–EXPERIENCE GAP

The resurgence of interest in experience-based decisions has not only focused on the whys, whether and hows of the 'gap' between description and experience-based choice. As Rakow and Newell (2010) discuss, this return to a focus on the kinds of 'small-feedback-based' decision tasks has brought back into vogue many of the key questions that vexed researchers from the 1930s to the 1960s, such as when and why people maximize versus probability match (Goodnow, 1955; Humphreys, 1939; Tversky & Edwards, 1966 – see Chapter 12 for additional discussion of this work). However, far from a regress, bringing the roles of experience, sampling, memory and learning to the fore further facilitates the integration of 'typical' judgment and decision-making phenomena with related areas in cognitive psychology (cf. Hertwig, in press).

Research within the sampling paradigm in particular has led to important insights into the ways people search for information and how patterns of search and features of the environment predict or affect choices (e.g. Hertwig & Pleskac, 2010; Hills & Hertwig, 2010; Lejarraga, Hertwig & Gonzalez, 2012). For example, Lejarraga et al. demonstrated that participants facing losses searched (a little) more than those facing gains – perhaps indicating a tendency for loss-aversion. Participants also searched more when they experienced more than one outcome in the payoffs from a particular option (i.e. payoff variance). Hadar and Fox (2009) report a similar effect in which exploration and choice differ as a function of the order in which participants experience problems that have either high, low or no variance in payoff.

More broadly, interest in experience-based decisions has led researchers to ask an increasingly wide set of questions such as how sampling affects preferences for ambiguity (Güney & Newell, in press), how choices change when they are played out over longer time horizons (Camilleri & Newell, 2013), in dynamic environments (Rakow & Miler, 2009), or even when the same choices are compared across species (e.g. Shafir et al., 2008). Many of these studies are building a rich and varied understanding of how our experience determines our preferences. There is also clear and already realized potential for these insights from the laboratory to inform strategies for risk communication in the world outside the laboratory (e.g. Barron, Leider & Stack, 2008; Li, Rakow & Newell, 2009; Yechiam, Erev & Barron, 2006).

SUMMARY

Erev and Haruvy (in press) emphasize that the study of decisions from experience is not designed purely to test or refine theories based on modifications of expected utility theory (e.g. prospect theory). Thus although much of the initial interest in this area came from the 'call to arms' for a new theory to explain surprising patterns of behaviour – under-weighting where over-weighting was expected, the reversal of the certainty effect – subsequent research has used the 'money-machine' task to achieve what Erev and Haruvy argue is the more important goal, namely 'to expand the set of situations that can be addressed with economic models that provide clear and useful predictions' (p. 2). To that goal we would add another, namely to develop psychological models that aim to elucidate and emphasize the key role that learning plays in all of the decisions that we make – a theme that runs throughout this book.

Suggested further reading

- Barron, G., & Erev, I. (2003). Small feedback-based decisions and their limited correspondence to description-based decisions. *Journal of Behavioral Decision Making, 16,* 215–233. The empirical paper that provided the first demonstration of divergence between decisions from experience and description.
- Hertwig, R., & Erev, I. (2009) The description–experience gap in risky choice. *Trends in Cognitive Science, 13,* 517–523. A brief review of when and why a 'gap' emerges between decisions made from experience and description.
- Rakow, T., & Newell, B. R. (2010). Degrees of uncertainty: An overview and framework for future research on experience-based choice. *Journal of Behavioral Decision Making, 23,* 1–14. A longer summary and introduction to a special issue of the *Journal of Behavioral Decision Making* on experience-based choice.

11 Decisions across time

Chapter highlights

- Discussion of hindsight and projection biases, duration neglect and the peak–end effect
- The notion of discount functions and the consequences for decision making when they cross
- Factors that influence discount rates
- Evaluation of anticipated emotions and visceral influences on choice.

Confronted with the prospect of marriage to Emma Wedgwood, Charles Darwin famously wrote down lists of pros such as companionship in old age and cons such as disruption to his scientific work, and embarked upon a cost–benefit decision analysis to help him make up his mind. Of course, these prospects were all in the future for him, but their remoteness varied enormously. The pleasure to be derived from having a companion in old age was at least 20 years off, whereas disruption to his work (from having to visit his wife's relatives, say) might be only one or two years in the future. Thus, like many decision problems, time was a critical variable. Alternatives often have to be compared which will be realized at very different points in the future. In this chapter we consider some of the problems raised by these so called 'intertemporal' choice situations. (Thankfully – for the reputation of decision analysis – Charles and Emma were married in 1839.)

We begin, however, by considering an indirect influence of time on choice, namely via its common biasing effects on memory. We do not always remember events in a way that accurately reflects how they were experienced – indeed, our recollections often dramatically distort past events and how enjoyable or unpleasant they were. As an example, when students evaluated the enjoyment they were having during a particular type of vacation, their ratings did not predict how likely they were to repeat that type of vacation. That is to say, ratings taken during the vacation, as it was being experienced, did not determine future behaviour (Wirtz et al., 2003). Instead, recollections of how enjoyable the vacation was did predict future behaviour. Moreover, ratings of expected enjoyment given before the vacation influenced later recalled enjoyment independently of experienced enjoyment during the vacation: one's expectations have a long-lasting effect and are not overwritten by the actual experience. This raises the striking paradox that if you want to determine how likely it is that someone will repeat an experience such as revisiting a restaurant, asking them during the experience will be less useful than seeking their subsequent remembered experience: how much they are enjoying the meal when they are actually in the restaurant will be less predictive than their later recollections of how enjoyable it was.

HINDSIGHT AND OTHER TIME-RELATED BIASES

'Hindsight' and related 'self-serving' biases often influence recollections of attitudes and can lead to distortions whereby people tend to be biased to take credit for favourable outcomes and avoid blame for unfavourable ones. For instance, imagine that you have to organize a restaurant dinner for a large group of people from work. Beforehand, you are a little anxious about the complexity of the arrangements and whether the evening will be successful (will everyone like the food?). If asked, you would rate the likelihood of a good meal at about 0.7. The meal in fact turns out to be a success. Congratulating you, your boss asks you how confident you were that it would all work out. Your reply ('oh, about 95%') represents a hindsight (or 'I-knew-it-all-along') bias: knowing the outcome makes it very difficult to imagine what your judgment would have been if you had not known the outcome. You also feel a warm glow of satisfaction that the evening was a success *because* of you. But if it had been a failure, you would have blamed the restaurant (the service was poor) or the people in your party (they had no sense of humour). This is a 'self-serving' bias: the tendency to take credit for good outcomes while avoiding blame for bad ones.

In the context of financial purchase decisions, Louie (1999) asked individuals to decide whether or not to purchase a company stock prior to giving them information that the stock either increased or decreased in value. When the stock value increased, participants over-estimated what they thought they would have judged the likelihood of an increase to be (hindsight bias) and they credited themselves with the favourable outcome (self-serving bias).

Similarly, Conway (1990) asked a group of students to report prior to an exam how well prepared they thought they were for the exam and what their expected grade was. After the exam they were asked to recall as accurately as possible their earlier ratings. Conway found that students who did worse than they expected reported having prepared less and having expected a lower grade than they truly had. These students were motivated to avoid blame for a poor outcome by misremembering a smaller amount of preparation. In contrast, students who did better than they expected reported having prepared more and having expected a higher grade than they actually had.

It seems likely that these biases are often due to the more general difficulty people have with counterfactual thinking (that is, thinking about something that's inconsistent with reality). When you learn something, this doesn't simply add one piece of information to your memory, but instead it causes a cascade of inferences, which are often automatic and hence difficult to reverse. When your restaurant meal turns out to be successful, a lot of information in your memory changes, over and above the fact that the evening was a success: you learn that the food in the restaurant is exceptional, that the people in your party are very relaxed, and so on. Accurately gauging what the prior likelihood was of a successful evening requires negating all these new facts that you've learned and, hardly surprisingly, this is extremely hard to do.

This is well illustrated by Harley, Carlsen and Loftus's (2004) striking demonstration of visual hindsight bias. These researchers offered the following example of how perceptual judgments might be biased in hindsight. Imagine that radiographer A examines a patient's X-ray and declares it to be clear. Some time later the patient dies of a tumour, and a court case is brought for negligence against A for not having detected the tumour. Radiographer B, examining the X-ray, declares that A should have been able to detect it, and the court finds A guilty of negligence and awards compensation. The problem is that whereas A studied the X-ray without knowing whether or not it contained a tumour, B later studied it knowing that it did. Thus there is the possibility that radiographer B's conclusion that the tumour should have been visible to A may be biased by hindsight.

To test for the possibility of bias in such situations, Harley et al. showed participants sequences of photographs of famous people such as Harrison Ford. These photographs started out highly blurred but participants saw progressively clearer and clearer images until they were able to identify the famous person. Then in a second stage they saw the faces again, this time with their names alongside, and indicated at what level of blurriness they thought they had been able to identify them in the first stage. This is a test of hindsight bias in that on the second viewing participants had to engage in counterfactual thinking, namely 'if I didn't know that these blurry images are Harrison Ford, at what point would I have identified him?' Harley et al. found a strong tendency for participants to think they identified the face earlier (i.e. in a more blurry image) than they actually did, and that this tendency persisted even when participants were told about hindsight bias and given instructions to try to avoid it.

Further examples of biased recall are very easy to find (see Hawkins & Hastie, 1990). For instance, several studies reviewed by Ross (1989) asked people to report their attitudes on two occasions, separated by several years, to such things as government spending, equality for women and political opinions. Most people's views on such things tend to change over long time periods, but Ross's key finding was that when the individuals were asked on the second occasion to recall their earlier attitudes, those recollections were biased towards their later attitudes. Thus someone who is initially somewhat liberal politically but becomes more conservative is subsequently likely to misremember themselves as having previously been more conservative than they actually were. To recall accurately what one's earlier attitudes were requires undoing several years of new inferences and perspectives, an unfeasible act.

Given this evidence for biased recall of attitudes and judgments, it is perhaps not surprising that similar distortions pervade recall of decisions and of the criteria used for reaching those decisions (Pieters, Baumgartner & Bagozzi, 2006). Situations often occur in which we consider a range of reasons for or against a particular choice, make our choice, and then later try to recall what our reasoning was. Can we accurately recall why we selected a degree course which turned out well or why we accepted a job offer which didn't? If we hope to learn from our experiences and avoid repeating poor decisions, accurate recall would seem crucial. One clear result is that people's current views of how they should have reasoned tend to colour their recall of how they actually reasoned – in other words, people reconstruct their memory for a decision on the basis of their current beliefs and attitudes. Of course the decision can turn out to be a good or a bad one and this also appears to influence recall.

Galotti (1995) studied these issues in a naturalistic setting by asking high-school students to describe the criteria they were using to decide which university to go to, and for each criterion, they rated how important it was in their decision making and how each of the universities they were considering scored on that measure. Thus one university might have scored well on campus appearance and another poorly on financial aid. When they were at university some 8–20 months later the students were asked to recall the factors they had considered as well as the factors in retrospect they felt were most important.

Galotti's key finding was that while recall of the factors was moderate (about half were recalled), there was a significantly greater tendency to recall factors which the student *now* thought were important. For example, students rated type of institution (public/private/single sex, etc.) as quite an important factor at the time they were making their decisions, but after arriving at university they believed this to be much less important and tended not to recall basing their decisions on it, despite the fact that they patently had. Conversely, campus atmosphere was not heavily weighted initially but was thought later to be an important factor, and the students were much more likely to recall (or more accurately, falsely recall) taking this into consideration in their original decision. Thus people are prone to 'recall' factors which in truth they did not put emphasis on but which after the fact seem significant to them.

Distortions of recollection are only one type of biasing mechanism in our judgments and choices. We may sometimes also be influenced by our (incorrect) lay theories about how our preferences change over time. People are poor, for example, at predicting how much they will enjoy future events such as eating yoghurt every day for a week, believing that their enjoyment will decline, when objectively it will not (Kahneman & Snell, 1992). Yet being able to predict one's future preferences is very important in many decision contexts.

Consider a person who, having enjoyed a skiing holiday, is considering buying an apartment in that location. Will her enjoyment of skiing on subsequent visits be equally positive? Or will she become bored with skiing and regret the purchase? Unless one can make accurate forecasts of one's future likes and dislikes, significant mistakes about property purchases, job decisions, marriage or other major choices might ensue. Loewenstein and Angner (2003) have suggested that a common reason why people make unsatisfactory decisions is that they tend to regard their current preferences as much more stable and intrinsic than they actually are. In truth, many of our likes and dislikes are highly fluid (as discussed above) and are determined by ever-changing external and cultural influences (think of clothes). This means that our preferences are likely to change with external drivers, yet we may underestimate the extent of this change and believe ourselves to be more immune to the vagaries of external influences than we truly are. This in turn leads us to believe that our future self will be more like our current self in terms of likes and dislikes than it in fact will be.

Examples of this sort of 'projection' bias abound. For instance, people appear unable to predict the change in their future valuation of an object that will accompany owning it. People tend to place higher values on things when they own them than when they do not – recall the discussion of the 'endowment' effect with the coffee mugs in Chapter 9. Another example relates to the effects of visceral influences on decision making.

We are often not very good at taking account of the ways in which our future states of hunger, thirst, sexual arousal, and so on will motivate our behaviour. Read and van Leeuwen (1998) gave a choice of healthy or unhealthy snacks to office workers at times when they were either hungry or satiated. The choice was for a snack to be consumed in a week's time, which would be handed over either at a point during the day in which the individual was likely to be hungry (late afternoon) or satiated (after lunch). Read and van Leeuwen found, as might be expected, that individuals who expected to be hungry at the point of obtaining the snack were more likely to select an unhealthy one than those expecting to be satiated at the point of obtaining it. More interestingly, individuals who were hungry at the time of making the choice were also more likely to select the unhealthy snack than ones who weren't, suggesting that they projected their current desire onto their future selves and assumed that they would be hungrier at the point of obtaining the snack than they objectively would be.

PREDICTING PLEASURE AND PAIN

What is interesting about such examples is that they illustrate another type of irrationality, namely when a decision is inconsistent with an objective benchmark. The students in Wirtz et al.'s study of vacation enjoyment, for instance, genuinely enjoyed some holidays more than others, and should, on any reasonable grounds, have sought to repeat those vacations more than ones they enjoyed less. Yet their 'true' enjoyment did not determine their future choices. A famous experiment by Kahneman and his colleagues (Kahneman et al., 1993) illustrates this kind of irrationality even more graphically. Suppose you are asked to decide between the following two alternatives:

A: submerge your hand in very cold water for 60 seconds, or
B: submerge your hand in very cold water for 60 seconds, and then in mildly cold water for 30 seconds.

Presumably we will all agree that option A is preferable as it contains less total pain (30 seconds in mildly cold water is not as bad as 60 seconds in very cold water, but is still unpleasant). Normatively, to determine the pleasure or pain of an extended experience, one should simply add up (integrate) across all its constituent moments. Yet Kahneman et al. found that people forced to experience both options tended to prefer option B when they had to decide which one to repeat – hence this is another example of a preference reversal, in this case a reversal between what people would reflectively choose when fully briefed, and what they actually choose. The reason for this behaviour is that people (mis)remembered the longer episode as being less unpleasant (they were not given and had no access to objective information about the duration or temperature), presumably because the 30 seconds of mildly cold water partially overshadowed their recall of the earlier minute in very cold water (the 'happy end' effect). It is the passage of time that seems crucial here in introducing distortion between experience and recollection.

Kahneman and his colleagues (Redelmeier, Katz & Kahneman, 2003) have shown similar paradoxical choices in a much more painful real-world setting, where people are undergoing a colonoscopy for the detection of colorectal cancer. Some patients were given an extra period of a couple of minutes at the end of the procedure, in which the colonoscope remained inserted in the rectum, but in a way that was less painful than in the preceding period. Despite the fact that this extra period was undoubtedly unpleasant and made the longer procedure 'objectively' more painful, patients recalled the procedure as being less painful and were more likely to return for a follow-up colonoscopy when the additional period had been added. This behaviour seems irrational, because if one were to calculate the 'total pain' by integrating the moment-by-moment pain levels across the whole experience, the shorter procedure would yield less total pain.

The enjoyment or displeasure we obtain from everyday experiences such as eating an expensive meal, waiting in a queue or having a medical procedure are of course important not only in their own right but also insofar as they shape our likelihood of repeating these and similar experiences. Yet, as the examples above show, this relationship is far from straightforward. What is it precisely that determines the mapping between the pleasure or pain experienced during an event and the subsequently recalled level of pleasure/pain?

Quite a lot of evidence (see Ariely & Carmon, 2003) suggests that there are two particularly important features of any extended experience, namely its peak level of pleasure/displeasure and its end level, which together comprise the so-called 'peak-end' effect. Research has suggested that these are subjectively combined to produce an overall weighting. This function explains the results of the experiments of Kahneman and his colleagues, because whereas the contrasting conditions are equated for their peak displeasure, adding a less unpleasant period at the end reduces the end level of displeasure. The fact that the peak level of pain or pleasure is heavily weighted in global judgments of pleasantness or unpleasantness may seem entirely reasonable, and indeed it is. However, the combination of and reliance on peak and end levels can lead to strikingly irrational behaviour such as preference for sequences which include more total pain (described above) and for relative neglect of the duration of a pleasant or unpleasant event (discussed below).

Although the peak-end formula provides a good account of retrospective judgments of pleasantness or unpleasantness, additional complex features having to do with the ordering of events come into play when people make judgments ahead of time about how attractive an event will be. People tend, for instance, to have a very strong preference for improving sequences over ones that get worse.

Varey and Kahneman (1992), for instance, obtained judgments of the overall unpleasantness of sequences of aversive events, such as exposure to loud drilling, which were hypothetically experienced by individuals. Each sequence was described in terms of the individual's discomfort rating every five minutes (e.g. 2–4–6), where larger numbers indicate greater discomfort. Judgments were much greater for sequences of increasing discomfort such as 2–4–6 than for corresponding decreasing ones such as 6–4–2, possibly because in the latter, each period is an improvement on what came before it. (Although this may appear to be consistent with the peak-end formula, in that 2–4–6 ends with a worse level of discomfort than 6–4–2, it is important to bear in mind that we are considering here judgments made ahead of time, before the events are experienced, rather than recollections.) If experiences are evaluated in a relative rather than an absolute way, then such an outcome makes sense. Varey and Kahneman also found, consistent with the studies described above, that adding a painful period at the end of the sequence made the whole experience seem less painful, provided the added period was less aversive than what came before: sequences such as 2–5–8–4 were rated (again, ahead of time) as less unpleasant than ones like 2–5–8 which are subsets of them. In the case of positive events, like consuming foods or receiving money, improving sequences are again more attractive. People prefer jobs, for example, with increasing rather than decreasing wage profiles, even when the latter are objectively better.

A factor which seems to play surprisingly little role in judgments of pleasure/displeasure is the duration of an experience. Indeed, so minimal is this role in many circumstances that the term 'duration neglect' has been coined. In Kahneman et al.'s cold-water experiment, for instance, participants were generally accurate in recalling the relative durations of the two episodes, but recalled duration was only slightly correlated with recalled discomfort. Varey and Kahneman reported something similar: profiles of discomfort such as 2–3–4–5–6–7–8 (lasting for 35 minutes) were judged barely more unpleasant than ones like 2–5–8 (lasting 15 minutes), despite more than doubling the total duration of the discomfort.

However, the extent to which duration is neglected or under-weighted, and the implications of this for normative theories, has been the subject of some controversy (Ariely, Kahneman & Loewenstein, 2000). Ariely and Loewenstein (2000) have suggested that duration may be neglected when retrospective judgments about single extended experiences are made, but that this is often understandable. If someone asks you how painful a visit to the dentist was, the questioner is likely to be more interested in the peak pain level than in the duration. Furthermore, Ariely and Loewenstein argued that duration is much less likely to be under-weighted when the experience is compared to some reference point. More research is needed on this important topic.

Section summary

The preferences on which we act are not fixed but subject to numerous external influences. One of these is the distorting influence of memory, which can misrepresent events in striking ways: we can misremember the enjoyment of a vacation or the pain of a surgical procedure. We can misrecall the reasons why we made a decision. Moreover, people tend to be quite poor at anticipating their future preferences. What unites these distortions is that memory often tries to 're-write' the past in a way that is more congenial with our lay theories, expectations, desires, and so on. Thus our recall of a vacation is closer to how much we expected to enjoy it beforehand than to the actual pleasure it afforded us. Our recall of the reasons behind a decision is driven more by our current values than by the ones we actually held at the time.

DIRECT EFFECTS OF TIME

Whereas the influence of time in these studies is indirect in being mediated by memory, the bulk of research on intertemporal choice looks at more direct time-based influences. This reflects very many real decision problems in which the outcomes of different choices may be realized at different points in time. Any decision involving a choice between saving and spending is of this nature, as are decisions about whether to have a medical procedure now or in the future, whether eating a chocolate bar now will reduce the pleasure of this evening's meal, and so on. Addictions are probably the most unfortunate illustrations of the difficulties we face when making time-based choices: whether to consume a drug or carry out some behaviour which will have rewarding effects immediately, but longer-term harmful effects on our health and wealth.

Economists propose a simple extension of choice theory to deal with time-based decisions. Basically, the value of an outcome or commodity should be discounted as a function of how far into the future it is delayed, with the discount rate being like a subjective interest rate. Thus $10 in the future is equivalent to $10 × $d(t)$ now, where t is the delay and d is the discount function, assumed to be exponential in economic theory (that is, $d(t) = \exp(-\delta t)$). In other words, the present value of $10 at a delay of t is $10 × $\exp(-\delta t)$, where δ, the discount rate, is a constant.

The concept of discounting future events is understandable when one considers monetary assets and liabilities, for example. A bill that is due tomorrow does not have the same 'cost' as one due next year, and most people would pay to exchange the former for the latter (at least, if the amount involved was sufficiently large). This makes perfectly good economic sense. Rather than using your current wealth to pay the bill tomorrow, it would be financially beneficial to delay the bill and invest the wealth in something which accumulates interest. So long as the earned interest is greater than the cost of delaying the bill, it is prudent to choose the delayed bill. In other words, time dilutes the value of future outcomes. A discount rate (of, say, 100%) should be read as referring to the percentage increase in the magnitude or value of an immediate reward that would be required to make a person indifferent between having that reward now versus delaying it for one year.

A straightforward implication of the classic exponential model of discounting is that an individual's rank ordering of the value of various future outcomes cannot change with the passage of time. To see what this means, consider the choice between $100 in a year versus $120 in 13 months. Many people will prefer the latter. Exponential discounting implies that this preference ordering should be maintained regardless of when the events will occur, so long as they are separated by a month: counterintuitively, $120 in a month should be preferred to $100 today. To see this graphically, Figure 11.1 shows discount curves for these two monetary amounts. The horizontal axis of the graph indicates time, hence one moves rightwards along this axis as time passes. The vertical axis shows the current value of a future reward. Note that when the two monetary amounts are actually delivered (the vertical lines at the right of the graph), more value will be obtained from receiving $120 than from $100 – the bar for the former is higher.

At the point at which the delayed alternatives are being considered (month 13 on the x-axis), the two monetary amounts are a long way off in the future, 13 and 12 months respectively, and the larger amount is preferred. As time passes, the exponential curves reflecting their value gradually rise as receipt of the money becomes more imminent, but they never cross. Hence at month 1, when the smaller amount can be taken, it is not chosen because the larger amount is still preferred even though it is delayed for a further month. Choices between the same outcomes separated by the same amount of time must always be consistent on this model.

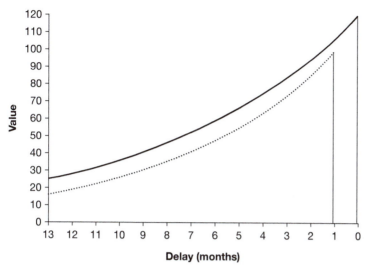

Figure 11.1 Exponential discount functions. In this example a choice is offered between
$120 delayed by 13 months from today and $100 delayed by 12 months.
Hence today is the point labelled 13 on the *x*-axis, and as time passes and
the payoffs get nearer, one moves rightwards along the axis. The bars at the
right indicate the value of each of the outcomes at the point of delivery.
The black line plots the discounting of the larger, more delayed outcome
by the function $d(t) = \exp(-\delta t)$ where δ, the discount rate, is 0.12, while
the dotted line plots that for the smaller, less delayed one with $\delta = 0.15$.
The important point to note is that these functions cannot cross.

Several violations of this normative account have been documented.
Consider a simple example from Rachlin (2000) that will undoubtedly resonate
with all of us. You set your alarm clock to wake up at 7 a.m., but when the
time comes and your clock rings, you turn it off and go back to sleep. In the
evening, your preference is to wake up at 7 a.m. rather than later but in
the morning your preference has reversed and you would rather stay in bed
till later. Given the prevalence of preference reversals as discussed in Chapter
9, it will perhaps come as no surprise that reversals such as the alarm clock one
can be demonstrated in intertemporal choices too. Such inconsistencies cannot
be explained by any model of choice that incorporates exponential discounting.
Returning to our monetary example, it is also common to find reversals such
that a person who prefers $120 in 13 months to $100 in a year will also prefer
$100 today to $120 in a month.

Such findings require that discount rate is descriptively modelled with
something other than an exponential function, something that will allow the
value curves to cross. One such function which has been applied to many studies
of intertemporal choice is the hyperbolic function (in which $d(t) = 1/(1 + kt)$,
where t is again the delay and k is a constant). Although this might seem like

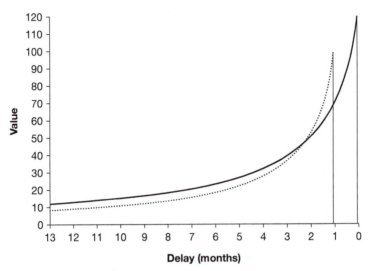

Figure 11.2 Hyperbolic discount functions plotting the same choice as in Figure 11.1
between $120 delayed by 13 months and $100 delayed by 12 months.
The black line plots the discounting of the larger, more delayed outcome
by the function $d(t) = 1/(1 + kt)$ where k is 0.7, while the dotted line plots
that for the smaller, less delayed one with $k = 0.9$. Unlike the exponential
curves in Figure 11.1, hyperbolic curves can cross. Hence the larger
payment is preferred at all delays until about a month before the smaller
payment becomes available, at which point the latter is preferred.

a mathematical detail, in fact it has quite profound consequences as the
exponential form is the only one which guarantees the avoidance of certain
choice anomalies. Hence from a rational economic perspective, hyperbolic
discounting is non-normative. However, these anomalies become perfectly
understandable given a hyperbolic function. Figure 11.2 shows hyperbolic
functions and the consequences that ensue when the value functions can cross.
When the payoffs are a long way off, the larger and more remote one ($120)
is preferred to the closer but smaller one. However, after about 10 months
have elapsed (month 2 on the *x*-axis), the smaller reward is preferred. The
rank ordering of different outcomes can reverse with the passage of time,
yielding the sorts of preference reversals described above.

Although hyperbolic discounting provides a good account of many aspects
of intertemporal choice, it is reasonable to ask what the underlying psychological
mechanisms are that yield such discount rates. One possibility, explored in detail
by Zauberman et al. (2009), is that its basis lies in the psychophysics of time
perception. If time is perceived, like many other dimensions, according to the
Weber-Fechner Law (for instance, three weeks is not perceived as being three
times as far in the future as one week), then future discounting would arise
from this basic psychological law.

DISCOUNT RATES

A second general finding from studies of intertemporal choice that is inconsistent with the normative exponential model is that discount rates tend to be larger for lower-valued outcomes than for higher-valued ones, larger for more immediate outcomes than for longer-delayed ones, and greater for gains than for losses of the same magnitude (see Frederick, Loewenstein & O'Donoghue, 2003). Chapman and Winquist (1998) asked participants to imagine that they had won a lottery and to indicate how much they would accept in three months instead of taking their winnings immediately. Conversely, in another condition participants imagined they had received a speeding fine and could either pay an amount now or a larger amount in three months. The average discount rates were about 400% for the fine (a loss) but around 2000% for the lottery (a gain). Hence with a loss of $100, indifference is reached when the fine is $500 at three months, while with a gain of $100, indifference is not reached until the delayed winnings reach $2100 (perhaps with real-money outcomes participants would have been slightly more conservative!). However, these average effects were moderated by a magnitude effect such that the discount rates were far higher for small than large amounts.

It is important to realize that this magnitude effect could lead to highly anomalous behaviour. An interest rate that would be unacceptable to a customer on a large bank loan would become acceptable if the loan was broken down into several smaller loans. In other work, Chapman (1996; see also Hardisty & Weber, 2009) has found that influences such as delay have very different effects on discount rates in different domains such as money versus health. Even when money and health are matched to be of equal value, the utility that results from money is not the same as that from health in decisions across time and does not yield comparable discount functions. Indeed, Chapman found very little correlation between discount rates in these domains. It is important to note, however, that the normative model only anticipates identical discount rates across all domains if the outcomes are what economists call 'fungible' – that is, freely exchangeable for one another. Although this is approximately the case for many domains (e.g. money and food), it is probably not true of money and health. One cannot simply trade a given amount of money for a given change in health level.

This might explain why, despite the fact that very low correlations between money and health discount rates are found, monetary discounting does correlate with another very important health-related behaviour, namely addiction. Indeed, quite a number of studies have documented this. In a typical experiment, money discount rates are measured in the usual way by offering varying (often hypothetical) amounts delivered either immediately or at a delay, and these rates are compared in sample groups of addicts and non-addicts. Studies of this sort have shown, for instance, that heroin addicts, heavy drinkers and smokers all have steeper money discount functions (see Chapman, 2003). This makes sense if one assumes that individual differences in susceptibility to substance abuse relate to the relative weighting given to events occurring at different time horizons: heroin offers an immediate highly pleasurable reward at the expense, inevitably, of future costs in terms of health, wealth, work, relationships, and so on.

The issue of cross-domain generalization aside, the observed properties of discount rates are plainly inconsistent with the normative model. In fact there are even examples of negative discount rates for some nonmonetary losses: people often prefer to take a loss immediately rather than to delay it, implying that a delayed loss is more painful than an immediate one, perhaps because the delay creates the unpleasantness of dread. Conversely, in the domain of gains, people sometimes prefer to delay a pleasurable event, presumably in order to savour it, but nonetheless demonstrating a negative discount rate. When students were asked when they would most like (hypothetically) to kiss their favourite film star, the median response was three days in the future rather than immediately (Loewenstein, 1987). These examples raise issues about visceral or emotional influences on decision making, which we return to later in this chapter and in Chapter 15.

A third non-normative finding is that people will pay less to bring forward an outcome than they will accept to delay it. Loewenstein (1988) found that people would pay on average $54 to receive immediately a video cassette recorder which they didn't expect to receive for a year, while others who expected to receive it immediately demanded an average of $126 to delay receipt for a year. This is inconsistent with the normative model as the same change in value should be measured regardless of the method.

To what extent should these many deviations from the normative exponential discounting model cause us concern? Do they constitute clear examples of irrational behaviour or are they better viewed as 'anomalies' rather than mistakes? This of course depends on how strongly one believes the exponential model to be normatively justified. In many domains of judgment and decision making, individuals will often agree, when the situation is fully explained to them, that their behaviour is irrational. For example, someone who is induced in an experiment to judge that a conjunction ('it will rain tomorrow and the next day') is more probable than either of its conjuncts ('it will rain tomorrow') is very likely to admit the invalidity of this on reflection.

For deviations from the normative model of time-based decisions, however, this seems rather less likely. To explain why the individual should discount money and food equally would not be an easy task. Many behavioural economists now dispute the normative status of the model (e.g. Frederick et al., 2003) and have turned their attention instead to more descriptive approaches to intertemporal choice. With great variability as a function of seemingly insignificant experimental details (e.g. the amounts under consideration or their delays), it has proven extremely difficult to find any stable measures of discount rates and this calls into question the whole normative approach to discount rates.

Psychological explanations of these 'anomalies' of intertemporal choice are beginning to be developed. To give a flavour of one of these, let us consider again Loewenstein's (1988) demonstration of asymmetries between how much we demand to be paid to delay an outcome versus how much we are willing to pay to bring it forward. 'Query' theory explains this asymmetry by reference to the reasons we bring to mind in each case. When individuals consider delaying receipt of something like a gift certificate, they query their memories and tend to think first of reasons favouring early receipt; only later (and more weakly) do they think of reasons favouring delayed receipt. The net effect is greater preference for early receipt.

When they instead consider bringing forward receipt of a delayed gift certificate, they tend to think first of reasons favouring late receipt and only later (and more weakly) of reasons favouring early receipt, the net effect being attenuated preference for early receipt. Consistent with this explanation, Weber et al. (2007) were able to completely eliminate the usual asymmetry by forcing participants to generate reasons in an unnatural order (for instance, first generating reasons for delaying receipt in the condition where they consider delaying a reward). Thus it is possible to develop accounts of intertemporal choice anomalies based on sound principles of such psychological processes as memory retrieval.

ANTICIPATED EMOTIONS

As alluded to above in the context of savouring the prospect of a kiss or bringing forward an unpleasant and dreaded event, emotions seem to play an important role in decision making and in particular may be critical in causing time-based preference reversals when an imminent event gains control of our behaviour against our more long-term objectives. This is reflected in the fact that as one moves away from the point of delivery of a valued event, the hyperbolic discount function is steeper than the exponential one, implying a greater impact of imminent events.

There is now quite a lot of evidence that there is something special about immediate outcomes. McClure et al. (2004) have shown, by way of illustration, that immediate and delayed outcomes evoke brain activity in two quite distinct brain regions and that the relative magnitude of activity in these regions predicts whether the individual will choose the immediate or delayed outcome. Their participants chose between small but immediate monetary amounts (immediate here meaning at the end of the experiment) and larger delayed amounts (up to six weeks later). When a choice involved an immediate outcome, the striatum and orbitofrontal cortex (limbic structures innervated by dopamine cells) became particularly active. With delayed outcomes, a different network including parts of lateral prefrontal and parietal cortices became active, irrespective of the delay involved. McClure and his colleagues referred to these systems as the β and δ systems, respectively.

The fact that immediate rewards can often have an excessive pull on our behaviour leads to many highly undesirable behaviours such as addictions. A craving for instantaneous pleasure from a drug often co-exists with a strong desire to give up the drug in the future. This is exactly what is depicted in Figure 11.2: a preference is one way round at a point in the future (not having the drug is preferred to having it) but reversed when immediate consumption is at issue (having the drug is preferred to not having it). Amongst young people, about 30% report that they expect to be still smoking in five years' time, but the true figure is about 70%, indicating a strong but erroneous tendency to believe that they will give up. A smoker prefers a cigarette today to no cigarette and plans to give up next month, without realizing that the choice next month will be the same as the one faced today. This is the paradox of addiction, that a desire to quit can coincide with continued consumption.

In an extensive theoretical treatment of the effects of immediate events on behaviour, Loewenstein (1996) has suggested that what he calls 'visceral' influences have several significant properties which distinguish them from other, more coldly valued, events. One is that they have a disproportionate effect on behaviour, and of course this is very obvious in the case of drug cravings, sexual compulsion or the urgent desire to escape pain. The brain-imaging data described above suggest a biological basis for this exaggerated influence which often runs counter to the individual's more reflective judgment.

Another feature is that these punishing or rewarding events tend to alter the attractiveness of other events or actions. A drug addict loses concern with career, social relationships, and so forth in the desire to obtain a drug. A particularly vivid illustration of this is the behaviour of rats in the famous experiments of Olds and Milner (1954) when allowed to self-administer electrical stimulation of the brain. This stimulation can be so pleasurable that some animals will ignore food and water to the point of death. Thirdly, Loewenstein pointed out that visceral influences on behaviour, although extremely powerful 'in the moment', are often profoundly under-weighted in memory and downplayed when future courses of action are under consideration. Someone who contemplates a future visit to the dentist may sincerely intend to avoid the use of anaesthetic despite on a previous occasion having abandoned such a resolution at the first sight of the dentist's drill. Memory for pain (e.g. during childbirth) is notoriously poor. Thus there are a variety of reasons to believe that immediate emotional or visceral events have a singular influence on behaviour, one which is often not easily accommodated within classical decision theory.

The extent to which the immediate rewarding or punishing attributes of an object influence behaviour can also depend on the focus of one's attention. This notion is captured in models of 'attentional myopia' developed in the context of alcohol consumption and eating behaviour. These models apply to any situations in which behaviours are subject to conflicting forces, with some influences promoting the behaviour and some inhibiting it. We have all had the experience of letting our best intentions slip and succumbing to temptation when our attention is diverted.

Suppose that one is considering consuming a highly attractive but unhealthy chocolate milkshake. Under normal circumstances, a whole range of features may be attended to and weighted in the course of forming a decision about whether to consume it: its perceptual qualities, the current context, one's mood and motivational state, as well as its dietary impact. Under conditions of low attention, in contrast, where attentional resources are partially diverted away from the milkshake, some of these attributes will fall outside the narrower focus of attention and only the most salient features will remain under consideration. If those features, as will often be the case, happen to be strongly tied to the visceral attractiveness of the object, then consumption is more likely to occur. For example, Ward and Mann (2000) showed that increased cognitive load (that is, requiring participants to attend to another task concurrently) caused dieters to become disinhibited and consume foods that they would not have under conditions of full attention.

If, however, the more salient aspects of the object are inhibitory ones, then narrowing one's attention may make it easier to avoid consumption. Just as decreased attention will increase selection of the object when the preponderance of salient features are promoting ones, so it should decrease selection when the majority of such features are inhibiting ones. Mann and Ward (2004) provided convincing evidence in support of this prediction in a study in which dieters were required to taste a milkshake unobserved and the amount consumed was measured. Under conditions of reduced attention, participants had to remember a nine-digit number during the test. The critical manipulation was that some subjects were primed before the test to think about features of the milkshake associated with its visceral properties (specifically, they were led to believe they were taking part in a taste memory experiment and therefore focused on the milkshake's taste) whereas others were primed to think about inhibiting factors – specifically their own diets and the high fat content of the drink. Consistent with the attentional myopia model, when diet was made salient, participants consumed *less* of the milkshake under conditions of distraction than when devoting full attention. The opposite trend was observed, as in the earlier Ward and Mann (2000) study, when the visceral properties were made salient.

These results have both theoretical and practical implications. On the theoretical front, they emphasize again that visceral events can exert a powerful sway on behaviour and that this sway can be increased when an individual cannot fully weigh up all the relevant factors in reaching a decision. But they extend this by suggesting that the reason for this outcome is that the most powerful and attractive features of an object tend to be highly salient in decision making. If, in contrast, the salience of inhibiting features can be enhanced, then reduced attention will tend to cause greater weighting of those features in the choice process and hence avoidance of the object. From a practical perspective, the findings suggest a simple method for helping people to avoid attractive foods, drugs, and so on, when they come under attentional pressure by enhancing those attributes associated with avoidance.

Setting deadlines

Returning to the issue of temporal discounting, one important way to avoid the consequences of crossing discount functions and addictive behaviour is to make a commitment. In the example of setting an alarm to wake yourself up in the morning, you could decide to place the alarm clock on the other side of the room in order to force yourself to get up. You know when you set the clock in the evening that your preferences will reverse during the night and that at 7 a.m., staying in bed will be preferable to getting up. However, when you set the alarm your preferences are the other way round and hence you might thwart your future self by doing something which will change the value of the alternatives when they are available. Putting the clock on the other side of the room will reduce the pleasure of staying in bed (as it will be ruined by having the clock going off) and will increase the value of getting up (it's easier to stay up once you're forced by the clock to get out of bed). Commitments such as this are very common ways of controlling our intertemporal decision making. Putting aside a regular savings amount each month is a form of commitment if it prevents you from impulsive spending.

Commitment does, however, require self-awareness. You have to be aware that your future preferences may not coincide with your current ones. Some people are more insightful about this than others. Perhaps one can learn to be more insightful in an appropriately structured environment? Some would doubtless argue that this is part of the value of education in general. There has not been a great deal of research on this topic, but some evidence suggests that people are sometimes aware of the value of costly commitments but perhaps not optimally so.

Evidence for this claim comes from Ariely and Wertenbroch's (2002) study of self-imposed deadlines, a form of commitment used to overcome the tendency for value functions to cross. We commonly face situations where we agree to do some task by a particular time, such as agreeing to write a book or organize a party or have a difficult confrontation with a colleague, yet don't start the task immediately because with the deadline far in the future the pleasure from doing the task is lower than that of all other activities. That is to say, at time t_0 the value function for doing the task is lower than that of everything else. As time passes, however, the value functions cross as in Figure 11.2 until a point is reached (t_1) where the value of doing the task exceeds that of all other activities that can substitute for it, and we finally get around to doing it. Setting a deadline is a way of committing to do the task. For example, you might organize a meeting with your co-authors on a particular deadline day to discuss the draft of your book. A co-author who fails to meet this dead-line risks embarrassment and opprobrium – in other words, the deadline is costly in the same way that having to get out of bed to switch off an alarm clock is costly.

Ariely and Wertenbroch recruited participants to proofread long essays containing grammatical and spelling errors. These individuals were set the task of correcting three such essays either at weekly deadlines, or they were allowed to submit all the corrected essays at the end of three weeks, or they were required to commit to their own deadlines for the three pieces of work in advance. Participants in this latter condition could have chosen to give the final day of the three-week period as their deadline for all pieces of work, but in fact chose to set deadlines spaced throughout the period despite the fact that this was costly for them: by having the latest possible deadline, they would have had more time to do the work and had more flexibility about their workload.

This suggests some awareness that a deadline is needed, to avoid having to do all the work at the last minute. Consistent with this, participants who set themselves deadlines detected more errors in the essays, missed fewer deadlines and earned more from the task (their earnings related both to errors detected and to getting the work in on time). Hence there are tangible benefits to commitments, and people seem to be aware of this and able to use commitments to boost their performance. Yet they are not always perfect at this: the participants in Ariely and Wertenbroch's study who set their own deadlines did not perform as well as those who were forced to abide by external deadlines (one essay marked per week). Thus, by an objective measure, they could have improved their performance and earnings but failed to do so because they did not space their deadlines in the most efficient way. Lastly, and in accord with experience that we doubtless all share, the participants who worked towards a single final deadline put less time into the task in total than those who committed to deadlines (who in turn worked less than those with evenly spaced deadlines). As we all know, waiting till the last minute usually means that a job is done poorly.

SUMMARY

In the context of time-based decisions, violations of the normative theory (in this case, the exponential discounting model) are easy to find. Crossing discount functions, which describe many problems of self-control such as dieting and addiction, can be modelled by hyperbolic discount functions. In addition, an important concept for understanding behaviour in these circumstances is the notion of visceral influences on behaviour, those influences that are associated with powerful biological drives. In the past few years a considerable body of research has illustrated how these may affect behaviour.

This discussion of the effects of time on decision making brings us to the end of the chapters concerned with analysing and describing models of choice. In the next two chapters our attention turns to the fundamental processes underlying learning. We examine how we learn about the environments in which we make decisions and how this learning can improve our decision making. Put another way, we investigate the mechanisms that facilitate *straight choices*.

Suggested further reading

- Bechara, A. (2005). Decision making, impulse control and loss of willpower to resist drugs: A neurocognitive perspective. *Nature Neuroscience, 8,* 1458–1463. Discussion of the roles of impulse and reflection, and their brain mechanisms, in addiction.
- Loewenstein, G. (1996). Out of control: Visceral influences on behavior. *Organizational Behavior and Human Decision Processes, 65,* 272–292. Discussion of some of the ways in which visceral reactions can influence our decisions.
- Loewenstein, G., Read, D., & Baumeister, R. (Eds) (2003). *Time and decision: Economic and psychological perspectives on intertemporal choice.* New York: Russell Sage Foundation. A comprehensive collection of papers by leading researchers.
- Scholten, M., & Read, D. (2010). The psychology of intertemporal tradeoffs. *Psychological Review, 117,* 925–944. Recent theorizing about the psychological mechanisms that govern intertemporal choices.

12 Learning to choose, choosing to learn

Chapter highlights

- Revisiting the basic binary decision task (Chapter 10) and introducing the linear model
- Probability matching can be overcome by feedback and incentives
- Extending the linear model to multiple-cue probability learning.

Imagine you're at a horse race-track and want to bet on the outcome of a two-horse race. What factors are likely to determine the winner? Of course, the horses themselves will differ in ability and their past records will give some clues about how they compare. But just because horse A has a better recent record than horse B does not mean that it will prevail – its wins may have been against poor horses, while B's losses may have been against good ones in which case past record will be a very poor clue as to the race outcome. Other factors will include the ability of the respective jockeys, the weather conditions, and so on. In a striking study, Ceci and Liker (1986) showed that expertise at predicting the outcome of such races can develop even in individuals of low intelligence (as measured by IQ) and can be based on extraordinarily complex decision rules which take account of numerous cues, with the cues often interacting with each other. How can such learning be accomplished?

The goal in this chapter is to describe developments over the last few years in our understanding of learning in decision problems and the way this has influenced theories of decision making. The review, however, will be conceptual rather than historical. Learning models now exist which encompass an enormous range of empirical phenomena. Of course, the horse-race scenario is just one of a potentially endless catalogue of examples which range from complex medical, financial and legal decision learning at one extreme, to the basic ability which all of us possess to make category decisions about unfamiliar objects or situations: recognizing an object as a chair, or a facial expression as an example of jealousy involve learning about subtle cues and combining them to make a decision.

It will be useful in this chapter to focus on a simple choice situation, essentially the same as the 'money-machine' described in Chapter 10, in which an individual is faced with a repeated choice between two alternatives or commodities, A_1 and A_2. On each trial A_1 is the correct choice with probability $p(A_1)$ and A_2 is correct with probability $p(A_2)$. Often (but not always) it will be the case that the options are exclusive and only one alternative is correct, that is $p(A_1) = 1 - p(A_2)$. If the correct alternative is selected, a reward or reinforcer is delivered. This basic set-up distils the key decision-learning aspects of numerous real-life choice situations. Examples would be a doctor choosing between two alternative diagnoses for a patient, with the reinforcer being the alleviation of the patient's symptoms, or a financial expert choosing whether to buy or sell a particular stock, with the reinforcer being financial gain or loss.

The starting point for understanding how learning proceeds in such situations is the so-called *linear* reinforcement learning model of Bush and Mosteller (1955), which serves as a parent of almost all subsequent models (see Bower, 1994, for a historical overview; Yechiam & Busemeyer, 2005, describe recent developments and tests of this model). What we would like to know is how the individual's probability of choosing A_1 on trial t, which we denote $P(A_1)_t$, is related to the actual probability $p(A_1)$ of A_1 being the correct choice. The basic idea is simple: if A_1 is chosen and rewarded, then there should be a small increment to the probability of it being emitted on the next trial, and this increment depends on how far the probability is from a value of 1 (if $P(A_1)_t$ is close to zero on the current trial, the increment should be larger than if it is already close to 1). Conversely, if A_1 is chosen but not rewarded, then there should be a small decrement to the probability of it being chosen on the next trial. Specifically, in this model it is assumed that

$$P(A_1)_t = P(A_1)_{t-1} + \lambda[1 - P(A_1)_{t-1}]$$

on rewarded or correct trials and

$$P(A_1)_t = (1 - \lambda)\, P(A_1)_{t-1}$$

on non-reinforced or incorrect trials, where λ is a learning-rate parameter which is assumed to vary from task to task and from one person to another. The probability of choosing A_2 is simply $1 - P(A_1)_t$. These two equations can be rewritten as a single one

$$P(A_1)_t = P(A_1)_{t-1} + \lambda[d - P(A_1)_{t-1}] \tag{1}$$

in which d codes the magnitude of the reinforcer: $d = 1$ on rewarded trials and $d = 0$ on non-rewarded ones. Note that although $p(A_1)$ does not appear in this equation, it is nonetheless the case that it influences the evolution of $P(A_1)$. It does so via determining the distribution of d across trials, with d in turn influencing the individual's behaviour.

The simplicity and elegance of this model masks a deceptively broad degree of empirical power. Note, first, that the model captures basic properties of rewarded choice. Assuming that the individual guesses on the first trial, chooses A_1 and is rewarded, then $P(A_1)$ is incremented and A_1 accordingly becomes the more likely choice on the next trial. This will continue, with $P(A_1)$ approaching 1, until reward is omitted, at which point $P(A_1)$ is reduced and choice of A_1 becomes slightly less likely (choice of A_2 becoming correspondingly more likely). With repeated trials, it can be shown that the asymptotic value of $P(A_1)$ is $p(A_1)$, the true probability of a reinforcer on trials on which A_1 is chosen. If the alternatives are exclusive $[p(A_1) = 1 - p(A_2)]$, then the asymptotic likelihood of selecting A_2 is $p(A_2)$. The learning rule therefore allows the individual to track the true reward probabilities, homing in on a pattern of behavioural allocation which perfectly matches the true probabilities. If these happen to change during the course of learning, the rule will allow adaptation to the new probabilities with the speed of adaptation being governed by the parameter λ.

Fifteen or so years after the introduction of the linear model, Rescorla and Wagner (1972) introduced a small but important modification. They proposed that the primary goal of mathematical models of learning is not to predict response probabilities per se, but internal association strengths or weights. It is a person's belief about an association between an action and an outcome that we want to understand, rather than the superficial manifestation of that belief. After all, many factors having nothing to do with learning (such as one's level of motivation) will determine whether a response is made. Whereas response probability is a purely behavioural descriptor, the idea of a weight is intended to refer to an internal mental construct something like the preference for choosing A_1.

Hence Rescorla and Wagner rewrote the model with weights, w, replacing response probabilities. With this change, it is easier to see how the model incorporates one of the truly great discoveries of modern cognitive and biological psychology, namely the idea that learning is driven by a process of error-correction or gradient-descent. This insight was hit upon independently by a number of researchers in different fields but credit is usually given to Widrow and Hoff (1960). The model computes an error in the sense that the critical term $[d - P(A_1)]$, now written as $(d - w_1)$, represents the error or discrepancy between the actual outcome of a learning episode, d, and the person's expectation of that outcome, w_1. The idea therefore is that learning should proceed via the very elementary process of trying to minimize this error, and the linear model achieves this by adjusting w across trials. Another way of thinking about this is that learning always moves in the steepest direction down a gradient towards a point which minimizes the discrepancy between expectancy and outcome. An enormous amount is now known about the computation of error signals in the brain in terms of the neuroanatomy of the reward and error-calculation systems (Schultz & Dickinson, 2000). Signals can be detected in brain-imaging studies which function exactly as expected on the basis of error-detection (Fletcher et al., 2001).

As noted above, the asymptotic pattern of behavioural allocation in the model perfectly matches the true reward probabilities. Unfortunately, this means that the model predicts *probability matching*, which we briefly introduced in Chapter 10. As we will see in the next section, this is a serious problem with the model. It can be remedied, however, by a further modification which greatly expands its explanatory scope.

PROBABILITY MATCHING

Imagine you are in Caesar's Palace and simultaneously playing two slot machines. You feed coins into each machine, pull the levers, watch the reels spin, and occasionally win. You notice that the machine on the left pays off more regularly than the one on the right. In terms of the amounts you feed into each machine, what should you do? A striking violation of rational choice theory is commonly observed in simple repeated binary choice tasks like this in which a payoff is available with higher probability given one response than another. In such tasks people often tend to 'match' probabilities: that is to say, they allocate their responses to the two options in proportion to their relative payoff probabilities. In the slot machine example, this amounts to feeding money into the machines in proportion to how often they are paying out. Suppose that a payout of fixed size is given with probability $P(L) = .7$ for choosing the left machine and with probability $P(R) = .3$ for choosing the one on the right. Probability matching refers to behaviour in which coins are inserted into the left machine on about 70% of trials and into the right one on about 30%. In fact, the optimal thing to do is to put all your money into the higher-paying machine.

This is easy to see. After an initial period of experimentation and assuming that the payoff probabilities are stationary (they don't systematically change over time), the best strategy for *each separate decision* is to select the machine associated with the higher probability of payoff. On any trial, the expected payoff for choosing the left machine is higher than the expected payoff for choosing the right one. There is never a time at which the expected payoff is higher for the lower-yielding machine. Even if the payoff probabilities are very close (say .31 versus .29), it is still irrational to put *any* money into the lower-yielding machine (except to explore its payoff behaviour).

Choice behaviour in this sort of game has been studied in an enormous number of experiments and demonstrations of probability matching are very robust (in the statistics literature these situations are called *bandit problems* by analogy with slot machines). For instance, in Neimark and Shuford's (1959) study, one response alternative was correct on 67% of trials and the other on 33%, and at the end of 100 trials participants were choosing the former on about 67% of trials. However, there are also many studies reporting 'over-matching' – that is, a tendency to choose the option with the higher probability of payoff with probability closer to 1.0. In Edwards' (1961) study, for example, participants' asymptotic choice probability for a response that had a payoff probability of .7 was .83.

The fact that participants fail to maximize their payoffs in these choice tasks has attracted the interest of many theorists concerned with the implications of this phenomenon for rational choice theory. Thus the Nobel Prize-winning economist Kenneth Arrow (1958, p. 14) noted that:

> The remarkable thing about this is that the asymptotic behavior of the individual, even after an indefinitely large amount of learning, is not the optimal behavior . . . We have here an experimental situation which is essentially of an economic nature in the sense of seeking to achieve a maximum of expected reward, and yet the individual does not in fact, at any point, even in a limit, reach the optimal behavior.

What is particularly striking is that participants fail to maximize despite the apparent simplicity of the problem facing them. Keeping track of payoff probabilities across two response options should hardly tax working memory, nor would one expect the comparison of these probabilities to be very demanding. Moreover, unlike many examples of apparently irrational choice behaviour, such as preference reversals, participants make repeated choices and receive a steady flow of feedback from their behaviour, which should provide a strong impetus to help them find the optimal choice strategy.

In response to this somewhat pessimistic perspective, a number of objections can be raised to the conclusion that people inherently behave irrationally in these probability-learning tasks. First, many studies used sequences that were not truly random (i.e. not independent and identically distributed) and this often means that the optimal strategy is no longer to choose one option with probability 1.0 (see Fiorina, 1971). Secondly, quite a large number of studies used either non-monetary outcomes or else payoffs of such low monetary value that the difference in expected cumulative earnings from maximizing compared to matching is negligible, and there is some evidence that monetary payoffs promote responding that is more nearly optimal (see Vulkan, 2000). Thirdly, given participants' common suspicion about psychological experiments, they may be reluctant to believe that the payoff probabilities are constant and may seek sequential dependencies and predictable patterns across trials (Peterson & Ulehla, 1965; Wolford et al., 2004). Fourthly, almost all studies have reported group rather than individual-participant data, with the obvious danger that probability matching at the group level masks wide variations at the individual-participant level.

How does all this relate to the linear model? As mentioned earlier, that model predicts matching, and early studies which appeared to demonstrate matching were therefore taken as supportive of the model. But demonstrations of overmatching, and the demonstrations of maximizing we describe below, clearly present a challenge to the model.

Friedman (1998, p. 941) asserted that that 'every choice "anomaly" can be greatly diminished or entirely eliminated in appropriately structured learning environments'. This appears to be the case with probability matching. Shanks, Tunney and McCarthy (2002) presented evidence against the pessimistic conclusion that people's natural behaviour in probability-learning tasks is suboptimal. They explored simple probability-learning tasks in which large performance-related financial incentives were provided, together with meaningful and regular feedback, and extensive training in the hope of obtaining evidence that this particular choice anomaly, like others, can be eliminated. Participants were given an enormous number of learning trials (up to 1800 in one experiment). The results were fairly clear in demonstrating that large proportions of participants (about 70%) can maximize their payoffs when maximizing is defined as a run of at least 50 consecutive choices of the optimal response. Many participants quite comfortably exceeded this criterion. Each of the three factors mentioned above contributed to participants' ability to maximize: both feedback and payoffs affected the overall likelihood of exclusively choosing the best alternative, and stable performance was not reached until after many hundreds of trials.

In Chapter 10 we discussed the important contrast between decisions from description and decisions from experience. The evidence concerning probability matching described above comes entirely from experiments in which participants made decisions from experience – that is to say, they made repeated choices and received feedback on the outcomes of those choices and this permitted them to learn about the reward contingencies in the task. But it is natural to ask whether probability matching is found when people make decisions from description. Is this another situation in which we see a 'gap' between behaviour in described versus experienced versions of the same decision problem?

Surprisingly, probability matching is readily observed when people make decisions from description. Imagine that you are given the following problem:

> A die with 4 black faces and 2 white faces will be rolled 60 times. Before each roll you will be asked to predict which colour (black or white) will show up once the die is rolled. You will be given one dollar for each correct prediction. Assume that you want to make as much money as possible. What strategy would you use in order to make as much money as possible by making the most correct predictions?
>
> A: Go by intuition, switching when there have been too many of one colour or the other.
> B: Predict the more likely colour (black) on most of the rolls but occasionally, after a long run of blacks, predict white.
> C: Make predictions according to the frequency of occurrence (4 of 6 for black and 2 of 6 for white). That is, predict twice as many blacks as whites.

D: Predict the more likely colour (black) on all of the 60 rolls.

E: Predict more black than white, but switching back and forth depending on 'runs' of one colour or the other.

Strategy D is the maximizing strategy, the correct answer in the sense that it will yield more correct predictions than any of the other strategies. It will yield around 40 correct predictions (4/6 × 60), a level that cannot be exceeded given the randomness of the outcomes. Strategy C is the matching strategy and is expected to yield only around (4/6 × 4/6 × 60) + (2/6 × 2/6 × 60) = 33 correct predictions, because whenever a white outcome is predicted there is only a 1 in 3 probability that it will occur. Such predictions are 'wasted' because a black outcome is twice as likely. Yet people seem to find this problem quite difficult: Newell and Rakow (2007) for example found that a majority of their participants chose Strategy C. Why is this?

Subsequent research (e.g. Newell et al., 2013) has examined two factors which seem to be important. Without being explicitly encouraged to consider different ways of responding, a proportion of participants simply fail to realize that maximizing is the optimal response, and so are seduced into responding in a way that is 'representative' of the probabilities underlying the task. When a hint is provided to explicitly contrast the matching and maximizing strategies, and to consider how frequently each would pay off, some participants are pushed towards maximizing. This is consistent with the idea that maximizing simply does not come to mind spontaneously as a valid and potent strategy.

Newell and Rakow (2007) observed a second striking influence on behaviour. They gave participants the scenario above, but also allowed some participants to see the outcome of each roll after making their prediction. This therefore yields a hybrid choice problem combining a decision from both description (the scenario above) and experience (outcome feedback). This led to an increasing rate of maximizing across the trials. This facilitative effect of feedback was observed despite the feedback being completely uninformative, and therefore normatively irrelevant – the die was fair, the probabilities were stationary and the relevant outcome probabilities were already precisely known before any feedback was received.

The finding that feedback nonetheless influenced the rate of maximizing is puzzling, because it suggests that people only gradually 'learn' to choose optimally in a task that (normatively) requires no learning. Feedback seems to trigger a trial-by-trial search for alternative choice strategies that helps at least some participants discover the maximizing strategy. Importantly, this period of discovery takes time; the effect of outcome feedback took many trials to emerge.

THE LINEAR MODEL

Returning to the linear model, it is clear that the ability of people to maximize under appropriate conditions is a problematic result as the model necessarily predicts matching. This can be handled, however, by assuming a non-linear transformation of beliefs into behaviour. In terms of weights, the model is:

$$w_t = w_{t-1} + \lambda(d - w_{t-1}) \tag{2}$$

and we now explicitly incorporate a separate decision function to translate weights into behaviour:

$$P(A_1)_t = 1 / [1 + \exp(-\theta w_t)] \tag{3}$$

In this equation, θ is a scaling parameter. If θ is small (<1), responding is predicted to be quite close to probability matching, but provided θ is sufficiently large, maximizing is predicted since $P(A_1)$ follows a step function.

This, then, is the essence of the linear model. It has been remarkably influential in the history of learning research stretching back over more than 30 years. The remainder of the chapter attempts in a non-technical way, first, to show how it can be expanded to deal with situations involving multiple predictive cues, and secondly, to highlight some of the ways in which additional processes might need to be added to construct a more complete model of decision learning.

Choices informed by multiple cues

The classic probability-learning task is one of the most stripped-down decision problems it is possible to imagine and hence omits numerous features of significance in natural decision making. In real life we are rarely confronted with exactly the same problem repeatedly; instead, there are usually cues which vary from occasion to occasion and which give us information about the likely correct choice at that particular moment. A stock analyst, for instance, does not make a decision on whether or not to purchase a stock simply on the basis of past history of success with that stock: he or she takes into account numerous cues such as the overall economic climate, the company's current financial position, and so on, some of which increase the analyst's belief that the stock will increase in value and others of which predict that it will decrease. Decision making therefore needs to be situated within a framework for determining the role that such cues have on behaviour. The simple situation we have considered thus far needs to be generalized to include the informational role of such cues. In Chapter 3 we introduced multiple-cue tasks in the context of the lens model framework for thinking about the stages involved in judgment, but now we examine the specific learning mechanisms underlying performance in these situations.

Research on probability matching dwindled considerably after the mid-1970s, but since a seminal article by Gluck and Bower (1988), a growing number of studies have used versions of a multiple-cue probability-learning

(MCPL) task to examine rational choice in probability-learning situations. In the prototypical experiment resembling the horse-race example described earlier, participants are presented with a cue or set of cues which vary from trial to trial and which signal independent reinforcement probabilities for the choice alternatives. For example, in one condition of a study by Myers and Cruse (1968), one cue signalled that left was correct with probability .85 and right with probability .15, while another cue signalled probabilities of .15 and .85 for left and right, respectively.

In a common cover story, participants imagine themselves to be medical practitioners making disease diagnoses about a series of patients. Each patient presents with some combination of the presence or absence of each of four conditionally independent symptoms (e.g. stomach cramps, discoloured gums) and is either suffering or not suffering from a disease. Thus each symptom pattern can be described by a set of 1's and 0's referring to whether each symptom is present or absent. The person's task is to predict whether the disease is present ($d = 1$) or absent ($d = 0$) for each of many such patients, receiving outcome feedback (the actual value of d) on each trial. The structure of the task is such that for each of the possible symptom patterns there is some fixed probability that patients with that pattern have the disease and the complementary probability that they have no disease. The standard probability-learning experiments reviewed in the last section can be thought of as special cases of this sort of task in which the number of symptoms (cues) is zero.

To maximize the number of correct diagnoses, participants should always choose the outcome (disease or no disease) that has been more frequently associated with that particular symptom pattern. Just as with the basic probability-matching problem, there has been a lot of debate about whether people are capable of achieving optimal performance or whether instead they are inevitably drawn towards suboptimal decisions. Recent evidence has tended to paint a more encouraging picture with behaviour approaching – if not actually reaching – optimality so long as enough learning periods are included and informative feedback and significant incentives are provided.

The linear model can be applied fairly straightforwardly to MCPL tasks. All that is required is an algorithm for specifying how the propensity or weight w for each of the various choice alternatives varies as a function of the set of cues present on a given occasion. Suppose again that there are two choice options, A_1 and A_2. Picking up on another key proposal introduced by Rescorla and Wagner (1972), Gluck and Bower (1988) proposed that the weight for one of these options is the linear sum of the weights of the individual cues for that alternative, $\sum w$. That is to say, the total propensity to choose alternative A_1 is simply the sum of the weights for A_1 of all the cues present on that occasion. This combined weight is converted to a response probability via the same rule as previously:

$$P(A_1)_t = 1 \; / \; [1 + \exp(-\theta \textstyle\sum w_i)] \tag{4}$$

where θ is a scaling parameter. The only difference between this and equation 3 is that we now sum all the weights of the separate cues. As before, if θ is small (<1), responding is predicted to be quite close to probability matching, but provided θ is sufficiently large, maximizing is predicted. Lastly, each individual weight is updated by the original linear rule, that is:

$$w_t = w_{t-1} + \lambda(d - \Sigma w_{t-1}) \tag{5}$$

where λ is a learning-rate parameter and d is the reinforcement (1 if the payoff is positive, 0 otherwise). Figure 12.1 provides a graphical illustration of the contributions of the cue weights to choice between the alternatives.

The linear model bears a very important relationship to the classic cue-integration model of MCPL (Juslin, Olsson & Olsson, 2003). This 'normative' regression model proposes that people adopt a linear independence assumption (i.e. that the outcome is a linear function of the input values). The linear model is essentially a learning model for this cue-integration approach (Stone, 1986).

Despite its simplicity, the linear model of MCPL has been strikingly successful in predicting decision behaviour in laboratory learning experiments (although, as we discuss below, it also faces several problems). In a sense this success should not be surprising as the model is a very close relative indeed of a model, the Rescorla–Wagner (RW) theory, which has been enormously influential in another domain of simple learning, namely Pavlovian conditioning. The linear model can be thought of as extending the RW theory to situations in which associations are concurrently learned between multiple cues and outcomes rather

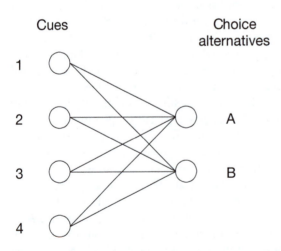

Figure 12.1 Application of the linear model to a multiple-cue probability-learning (MCPL) situation. Each cue possesses weights for each of the choice alternatives and these weights are incremented and decremented as a function of the error term in Equation 5.

than to a single cue (the conditioned stimulus) and outcome (the unconditioned stimulus), and the reason why Gluck and Bower's (1988) study was so influential was because it drew attention to this connection.

Gluck and Bower introduced the medical decision-making task described above in which hypothetical patients present with some combination of four symptoms (bloody nose, stomach cramps, puffy eyes, discoloured gums). The participant's task was to decide for each patient whether he or she had fictitious disease R or C, and having made a choice, feedback was provided (each patient had one disease or the other). Participants saw 250 such patients and thus had extensive opportunity to learn the basic probabilistic structure of the task; that is, the probabilities of the two diseases given each symptom combination. One symptom was particularly associated with disease C, another with disease R, while the other two fell in between. These probabilities, however, were never 0 or 1, so, as in many real decision problems, participants could never be 100% correct. The presence and absence of each of 4 symptoms means there were 16 different patterns in total, but Gluck and Bower eliminated cases in which no symptoms were present, leaving 15 patterns in the experiment.

Figure 12.2 shows participants' choices of disease R across the final 50 cases. Each symptom pattern is denoted by a string of 0's and 1's, where 0 means the symptom is absent and 1 means that it is present; hence pattern 1010 means the patient in question had a bloody nose and puffy eyes but not stomach cramps or discoloured gums. The figure shows the true objective probability of the disease together with participants' mean choice of the disease and the predicted probability from the pattern model with θ set to a value of 3.2. This value implies fairly deterministic responding in this situation; later in the chapter we will consider some of the determinants of the value of this parameter. It is clear not only that participants were quite good at this task – choosing the alternatives in approximate accord with the true probabilities – but also that the model did a good job of predicting their behaviour. This fit was supported in a number of follow-up studies.

Several of these studies also examined the role of base rates in learning about cue weights. Base rate refers to the overall probability of an event within a population, independently of any cues that might signal the presence of that event. As we saw in Chapter 6, much research has been concerned with evaluating people's sensitivity to base rates (Koehler, 1996).

Gluck and Bower's study incorporated a base-rate manipulation and this allowed a strikingly simple but compelling prediction of the linear model to be tested. In the basic design employed by Gluck and Bower the two diseases did not occur equally often: one was much more common than the other (indeed the labels R and C mean 'rare' and 'common'). This allows a situation to be created where a particular symptom s is paired with these diseases with equal probability:

$$P(C/s) = P(R/s)$$
$$= .5$$

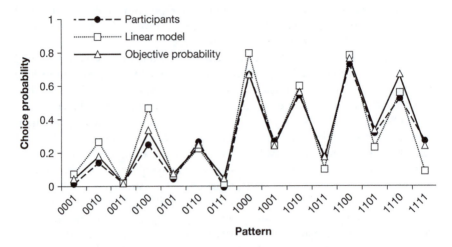

Figure 12.2 Results of Gluck and Bower's (1988) simulation using the linear model.
The graph shows the objective probability of disease R given each
symptom pattern. These are denoted by a string of 0's and 1's representing
the 4 symptoms, where 1 means the symptom is present and 0 means that it
is absent. Also shown is the mean probability with which participants chose
the disease and the corresponding probability predicted from the linear
model.

Adapted from Table 1 of Gluck, M. A., & Bower, G. H. (1988). From conditioning to category
learning: An adaptive network model. *Journal of Experimental Psychology: General, 117*, 227–247.

but where the probabilities of these diseases in the absence of the symptom
are not equal. For instance, in a study by Shanks (1990) they were:

$$P(C/\sim s) = .86,$$

$$P(R/\sim s) = .14$$

From a normative point of view, when seeing a patient who only has symptom
s, the two diseases are equally likely. However, participants did not choose
them with equal frequency: instead they chose the rare disease on about 63%
of occasions in Shanks' (1990) experiment.

Importantly, this is precisely what the linear model predicts. Why is this?
The reason is that although the rare and common diseases were equally likely
given the target symptom, this symptom was in another sense a much better
predictor of the rare disease because the latter occurred only rarely in the absence
of this symptom. An analogy may help to explain this. Think of the influence
of a particular player on the success of a football team. Objectively, the team
is as likely to win as to lose when he plays. However, when he is not playing,
the team is overwhelmingly more likely to lose than to win. It seems clear that
the player is having an influence on the success of the team, raising *P*(win)
from a low level when he is absent to a much higher level (.5) when he is

playing. What Gluck and Bower (1988), Shanks (1990), Nosofsky, Kruschke and McKinley (1992) and others found was that such a situation induces a decision 'error' whereby people tend to select the event which is rarer overall (winning in this example, disease R in the laboratory experiments) when the cue is present despite the fact that on such occasions the two outcomes are objectively equally likely.

Another illustration of the same effect was provided by Kruschke (1996). The basic design is shown in Table 12.1. Each row in the table can be thought of as representing a case such as a patient. The cues across the top refer to cues such as medical symptoms. It can be seen in the table that 3 out of 4 patients have the common disease C1 while one has the rare disease R1. Thus the base rate of C1 is higher than that of R1. All patients have symptom X which is therefore unpredictive. In contrast symptom Y is a perfect predictor of C1. The critical symptom is Z which occurs with equal prevalence in the two diseases. Kruschke trained participants on this structure by showing them hypothetical patient records indicating the symptoms and requiring them to predict the correct disease prior to feedback. After many such training trials Kruschke presented the critical case which comprised a patient presenting with just symptom Z. As is clear from the table, the probabilities of diseases C1 and R1 are both .5 in patients with this symptom, yet Kruschke's participants, like those in Gluck and Bower's probabilistic version of this design, were biased to choose disease R1, preferring this nearly six times as often as C1.

The pattern model predicts the base-rate neglect result in Table 12.1 because it allocates weight to a cue as a function of its predictive value, not merely as a function of the probability of the outcome given the cue. Formal analyses of the linear model (e.g. Stone, 1986) have documented its relationship to statistical methods such as multiple linear regression, in which cues are weighted in accordance with their partial correlations with the outcome event. Clearly the presence of the footballer in the example above is correlated with winning and for this reason would be chosen by a statistical model, such as regression, as a predictor of the outcome.

Table 12.1 Design of Kruschke's (1996) experiment

	Symptoms		
X	Y	Z	*Disease*
1	1	0	C1
1	1	0	C1
1	1	1	C1
1	0	1	R1

The table illustrates a situation in which a cue (Z) is objectively equally associated with two alternatives (C1 and R1) but where one of the alternatives (C1) is more common than the other in the absence of that cue. Presented with cue Z alone, people tend to choose alternative R1 over C1.

CHOICE RULES

As we have already mentioned, despite the fact that probability matching is often observed in simple choice tasks, people can be induced to maximize or nearly maximize their payoffs via selecting only the higher-probability response alternative. Within the linear model this is captured by variation of the θ parameter. Conditions in which participants probability match are characterized by a low value of θ whereas ones in which they maximize are described by setting θ to a higher value. But is there any direct evidence concerning the psychological reality of this response determinism parameter? In the present section we elaborate on the theoretical interpretation of this aspect of the linear model.

Friedman et al. (1995), Kitzis et al. (1998) and Friedman and Massaro (1998) reported some important studies using multiple-cue choice tasks which considerably clarify our understanding of the factors that might drive participants towards more nearly optimal performance, or in other words, which might influence the value of the θ parameter. In their initial study (Friedman et al., 1995), very clear probability matching was obtained with correlations between asymptotic choice and actual probabilities in excess of .88. In a later study (Friedman & Massaro, 1998; Kitzis et al., 1998), however, the payoff conditions and provision of information about prior relevant cases were systematically varied. Some groups were provided both trial-by-trial and cumulatively with a score based on their accuracy, others were in addition paid on a performance-related basis, and others received neither the score nor monetary payoff. An interesting aspect of the score information was that it included information about how well an ideal Bayesian expert would have done, thus allowing participants to see how close or far their performance was from that achievable by the optimal but unspecified algorithm. Orthogonal to the score and payoff manipulation, some groups were able to access on each trial a summary table providing information about the outcomes of previous cases with the same pattern of symptoms as the current patient. Other groups did not have access to this information.

Friedman and Massaro (1998) found that the provision of history information pushed participants significantly closer to maximizing. The score conditions had a similar beneficial effect, but providing a payoff (somewhat surprisingly) had no such effect. The effects of providing a score, however, strongly suggest that one reason why probability matching occurs in many situations is because participants have not been adequately motivated to search for the optimal response strategy, and that when appropriate outcome feedback is provided, maximizing might be observed.

A natural interpretation of these findings in terms of the θ parameter is that the provision of history and score information increases the effective value of θ. In the study by Shanks et al. (2002), both feedback and monetary payoffs increased the likelihood of maximizing, so these also appear to increase the extent of response determinism. In sum, the linear model seems to fit the results of these studies quite well provided that allowance is made for variations in the degree of response determinism.

SUMMARY

The basic features of repeated decision learning with feedback are captured by the example of playing slot machines and receiving occasional payoffs. Probability matching, commonly observed in such situations as well as in one-shot decisions, is suboptimal but can be overcome when individuals are given enough feedback and adequate incentives.

This scenario can be extended by incorporating cues which vary from moment to moment and which signal changes in the payoff conditions. For such situations, a formidable body of normative theoretical and statistical work has attempted to describe the ideal learning process, whereas psychological research has concentrated on descriptive models of actual behaviour (the linear model and its variants). Actually, the distinction between normative and descriptive approaches is quite narrow here because the linear model (under certain assumptions) is equivalent to the statistical method of multiple linear regression, a common technique for identifying which cues are predictive of some criterion. The linear model captures many striking properties of people's choice behaviour.

Suggested further reading

- Gluck, M. A., & Bower, G. H. (1988). From conditioning to category learning: An adaptive network model. *Journal of Experimental Psychology: General, 117*, 227–247. Seminal application of the linear model to multiple-cue decision making.
- Koehler, D. J., & James, G. (2014). Probability matching, fast and slow. *The Psychology of Learning and Motivation, 61*, 103–132. An up-to-date assessment of the implications of probability matching, from a two-systems perspective.
- Yechiam, E., & Busemeyer, J. R. (2005). Comparison of basic assumptions embedded in learning models for experience-based decision making. *Psychonomic Bulletin & Review, 12*, 387–402. Extensive discussion of learning models for decision making.

13 Optimality and expertise

Chapter highlights

- A discussion of how the linear model can be extended to more complex dynamic tasks
- Introduction to exemplar theories as an alternative to associative approaches to learning in decision problems
- What characterizes expertise and how do experts and novices differ in their judgments?
- A discussion of naturalistic decision making: how are decisions made by experts in their domains of expertise?

At the heart of the debate on the nature of human rationality is the question of whether people are intrinsically bound to commit decision errors or whether in contrast they can make optimal decisions. In the context of our emphasis on the relationship between learning and choice, this translates into a question about the long-term outcome of exposure to a decision environment. With sufficient exposure can people always find the optimal decision strategy or do they inevitably and unavoidably, even after extensive experience, fall prey to decision errors? Proponents of both sides in this debate have been able to marshal powerful evidence to support their views. The present chapter considers these important issues.

HOW CLOSE CAN A DECISION MAKER GET TO OPTIMALITY?

Perhaps the simplest question is what happens in the long run when people are exposed to simple choice tasks of the sort we focused on in the previous chapter. We have already seen that in binary problems like the slot machine examples, people can achieve near-optimal behaviour, that is to say, maximizing (Shanks et al., 2002). A number of factors have to come into alignment for this to happen (e.g. the incentives must be adequate), but the evidence suggests that there is no intrinsic limit to people's competence in simple binary-choice tasks.

What about multiple-cue tasks in which cues vary from trial to trial and signal changes in the likelihood of reward? Here there is less evidence, but again there are persuasive examples of optimal behaviour. The work of Gluck and Bower has already been discussed in the previous chapter. In the studies by Friedman et al. (1995) and Kitzis et al. (1998) participants saw cue patterns containing binary information about medical symptoms and on the basis of these cues judged which of two hypothetical diseases a patient had. Friedman and his colleagues compared decision behaviour across 240 learning trials, taking a Bayesian model as the yardstick for optimal behaviour. This model essentially assumes that a record is kept of the frequency with which each cue is associated with each outcome and then combines information across the cues present on each trial. The striking outcome was that behaviour approximated the predictions of the Bayesian model remarkably well.

Another way of specifying what counts as 'optimal' is to use linear regression. In tasks with a dichotomous outcome, participants predict the outcome on a trial-by-trial basis and learning performance is measured in terms of correct predictions. Standard analyses then average across both individuals and trials to produce a mean percentage correct for the whole task. While this kind of approach is useful for broad comparisons across different tasks, it does not provide much information about the learning process. It ignores the possibility of individual differences in judgment or learning strategies, and that these strategies may evolve or change during the course of the task. As we have already seen in Chapter 3, a richer approach to the analysis of the judgment process is provided by the lens model framework. This is founded on the idea that people construct internal cognitive models that reflect the probabilistic structure of their environment. A central tenet of this approach is that people's judgmental processes should be modelled at the individual level before any conclusions can be drawn by averaging across individuals. This is done by inferring an individual's judgment policy from the pattern of judgments that they make across a task. More specifically, a judge's policy is captured by computing a multiple linear regression of their judgments onto the cue values across all the trials in the task. The resultant beta-coefficients for each cue are then interpreted as the weights that the judge has given to that cue in reaching their judgments (cue–utilization weights).

Each judge's policy model can be assessed against the actual structure of the task environment. This is done by computing a parallel multiple linear regression for the actual outcomes experienced by the judge onto the cue values (again across all task trials). The resultant beta-coefficients are interpreted as the objective cue weights for the judge's environment. If all the participants have been exposed to the same environment then the objective cue weights revealed by this computation will be the same for everyone. However, this technique allows for the possibility that different individuals experience different environmental structures. A judge's policy (their cue–utilization weights) can then be compared with the objective weights to see how well they have learned the task environment. This is illustrated by a lens model in which one side of the lens represents the structure of the environment, and the other side represents an individual's cue utilization (see Figure 3.1).

The lens model framework thus provides a means to analyse individual judgmental processes. However, although it avoids the loss of information incurred by averaging over participants, it still loses information by averaging over trials. It fails to capture the dynamics of a learning task – in terms of both potential changes in the environment and potential changes in a judge's policy. In particular, the reliance on global weights ignores the fact that both the actual weights experienced by the judge, and the judge's own subjective weights, may vary across the course of the task. This is a problem even when the under-lying structure of the environment is stationary (as it usually is in multiple-cue tasks), because the cue-outcome patterns that someone actually experiences (and therefore the environmental weights) may not be representative of the underlying probabilistic structure, especially early on in a task. Analysing indi-vidual judgment policies just in terms of their averaged performance across all the trials ignores this possibility, and as a consequence may underestimate someone's performance. Moreover, it overlooks the possibility that the person's judgment policy may change over trials, and that such changes may track variations in the actual environment.

A related shortcoming is that these global analyses assume that the judge has a perfect memory for all task trials, and that they treat earlier trials in the same way as later ones. But both of these assumptions are questionable – people may base their judgments on a limited window of trials, and may place more emphasis on recent trials (Slovic & Lichtenstein, 1971).

The need for dynamic models of optimal performance is now widely recognized, and a variety of different models have been proposed. A natural extension to the lens model (and very closely related to the linear model) is the 'rolling regression' technique introduced by Kelley and Friedman (2002) to model individual learning in economic forecasting. In their task, participants learned to forecast the value of a continuous criterion (the price of orange juice futures) on the basis of two continuous-valued cues (local weather hazard and foreign supply). Individual learning curves were constructed by computing a series of regressions (from forecasts to cues) across a moving window of consecutive trials. For example, for a window size of 160 trials, the first regres-sion is computed for trials 1 to 160, the next for trials 2 to 161, and so on. This generates trial-by-trial estimates (from trial 160 onwards) for an individual's cue-utilization weights, and thus provides a dynamic profile of the individual's learning (after trial 160).

Each individual learning profile is then compared with the profile of an 'ideal' learner exposed to the same trials. Regressions for each ideal learner are also computed repeatedly for a moving window of trials, but in this case the actual criterion values (prices) are regressed onto the cues. The estimates of the ideal learner thus correspond to the best possible estimates of the objective cue weights for each window of trials. The rolling regression technique thus provides dynamic models of both actual and ideal learners, and permits trial-by-trial comparisons between the two as the task progresses. For example, in analysing the results in their orange juice task, Kelley and Friedman (2002) compared actual and ideal learning curves to show that while ideal learners converged quickly to the objective weights, participants learned these weights more slowly, and their final predictions tended to over-estimate the objective cue weights.

Lagnado, Newell et al. (2006) applied the rolling regression technique in a slightly more complex task in which participants learned to predict the weather (rainy/sunny) on the basis of four binary predictors. As with the orange juice task, participants learned in a manner that corresponded quite well to the optimal regression model, although their learning was somewhat slower and the final weights overshot the objective ones. This latter finding is consistent with probability maximizing, however. An individual who, on the basis of the regression weights, decides that a particular outcome is more than 50% likely and who then maximizes by selecting that outcome on every trial will appear to have extracted weights that are larger than the true regression weights. Such maximizing behaviour is of course captured by Equation 4 from Chapter 12.

Answering the question 'is human decision learning optimal?' requires first of all a specification of what an ideal learner would do. Bayesian and regression models, amongst others, provide one such set of yardsticks which can then be used in comparisons with human behaviour. Although much work needs to be done on this important question, the studies described above suggest that we should not be too pessimistic. In many quite difficult learning problems, people's decisions come close to converging with the optimal ones. Moreover, the optimal models we have briefly sketched link back nicely to the linear model: there are very close and deep relationships between learning models based on error-correction and rational statistical or Bayesian inference (McClelland, 1998; Stone, 1986).

CAN EXPERTS OVERCOME DECISION BIASES?

This perspective – that decision learning approximates optimal behaviour in the long run – implies that in real-world decision settings, experts should be much less susceptible to biases than non-experts. Several studies confirm this prediction. An enormous amount of research has examined expert decision making and although biases are often obtained, it is also true that experts seem less prone to such biases than non-experts. The tendency to ignore information about base rates (see Chapter 6) is largely eliminated in repeated-decision situations in which individuals have enough experience to become 'experts' (Goodie & Fantino, 1999). Proneness to hindsight bias – the tendency to distort one's estimate of the likelihood of an event as a result of knowing how it turned out – is markedly attenuated in experts (Hertwig, Fanselow & Hoffrage, 2003).

Another example relates to the 'sunk cost' effect, the irrational tendency we have to continue with a plan of action in which we have invested resources, despite the fact that it has become suboptimal. From a rational perspective, previous investment that has been irretrievably sunk should not influence one's current evaluations of the utilities of the different options, yet we all know that this bias is hard to avoid. The effect is sometimes also called the Concorde fallacy in honour of the supersonic jet. Long after it had become an economic white elephant, politicians in Britain and France continued to invest millions in the development of the airliner because they feared the political consequences of abandoning the project. Such a desire to appear consistent (or to avoid being inconsistent) is not in itself irrational, but that doesn't alter the fact that if one's only motivation is to make a good decision, then past investment should be discounted. Another way in which people sometimes justify sunk-cost reasoning is because of a desire not to waste resources already committed.

Importantly, there is evidence that the sunk-cost effect diminishes with expertise. Bornstein, Emler and Chapman (1999) asked medical experts (residents) or non-experts (undergraduates) to judge the attractiveness of various options in medical and non-medical settings. For instance, in a medical setting, participants were asked to decide what to do in the case of a patient prescribed a drug which was proving ineffective: either to stick with the treatment or discontinue it. In one case (high sunk cost) the patient was described as having purchased a supply of the drug for $400; in another case (low sunk cost) the supply cost $40.

For these medical decisions, the experts showed no sunk-cost effect: their choices were unaffected by the investment. This is heartening as it suggests that experience can help people to avoid decision biases. However, this only applies to the specific area of expertise. Bornstein et al. found that the experts and non-experts were equally prone to the sunk-cost effect in reasoning about non-medical scenarios. Arkes and Ayton (1999) argued that the effect does not occur in animals and that when it occurs in humans, it does so for a simple reason, namely people's keenness to adhere to a 'don't waste' rule. Resources that have already been invested in an option go to waste if a different option is selected, and people often find this disagreeable.

A related finding has been described by Christensen et al. (1995) in the context of the framing effect which we discussed in Chapters 1 and 9. This effect refers to the tendency for decisions to be influenced by the way in which they are couched. For example, when presented with scenarios, students are more willing to accept risk when a medical treatment is described in terms of a potential loss and less willing to accept risk when the very same treatment is described in terms of gain (Tversky & Kahneman, 1981). Yet, Christensen et al. reported that framing effects tend to be small and highly variable from one scenario to another when medical experts are asked to make choices relating to their domain of expertise.

Lastly, recall the evidence (described more fully in Chapter 9) that experts are better able than novices to avoid making preference reversals. List (2002) asked professional dealers in baseball cards and less-experienced collectors to value a 10-card bundle and a 13-card one which included the same 10 cards plus 3 inferior ones. The less-experienced collectors preferred the 10-card bundle when valuing the bundles in isolation but preferred the 13-card one when comparing them side by side. The professional dealers, in contrast, were able to avoid this irrational preference reversal.

LIMITATIONS OF THE LINEAR MODEL

Despite the many successes of the linear model as applied both to simple choice tasks and to more complex MCPL problems, there are some fairly serious difficulties which this model faces and which have been taken as the starting point for alternative approaches. Perhaps the simplest problem is caused by the fact that the propensity to choose alternative A is an increasing function in Equation 4 (Chapter 12) of the independent weights of the cues present on a given occasion.

It seems natural at first glance to assume that if two cues X and Y each have some positive weight for A – that is to say, they each imply that A is the likely correct choice – then the presence of both X and Y should increase the likelihood of choosing A over and above what would happen if only one cue were present. But it is trivial to set up a situation in which this would not be objectively correct. Suppose that cue X indicated that A will be reinforced as the correct choice, that cue Y signals the same, but that when X and Y are both present, A will be the incorrect choice. An example is provided by a classic experiment by Bitterman, Tyler and Elam (1955): humans and animals can readily learn discriminations in which two red stimuli are shown on some trials and reward depends on choosing the right-hand one, while on other trials, a pair of green stimuli is presented and reward is given for choosing the left-hand stimulus. Such a discrimination cannot be solved by the linear model because each element (red, green, left, right) should be equally associated with reinforcement.

The linear model is unable to deal with such situations because weights necessarily add together linearly (see Equation 4 in Chapter 12): no set of weights can be constructed which would point towards A in the presence of X or Y but not in the presence of X and Y (this is called an XOR problem). One way around this problem is to assume that in addition to learning direct associations between the outcome and the separate elements that make up the stimulus, intermediate representations of the stimulus can also be involved in associations with the outcome. This is the essence of connectionist models incorporating a layer of 'hidden' units that intervene between the input and output units, as shown in Figure 13.1.

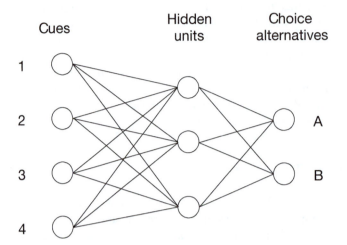

Figure 13.1 Architecture of a backpropagation model to a multiple-cue probability-learning (MCPL) situation. Each cue possesses weights, but instead of connecting directly with the choice alternatives, these are relayed via intermediate hidden units. Connections in both layers are incremented and decremented as a function of the error term shown in Equation 5 of Chapter 12.

One particular type of hidden–unit network has been extremely widely investigated and has been shown to have some very powerful properties. In such a 'backpropagation-of-error' network, the linear rule applies exactly as before except that it is refined in order to determine how much the input–hidden weights and the hidden–output weights should be changed on a given trial. The precise calculations are not critical here, but the key point is that the development of multi-layer networks using this generalized version of the linear model has provided a major contribution to recent connectionist modelling since phenomena such as the learning of non–linear classifications that are impossible for single-layer networks can be easily dealt with by multi-layer networks. This class of models has been enormously influential in cognitive psychology (Houghton, 2005; McClelland & Rumelhart, 1986; Rumelhart & McClelland, 1986).

In the context of decision making, neural network models based on the architecture shown in Figure 13.1 and using the backpropagation algorithm have been applied to many real-world problems. Some of these have involved medical decisions. A common technique has been to use databases of information on predictors of particular medical conditions and use these as training sets for network models. Databases have included predictors of heart disease, diabetes, hepatitis, psychiatric admission, back pain, and many more. In one application, for instance, Baxt (1990) trained a network on 356 cases relating to patients admitted to a hospital emergency department, which included 236 in which myocardial infarction was ultimately diagnosed and 120 in which it was not. Each case provided numerous predictors or cues such as the patient's age, past-history variables such as diabetes or high cholesterol, and test results such as blood pressure and electrocardiogram indicators. Half of the cases were used as training examples for the neural network, with this corpus being presented repeatedly to the model until the weights were stable, and the model was then tested on the remaining cases.

Baxt reported that previous decision models had achieved at best a detection rate of about 88% (patients with the condition correctly diagnosed as such) combined with a false alarm rate of 26% (patients without the condition incorrectly diagnosed as having it) and that this is about the level of accuracy achieved by expert physicians. In contrast, the neural net model achieved a detection rate of 92% and a false alarm rate of 4%. Bear in mind that this highly impressive level of performance is achieved on a sample of cases different from the ones used in training. Numerous similar studies have compared the success of neural network models on real datasets both against human performance and that of statistical models such as logistic regression.

Hence there is no question about the power of this sort of connectionist network for learning predictive relationships and applying this knowledge to make decisions. But the question remains, does it learn in the same way as humans? The fact that such models can outperform human experts hints that the answer might be 'no', and one reason for this seems to be their neglect of important processes concerned with selective attention. This has been taken into account in the construction of a powerful model called ALCOVE (Kruschke, 1992; Nosofsky & Kruschke, 1992), which is major alternative to standard backpropagation. Briefly, in models such as ALCOVE it is acknowledged that learning takes place at two levels: there is basic learning about the predictive utility of each cue (or configuration of cues), but there is also more generalized learning about how useful it is to attend to each cue. It is generally helpful to learn to attend more to those cues which have strong connections to an outcome, but learning to attend and learning the weight of a cue are not the same thing: one could ignore a cue – perhaps because it has not been useful in the past – that in fact is now highly predictive. Models which separate out these two types of learning have proven better able to capture aspects of decision learning than standard backpropagation models.

EXEMPLAR THEORIES

Up to this point, we have concentrated solely on associative approaches to decision learning. This family of models is based on the assumption that knowledge of the structure of a decision problem is captured by a set of weights connecting cues to choice alternatives, either directly (in the linear model) or indirectly (in multi-layer neural network models). Accordingly, such models construe the learning process as involving the updating of these associative weights on a case-by-case basis and it is almost universal that such updating is based on the sort of error term captured in Equation 5 in Chapter 12. An entirely different approach to decision making, in contrast, emphasizes memory processes rather than learning. So-called 'exemplar' models conceive of decisions as being based on retrieval of past cases from memory, with the decision being pulled towards more similar previous cases. The exemplar approach is also known in the machine learning literature as 'case-based' reasoning. Hence we turn now to a consideration of the successes of such models in simulating and predicting human performance. At the end of the section we discuss the relationship between connectionist and exemplar-based theories.

There is a wealth of evidence that exemplar or instance memorization plays a role in decision making. Much of this evidence comes from studies of categorization, a simple variety of decision making in which a person judges which of several potential categories an object belongs to. An illustration would be making a diagnostic decision in a medical context: on the basis of a set of indicators, a medical expert decides whether a patient belongs to the category of diabetic people, for instance. Indeed, several of the tasks discussed previously, such as that used in Gluck and Bower's (1988) study, are categorization tasks. Categorization research has shown that decisions are heavily influenced by similarity to previously seen cases. As discussed in Chapter 3, Brooks et al. (1991), for example, found that dermatologists were heavily influenced by prior cases in classifying skin disorders. A given disorder was more likely to be diagnosed if a similar case of that disorder had been seen previously, and this influence persisted across several weeks. Such facilitation was not induced by a dissimilar example of the disorder.

On the basis of evidence that memorized exemplars play a crucial role in category decision making, Medin and Schaffer (1978) proposed that a significant component of the mental representation of a category is simply a set of stored exemplars or instances. The mental representation of a category such as *bird* includes representations of the specific instances belonging to that category, each presumably connected to the label *bird*. In a category-decision learning experiment, the training instances are encoded along with their category assignment.

The exemplar view proposes that subjects encode the actual instances during training and base their classifications on the similarity between a test item and stored instances. When a test item is presented, it is as if a chorus of stored instances shout out how similar they are to the test item. Research has shown that this sort of conception of decision making can be very powerful, with complex sets of behaviour being well predicted by formal exemplar theories. Studies by Juslin and his colleagues have also explored factors which might promote instance-based versus cue-integration modes of decision learning. Juslin, Jones et al. (2003) used a task in which participants judged the toxicity of a secretion from a frog. Four binary cues (e.g. the frog's colour), differing in their predictive validity, allowed the level of toxicity to be judged. Juslin and his colleagues found that participants' performance was well reproduced by a version of the linear model when the feedback about toxicity provided on each trial was both binary (harmless/dangerous) and continuous-valued on a scale from 0 to 100 ('its toxicity is 40'). However, when only the binary feedback was provided, performance was better modelled by an exemplar process.

It thus appears as though people can employ different strategies for learning a repeated-choice decision problem: they can either abstract the cue weights according to the sort of process captured by the linear model, or they can memorize specific training exemplars. Other processes may be possible too. Juslin et al.'s work suggests that various features of the task, such as the type of feedback provided, may encourage one process or another (see also Juslin et al., 2008).

But perhaps there is another way to think about these findings. Rather than adopting a multiple-process account of learning, it may be appropriate to think of cue abstraction and exemplar memorization as emerging from a common mechanism. Indeed, the ALCOVE model briefly mentioned in the previous section is both an associative learning model – in that cue weights are incrementally adjusted according to an error-correcting learning algorithm – and an exemplar model, in that hidden units in the network represent specific training items. On this approach, it may be possible to subsume both types of process within a unitary, more general model. Whether Juslin et al.'s data can be adequately accounted for by ALCOVE is yet to be established but considerable effort is currently being put into trying to distinguish between multiple-system versus unitary models of decision learning (e.g. Maddox & Ashby, 2004; Newell, Dunn & Kalish, 2011; Nosofsky & Johansen, 2000).

EXPERTISE

The models of learning discussed so far in this chapter invariably predict improved performance with more and more experience and feedback. Thus it is natural to ask whether the general perspective they give for the development of expertise is empirically correct. We will not attempt to review here the very substantial literature on the development of expertise (which connects with many branches of psychology in addition to judgment and decision making, for instance memory and perception) but will briefly look more at the broad properties of expertise.

One way in which the performance of error-correcting models improves is via steadily increasing discrimination. In the early stages of learning, the same response is often given in response to different cue configurations. A naïve person trying to learn how to determine the sex of day-old chicks simply doesn't see differences between them (they all look alike) and hence can't discriminate between them. An expert, in contrast, instantly focuses on the features which tell them apart and hence is able to make different decisions in the face of quite similar objects (Biederman & Shiffrar, 1987). Error-correcting models capture this aspect of discrimination quite readily as feedback provides the driving force for a set of weights to be formed which is sensitive to small but potentially significant differences between objects. Selective attention to the most important attributes or features amplifies this effect.

Weiss and Shanteau (2003) have proposed that discrimination is only one of the critical ingredients of expertise. Another is consistency. An expert in marking student exams, for example, would give approximately the same mark to the same piece of work on two different occasions, whereas a novice, whose benchmarks are yet to develop fully, might give quite different marks. In an analysis of doctors, auditors and personnel selectors, Weiss and Shanteau showed that a measure which took both discrimination and consistency into account seemed to distinguish levels of expertise well. The importance of consistency is less well captured in formal models of decision learning, however. As we have couched them, these models would behave in the same way to the same input pattern on different occasions (except insofar as new learning might occur in the intervening period). To deal with this, these models would have to be supplemented by an account of performance error. The idea would be that the output of the linear model is combined with error to generate the observed behaviour, with this error diminishing in influence as the individual becomes more expert in the domain.

Yet a third feature of human expertise is its remarkable narrowness. A chess expert is unlikely to be outstanding at poker, the stock tips of an expert weather forecaster are probably not worth undue attention, and an outstanding golfer will probably be average at soccer. Research has consistently failed to find general skills or abilities which underlie expert performance. For instance, basic cognitive processes such as working memory, attention and learning speed are not *in general* better developed in experts. Put differently, becoming an expert does not entail an improvement in any of these basic processes (Ericsson, 1996). What does improve are the perceptual, memory and cognitive components that the task places demands on. Thus an expert chess player has a vastly superior memory and perceptual capacity for chess positions than a novice. Consistent with the linear model, becoming an expert does not intrinsically require the development of basic cognitive, perceptual or motoric processes – it is specific to the domain in question and the cues and outcomes intrinsic to that domain.

The sorts of laboratory learning experiments reviewed in this chapter induce expertise by their very nature. After many trials in which some decision is made and feedback provided, performance inevitably improves – the participant becomes more expert at that particular task.

But of course real experts have skills that go beyond simple learning, discrimination and consistency. They typically are better teachers than non-experts, they can reflect more deeply on the structure of the environment in which their expertise is embedded, and they usually have deeper insight about their own performance. However, the core of most types of expertise does seem to be some sort of learning process similar to that exemplified by the linear model and its variants. In recognition of the skills that real experts have, one branch of research in judgment and decision making has turned to experts as a source of data and theories about how decisions are made. This area has become known as *naturalistic decision making* and in the next section we provide a brief overview of the advantages and disadvantages of studying decision making 'in the wild'.

NATURALISTIC DECISION MAKING

A report of flames in the basement of a four-storey building is received at the fire station. The fire chief arrives at the building: there are no externally visible signs of fire, but a quick internal inspection leads to the discovery of flames spreading up the laundry chute. That's straightforward: a vertical fire spreading upward, recently started (because the fire has not reached the outside of the building) – tackle it by spraying water down from above. The fire chief sends one unit to the first floor and one to the second. Both units report that the fire has passed them. Another check of the outside of the building reveals that now the fire has spread and smoke is filling the building. Now that the 'quick option' for extinguishing the fire is no longer viable, the chief calls for more units and instigates a search and rescue – attention must now shift to establishing a safe evacuation route.

This vignette, adapted from Klein (1993), is typical of the kinds of situations that have been analysed in the development of models of naturalistic decision making (NDM). NDM emphasizes both the features of the context in which decisions are made (e.g. ill-structured problems, dynamic environments, competing goals, high stakes, time constraints) (Orasanu & Connolly, 1993), and the role that experience plays in decision making (Pruitt, Cannon-Bowers & Salas, 1997). Zsambok provides a succinct definition: 'NDM is the way people use their experience to make decisions in field settings' (Zsambok, 1997, p. 4).

Cognitive task analyses of fire-fighters' reports such as the one described in the vignette are a key aspect of the NDM methodology. The fascinating aspect of these task analyses, according to Klein (1993), is the *lack* of decisions. The chief sees the vertical fire and he knows what to do straight away – there is no process of generating varieties of options or of attempting to 'maximize utility' by picking the best option. Even when the course of action is negated by the spread of the fire, the chief knows instantly what to do next – switch to a search-and-rescue strategy. The chief never seems to *decide* anything.

Observations such as these led to the development of the prototypical model in the NDM framework, the Recognition-Primed Decision Making model (RPD; Klein, 1993; 1998). The RPD has three variants (Lipshitz et al., 2001). In the simplest version a decision maker 'sizes up' a situation, recognizes which course of action makes sense and then responds with the initial option that is generated or identified. The idea is that a skilled decision maker can typically rely on experience to ensure that the first option generated is a feasible course of action. In a second version of RPD the decision maker relies on a story-building strategy to mentally simulate the events leading up to the observed characteristics of a situation. Such a strategy is invoked when the situation is not clear and the decision maker needs to take time to carry out a diagnosis. Finally, the third variant explains how decision makers evaluate single courses of action by imagining how they will play out in a given situation. This mental simulation allows the decision maker to anticipate difficulties and amend the chosen strategy.

Expertise plays a key role in all three of these versions. Expertise is required for recognizing the 'typicality' of the situation (e.g. 'it's a vertical fire'), to construct mental models that allow for one explanation to be deemed more plausible than others, and for being able to mentally simulate a course of action in a situation (Lipshitz et al., 2001). This latter skill – mental simulation – has been documented in chess masters and is often described as 'progressive deepening' – playing a move in the mind, to see how it would work (deGroot, 1965). Mental simulation in the RPD is also closely related to the *simulation heuristic* (Kahneman & Tversky, 1982a), by which people build a simulation or story to explain how something might happen, and disregard the simulation as implausible if it requires too many unlikely events. In fact, as Klein (1993) points out, the RPD model could be described as a combination of the *representativeness* and *availability* heuristics – for recognizing the typicality of a situation – and the simulation heuristic for diagnosis and evaluation of a situation. (Recall our discussion of these heuristics and their role in mental simulation in Chapters 6 and 7.)

The RPD model has been applied to a variety of different experts and contexts, including infantry officers, tank platoon leader, and commercial aviation pilots. Consistent with the initial studies of the fire-fighters, RPD has been shown to be the most common strategy in 80–95% of these environments (Lipshitz et al., 2001). These are impressive results, suggesting that the RPD model provides a very good description of the course of action followed by experienced decision makers, especially when they are under time pressure and have ill-defined goals (Klein, 1998).

Klein (2009) offers the 'miracle' landing of US Airways Flight 1529 on the Hudson River in New York in January 2009 as a compelling example of recognition-primed decision making in action. Klein (2009) suggests that Captain Chesley B. 'Sully' Sullenberg III rapidly generated three options when he realized that birds flying into his engines had caused a power failure: (1) return to LaGuardia airport; (2) find another airport; (3) land in the Hudson River. Option 1 is the most typical given the circumstances, but was quickly dismissed because it was too far away; option 2 was also dismissed as impractical, leaving the 'desperate' but achievable option of ditching in the river as the only remaining course of action. Sully did land in the river, and saved the lives of all on board. Klein claims that Sullenberg was 'satisficing, looking for the first option that would work' (p. 92).

The descriptive power of RPD is not in question but can RPD be used to generate testable hypotheses? Some confirmation of the predictions of the RPD model has been found in the analysis of chess players (Calderwood, Klein & Crandall, 1988; Klein et al., 1995). For example Klein et al. (1995) asked whether skilled chess players could generate reasonable moves as the very first one they considered in a chess problem (in much the same way as the fire chief seemed to know what to do straight away when confronted with a fire situation).

Klein et al. gave chess players four chess boards displaying different configurations of pieces. For each board a chess master had previously determined the quality of next moves that a player could make. The results indicated that the number of high-quality first moves generated was much greater than if players had simply been selecting randomly from the population of all possible legal moves. It seems that expertise was used to generate a good move as the first one that was considered. Such findings are suggestive but perhaps not decisive (what theory would predict the opposite, namely that people randomly generate options? cf. Lipshitz et al. (2001)), but if the general remit of NDM is decision analysis in 'messy' field settings, does it matter that it is difficult to test its specific predictions?

This inability is not necessarily a problem for NDM – after all, its entire goal, in a sense, is to *describe* how proficient decision makers make decisions in the field. But it is important that the techniques employed by NDM in collecting and analysing these qualitative data are rigorous and defensible. Failure to adopt such methods will impede the acceptance of NDM methods by other scientists (Klayman, 2001). Such rigour can be adopted. For example, Hoffman, Crandell and Shadbolt (1998) demonstrated 82% retest reliability in the reports of fire commanders across several months. Furthermore, extensive use of protocol analysis in cognitive science (e.g. Ericsson & Simon, 1984) is testament to their usefulness as sources of data. As Lipshitz et al. (2001) concluded, developing better understanding of and methods for rigorous observation and knowledge elicitation is a key challenge for the future of NDM.

Can NDM and more traditional laboratory-based methods for examining judgment and decision making be unified into a 'decision-science' (cf. Cooksey, 2001)? Although NDM has taken a rather confrontational position against laboratory-based studies, as Klayman (2001) and Cooksey (2001) both suggest, it would perhaps be more beneficial to develop a synergy that uses both observation and experimentation to examine the behaviour of novices and experts in the lab and in the field.

SUMMARY

In this chapter we have followed a path through theory development from the original linear model for simple binary choices to models which incorporate internal representations, along the way discussing expertise and optimality, and exemplar representation. The linear model is an extraordinarily compelling yet simple way of accounting for how people learn to assign weights to cues in a decision environment, and its scope suggests that error-driven learning in some form or other plays a central role in the learning process. The model often predicts convergence to optimal behaviour in the long run, and this appears to be consistent with expert performance.

In many settings, both in the laboratory and in real life, experts seem able to iron out many biases such as base-rate neglect. Although experts can be outperformed by statistical tools (as we saw in Chapter 3), we should take heart from the capacity of the brain to incorporate incredible amounts of complex data into accurate decisions. The naturalistic approach to studying decision making takes advantage of these achievements and turns to experts as a source of data and theories. The RPD model which emerges from this approach blends rapid, intuitive processing based on the availability and representativeness of situations and cues with more deliberative mental simulation to produce 'satisficing' responses in real-world situations. The juxtaposition of intuitive and deliberative processing enshrined in the RPD model is characteristic of a much broader conceptualization of the mental operations underlying judgment and decision making. These so-called two-system or dual-process frameworks are evaluated in depth in the next chapter.

Suggested further reading

- Juslin, P., Karlsson, L., & Olsson, H. (2008). Information integration in multiple cue judgment: A division of labor hypothesis. *Cognition*, *106*, 259–298. Compares exemplar and linear cue-abstraction models in their ability to model judgment.
- Klein, G. A. (2009). *Streetlights and shadows: Searching for the keys to adaptive decision making*. Cambridge, MA: MIT Press. An accessible account of naturalistic decision making by one of the founders of the field.
- Lagnado, D. A., Newell, B. R., Kahan, S., & Shanks, D. R. (2006). Insight and strategy in multiple cue learning. *Journal of Experimental Psychology: General*, *135*, 162–183. Explores how the lens model approach can be applied to learning more complex tasks.

14 Two systems of judgment and decision making?

Chapter highlights

- Introduces the 'intuitive' System 1 and the 'deliberative' System 2 and discusses their key characteristics
- Gives a flavour of the debate between dual- and single-system theorists
- Critiques the evidence for unconscious influences on decision making.

Consider the following question:

> If a bat and a ball cost $1.10 in total and the bat costs $1 more than the ball, how much does the ball cost?

If you are like many people, your immediate answer would be '10 cents' (Kahneman & Frederick, 2002). You'd be wrong. Think a little more and you'll see why.

The bat-and-ball question is one of three similar items in the so-called 'cognitive reflection test' (CRT) devised by Frederick (2005). As the name suggests, the CRT is designed to measure people's ability to inhibit an initial response and to engage in some additional deliberation ('cognitive reflection') in order to identify the correct answer. For protagonists of what has become known as the dual-system perspective on judgment and decision making, the CRT provides compelling evidence for two types of thinking. The first type, often credited to 'System 1', is depicted as fast and intuitive and is contrasted with the second type, a product of 'System 2', which is slower, analytic and reflective (e.g. Evans, 2008; Kahneman, 2003, 2011; Kahneman & Frederick, 2002; Sloman, 1996; Stanovich & West, 2000).

The basic dual-system perspective suggests that intuitive answers are proposed by System 1 (e.g. 'The ball must cost 10 cents'), but are in some way monitored by System 2, and if necessary (and circumstances permit) can be over-ridden (e.g. 'It can't be, because then the total would be $1.20'). This characterization leads to important questions about how such monitoring happens and what determines which system we 'listen to' in giving our final response, such as what are the circumstances that permit endorsement, correction or the over-riding of System 1 by System 2? In this chapter we discuss some of the evidence for this dual-system characterization and reflect on the vociferous debate about whether dichotomizing thinking as 'fast' and 'slow' (Kahneman, 2011) represents theoretical progress or regress. We then turn to one specific characteristic that is often used to diagnose the involvement of different systems – conscious insight – and evaluate evidence suggesting that unconscious influences have an important role in decision making.

CHARACTERISTICS OF THE TWO SYSTEMS

The vast majority of research discussing dual-system perspectives on judgment and decision making begins by presenting a taxonomy of the features or attributes associated with each system. Table 14.1 is one such taxonomy, adapted from Evans and Stanovich (2013a) – two of the leading proponents of dual-systems theory. As noted above, the basic distinction is between fast, relatively effortless, intuitive thinking and slow, more effortful, deliberative thinking. The additional clusters of features have been derived from multiple lines of experimental evidence in which the characteristics of tasks, mental resources, time, and so on have been manipulated and measured in an effort to identify which kinds of features 'load' on to the different systems. If you recall the discussion in Chapter 11 on intertemporal decision making, you might also align impulsive choices involving immediate outcomes with System 1 and reflective choices involving future outcomes with System 2, especially given evidence that these depend on partially distinct brain systems (McClure et al., 2004).

An illustrative example comes from a study by Bonner and Newell (2010). These authors examined a phenomenon known as the 'ratio-bias' (Denes-Raj & Epstein, 1994). Consider the following problem: in front of you are two bowls containing different numbers of jelly beans. The small bowl contains 1 red bean and 9 white beans, while the large bowl contains 7 red beans and 93 white beans. If you select a red bean you will win $1. The bowls will be shielded from view when you make your selection (it is not that easy!) but you have to decide which bowl you would like to select from – the large one or the small one?

Much like the 'bat-and-ball' problem, you might experience some tension between a more intuitive response ('pick the bowl that has more red beans: 7/93') and a more deliberative one ('pick the bowl that has the *higher chance* of winning: 1/10). Bonner and Newell (2010) gave their participants a series of choices of this kind in which the ratio of winning beans to the total in the bowl varied across trials. Sometimes the ratios were in 'conflict' with each other, as in the example above where the bowl with the higher numerator (7/93) conflicts with the bowl with the better chance of winning (1/10). On other trials the numerator and the chance were in 'harmony', such as in a choice

Table 14.1 Attributes and features typically associated with dual-process theories of judgment and decision making

System 1 (intuitive)	System 2 (deliberative)
Working memory independent	Working memory dependent
Autonomous	Mental simulation
Fast	Slow
High capacity	Capacity limited
Non-conscious	Conscious
Biased responses	Normative responses
Contextualized	Abstract
Automatic	Controlled
Associative	Rule based
Independent of cognitive ability	Correlated with cognitive ability

Based on Table 1 in Evans & Stanovich, 2013a.

between a bowl offering a 21/100 chance with one offering a 2/10 chance. Bonner and Newell then measured the accuracy and optimality of choices and the time participants took to choose on conflict and harmony trials.

According to a dual-process perspective, on conflict trials in which participants are perhaps trying to resolve the tension between two possible answers, they should take longer to respond than on harmony trials in which both systems produce the same answer. The results were broadly consistent with this prediction. First, a higher number of optimal choices was observed in harmony than in conflict trials – that is, people chose the bowl with a better chance of winning more often when both the numerator and the ratio favoured the same bowl. Second, reaction times on these harmony trials were faster than on the conflict trials, perhaps implying that some additional time was needed to 'resolve' the conflict between the two possible responses. Moreover, those participants who made more non-optimal choices across all trials responded more rapidly than those who made fewer, again suggesting that the intuitive response was characterized by fast, non-reflective thinking.

Competing systems: parallel process or default intervention?

The kind of explanation of Bonner and Newell's data offered above begs the question of how the apparent conflict between systems is resolved. Evans (2007) proposed two possibilities for the way in which dual processes might interact. The Default-Interventionist (DI) model proposes a serial framework in which intuitive processes (and thus responses) are the default and that these are only intervened upon later in processing by deliberative processes when some conflict is detected – thus monitoring is somewhat 'lax' (De Neys & Glumicic, 2008). In contrast, parallel models (e.g. Denes-Raj & Epstein, 1994; Sloman,

1996) suggest that heuristic and analytic processes occur simultaneously, leading to constant and effective monitoring and the experience of conflict.

However, as De Neys and Glumicic (2008) correctly point out, neither an extreme 'serial' DI model nor a pure parallel model make sense once their underlying assumptions are scrutinized. In the DI model, *some* analytic processing must be occurring all the time for a conflict to be detected. It makes no sense to say that analytic processes will be engaged only *when* a conflict is detected. How could conflict be detected unless minimal analytic monitoring was already operating (see also Kahneman, 2011)? For the parallel model, the principle of cognitive economy would suggest that analytic processes would be redundant in those instances where both intuitive and analytic routes lead to the same answer (e.g. harmony trials in the Bonner and Newell experiments). Why would a system bother with the slower, more capacity-intensive process when an 'easy' intuitive solution presents itself?

One potential solution to the perceived inadequacies of these 'pure' accounts is to propose a 'hybrid two-stage model' characterized by a 'shallow analytic monitoring process' and an 'optional deeper processing stage' to accompany the ever-present intuitive processing (De Neys & Glumicic, 2008). The basic idea is a model in which shallow analytic processing is always engaged in order for conflict to be detected, and deeper analytic processing is only sanctioned once there *is* a conflict between the shallow processing and the intuitive response (see also Evans & Stanovich, 2013b, for discussion of this kind of model, and V. A. Thompson, 2013, for similar arguments). Such a hybrid model would fit the Bonner and Newell data. The shallow analytic processing is always engaged – this is especially likely given the within-subjects manipulation of conflict and harmony trials – while deeper, more time-consuming analytic processing is invoked when a detected conflict needs to be resolved (that is, on conflict trials). Thus the longer response times on conflict trials are due to the attempt to resolve the conflict, arguably via inhibition of the intuitive response.

But is all this discussion of interacting systems, and qualitatively different processes necessitated by the data? The increased response times for conflict relative to harmony trials could be attributed to the fact that two possible answers are apparent on conflict trials, but only one is apparent on harmony trials. The availability of two possible answers could simply require *more* (but not *different*) processing, resulting in longer response times. Similarly, the increase in response times for those individuals who gave more optimal responses could be the result of them thinking about (processing) the problem for longer and hence being more likely to decide on the higher percentage (cf. Evans' (2007) discussion of the *quality* versus *quantity* of processing). In fact, in a second experiment, Bonner and Newell failed to find a significant effect of memory load on the proportion of optimal responses in the ratio-bias task. As highlighted in Table 14.1, working memory involvement is often held up as a signature indicator of System 1 versus System 2 responding (Evans, 2008; Evans & Stanovich, 2013a), so this failure to find a difference could be taken to suggest that the processes underlying optimal and non-optimal responding are only quantitatively and not qualitatively different.

EVIDENCE FOR TWO SYSTEMS OR THEORETICAL 'STONE SOUP'?

These difficulties in determining whether a particular response should be interpreted as the product of System 1 or System 2 and the problems associated with understanding the interaction between the systems has led some theorists to argue strongly against the usefulness of the dichotomy (e.g. Keren, 2013; Keren & Schul, 2009; Kruglanski, 2013; Kruglanski & Gigerenzer, 2011; Osman, 2004, 2013). Keren (2013) provides the emotive analogy with a folktale in which a person teaches a 'fool' how to make a delicious soup from nothing but a soup stone. Apparently, all one needs is to place the soup stone into boiling water, but to make the soup tastier one should add some vegetables, some meat, salt and pepper, and so on. Keren (p. 257) argues that:

> inspecting the different labels proposed and the various terminologies employed to characterize the presumed two systems and their corresponding alleged processes strongly suggest that it has become a stone soup where everything goes.

The key complaint of Keren and other commentators is that the desire to dichotomize creates confusion and impedes rather than fosters theoretical progress. To evaluate the force of these critiques it is important to understand what proponents of the dual-process view take as the strongest evidence for the kind of characteristics highlighted in Table 14.1. As we've seen, one illustrative set of experiments – Bonner and Newell (2010) – provided evidence that could be taken to support a dual-process perspective, but by no means compelled that interpretation. What is the 'best evidence' for the distinction?

The 'best evidence' for dual-process theories

Evans and Stanovich (2013a) cite three lines of evidence: (1) experimental manipulations designed to selectively affect System 1 or System 2; (2) neuroscientific evidence that claims to show differential involvement of brain regions in System 1 and 2 processes, and (3) selective correlations between System 2 processes and cognitive ability. As an example of (1), Evans and Stanovich cite evidence from De Neys (2006), who demonstrated that participants who made the classic conjunction fallacy error when given the famous Linda problem (see Chapter 6), responded more rapidly than those who did not make the error. Moreover, when a concurrent working memory load was introduced in a second experiment, the number of correct responses on the Linda problem dropped. But as we have discussed, such changes as a function of cognitive load or time pressure do not constitute clear evidence for the involvement of qualitatively different systems or processes, because several other accounts that make a distinction in the quantity but not the type of processing could also explain such patterns (Bonner & Newell, 2010; Kruglanski & Gigerenzer, 2011; Keren & Schul, 2009; Osman, 2004, 2013).

Turning to the neuroscience evidence, Evans and Stanovich suggest that responses based on deliberation reveal different areas of activation compared to responses based on intuition. They cite studies of delay-discounting, of the kind discussed in Chapter 11, as providing evidence that decisions about delayed or deferred rewards involve different neurobiological systems than those concerning immediate rewards (McClure et al., 2004). Specifically, delayed decisions led to activation of the prefrontal cortex, whereas immediate ones were associated with the limbic system. According to Evans and Stanovich, only the former require the involvement of System 2 – because of the need for mental simulation for thinking about future consequences – and thus finding activation of the prefrontal cortex is entirely consistent with dual-process theories because executive control and other kinds of deliberative processing are thought to be the domain of the prefrontal cortex.

There are, however, significant difficulties in drawing such conclusions on the basis of neuroscientific evidence. Poldrack (2006) identified the problem of 'reverse inference' whereby researchers argue that because a particular task A appears to activate brain area Z, while in other studies when some cognitive process X was putatively engaged, area Z was also active, then the activity of Z in the current study demonstrates the engagement of cognitive process X. This inference is not deductively valid, and yet it appears to be the kind of inference Evans and Stanovich make in discussing the neuroscience evidence 'supporting' dual processes. Decisions about delayed rewards may activate prefrontal cortex, and numerous executive control tasks may also activate this region, but it does not follow from these premises that decisions about delayed rewards engage executive control processes.

Moreover, as Henson (2006) has pointed out, even if such fallacious reverse inferences are replaced with 'forward inferences', any inferences from brain activation to cognitive theories are only as good as the theories to which they pertain. One needs to be very careful to rule out differences in tasks, procedures, instructions and participants, before making strong claims that differences in brain activation are due to the recruitment of qualitatively different cognitive processes (see also Gureckis, James & Nosofsky, 2011). Of course, this same basic argument applies to any (non-neuroscience) behavioural study that attempts to isolate selective involvement of a cognitive process by way of dissociation, such as demonstrating that a variable, perhaps working memory load, impacts on one type of cognitive process but has no or an opposite effect on another. Such dissociation logic is fraught with interpretational difficulties and it is only under the most stringent conditions that it supports valid conclusions about the involvement of different systems or processes (e.g. Chater, 2003; Dunn & Kirsner, 1988; Newell & Dunn, 2008).

The final source of 'best' evidence comes, according to Evans and Stanovich (2013a), from studies showing that individuals who are more likely to respond with the 'System 2' answer are also more likely to show higher levels of intelligence and working memory capacity. Thus, those people who give the right answer to the bat-and-ball problem (5 cents, in case you were still wondering), tend to display higher cognitive ability on standard intelligence tests such as the Wechsler Abbreviated Scale of Intelligence (WASI) (e.g. Toplak, West & Stanovich, 2011).

At first glance, this evidence appears straightforward, but Evans and Stanovich are keen to emphasize that a simple dichotomy in which 'System 1 = irrational or non-normative' and 'System 2 = normative' is inaccurate. Indeed they suggest that such identification of System 1 as 'bad' and System 2 as 'good' is 'perhaps the most persistent fallacy in the perception of dual-process theories' (p. 229). They argue that System 1 can, in fact, lead to correct answers and System 2 to incorrect ones in some circumstances. This flexibility is, however, an undoing for the force of the dual-systems account. As Kruglanski (2013) notes, once one eschews the idea that System 1 processing is in some sense less normative than System 2 – that normativity of responding is a defining characteristic of different systems – then it makes little sense to argue that correlations between intelligence and System 2 processing are strong evidence for the dichotomy. To paraphrase Kruglanski (2013): you can't have it both ways! Either System 2 processing and normative responding are systematically and positively related or they are not, and if they are not, then evidence that people with higher cognitive ability tend to provide more normative answers is entirely non-diagnostic regarding the existence of different systems of thinking.

AWARENESS, INSIGHT AND UNCONSCIOUS INFLUENCES

One of the typical correlates in many dual-system perspectives on judgment and decision making is consciousness and insight (see Table 14.1). Some theories place the 'conscious/non-conscious' distinction at the heart of the dichotomy (e.g. Lieberman, 2009) while others suggest this characterization is questionable and argue specifically against the conflation of System 1 and System 2 with non-conscious and conscious processing, respectively (e.g. Evans, 2014). Regardless of its centrality to dual-process theories, there can be few issues in psychology that capture people's attention as much as questions about the extent to which we know our own minds when making decisions. Everyday notions such as 'gut instinct' and 'intuition' capture the idea that subtle influences falling outside awareness can bias behaviour. Claims that 'People possess a powerful, sophisticated, adaptive unconscious that is crucial for survival in the world' (Wilson, 2002, p. vii) and that we should think less rather than more about complex decisions (Dijksterhuis et al., 2006) have a strong grip on both theoretical perspectives and the public imagination (e.g. Gigerenzer, 2007; Gladwell, 2005; Lehrer, 2009).

In the remaining sections of this chapter we review and critique some of the evidence on which these claims for unconscious influences on decision making have been built. The review is based on the comprehensive coverage of the topic provided in the article by Newell and Shanks (2014) and the accompanying commentaries and reply (see suggested further reading at the end of the chapter).

The legacy of Nisbett and Wilson

The willingness of many researchers to embrace the possibility of unconscious influences on decision making can be traced to the highly influential work of Nisbett and Wilson (1977). Nisbett and Wilson launched a powerful series of arguments that people typically lack insight into their own mental processes. One of their key claims was that people often misreport causal influences on their choices, falsely reporting factors that did not in fact influence their performance and failing to acknowledge factors that truly were causal. Nisbett and Wilson argued that when people do give veridical reports, it is because they make use of a priori implicit theories about causal relationships between stimuli and responses, rather than because they have privileged conscious access to their own mental processes.

One of the many illustrations of this basic point is an experiment in which participants chose between (and justified their choice from) four consumer products which were in reality identical. Nisbett and Wilson (1977) found that participants tended to select the right-most of four alternatives (e.g. pairs of stockings) but did not mention position when justifying their choice, or flatly denied being influenced by position when asked directly. Indeed, Nisbett and Wilson reported that some participants 'felt either they had misunderstood the question or were dealing with a mad-man' (p. 244) when asked about the possible effect of the article's position on choice. Instead participants mentioned attributes such as the quality of the stockings. The problem with this finding is that asking participants about position fails to tap into the information that is relevant for the choice the person has made, as position is almost certainly not a proximal or immediate cause of choice (this argument was originally made by Smith & Miller, 1978). It is at best a distal cause, whose influence is mediated via the participant's true decision rule.

In such sequential choice situations, people tend to study the options one at a time, usually (but depending on culture) from left to right. Suppose that the decision rule is that *if the current item is no worse in terms of quality than the previous item, then prefer the current item.* After the initial item, each subsequent one is mentally compared with its predecessor (Li & Epley, 2009; Mantonakis et al., 2009) and because the items are identical, the resulting final choice is the right-most pair of stockings. Even though the rule may lead (wrongly) to the belief that one item is superior to the others, the choice is in no sense determined by spatial position. Spatial position only has an influence insofar as it affects how the items are sequentially sampled.

Indeed, under such circumstances it is perfectly correct for participants to report quality as the basis of their decision, as their decision rule incorporates judgments of quality, and to deny being influenced by position. To establish that the choice is being driven by unconscious influences, it would be necessary to show that participants deny employing a sequential comparison process, but this is not what Nisbett and Wilson (1977) asked their participants. Claiming that their participants were unconsciously influenced by position is like claiming that an individual who chooses the apartment she saw on Friday, after seeing others on Monday, Tuesday, Wednesday and Thursday, is unconsciously influenced in her choice by the day of the week.

Insight in multiple-cue judgment

Similar claims for the reliance on unconscious or implicit knowledge have been made in multiple-cue judgment tasks of the kind discussed in Chapters 3, 4 and 13 that have employed the lens model framework to examine judgment (see Chapter 3, Figure 3.1). In a standard study participants make judgments about a series of 'cases' (e.g. patients) for which information is available from a set of cues. Multiple linear regressions are then performed from the judgments to the cues to measure the 'policies' that judges adopt. The beta weights obtained from these regressions give an indication of the cues that influenced the judge, as well as the relative extent of this influence. These beta weights are described as the implicit or tacit policy underlying judgment.

To examine the extent of insight into judgments, these implicit policies are then compared with self-assessments of the importance of cues for determining judgments. The strength of the correlation between these ratings of importance and the beta weights derived from multiple regression is taken as indicating the extent of insight. A widely accepted consensus from this research is that there is often a lack of correlation between the two measures of the usage of cues, reflecting judges' poor insight (Arkes, 1981; Evans et al., 2003; Rolison et al., 2011; Slovic & Lichtenstein, 1971).

A simple experimental demonstration of this apparent dissociation is provided in Gluck, Shohamy and Myers' (2002) study of multiple-cue learning and judgment. They found that while participants attained high levels of predictive accuracy (well above chance), they demonstrated little explicit knowledge about what they were doing. In particular, in questionnaires administered at the end of the task, they gave inaccurate estimates of the cue-outcome probabilities, and there was little correspondence between self-reports about how they were learning the task and their actual task performance. The lack of self-insight on this task is thus explained by the operation of implicit or 'System 1' processes to which participants lack conscious access.

It is important to distinguish between someone's insight into the structure of a task *(task knowledge)* and their insight into their own judgmental processes *(self-insight)*. In the case of a multiple-cue learning task, this translates into the difference between a learner's knowledge of the objective cue-outcome associations, and their knowledge of how they are using the cues to predict the outcome. There is no guarantee that the two coincide. Someone might have an incorrect model of the task structure, but an accurate model of their own judgment process. For instance, think of a pathologist whose job is to screen cell samples in order to detect a particular disease. This person might have complete and accurate awareness of the features she is looking for and how much weight to give them, and she might be very good at passing on her understanding to students. She thus has excellent self-insight. However, her actual success in detecting abnormal cells might be poor or non-existent if the features and weights she is using are not objectively valid. This would imply weak task knowledge.

Though distinct notions, there is a tendency in lots of research to run the two together. Thus it is not always clear whether claims about the dissociation between insight and learning refer to a dissociation between self-insight and learning, task knowledge and learning, or both. Further, this conflation can infect the explicit tests given to participants. Questions that are designed to tap someone's insight into their own judgment processes may instead be answered in terms of their knowledge about the task. Such confusion needs to be avoided if firm conclusions are to be drawn about the relation between learning and insight.

There are several other problems with the explicit tests commonly used to measure task knowledge and self-insight. First, these measures tend to be retrospective, asked after participants have completed a task involving numerous trials, and this can distort the validity of the assessments that people give. The reliance on memory, possibly averaged across many trials, can make it difficult to recall a unique judgment strategy. This is especially problematic if people's strategies have varied during the course of the task, making it hard if not impossible to summarize in one global response. In general it is better to get multiple subjective assessments as close as possible to the actual moments of judgment (Ericsson & Simon, 1980).

A second common problem with tests of explicit knowledge is that they are too vague (Lovibond & Shanks, 2002; Newell & Shanks, 2014). Rather than focus on specific features of the task necessary for its solution, they include general questions that are tangential to solving the task. Once again this reduces the sensitivity of the test to measure people's relevant knowledge or insight. This problem can lead to an over-estimation of insight (because someone may be able to recall features of the task that are irrelevant to good performance on it) or to under-estimation (because the questions fail to ask about the critical information) (e.g. asking about position instead of a sequential comparison choice rule in the Nisbett & Wilson studies).

In recognition of the problems of retrospective interrogation of explicit knowledge, Lagnado, Newell et al. (2006) used an approach in which participants learning a multiple-cue judgment task were probed throughout training trials for the explicit basis of their predictions. On each trial participants were asked to rate how much they had relied on each cue in making their prediction. The 'explicit' cue ratings were then compared with the 'implicit' weights derived from running 'rolling' regressions, a series of regressions from predictions to cues across a moving window of consecutive trials (cf. Kelley & Friedman, 2002 – see discussion of this study in the previous chapter for more details).

The take-home message from the analysis of these data was that participants distinguished clearly between strong and weak predictors on *both* the implicit and explicit measures of cue reliance. This ability occurred fairly early in the task and was maintained or increased across training. Lagnado, Newell et al. (2006) also reported strong positive correlations between individuals' cue reliance ratings and implicit regression weights. The overall pattern suggested that people had access to the internal states underlying their behaviour and that this access drove both online predictions and explicit reliance ratings. Note that it is unlikely that the requirement to make online ratings altered participants' judgment strategies, as an additional experiment demonstrated that overall accuracy in the task was unaffected by the inclusion of the online ratings.

In a more recent study, Speekenbrink and Shanks (2010) extended this approach by using a 'dynamic lens model' to assess participants' insight in an environment in which cue validities changed across the course of an experiment. Consistent with Lagnado, Newell et al.'s (2006) results, Speekenbrink and Shanks found little evidence for any contribution of implicit processes: participants learned to adapt to changes in the environment, and their reports of *how* they changed their reliance on cues reflected their *actual* reliance on those cues as evidenced by their predictions.

Similar optimistic conclusions about the extent of insight appear to hold for naturalistic multiple-cue judgments too. Although Slovic and Lichtenstein (1971) were early to note that there were 'serious discrepancies' (p. 649) between the explicit weights provided post hoc by judges (such as stockbrokers) and the implicit weights they placed on cues, as we have seen, the strength with which such conclusions can be drawn depends crucially on the methods used to elicit the ratings and weightings. It is quite possible that judges have good insight, but that they have not been provided with sufficient opportunities to report the knowledge that they possess. It is also possible that judges confuse questions about the 'importance' of cues for the task environment with their 'importance' for their own judgment process (cf. Lagnado, Newell et al., 2006; Speekenbrink & Shanks, 2010; Surber, 1985). Studies by Reilly and Doherty (1989; 1992) and Harries, Evans and Dennis (2000) support this general contention. When other opportunities are provided for expressing insight, such as 'recognition' tests that involve identifying one's own policy from an array of possible policies, judges have been found to show an 'astonishing degree of insight' (Reilly & Doherty, 1989, p. 125).

Decisions under uncertainty, but outside of awareness?

In Chapter 10 we discussed an area of research that has become subsumed under the label 'decisions from experience'. In decisions from experience the payoffs associated with different choice alternatives are initially unknown but can be learned via repeated sampling. Most of the tasks we considered in that chapter involved choices between two alternatives. Now imagine a game in which there are four options (or four decks of cards) on every trial. This is the set-up facing participants given the Iowa Gambling Task (IGT; Bechara et al. (1994)) and their job is to figure out which deck will earn them the most money. The IGT has become very popular in the literature on decision making, not least because of claims that people can learn to choose optimally in the absence of a conscious basis for their choices.

The basic task involves four decks of cards and 100 card selections (trials). Two of the decks (the 'bad decks') have a reward/punishment schedule which results in a net loss over the course of the experiment, whereas the other two decks (the 'good decks') have a schedule that results in a net gain. However, the key feature of the design is that the immediate reward associated with the bad decks is higher than that associated with the good decks. One interesting question is whether participants learn to choose from the decks that are advantageous in the long term or are more influenced by the immediate gains from the long-term disadvantageous decks. Further, a crucial question is whether awareness of the properties of the decks correlates with choice.

Bechara et al. (1997) claimed to observe an absence of correlation, concluding that 'normals began to choose advantageously before they realized which strategy worked best' and that 'in normal individuals, non-conscious biases guide behavior before conscious knowledge does' (p. 1293). Elsewhere, it has been claimed that 'this biasing effect occurs even before the subject becomes aware of the goodness or badness of the choice s/he is about to make' (Bechara, Damasio & Damasio, 2000, p. 301).

However, these strong claims for unconscious influences in the IGT have not withstood further scrutiny. Maia and McClelland (2004) in a replication and extension of the Bechara et al. study employed a much more careful assessment of awareness of the nature of the task at regular intervals across trials. Rather than simply recording responses to open-ended questions regarding what they thought and felt about the task, as Bechara et al. (1997) had done, Maia and McClelland required their participants to rate each deck on a numerical scale, to explain their numerical ratings, to report in detail what they thought the average net winnings or losses would be if 10 cards were selected from each deck, and to state which deck they would choose if they could only select from one deck for the remainder of the game. Answers to these questions provided a range of assessments of awareness against which actual card selections could be compared. In addition, Maia and McClelland ensured that the classification of decks as good or bad was based on the actual payoffs experienced by the individual participant to that point. Bechara et al. (1997) fixed the sequence of payoffs from each deck in the same way for each participant and scheduled very few penalties on the bad decks across the early trials. Thus a participant selecting early on from the bad decks might actually be making good choices, because the penalties that ultimately make such decks bad have not yet been experienced. Plainly, it is crucial to classify selections as good or bad in relation to what the participant has actually experienced, not in relation to the long-term but unknown average.

When card selections were compared with reported awareness under Maia and McClelland's (2004) improved method, it was apparent that awareness if anything was more finely tuned to the payoffs than the overt selections were. Far from observing selections from the good decks in participants who could not report which were the good decks, Maia and McClelland found that conscious reports about the decks were more reliable than overt behaviour. This might indicate that participants were still exploring the task and acquiring further information about the decks, but it clearly provides no support for the claim that unconscious biases occur before individuals have relevant conscious knowledge. Konstantinidis and Shanks (2014) have reported similar findings with a broader range of methods for assessing awareness.

Criteria for the assessment of awareness

Maia and McClelland's (2004) study provides a particularly striking illustration of the dangers of employing an unreliable or insensitive test of awareness. Consistent with findings from the multiple-cue judgment literature, and research from further afield such as implicit learning (e.g. Shanks & St John, 1994), human conditioning (Lovibond & Shanks, 2002) and category learning (Newell, Dunn & Kalish, 2011), time and again research suggests that when appropriate tests of awareness are administered, the evidence for unconscious, implicit, influences on higher-level cognition appears very thin (Newell, 2015). In an effort to emphasize and systematize measures of awareness, Newell and Shanks (2014), building on earlier recommendations (e.g. Dawson & Reardon,

Table 14.2 Criteria for adequate assessments of awareness

Criterion	Explanation
Reliability	Assessments should be unaffected by factors that do not influence the decision (e.g. experimental demands, social desirability).
Relevance	Assessments should target only information relevant to the decision.
Immediacy	Assessments should be made concurrently (so long as they do not influence the behaviour) or as soon after the decision as possible to avoid forgetting and interference.
Sensitivity	Assessments should be made under optimal retrieval conditions (e.g. same cues are provided for measuring awareness as for eliciting decisions).

Adapted from Newell & Shanks, 2014.

1973; Ericsson & Simon, 1980; Lovibond & Shanks, 2002; Shanks & St John, 1994), suggested that the more *reliable, relevant, immediate,* and *sensitive* an awareness assessment is, the less likely it is to be distorted by bias or error. Table 14.2 provides brief explanations of these criteria. As we've noted throughout this section, many studies fail to employ methods that satisfy these criteria (e.g. Bechara et al., 1997; Gluck et al., 2002; Slovic & Lichtenstein, 1971), but those studies that do (e.g. Lagnado, Newell et al., 2006; Maia & McClelland, 2004; Reilly & Doherty, 1992), often find little evidence for the impact of information that is outside of awareness.

Deliberation without attention?

One final area of research that merits some discussion in our consideration of the potential role for unconscious processes in decision making is the set of bold claims made by Dijksterhuis and colleagues regarding the power of 'unconscious thought'. Here, the influence of unconscious processes is not demonstrated via claimed dissociations between performance and awareness; instead the idea is that 'cognitive and/or affective task-relevant processes [which] take place outside of consciousness awareness' (Dijksterhuis, 2004, p. 586) act to improve our decision making. What is the evidence?

The standard experimental paradigm is much like the multi-attribute decision tasks we have considered in other chapters. Participants are presented with information about three or four objects (e.g. apartments) described by 10 or more attributes (e.g. rental cost) and are asked to choose the best one. In most experiments *best* is determined normatively by the experimenter assigning different numbers of positive and negative attributes to each option. Attribute information about the four options is presented sequentially and typically in a random order. Following presentation of the attributes, participants are assigned to one of three (or sometimes only two) conditions. In the unconscious thought condition, participants are prevented from making a decision for a few minutes by engaging in some distracting activity such as solving anagrams. This displacement of attention is what is claimed to allow the superior implicit processes (unconscious thought) to operate. In the conscious thought condition participants are asked to think carefully about their choice for a few minutes, while in the immediate condition participants are simply asked to make their decision as soon as the presentation phase has finished.

The key result is that participants who have been distracted make better choices than those in either the conscious thought or the immediate decision conditions. For example, Dijksterhuis et al. (2006) reported that 60% of participants chose the best car after being distracted, compared to only 25% following conscious deliberation.

Newell and Shanks (2014) examined the deliberation-without-attention literature in some detail and drew the following three conclusions. First there are clear question marks surrounding the replicability of the key result: several studies show no advantage for decisions following distraction (e.g. Newell &

Rakow, 2011; Newell, Wong, Cheung & Rakow, 2009), even when the experimental conditions and moderators are set in such a way as to maximize the chances of obtaining the effect (e.g. Nieuwenstein & van Rijn, 2012). Indeed, one paper demonstrated, using Bayes Factor analysis, that there was in fact evidence *for the null hypothesis* of no difference between conscious and unconscious thought conditions in a sample of over 1000 participants from two different laboratories (Newell & Rakow, 2011). Second, several of the studies that show an advantage following distraction do not include the relevant control conditions (for instance, they omit the immediate condition), making it impossible to determine whether distraction was beneficial or deliberation was detrimental (e.g. McMahon et al., 2011). Third, some studies that do find the effect have offered alternative explanations that do not involve the operation of implicit processes during distraction (e.g. Payne et al., 2008; Rey, Goldstein & Perruchet, 2009). For example, Payne et al. (2008) demonstrated that allowing participants to think consciously for as long they liked (rather than for a forced amount of time) led to decisions that were superior to those made following distraction.

Although some interesting exceptions remain (e.g. Usher et al., 2011), the overall picture emerging from work on 'unconscious thought' suggests that the case for improving decision making via the disengagement of explicit thinking has been overstated. This view is echoed by some commentators (Evans, 2014; Hogarth, 2010; Thompson, 2014) but vehemently opposed by others (e.g. Dijksterhuis et al., 2014). Clearly more work is needed on this controversial topic.

SUMMARY

Despite the voluminous research and the obvious allure of the dual-system framework, there is debate about the explanatory value that such a framework can provide. The advantages of describing processes and heuristics as under the operation of System 1 or System 2 are, some argue, outweighed by the disadvantages for theoretical progress. A key problem in the dual-system literature is the plethora of often vague and imprecise terms used to describe the characteristics of the systems, and a failure to specify the manner in which systems interact and/or exchange information. This has led, arguably, to an illusion of convergence whereby researchers appear to be describing similar models and frameworks that in fact differ in many crucial aspects (Evans, 2008). This tendency could impede progress on understanding the phenomena of interest through a (potentially misguided) desire to dichotomize (e.g. Bonner & Newell, 2010; Keren, 2013; Keren & Schul, 2009; Kruglanski & Gigerenzer, 2011; Osman, 2004, 2013).

Nevertheless, some argue that even imprecise frameworks such as those offered by dual-process protagonists are useful because of their potential to guide search for commonalities in processes, identify analogies across domains, and prevent overly narrow interpretations of phenomena (e.g. Evans & Stanovich, 2013b; Kahneman, 2003, 2011). Time will tell whether such optimism is warranted.

Taking 'conscious versus non-conscious' as a diagnostic characteristic of the two systems does not appear to be a fruitful approach. Newell and Shanks' (2014) review suggests that many key decision-making tasks and paradigms have so far failed to yield clear, replicable and unequivocal demonstrations of unconscious influences. On the contrary, many careful experiments have documented consistently high levels of conscious access in people's causal reports on their behaviour.

Given these conclusions, it is surprising (to us) that there remains a pervasive view in the field that unconscious processes serve an important explanatory function in theories of decision making – not least in those that espouse a dual-system perspective.

Why, then, do explanations that invoke unconscious mental states remain so popular? A superficial answer is that they make good stories that have clear appeal to a wide audience, especially when they involve expert decision making (e.g. Gladwell, 2005; Lehrer, 2009). A more considered answer acknowledges that as a field of study, the issue of unconscious influences is a challenging one to look at impartially because we all have such strong *ex ante* beliefs about the causation of our choices and the circumstances in which we are unaware of their determinants. We argue that many reports of unconscious biases have been influential in part because the audience has been strongly predisposed to believe them, even when alternative interpretations are available. Thus claims about the role of unconscious processes have not always been treated quite as critically by the academic community (including journal editors) as claims for which our intuitions are weaker.

This perspective does not deny that there are differences (phenomenological and otherwise) between a deliberation-based and an intuition-based decision. Nor is it to deny that sometimes deliberated decisions can be bad (e.g. Ariely & Norton, 2011; Wilson & Schooler, 1991) and fast decisions can be good (e.g. Goldstein & Gigerenzer, 2002).

With regard to the second claim – that fast decisions can be good – Simon's succinct statement that intuition is 'nothing more and nothing less than recognition' (Simon, 1992, p. 155) is a useful insight here (cf. Kahneman & Klein, 2009). Simon's analogy with recognition reminds us that intuition can be thought of as the product of over-learned associations between cues in the environment and our responses. Some decisions may appear subjectively fast and effortless because they are made on the basis of recognition: the situation provides a cue (e.g. no clouds in the sky), the cue gives us access to information stored in memory (rain is unlikely), and the information provides an answer (don't take an umbrella) (Simon, 1992). When such cues are not so readily apparent, or information in memory is either absent or more difficult to access, our decisions shift to become more deliberative (cf. Hammond, 1996; Hogarth, 2010). The two extremes are associated with different experiences. Whereas deliberative thought yields awareness of intermediate steps in an inferential chain, and of effortful combination of information, intuitive thought lacks awareness of intermediate cognitive steps (because there aren't any) and does not feel effortful (because the cues trigger the decision). Intuition is, however, characterized by feelings of familiarity and fluency. Again, the simple point is that in neither situation do we need to posit 'magical' unconscious processes producing answers from thin air (cf. Hogarth, 2010; Kahneman & Klein, 2009). As we have seen, when one undertakes a critical examination of the empirical evidence for 'genuine' unconscious influences on decision making, the evidence is remarkably weak.

In the next chapter we turn to the issue of how emotions can influence our decision making. This topic is closely related to the studies discussed here, because decisions can be characterized as driven by affective or deliberative processes. How do 'hot' (emotion-laden) judgments and decisions differ from 'cold' (analytic/deliberative) ones? How do emotion and cognition combine? We consider these questions next.

Suggested further reading

- Dijksterhuis, A., Bos, M. W., Nordgren, L. F., & van Baaren, R. B. (2006) On making the right choice: The deliberation-without-attention effect. *Science, 311,* 1005–1007. Provides some intriguing demonstrations of the benefits of unconscious thought.
- Evans, J. St B. T., & Stanovich, K. E. (2013a). Dual-process theories of higher cognition: Advancing the debate. *Perspectives on Psychological Science, 8,* 223–241. A summary of recent thinking on dual-process theories and models from two of the most influential proponents.
- Maia, T. V., & McClelland, J. L. (2004). A reexamination of the evidence for the somatic marker hypothesis: What participants really know in the Iowa Gambling Task. *Proceedings of the National Academy of Sciences, 101,* 16075–16080. Exemplifies the importance of using appropriate measures of awareness.
- Newell, B. R., & Shanks, D. R. (2014). Unconscious influences on decision making: A critical review. *Behavioral and Brain Sciences, 37,* 1–63. A comprehensive review and critique of the literature on the effects of unconscious influences on decision making.

15 Emotional influences on decision making

Chapter highlights

- Introduces the challenge of predicting our future feelings and emotions (affective forecasting) and presents examples of impact bias, the tendency to exaggerate future feelings and emotions
- Discusses evidence for the somatic marker hypothesis, the idea that unconscious bodily reactions can signal risky choices and deter us from making them
- Presents the affect heuristic and the notion of risk as feelings
- Evaluates the role of imagery in emotion and decision making.

In January of 2005 some tragic events occurred in Italy. A woman drowned herself in the sea off Tuscany, a man from Florence shot his wife and children before turning the gun on himself, and a man in Sicily was arrested for beating his wife. These and many other incidents were connected by the 'Venice 53', an elusive and unlucky number in the Italian national lotto.

Italians are invited to bet any amount of money on numbers from 1 to 90 in bi-weekly draws of the lotto. The draws take place in 10 cities throughout Italy, with five numbers picked in each of the 10 cities. By the beginning of February 2005, the number 53 had not been drawn in Venice in almost two years. A '53 frenzy' gripped the nation, with €671 million bet on the number in January alone. The unfortunate 'victims of 53' were so convinced that the number's time had come that they bet their entire family savings on '53', all to no avail. Finally on Wednesday 9 February '53' was pulled from the basket in the Venice lottery and the nation sighed in relief.

The belief that a number's time has come is, of course, fallacious – the lottery has no memory for previous outcomes, so any number is just as likely to be picked on every occasion. Adhering to such a belief is an example of the well-documented 'gambler's fallacy'; that is, believing that after a long run of one outcome – '53' not being drawn – the other outcome – '53' being drawn – is more likely to occur (see Ayton & Fischer, 2004, for a discussion of this phenomenon). The tragic examples illustrate, however, the degree to which people are swayed by such fallacious beliefs. What causes people to hold on to these beliefs so strongly, and to go to such extremes?

In the preceding chapters we have considered several explanations for why, when and how people might fall off the 'straight and narrow' road of good decision making, but in most of our discussions (with the exception of the evaluation of visceral influences in Chapter 11) we have taken a cognitive perspective and focused on the decision maker as a 'cold information-processor'. But when a person commits suicide because a number has not appeared in a lottery, it seems too simplistic to explain this away as solely due to a misunderstanding of randomness, or in terms of the 'gambler's fallacy'. For such an extreme action to be provoked, 'hot' feelings and emotions must have played a fundamental role.

For quite some time, many decision researchers have been making this point, urging that decision making does not occur in an emotional vacuum and that therefore it should not be studied in one either (e.g. Finucane, Peters & Slovic, 2003; Loewenstein et al., 2001). In this chapter we move away from the cold analysis of the learning underlying decision making that was the focus of Chapters 12–14 and examine the effects of emotions on judgment and choice. Our change in focus is in acknowledgement that if we want to improve our decision making in the real world, then we will need to understand more about 'hot' cognition – that is, cognition influenced by emotion and affect.

AFFECTIVE FORECASTING

Classical theories of decision making focus on subjective assessments of outcomes or prospects in terms of their probabilities and utilities, but pay scant regard to the feelings or emotions those outcomes might induce. Yet it is beyond dispute that anticipated feelings and emotional reactions steer us towards pleasant and away from unpleasant outcomes. How many of us have delayed an appointment to visit the dentist because of the anxiety we feel about the painful procedures we will have to undergo? Regardless of the positive value we might put on dental treatment weeks in advance, as the time approaches, our dread causes us to invent excuses to postpone the appointment.

Putting aside for the moment the issue of how to build emotion into theories of decision making, research on *affective forecasting* – our ability to predict in advance how much pleasure or pain an experience will give us – has asked how accurate we are generally in our anticipations of future emotional reactions. This question is fundamental, as rational behaviour hinges on us being reasonably accurate in our expectations. Consider young Barack, a lawyer contemplating a career in politics. If Barack incorrectly anticipates that he will feel extreme anxiety whenever he is required to speak in public, a promising career may be abandoned at the outset. Or consider someone who ends a relationship not because it is unhappy but because she feels a more fulfilling one might be around the corner. The saying that the grass is always greener on the other side of the fence captures precisely the notion that we sometimes over-estimate the pleasure to be had from life-changing courses of action.

Indeed there is now a considerable body of evidence that people tend to over-estimate the emotions and feelings, whether positive or negative, they will experience from future outcomes. In a typical study, participants estimate (say on a 10-point scale) how much pleasure or discomfort they will experience from an episode or outcome, and later, after it has occurred, they state how much they actually experienced. For example, trainee parachutists over-estimated how much fear they would experience during a difficult jump (McMillan & Rachman, 1988) and anxious individuals anticipated more pain during dental treatment than they actually later experienced (Arntz, van Eck & Heijmans, 1990). Nor is it the case that anticipated emotions are simply too extreme: a recent meta-analysis (Mathieu & Gosling, 2012) concluded that they are poorly calibrated as well, with the average correlation between predicted and experienced emotions being about $r = .3$.

The tendency to exaggerate future feelings and emotions has been termed *impact bias* and is related to the evidence discussed in Chapter 11 concerning biases in recall of past experiences, where we saw that the peak and end levels of emotion or feeling seem to have a disproportionate impact on subsequent recollections. One potential explanation for the exaggerated impact of future events is that people fail to appreciate that the focal topic or event will be much less prominent in their future lives than they imagine *(focalism)*.

Suppose you have applied for a job and you try to estimate how you will feel if you are or are not offered it. It is hard to appreciate that the outcome – success or failure – will only be one event in your busy life: you will still have to fill your day with your usual routines and distractions, and although the outcome of the job application will occupy your mind for a short while, it will soon be replaced by other concerns. Our lives are not vacuums. Failure to appreciate the extent of these distractions will cause you to over-estimate the impact of learning the outcome of your job application. This explanation for the over-estimation of future emotions has been supported by evidence that the tendency is reduced or eliminated by inducing people when they make their initial estimates to think in detail about all the other events that will be occupying them at the point in the future when the outcome in question is decided (Wilson et al., 2000). Reminding people that the focal outcome will be only one of numerous events competing for their attention tends to reduce affective forecasting errors.

It must be acknowledged that some have questioned the evidence for impact bias and suggested that people may be more accurate in forecasting their emotions than they have been given credit for. One reason for taking a slightly more optimistic view of affective forecasting is that some (possibly many) studies have inadvertently conflated forecasts of *specific* emotions with later reports about *general* well-being. In a typical study, participants might be asked to predict how they will feel about an important outcome such as an election. This focuses them on a specific event and how they will feel about it. Later on, after the election, they are asked how they feel *generally*. Thus the two questions are not quite the same. Someone might feel perfectly happy in general, but deeply unhappy about the fact that Barack Obama was elected President.

Levine and her colleagues (Levine et al., 2012) demonstrated the potential consequences of this sort of conflation of specific and general questions in a study in which participants estimated how they would feel about the outcome of the 2008 US presidential elections. Before the election they were asked, 'Imagine that it is the week of November 4th, just days after the presidential election, and that Barack Obama won the election and will be the next President,' and then rated how happy they thought they would feel. Similar questions were asked about John McCain. Naturally, Obama supporters expected that they would feel happy about an Obama victory and unhappy about a McCain one, and *vice versa* for McCain supporters. A few days after the election, some participants were asked (following the typical format of affective forecasting studies), 'In general, how happy are you feeling these days?' For these individuals, profound forecasting error was observed in that Obama supporters experienced considerably less happiness than they had anticipated before the election and McCain supporters considerably less unhappiness. Forecast happiness also correlated quite weakly with experienced happiness ($r = .3$).

For other participants, however, the question regarding their post-election experienced happiness was phrased rather differently. Instead of being asked how they were feeling in general, they were asked, 'How happy do you feel about Barack Obama being elected President?' Now a very different pattern of accuracy emerged: these ratings correlated very highly ($r = .89$) with the pre-election forecasts and showed no evidence of over-estimation. Thus when people are asked to forecast how they will feel about a specific state of affairs, and subsequently rate their experienced emotion regarding that very same state of affairs, the two judgments tend to align quite well. Although this conflation of specific and general questions does not explain all instances of impact bias (Wilson & Gilbert, 2013), it is clear that our ability to forecast our future emotions may not be as poor as research on affective forecasting has tended to claim.

DECISIONS AND EMOTIONS

How exactly do emotions alter or influence our decisions? One of the first people to emphasize the importance of understanding the link between decision making and emotion was Robert Zajonc. In a classic paper published in 1980 Zajonc argued that affective reactions to stimuli may precede cognitive reactions and thus require no cognitive appraisal; or as Zajonc (1980) rather pithily described it: 'preferences need no inferences.' He went on to argue that we sometimes delude ourselves into thinking that we make rational decisions – weighing all the pros and cons of various alternatives – when in fact our choices are determined by no more than simple likes or dislikes: 'We buy the cars we "like", choose the jobs and houses we find "attractive" and then justify these choices by various reasons . . .' (p. 155). If Zajonc's 'primacy of affect' argument is correct, then it has strong implications for our understanding of how we make decisions effectively and efficiently in our increasingly complex world (cf. Finucane et al., 2003).

One highly influential account of the role of affect in decision making comes from the work of Damasio, Bechara and colleagues (Bechara et al., 1994; Bechara et al., 1997; Damasio, 1996, 2000). In a series of experiments these researchers investigated the reasons behind the defective choices made by some brain-damaged individuals. Specifically, they were interested in why some individuals with damage to the prefrontal cortex of the brain are unable to learn from their mistakes, and often make decisions that lead to negative consequences, despite displaying intact general problem-solving and intellectual abilities.

As described in the previous chapter, in Bechara and collegues' Iowa Gambling Task, participants (both normal and brain damaged) sit in front of four decks of cards (A, B, C and D) and are asked to turn over cards one at a time from any of the four decks. The trick to learning the task is to discover what kind of monetary reward or punishment is associated with each deck. The interesting question is whether participants learn to choose from the decks that are advantageous in the long term, but have smaller immediate rewards (C and D), or are more influenced by the immediate gains from the long-term disadvantageous decks (A and B).

Damasio, Bechara and colleagues' results showed a clear difference between the performance of normal and brain-damaged individuals on the IGT. While normal participants learned to choose from the 'good decks' – choosing from C or D on approximately 70% of the trials – brain-damaged individuals showed the reverse pattern, choosing from A or B on around 70% of trials (Bechara et al., 1994). Why are the brain-damaged individuals insensitive to future consequences? Damasio (2000) has suggested that in these individuals 'the delicate mechanism of reasoning is no longer affected . . . by signals hailing from the neural machinery that underlies emotion' (p. 41). According to Damasio, the damage these individuals have suffered to specific areas in the brain results in the loss of a certain class of emotions and the loss of the ability to make rational decisions.

These ideas are encapsulated in what Damasio describes as the 'somatic marker hypothesis'. The central claim of the hypothesis is that in normal individuals, somatic or bodily states provide a 'mark' indicating the affective valence (positive or negative) for a cognitive scenario. Although Damasio further assumed that these somatic markers are unconscious (a claim that we questioned in the previous chapter), individuals with prefrontal cortex damage have lost the ability to mark scenarios with positive or negative feelings and so do not exhibit the appropriate anticipatory emotions when considering the future consequences of decisions. Put simply, the hypothesis explains the patients' gambling behaviour by suggesting that they failed to anticipate the catastrophic losses incurred by perseverance on the bad decks.

The IGT assesses decision making under uncertainty (or ambiguity), in the sense that at the outset of the task participants are ignorant of the probabilities of gains and losses (risks) associated with each deck. Neuroscience studies (e.g. Lee, 2013) have yielded considerable insight into the basic brain mechanisms of decision making under risk (where the probabilities are known a priori, as in studies of description-based decision making). Interestingly, recent work has suggested that the brain systems engaged in decision making under risk and uncertainty may be largely overlapping (Levy et al., 2010).

Another card game, the Columbia Card Task (CCT), has been developed in two versions designed specifically to examine differences between 'hot/ affective' and 'cold/deliberative' decision making (Figner & Weber, 2011). In the 'hot' version, participants are shown 32 cards face down on a computer screen and are asked to turn over as many cards as they like, one at a time, in an attempt to win points. Feedback is given after each card is turned, with some cards indicating a gain and others a loss. Each round continues until a participant decides to stop or when she turns over a loss card. In the 'cold' version of the game, rather than making card selections sequentially, participants indicate at the start of the round how many cards (out of 32) they would like to turn over. Feedback is then withheld until the completion of all rounds. In both versions the variable of interest is the number of cards a participant turns over: this variable is an indication of risk-taking because as more cards are turned over, the chance of turning over a loss card increases and the chance of revealing a gain decreases. Figner and colleagues argue that the 'hot' version with its stepwise, incremental decisions and immediate feedback raises the affective or emotional stakes of the game, whereas the 'cold' version emphasizes planning and deliberative information processing. Self-report and skin-conductance measures appear to support the claim that the hot CCT evokes stronger affective reactions (Figner & Murphy, 2011).

Perhaps more interestingly, these hot and cold versions of the task index different levels of risk-taking across age groups. Specifically, adolescents take more risks (turn over more cards) than children and adults in the hot version but not in the cold version. Moreover, they appear to be less sensitive to changes in the magnitudes of loss incurred by turning over the loss cards (a finding that is reminiscent of perseverance on the bad decks in the IGT) (Figner & Weber, 2011). These results serve to highlight that emotional influences on decisions are not only tied to characteristics of the task, but also to characteristics of individuals, such as their level of maturity (see also Peters et al., 2006). One final consideration is that the *domain* in which a decision – especially a risky one – is made can also influence the extent to which emotions are involved. Weber, Blais and Betz (2002) provide evidence for domain-specific attitudes to risk with important differences emerging across areas such as gambling, investing, ethical choices, health and safety and recreation.

THE AFFECT HEURISTIC AND RISK AS FEELINGS

Slovic and colleagues have investigated many of these ideas about emotional markers and differences in perception of risks across domains and individuals, and have suggested that 'mental representations of decision stimuli evoke online affective experiences that influence people's perceptions and consequently their judgments and decisions' (Finucane et al., 2003, p. 341). They propose an 'affect heuristic', arguing that in the same way that memorability and imaginability might be used as rules of thumb in probability judgment (for instance, the availability heuristic), so affect can be used as a cue for a variety of important judgments.

Empirical evidence supporting the operation of such a heuristic comes from research by Finucane et al. (2000). In one study they demonstrated that participants' judgments about the risks and benefits of an option could be altered by manipulating its global affective evaluation. For example, they suggest that nuclear power may appear more favourable in the light of information indicating that it has either high benefit or low risk. The notion here is that if you are given information about the benefits of nuclear power, your affective evaluation of nuclear power rises and so you infer – via the 'affect heuristic' – that the risks associated with nuclear power are low. In a similar fashion, if you are told that risks are high, your affective evaluation is lowered and you infer that nuclear power has low benefit. Finucane et al. contrast this affective account with a more cognitively derived prediction that inferences pertaining to the attribute that you did not receive any information about would remain unaffected (that is, if you only learned about the risks of nuclear power, your attitudes to its benefits should remain unchanged).

To test this idea Finucane et al. (2000) presented participants with vignettes designed to manipulate affect by describing either the benefits or risks of nuclear power. They then collected perceived risk and benefit ratings. The general pattern of results was that information about one attribute (e.g. risk) had a carryover effect on the attribute about which nothing had been learned directly (e.g. benefit). Finucane et al. interpreted this pattern in terms of people 'consulting their overall affective evaluation of the item when judging its risk and benefit' (p. 13) – in other words, people relied on an affect heuristic to make risk/benefit judgments.

A similar notion to the affect heuristic has been proposed by Loewenstein and colleagues (Loewenstein et al., 2001) with the 'risk as feelings' hypothesis. The hypothesis overlaps with the affect heuristic in proposing that emotional reactions and cognitive evaluations often work 'in concert to guide reasoning and decision making' (p. 270); but the hypothesis also states that cognitions and emotions may diverge and emotions may sometimes lead to behavioural responses that depart from ones that a purely cognitive appraisal might lead to.

A good example of the kind of evidence that Loewenstein and colleagues draw on in formulating the risk-as-feelings hypothesis is their interpretation of one of the most robust findings in the decision-making-under-uncertainty literature – the over-weighting of small or extreme probabilities. As we saw in Chapter 9, a change of .01 in the probability of an event occurring is deemed trivial if the probability of occurrence is already .49, but if it is a change from 0 to .01 it is interpreted as far more important. Kahneman and Tversky (1979a) described these non-linearities in probability weights in terms of a *certainty effect*. Loewenstein et al. (2001) argue that by including emotion in the 'prediction equation' this effect can be readily explained. Their suggestion is that an increase from 0 to .01 represents the crossing of a threshold from a consequence of no concern to one that becomes a source of worry (or hope, depending on the context); once this threshold has been crossed any subsequent increments in probability have a much lower emotional impact and thus tend not to influence choice (recall the Russian roulette example from Chapter 9 as an extreme illustration of such an effect).

An empirical investigation of the relation between emotion and over-weighting was reported by Rottenstreich and Hsee (2001). They were interested in whether the affective quality of an outcome influenced people's choices under conditions of certainty and uncertainty. Rottenstreich and Hsee's study had two conditions: a certainty condition in which participants were offered the choice between $50 in cash or the opportunity to meet and kiss their favourite movie star, and an uncertainty condition in which participants chose between two lotteries offering a 1% chance to win either the movie-star kiss or the cash. The authors proposed that if emotions impact on choice, then participants would prefer the more affect-laden option (kiss) to the affect-poor option (cash) in the uncertainty condition but show the opposite preference when the outcomes were certain. Note that a purely psychophysical analysis of this choice focuses solely on the given impact of a probability and not on the outcome to which that probability is attached. This means that both expected utility theory and prospect theory (see Chapters 8 and 9), which posit separate functions for the evaluation of outcomes and probabilities, predict no differences in preference between the certain and uncertain conditions.

The results provided support for Rottenstreich and Hsee's contention that the affective quality of the outcome would impact choice. In the uncertainty condition 65% of participants preferred the kiss lottery over the cash lottery. This was despite the fact that in the certainty condition 70% of participants preferred the $50 cash. This striking probability-outcome interaction (another example of a preference reversal) was interpreted as indicating that the weight assigned to a 1% probability is greater for the affect-rich kiss than for the affect-poor cash. In two follow-up experiments Rottenstreich and Hsee replicated this same basic finding using more comparable prizes (a $500 coupon redeemable either for tuition fees or a European holiday) and negative outcomes (an electric shock). Overall the results provided strong support for the notion that people are more sensitive to departures from certainty and impossibility for affect-rich than for affect-poor prizes.

Pachur, Hertwig and Wolkewitz (2014) followed up on the idea of a 'gap' between affect-rich and affect-poor decisions by inviting their participants to make choices between drugs with different probabilities of adverse side effects (affect–rich) or their monetary equivalents (affect–poor), elicited via contingent valuation. Consistent with Rottenstreich and Hsee's thesis, Pachur et al. found that choices differed between the two contexts and that they were more in line with standard expected value models (e.g. cumulative prospect theory) in the affect-poor cases than in the affect-rich ones.

Specifically, Pachur et al. reported that choices in affect-poor scenarios were best accounted for by an expected value strategy, whereas those in affect-rich scenarios were better captured by heuristics that ignore probabilities and choose solely on the basis of outcomes (e.g. minimax – a strategy which chooses the option with the more attractive worst outcome, irrespective of probabilities – see Savage, 1951). In a final experiment Pachur et al. demonstrated using a process-tracing task (or information board – see Chapter 3) that affect-rich choices led participants to examine outcome information more often than probability information; in affect-poor choices both types of information were looked at equally often. This pattern of findings led Pachur et al. to conclude that the psychological impact of probability information is diminished when options trigger strong affective reactions. This conclusion sits uneasily with Rottenstreich and Hsee's claim that small probabilities are given *more weight* when affect is involved. Clearly further research is needed to establish the relative roles of probabilities and outcomes in determining affectively laden choices.

IMAGERY, AFFECT AND DECISIONS

An important thread running through the approaches we have reviewed so far is the role of vivid imagery in determining emotional reactions and the decisions based on those reactions. Damasio's somatic marker hypothesis has at its core the notion that 'images' (loosely constrained to include real and imaginary visual images, as well as sounds and smells) are marked with positive and negative feelings throughout the course of our lives. Finucane et al. (2003) describe the 'basic tenet' of the affect heuristic as being the idea that positive and negative feelings are attached to images which subsequently influence judgments and decisions. The risk–as–feelings perspective (Loewenstein et al., 2001) proposes that a key determinant of feelings is the vividness of evoked imagery.

One factor, discussed by proponents of both the affect heuristic and risk-as-feelings perspective, that is claimed to influence the vividness of images, is whether statistical information is presented in terms of frequencies or in terms of probabilities. For example, Slovic, Monahan and MacGregor (2000) demonstrated that clinicians provided with recidivism risks presented as frequencies (e.g. 20 out of 100) judged mental patients as posing higher risks than when the same information was presented as probabilities (e.g. 20%). The explanation was that only the frequency presentation generated a 'terrifying image' of the 20 recidivists in the mind of the clinician and that the affect associated with this imagery led to the more extreme judgments (Slovic et al., 2000). In a similar vein, Purchase and Slovic (1999) reported that individuals were more frightened by information about chemical spills framed as frequencies (e.g. out of 1,000,000 exposed people, there will be 1 additional cancer death) than as probabilities (e.g. each exposed individual has an additional chance of .0001% of getting cancer). In a related set of findings Yamagishi (1997) demonstrated that participants rated a disease that kills 1,286 people out of every 10,000 as more dangerous than one that kills 24.14% of the population (despite the former number obviously being equivalent to only 12.86%!).

It is worth noting that although these format effects are interpreted as being due to evoked imagery, there is often no independent evidence that participants given frequency formats do indeed experience more vivid imagery than those given probability formats. However, Slovic et al. (2000) refer to an unpublished study which does provide support for this interpretation. Participants were given scenarios in which patients were described as having either a '10% probability of committing a violent act' or in frequentist terms as '10 out of 100 similar patients are estimated to commit an act of violence'. They were then asked to 'write a few brief thoughts or images that come to mind as you evaluate the risk posed by this patient' (p. 289). The frequency format produced images of violent acts in participants' reports, whereas the probability format did not. Newell, Mitchell and Hayes (2008) also found some evidence for an increase in the 'imaginability' of outcomes when frequency as opposed to probability formats were used.

Koehler and Macchi (2004) speculated that particular statistical formats need not necessarily evoke terrifying or affectively rich imagery to influence probability judgment; it may be sufficient for the statistics to simply evoke thoughts about other examples of the target event. Their 'exemplar cuing theory' states that 'the weight decision makers attach to low probability events is, in part, a function of whether they can easily generate or imagine exemplars for the event' (p. 540). They suggest, for example, that a lottery ticket might be more appealing if a potential purchaser is induced to think about other winning lottery tickets.

According to exemplar cuing theory, however, the use of a frequency format is not the crucial factor underlying the imaginability of exemplars. Koehler and Macchi propose a 'multiplicative' mechanism for the facilitation of exemplar generation. This mechanism cues exemplars when the product of the size of the reference class for the event and its incidence rate is greater than 1. For example, a lottery ticket described as giving a 1% chance of winning, with a reference class of 500,000 tickets sold in a day, generates 5000 exemplars of winning tickets. Such a ticket is deemed to be more appealing than a ticket with a 1% chance in a lottery in which only 50 tickets are sold in a day, because this arrangement only generates 0.5 of a winning ticket. Importantly, this mechanism is unaffected by the format of the information – that is, by whether incidence rates are provided as percentages (1%) or frequencies (1 out of 100).

The reason that format does not affect exemplar generation is that the format does not identify a relevant sample space within which to search for exemplars (Koehler & Macchi, 2004). This sample space is provided by the reference class (e.g. the number of other tickets sold), a factor common to both formats.

Koehler and Macchi tested their exemplar cuing model in the context of DNA evidence in mock jury trials. Participants rated the evidence against a defendant as weaker when the product of the reference class cued exemplars of other possible matches. However, Newell et al. (2008) were unable to find any evidence for a multiplicative mechanism in other situations involving low-probability events. In fact, in situations where the event was positive (e.g. winning a lottery), participants were more willing to play when, according to exemplar cuing theory, no exemplars of winning tickets were cued. Newell et al. explained their results in terms of participants anchoring on the reference class (that is, preferring lotteries in which fewer tickets are sold) rather than any multiplicative process.

Newell et al. (2008) also found strong evidence for a frequency format effect, contrary to the prediction of exemplar cuing theory. Specifically Newell et al. found that when the low-probability event was positive (e.g. winning a lottery), participants were more willing to engage in the proposed behaviour when frequency formats were used, but when the low probability event was negative (e.g. suffering a side-effect of a vaccine), they were less willing to engage in the behaviour when frequency formats were used. Overall the results were better explained by the simple frequency format account than by the more complicated exemplar cuing theory (but see Koehler & Macchi, 2009, for an alternative interpretation).

One final piece of evidence concerning the effect of imagery that is relevant to our discussion is the tendency for people to 'image the numerator' when presented with probability ratios. We encountered this effect in the last chapter when discussing the ratio-bias results of Bonner and Newell (2010). Recall that when offered the choice between a small bowl containing 1 red bean and 9 white beans and a large bowl containing 7 red beans and 93 white beans many participants behave as if the latter offers a better chance of picking a red bean. What prompts this irrational behaviour? Denes-Raj and Epstein (1994) explain the effect in terms of participants 'imaging the numerator' – that is, focusing on the overall number of red beans in the bowl rather than the probability ratio. They noted that participants often made statements such as 'I picked the one with more red jelly beans because it looked like there were more ways to get a winner, even though I knew there were more whites and the percents were against me' (p. 823). Thus the affect (or System 1 response, to use the language of Chapter 14) associated with winning combined with the images of winning beans appears to drive participants to make non-optimal choices, even when they knew that they shouldn't.

Koehler and Macchi (2004) reported similar effects again, using DNA statistics. They found that participants were more convinced by DNA evidence when a probability ratio was expressed as 1 out of 1000 than as 0.1 out of 100.

The interpretation is that innocent matches can only be imagined with the integer numerator (1) and not with the fractional numerator (0.1) (what does 0.1 of a person look like?).

Providing the image

Our focus in this section has been on how different numerical formats affect judgments and decisions through evoked imagery. However, as we noted, the evidence for imagery is often indirect (the images are assumed to be in participants' heads). What happens if the image is provided to the participant? How do graphical representations of statistics influence judgment? A study by Stone, Yates and Parker (1997) asked this question in relation to perceived risk. Stone et al. (1997) described the following scenario to participants:

> A set of four standard tyres costs $225. The risk of a serious injury from a tyre blowout is 30 per 5 million drivers. How much extra would you be willing to pay for a set of improved tyres in which the injury risk is halved to 15 per 5 million drivers?

The key manipulation was that in one condition the risk was conveyed in numbers (e.g. 30 per 5,000,000) but in the other 'graphical' condition the numerator of the risk statistic (i.e. either 30 or 15) was conveyed using figures of 'stick men' drawn on the page. Stone et al. found that participants in the stick-figures condition were willing to pay significantly more ($125 in addition to the $225) for the improved tyres than those in the numbers-only condition ($102). Stone et al. explained the effect in terms of the graphical display increasing participants' estimate of the risk of the standard tyres relative to the improved ones. In follow-up work (Stone et al., 2003) the boundaries of this effect have been explored, with the evidence suggesting that when both the numerator and the denominator are displayed graphically the difference between graphical and numerical displays disappears. Thus it seems that the increase in risk perception might operate in the same way as the 'image the numerator' mechanism, and unsurprisingly, when the image of the numerator is *provided* rather than evoked the effects are stronger.

SUMMARY

An increasing number of researchers are beginning to recognize the importance of studying the role of affect and emotion in decision making. Empirical evidence collected to date suggests that affect plays a part in heuristic judgment as well as in the evaluation of the probabilities and outcomes involved in choice. A common mechanism underlying these effects appears to be the emotional reactions evoked via vivid imagery. Further research is needed to understand how, when and why such imagery is evoked and how it influences decision making.

One area that is rather beyond the scope of this chapter is that of moral judgment. Any situation that invites us to consider moral factors – be it capital punishment, abortion rights, aid for the poor or action on climate change – is likely to evoke considerable emotional and affective reactions. Some theorists argue that in these morally loaded situations the 'emotional tail wags the rational dog' (Haidt, 2001); in other words, emotions come to the fore in favour of rational considerations. The burgeoning literature exploring these claims is too large to review here; we recommend the interested reader to Baron (2008) for a solid grounding in the moral judgment and choice literature.

Suggested further reading

- Dunn, B. D., Dalgleish, T., & Lawrence, A. D. (2006). The somatic marker hypothesis: A critical evaluation. *Neuroscience & Biobehavioral Reviews, 30,* 239–271. A detailed description of the somatic marker hypothesis together with a comprehensive review of the relevant evidence for and against it.
- Levine, L. J., Lench, H. C., Kaplan, R. L., & Safer, M. A. (2012). Accuracy and artifact: Reexamining the intensity bias in affective forecasting. *Journal of Personality and Social Psychology, 103,* 584–605. An introduction to some of the current debate on the magnitude of affective forecasting errors.
- Loewenstein, G., Weber, E., Hsee, C., & Welch, N. (2001). Risk as feelings. *Psychological Bulletin, 127,* 267–286. The original discussion of the risk-as-feelings hypothesis and the evidence supporting it.
- Slovic, P. (2010). *The feeling of risk: New perspectives on risk perception.* London: Earthscan. A collection of papers by a pioneer of research on the role of emotion, feelings and imagery on risk perception.

16 Group decision making

Chapter highlights

- A review of methods for combining opinions and achieving consensus
- A discussion of the 'wisdom of crowds' phenomenon
- A critical evaluation of the 'groupthink' concept.

Imagine that you are a contestant on the popular TV game show *Who Wants to Be a Millionaire?* You have answered a few questions and have some money in the bank but now you are facing a tricky question. You still have all three life-lines in hand, so to get help with the answer you can either phone a friend, ask the studio audience or use the 50:50 option to eliminate two of the four multiple-choice answers. Which lifeline should you opt for?

The choice between 'phone a friend' and 'ask the audience' requires deciding whether to rely on the intelligence of a single person or on the 'wisdom of the crowd' (Surowiecki, 2005). Intuitively, we might expect that the expert friend at home, selected to be a knowledgeable person, would be a better bet than the random collection of individuals who just happen to be in the studio. Is this intuition correct? Surowiecki (2005) obtained statistics from the US version of *Millionaire* and discovered that in fact the opposite was true: experts were right on average 65% of the time, but the audience picked the correct option on an impressive 91% of occasions!

Surowiecki acknowledges that this anecdotal evidence would not necessarily stand up to scrutiny – for example it may simply be the case that the audience are asked easier questions than the experts – but the data do appear to suggest that several heads might be better than one when it comes to making certain types of decisions. (An interesting footnote to Surowiecki's observation is that one of the most successful contestants on the Australian version of the show used his 'ask the audience' lifeline on the penultimate and thus very difficult question, and chose the option voted for by the *fewest* members of the audience. Presumably, the contestant reasoned that for very difficult questions the obvious answer is often wrong so it is reasonable to go against the audience choice – he was right (or lucky) and went on to win the million dollars.) These observations from game shows are all very interesting, but as the saying goes, the plural of 'anecdote' is not 'data' – what do we know from controlled empirical tests about the merits or otherwise of group decision making?

INTELLECTIVE AND JUDGMENT TASKS

The received wisdom concerning group decision making is that by working together on a problem we will arrive at a better solution than if we ponder the problem alone. Why else would we have invented juries, think-tanks or brainstorming sessions? However, the literature on group decision making does not always concur with this 'wisdom'. In a review of over 50 years' worth of research on group decision making, Hill (1982) concluded that group judgments were about as accurate as the second best individual member of the group. In a later analysis, Gigone and Hastie (1997) echoed the earlier conclusion: 'For the most part group judgments tend to be more accurate than the judgments of typical individuals, approximately equal in accuracy to the mean judgments of their members, and less accurate than the judgments of their most accurate member' (p. 153). The same basic conclusion was drawn by Kerr and Tindale (2004) in a more recent review of the literature.

So what is the empirical basis for these conclusions about group performance? One class of problems commonly used to compare individual and group performance is known as 'eureka-type' problems or intellective tasks because they have a demonstrable solution (e.g. Laughlin, 1999; Lorge & Solomon, 1958; Maier & Solem, 1952). A good example of one of these problems is the rule induction task used by Laughlin and colleagues (Laughlin, 1999; Laughlin, VanderStoep & Hollingshead, 1991) which requires participants to induce a rule involving standard playing cards. The task begins with one rule-following card exposed face up on the table; participants are then asked to select a new card from the deck in order to test their hypotheses about the rule. For example, the eight of diamonds might be face up and the to-be-discovered rule might be 'two diamonds followed by two clubs'. If a participant selects a card consistent with the rule, the card is placed to the right of the first card; if it is inconsistent it is placed underneath the first card. Participants continue these trial-by-trial tests of their hypotheses and attempt to use the feedback to infer the rule. The interesting manipulation in the experiments reported by Laughlin et al. (1991) is whether participants are invited to test their hypotheses individually or as part of a co-operative four-person group.

Laughlin et al. (1991) found that the best individual participants generated significantly higher proportions of correct hypotheses than did the groups or second, third or fourth best individuals. The groups and second individuals did not differ significantly from each other but they did produce more correct hypotheses than the third and fourth individuals. This pattern showing group performance to be equal to the second best individual is consistent with most previous research (e.g. Gigone & Hastie, 1997; Hill, 1982; Kerr & Tindale,

2004). Laughlin et al. conjectured that the poorer performance of the group may have been due to restrictions in the amount of evidence available for hypothesis testing and in the time available to discuss potential rules. In a follow-up study they tested this idea by allowing groups 10 extra minutes to solve the problem and by providing the opportunity to obtain more information about the rule on each trial. These manipulations led to equivalent performance for the groups and best individuals: both produced the same proportion of correct hypotheses. Thus it appears that given sufficient time and information groups can solve intellective tasks at least as well as the best of an equivalent number of individuals (Laughlin et al., 1991; Laughlin, 1999).

At the opposite end of the spectrum from intellective tasks are those commonly referred to as judgmental tasks. These tend to involve evaluative, behavioural or aesthetic judgments and have no demonstrable solution (e.g. sales forecasting) (Laughlin, 1999). How does the performance of groups and individuals compare on these types of tasks? Can the group perform as well as the best individual, as they seem to be able to do in the intellective tasks? A study reported by Sniezek (1989) addressed this question. Sniezek presented sales-forecasting problems to four groups of five undergraduate students. The task involved predicting sales volumes for a general store on campus. The groups received time-series data for the preceding 14 months and were asked to predict sales for the following month. Sniezek was interested not only in the comparison of individual and group performance but also in different methods of group interaction.

First, all members of the group provided an independent individual sales estimate which were then collated to provide a 'collective mean' judgment for the group. Second, one of four different group-decision techniques was imposed on the group: dictator, consensus, dialectic or Delphi. The dictator technique required group members to decide, through face-to-face discussion, who was the best member of the group and then to submit his or her estimate as the group estimate. The consensus technique was a straightforward discussion aimed at coming to group agreement on the estimate. For the dialectic technique members were provided with the collective mean estimate and then asked to think of all possible reasons why the actual sales volume might be higher or lower than the estimate, and following this discussion a revised group estimate was decided upon. Finally the Delphi technique required group members to provide estimates anonymously in a series of rounds, with no face-to-face discussion, until a consensus was reached. (This technique is supposed to maximize the benefits of group decision making and minimize possible adverse effects such as one person monopolizing discussion.)

To measure accuracy Sniezek looked at the Absolute Percent Error (APE) between the collective mean estimate and the group estimates. All of the group interaction techniques led to slightly lower forecast error than the simple aggregation of individual estimates. The greatest improvement was shown by the dictator group (reduction of 7.5%) followed by the Delphi (−2.3%), dialectic (−1.3%) and consensus (−0.8%) groups. However, the APE reduction achieved by the best members was 11.6%, indicating that the best members considerably outperformed all of the group-decision techniques. It is also worth noting that although groups seemed to be successful in identifying their best member – hence the relatively good performance of the dictator group – the dictators tended to change their judgment following group discussion, and these changes were all in the direction of the collective mean and hence more error. On average the final dictator estimates had 8.5% higher APE than the initial ones.

Sniezek took care to point out that the generality of these results is not known. The groups were small, the participants were undergraduates and the techniques were only tested in a single context (sales forecasting); nevertheless the results suggest that group interaction and discussion can sometimes lead to improvements in judgment accuracy – at least to a level that is better than the collective mean judgment. If this is the case, then it is important to consider how these interactions might occur – that is, how is the consensus achieved?

ACHIEVING A CONSENSUS

Sniezek and Henry (1990) describe consensus achievement in terms of a revision and weighting model. They argue that this two-stage model involves the conceptually distinct processes of revision and weighting, which can both operate to transform the distribution of individual judgments into a consensus group judgment. Sniezek and Henry suggest that the fundamental difference between these two processes is that revision occurs at the level of the individual within a group, whereas weighting (i.e. the combination of multiple judgments) occurs at a group level. The evidence from two experiments that were similar in design to the Sniezek (1989) experiment discussed earlier suggested that the weighting process was the more important one for achieving consensus and improving group accuracy (Sniezek & Henry, 1989; 1990). Social interaction of group members during the revision process had little appreciable impact on judgmental accuracy; only when the revision process ended and the group engaged in weighting and combining multiple individual judgments were improvements in accuracy observed.

Gigone and Hastie (1997) built on the ideas of the revision and weighting model but introduced a Brunswikian lens model framework for conceptualizing the group-judgment process. In Chapter 3 we encountered the lens model and discussed how the idea of a 'lens of cues' through which a decision maker sees the world is a metaphor that has inspired many researchers (e.g. Hammond & Stewart, 2001). Gigone and Hastie extended the metaphor to think about how groups might arrive at consensus judgments. Figure 16.1 is a graphical representation of their model. Its similarity to the individual lens model shown in Figure 3.1 should be immediately apparent. The far left-hand side in both diagrams represents the environment containing the to-be-judged criteria (C); the centre represents the cues which are probabilistically related

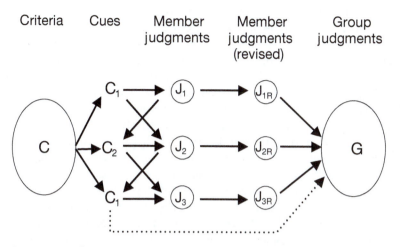

Figure 16.1 A lens model of the group-judgment process.

From Gigone, D., & Hastie, R. (1997). Proper analysis of the accuracy of group judgments. *Psychological Bulletin*, *121*, 149–167. Copyright 1997 by American Psychological Association. Adapted with permission.

to the criteria; the far right is the consensus group judgment (G) in Figure 16.1 and the individual judgment in Figure 3.1.

The clear difference between the individual and group models is that the latter has two extra layers or stages. In the group model the cues give rise to the initial member judgments and these are then revised before being combined into the group judgment. The advantage of using a lens model framework for thinking about group judgment is that the model lends itself readily to a variety of statistical techniques for analysing judgmental accuracy. For example, the 'lens model equation' (e.g. Cooksey, 1996) can be used to investigate the correlation between the best linear model of the environment (taking into account the validities of all the cues present) and the linear model used by each member of the group. Gigone and Hastie (1997) argue that a group's judgment accuracy depends fundamentally on the accuracy of individual member judgments, so examining individual judgments should be the starting point for understanding group performance.

The model can also be used to think about how accuracy is affected when the group convenes and discusses its judgment. For example, in group discussion a member might learn about a previously unknown judgment-relevant cue. If the member then weights this newly discovered cue appropriately, the result will be an increase in the overall correlation between the member's judgment and the environment. Successful combination of members' judgments depends partly on the way in which errors are distributed across the group (Hogarth, 1978). If group judgments converge towards those of a member whose judgment is highly correlated with the environment, then the group judgment will be accurate. However, if there is systematic bias in members' judgments, or a particularly persuasive individual in the group has low accuracy, then the combination process could result in poorer group judgment (Gigone & Hastie, 1997). Therefore if a group adopts an unequal weighting scheme, that weights some members' judgments more highly than others, it is very important for the group to be able to identify which of its members are most accurate. Recall that the Delphi technique, in which there is no interaction and judgments are made anonymously, was developed, in part, to counteract the negative impact of domineering but potentially inaccurate group members.

One final aspect of the model in Figure 16.1 that warrants mentioning is the possible direct influence that a cue can have on group judgments (depicted by the dashed line connecting the cues and the group judgment). There are at least two ways in which a cue might exert direct influence on the group judgment. One possibility is that there is an 'unshared' cue – that is, one that was only known by a single member of the group and did not come to light until the weighting and combination process. If that cue is a valid predictor, then its addition in the group judgment policy would increase the overall correlation with the environment. A second possibility is that during discussion the group might decide that a particular cue is very important and thus assign it more weight than did any group member in their individual judgments. Again, if the cue is valid, then correlational accuracy should improve.

These suggestions for how cue weights might be adjusted and integrated in group judgments are by no means exhaustive. As Plous (1993) notes, it is somewhat ironic that the complexity and richness of group research can hinder theoretical progress. The variety of different variables (tasks, group sizes, group members, decision rules) used in experimental studies often makes it very difficult to compare results or draw general conclusions. Gigone and Hastie's (1997) model is very useful in this regard as it provides a framework for applying a common methodology and for improving the ability to make precise comparisons of individual and group accuracy.

Despite the difficulty in drawing general conclusions about group perform-ance, one factor that does appear to be consistent in both intellective and judgmental tasks is the importance of identifying the best individual member of a group. In intellective tasks, such as the rule-induction task described earlier, identification of the best member should be straightforward because the solutions to these tasks are demonstrable. Once one member has 'got it' (a 'eureka moment'), he or she should be able to demonstrate the 'truth' of the solution. Indeed such a strategy is often described as a 'truth-wins' or 'truth-supported-wins' strategy (Hastie & Kameda, 2005).

In judgmental tasks the identification of best members is more difficult because there is not a demonstrable solution. In such tasks groups have to rely on intuitions about a member's credibility or likelihood of being able to generate an accurate estimate (Henry, 1993). An everyday example of this kind of phenomenon can be seen in group attempts to come up with an answer in trivia quizzes. Many of us will be familiar with the experience of being asked a general knowledge question at a trivia quiz and then trying to achieve a consensus by pooling the resources of the team. For example, if your team was asked, 'How long is the river Nile?', different members might attempt to justify their own estimates by claiming that they have been to Egypt and seen the Nile, or that they know the Amazon is so many kilometres and that the Nile is longer, and so on. In an experimental study using general knowledge questions, Henry (1993) provided evidence that groups were able to identify their best members at levels far exceeding chance expectations and that group members tended to engage in this process of identification as a normal part of the group-judgment process.

One finding that appears to contradict the general pattern of accurate identification of best members comes from a study of group-decision performance on a conjunction-error problem. Recall from Chapter 5 that the conjunction error is made when the probability of a conjunction (e.g. *P*(heart attack and over 55)) is rated as more probable than one of its conjuncts (e.g. *P*(heart attack)) (Tversky & Kahneman, 1983). Tindale, Sheffey and Filkins (1990, as cited in Kerr, MacCoun & Kramer, 1996) identified the number of persons in four-member groups who did and did not commit a conjunction error in individual pre-testing and then examined whether the group itself (following discussion of the problem) committed the error. Conjunction problems are intellective because they have a clear demonstrable solution (drawing a Venn diagram like the one shown in Figure 5.1 seems to convince most students) so one might expect that provided at least one member of each four-person group had not committed the error in pre-testing, the group as a whole would not commit the error.

This was not what Tindale et al. (1990) found. Seventy-three per cent of the groups containing one member who had not committed the error in pre-testing and three members who had, nonetheless committed the error when making a group judgment. Even those groups with even numbers of members who had and had not committed the error as individuals fared poorly – 69% still rated the conjunction as higher in probability.

Kerr et al. (1996) explained these results in terms of the normatively incorrect alternative (committing the error) exerting a 'strong functional pull' on groups. They argue that when a functional model of judgment (loosely defined as a 'conceptual system . . . that is widely shared and accepted in a population of judges' (p. 701)) operates in opposition to a normative model, the group discussion will tend to exacerbate any bias present in individual members. As we saw in Chapter 6, conjunction problems are sometimes interpreted in ways that are at odds with the normative model but consistent with everyday conceptions of language use (e.g. Gigerenzer, 1996; Hilton & Slugoski, 1986) and so it is quite plausible that a group member who knows the demonstrably correct answer might be persuaded that he or she has misinterpreted the question, thereby leading to a group tendency to commit the fallacy.

HARNESSING THE WISDOM OF THE CROWD

How might we be able to improve judgments in situations where *nobody* knows the answer? This is typical of many situations in which we try to make predictions or forecasts – be they about the weather, sport or world events. Consider the following question, posed to participants in a study on September 1, 2011: 'will there be a lethal confrontation (i.e. one resulting in at least one civilian death) of government forces in the South or East China Sea by December 31, 2011?' The context of this question was the rising escalations between Chinese fisherman and South Korean coastguards over allegations of illegal fishing. The question was one of many in the Intelligence Advanced Research Projects Activity (IARPA) forecasting tournament which ran between 2011 and 2013. Over 2000 participants answered hundreds of such questions on various geo-political events and provided their answers in terms of their certainty about whether an event would occur (0 *certain it will not occur*, 100 *certain it will occur*). The aim of the tournament was to identify the optimal way to combine the forecasts of all the individual participants – that is, to harness the wisdom of the crowd (Surowiecki, 2005).

The Good Judgment Project team (goodjudgmentproject.com), the group of researchers who won the tournament, developed statistical techniques that made predictions on the right side of 50/50 for 86.2% of all forecasts made (Tetlock et al., 2014). The methods they used echo some of the weighting and combination processes discussed above and in previous chapters (see Baron et al., 2014, for details), but in addition to the statistical methods, important psychological lessons were learned about how to get the best out of forecasters (Mellers et al., 2014). The researchers examined three factors: training, teaming and tracking. For training they contrasted forecasters who were randomly assigned to groups provided with no training, probability training or scenario training. Probability training highlighted many of the biases and fallacies that we have discussed throughout this book, such as base-rate neglect, over-confidence and confirmation bias. Scenario training made people aware of the importance of reference classes, the use of decision trees and subadditivity (see Chapter 6). Teaming was manipulated by assigning forecasters to work alone, in groups that could communicate, or in groups that had access to others' forecasts but in which discussion was not allowed. Finally, tracking involved monitoring performance and skimming off the top 2% of performers from the first year of the tournament and grouping them together as 'super forecasters' for the second year.

All of these factors proved to be important for improving individuals' forecasts, and in turn the accuracy of the statistical techniques for combining them. Probability training proved more effective than scenario training, and both were superior to no training. Working in a team that could communicate resulted in more accurate forecasts than working alone or in non-communicating groups. This result has important implications for understanding how the wisdom of crowds effect works – often aggregating estimates will be superior to individual ones because independent errors are uncorrelated and will cancel out in the aggregate. Sometimes the opportunity to discuss can be detrimental because it leads to correlated errors (as noted above – see Hogarth, 1978); but in the IARPA case it appears that the opportunity to share information was advantageous. This may have been due to a particular feature of the tournament: forecasters were allowed to update their predictions as many times as they liked prior to the event deadline. Thus in the case of the East China Sea question, one's early low-chance prediction might have elevated as events unfolded. Indeed, one of the key qualities of the super-forecasters – who ended up benefiting enormously from being grouped together – was the number of times they revised their estimates across time: an average of 7.8 predictions per question compared to around 1.5 for the 'standard' forecasters (Mellers et al., 2014).

An additional important observation that resonates with the themes of this book is that forecasters were remarkably well calibrated overall and that calibration improved significantly across the course of the tournament. Mellers et al. attribute this improvement to the regular provision of feedback on their performance and the opportunity to benefit from extended learning. However, even for the super-forecasters some events were just too unpredictable: on December 11, 2011, just before the question described above 'closed', a Chinese fisherman stabbed a South Korean coastguard officer to death – an event which took everyone by surprise and led to poorer answers by those trained, collaborative forecasters than the independent untrained ones.

Since the publication of Surowiecki's (2005) book there has been an explosion of interest in the 'wisdom of crowds' phenomenon. The IARPA project is just one example. Some researchers have sought ways to instantiate the wisdom of crowds 'in one mind' (e.g. Herzog & Hertwig, 2009), while others have examined how the inclusion of estimates of latent rather than observable knowledge can improve the wisdom of the crowd (e.g. Lee, Zhang & Shi, 2011). Extensions to this work are likely to prove a fruitful direction for future research, as is recent work examining the role of groups in strategic games, such as the Prisoner's Dilemma, the Ultimatum Game and the Dictator Game in which groups appear to behave more rationally than individuals (see Kugler, Kausel & Kocher, 2012; and Baron, 2008, for a more general discussion of the strategic interaction and social dilemmas literature). For the last section of this chapter, however, we turn to a well-documented situation in which combining heads appears to produce less rather than more wisdom.

GROUPTHINK: MODEL AND EVIDENCE

Consensus seeking is a good thing, providing all relevant and valid evidence is considered in the discussion (e.g. the dialectic technique used by Sniezek, 1989; or the probability training used by Mellers et al., 2014), but when there is a tendency to seek evidence that serves only to confirm an initial hypothesis or to support a pre-determined course of action, it can lead to disastrous consequences (cf. Wason, 1960).

The most provocative and influential work exploring such a tendency is that of Irving Janis. Janis (1972) coined the term 'groupthink' to describe the type of decision making that occurs in groups that are highly cohesive, insular and have directed leadership. Through the detailed analysis of a number of historical fiascos (the Bay of Pigs, President Johnson's decision to escalate the war in Vietnam, President Truman's decision to do the same in North Korea) and a comparison with major decisions that were successful (the implementation of the Marshall Plan after World War II), Janis identified the characteristics of groupthink-affected decision making: 'groupthink-dominated groups were characterized by strong pressures towards uniformity, which inclined their members to avoid raising controversial issues, questioning weak arguments, or calling a halt to soft-headed thinking' (Janis & Mann, 1977, p. 130).

More specifically, Janis (1972) proposed a model of groupthink with five antecedent conditions, eight symptoms of groupthink, and eight symptoms of defective decision making that result once groupthink has taken grip. The antecedents are those mentioned earlier: cohesiveness, insularity, directed leadership, along with two others – a lack of procedures for search and appraisal of information, and low confidence in the ability to find an alternative solution to the one favoured by the leader. The symptoms of groupthink are:

- the illusion of invulnerability creating excessive optimism and encouraging extreme risk-taking
- collective efforts to rationalize in order to discount warnings that might lead members to reconsider their assumptions
- an unquestioned belief in the inherent morality of the group, inclining members to ignore the ethical or moral consequences of decisions
- stereotyped views of rivals and enemies as too evil to warrant genuine attempts to negotiate
- direct pressure on any members who express strong arguments against any of the group stereotypes
- self-censorship of doubts or counterarguments that a member might have in order to create an illusion of unanimity within the group
- the emergence of self-appointed 'mindguards' who protect the group from adverse information that might shatter shared complacency about the effectiveness and morality of the group's decisions.

The groupthink concept has had a huge impact in both the academic literature (see for example the 1998 special issue of the journal *Organizational Behavior and Human Decision Processes*, 73/2) and popular culture (a Google search produced an incredible 1,730,000 hits for 'groupthink' (August 2014)). It is easy to understand the appeal of such a seductive concept. The eight symptoms of groupthink seem applicable to a vast variety of decision contexts, and appear to provide a useful framework for thinking about how defective decision making arises. Indeed, two of us were so struck by the similarities between the group-think symptoms and the characteristics of the decision making leading up to the invasion of Iraq in 2003 that we wrote to the *Psychologist* magazine stating that, 'at the time of writing (March 2003) it may just be the heads of state and government who are the victims, but if war results many more heads may be lost to groupthink' (Newell & Lagnado, 2003, p. 176). Tragically our predictions were correct and post-invasion Iraq is still suffering from many of the symptoms of defective decision making that Janis identified as resulting from groupthink-dominated decisions (e.g. the failure to work out the risks of a preferred strategy and the failure to develop contingency plans). We were not alone in our assessment of the influence of groupthink on the decision to go to war. After the invasion the US Senate Select Committee on Intelligence reported the following:

> Conclusion 3: The Intelligence Community suffered from a collective presumption that Iraq had an active and growing weapons of mass destruction (WMD) program. This 'group think' dynamic led Intelligence Community analysts, collectors and managers to both interpret ambiguous evidence as collectively indicative of a WMD program as well as ignore or minimize evidence that Iraq did not have active and expanding weapons of mass destruction programs. This presumption was so strong and formal-ized that Intelligence Community mechanisms established to challenge assumptions and group think were not utilized.
>
> Source: http://www.intelligence.senate.gov/108301.pdf

However, the seductiveness and applicability of the groupthink concept may also be its weakness. Aldag and Fuller (1993; Fuller & Aldag, 1998) have questioned whether groupthink is merely a convenient and over-used label and argued that direct empirical support for the groupthink model is almost non-existent. In a characteristic quote they stated, 'Our contention is that even the most passionately presented and optimistically interpreted findings on group-think suggest that the phenomenon is, at best, irrelevant. Artificially gathering a sampling of decision-relevant factors into a reified phenomenon has only resulted in the loss of valuable information' (Fuller & Aldag, 1998, p. 177). The lost information that Fuller and Aldag refer to is the advances that they suggest could have been made in understanding deficiencies in group decision making if so much research had not been constrained to fit within the groupthink framework. Fuller and Aldag go as far as suggesting that some researchers have unwittingly acted as virtual 'mindguards' of the groupthink concept.

To explain the lasting popularity of groupthink Fuller and Aldag invoke a rather esoteric but nevertheless instructive metaphor. They describe groupthink as an 'organizational Tonypandy' after the Welsh mining village which was reportedly the site of violent riots in 1910–11. The official story of the riots describes hordes of miners, who were striking for better pay and conditions, clashing with police and soldiers in a series of bloody incidents. In fact there was apparently no serious bloodshed and some doubt that army troops were even involved. Despite these doubts, stories about the riots have been perpetuated over time, and in some circles have taken on legendary status. Fuller and Aldag argue that the same thing has happened with groupthink. Proponents of the phenomenon, despite being aware of the lack of empirical evidence supporting it, continue to 'herald its horrors . . . building a mosaic of support from scattered wisps of ambiguous evidence' (p. 165/6).

The truth about groupthink probably lies somewhere in between the colourful language used by Fuller and Aldag (1998) and the rhetoric of its proponents. There is little doubt that the concept has proved to be very useful in focusing attention on the potential flaws of group decision making (e.g. Turner & Pratkanis, 1998), but the time to move on to testing other potential models of group functioning (e.g. the General Group Problem Solving model, Aldag & Fuller, 1993) and to break free from the constraints of groupthink theorizing is almost certainly long overdue.

SUMMARY

Research on group decision making is both appealing and frustrating. The richness of the environments tends to make controlled empirical testing difficult and thus theory advances slowly. A fair amount of research is concentrated on eureka/intellective and judgmental tasks. In both types of tasks group performance tends to exceed the collective mean but not reach the level of the most talented individuals in the group. The Brunswikian lens model provides a useful metaphor for conceptualizing the processes of group discussion, consensus seeking and revisions of estimates in judgmental tasks. The recent interest in the 'wisdom of the crowd' has seen several advances in understanding both the statistical and psychological basis of the phenomenon. One of the dangers of blinkered consensus seeking is groupthink, a concept that has inspired a great deal of research despite claims that underpinning empirical evidence for the concept is scarce.

Suggested further reading

- Herzog, S. M., & Hertwig, R. (2009). The wisdom of many in one mind: Improving individual judgments with dialectical bootstrapping. *Psychological Science*, *20*, 231–237. An empirical paper describing how individuals can attempt to harness the wisdom of the crowd within.
- Kugler, T., Kausel, E. E., & Kocher, M. G. (2012). Are groups more rational than individuals? A review of interactive decision making in groups. *Wiley Interdisciplinary Reviews: Cognitive Science*, *3*, 471–482. A recent review examining how groups decide in strategic games.
- Surowiecki, J. (2005). *The wisdom of crowds: Why the many are smarter than the few*. London: Abacus. An accessible account, written by a journalist, describing the evidence for the 'wisdom of crowds'.

17 Applying psychological insights to the world outside the laboratory

---

Chapter highlights

- Discusses how adopting an outside view can lead to improved judgment
- Examines the power of 'considering the opposite' when making judgments
- Promotes the usefulness of decision tools and support systems
- Explores the role of choice architectures and 'nudges'.

One of the aims of this book, and indeed the aim of many decision researchers, is to discover and highlight ways to improve decision making (e.g. Hogarth, 2001). With this aim in mind, this penultimate chapter will introduce three different approaches to improving decision making. The goal is to tie these approaches to specific examples that we have covered in the preceding chapters, and to provide some practical advice that can be used in the world outside the psychology laboratory. One of the major strengths of research into judgment and decision making is its applicability. Many of the researchers involved in the discipline are motivated by the potential for experimental findings to have real influence on the way decisions are made by individuals, companies and even governments (e.g. Kahneman, 2011; Thaler & Sunstein, 2008). We consider three approaches to improving or debiasing decision making, that can be loosely grouped under the headings individual, cultural (or institutional) and tools or resources.

INDIVIDUAL TECHNIQUES FOR IMPROVING DECISION MAKING

One of the most prevalent types of decisions that we face is predicting or forecasting the future on the basis of past experience. We have emphasized throughout this book that the probabilistic nature of the world makes such predictions difficult. Information in the environment can only be used as an imperfect indicator of an outcome of interest because cues and outcomes are typically only probabilistically related (e.g. Hammond, 1955). There is, however, one important technique that we can all adopt that can help to mitigate the noisiness and unpredictability of our uncertain world.

Adopting the outside view

An example used by Daniel Kahneman (e.g. Kahneman & Lovallo, 1993; Kahneman & Tversky, 1979b; Lovallo & Kahneman, 2003) provides an excellent introduction to our first technique. Kahneman tells the story of how he was involved in a project to design a curriculum on judgment and decision making for use in schools in Israel. About one year into the project the collection of academics and teachers that comprised the small group turned to the issue of how long they thought the project would take. Each member of the group was invited to make individual estimates of the number of months required to bring the project to completion. The estimates ranged from 18 to 30 months.

Kahneman recounts that at this point he asked the senior expert on curriculum development in the group the following question: 'We are surely not the only team to have tried to develop a curriculum where none existed before. Please try to recall as many such cases as you can. Think of them as they were in a stage comparable to ours at present. How long did it take them, from that point, to complete their projects?' (Kahneman & Lovallo, 1993, pp. 24–25). The answer was rather sobering and completely at odds with the estimates provided by the individuals. The expert first stated that around 40% of the groups given such a task eventually gave up, and furthermore that those that did complete successfully took between 7 and 10 years! He also noted that there was nothing about the composition of the current group that led him to believe that their performance would be any better than previous groups.

Kahneman and Lovallo (1993) suggest that this story serves to illustrate the adoption of two distinct modes of prediction. The individuals spontaneously adopted an 'inside view' to the problem, in which they tended to focus solely on the particular problem at hand, paying special attention to its unique or unusual features and extrapolating on the basis of its current status (cf. Lovallo & Kahneman, 2003). In contrast the expert, having been prompted by Kahneman's question, adopted an 'outside view' in which the details of the current project were essentially ignored and the emphasis was placed on generating a reference class of cases deemed to be similar to the current one and then placing the current project somewhere in that distribution of similar cases.

So which mode of prediction turned out to be more accurate? The 'results' could not have been more compelling: the team finally completed the curriculum 8 years later! And even then the resulting curriculum was rarely used (Lovallo & Kahneman, 2003). Thus the outside view with its prediction of 7–10 years was much more accurate than the optimistic estimates of 18–30 months generated via the inside view. Lovallo and Kahneman (2003) make a particular case for adopting an outside view in the context of managerial and executive decision making. They argue that many disastrous decisions made by executives can be traced to the 'delusional optimism' which results from taking an overly inside view of forecasting (cf. March & Shapira, 1987). They propose a straightforward five-step methodology for adopting the outside view, steps that they argue will improve forecasting accuracy considerably in organizational settings (see also Kahneman & Tversky, 1979b). The basic ideas are to identify a reference class of analogous past initiatives or projects, to determine the distribution of outcomes for those initiatives, and to place the current project at an appropriate point along that distribution.

Lovallo and Kahneman (2003) illustrate the five-step methodology with the example of a studio executive attempting to forecast the sales of a new film. In this context, the five steps would be something akin to the following:

1. *Select a reference class*: perhaps the most difficult step – this involves determining a set of other instances that are sufficiently similar and thus relevant to the problem you are considering, but sufficiently broad to allow for meaningful statistical comparison. For the studio executive this would amount to formulating a reference class that included recent films of a similar genre (action blockbuster), starring similar actors (Tom Cruise) and with comparable budgets ($50 million), and so on.

2. *Assess the distribution of outcomes*: attempt to document the outcomes of all members of your reference class as precisely as possible. This should involve working out an average outcome as well as some measure of variability. For the film example, the executive might find that of the films in the reference class, the average amount of money made through ticket sales was $30 million, but that 10% made less than $5 million and 5% made more than $100 million.

3. *Make an intuitive prediction of your project's position in the distribution*: use your own judgment to rate how the current project compares with all those in the reference class and position it accordingly. In other words the executive should try to weigh up everything he or she knows about the new film, compare it to all the others in the reference class and try to predict where sales of the new film would fall in the distribution. Lovallo and Kahneman (2003) suggest that the intuitive estimate made by the executive is likely to be biased (recall all the reasons why intuitive judgment may be poor that we discussed in Chapter 3) and so propose two further steps to adjust this intuitive forecast.

4. *Assess the reliability of your prediction*: the aim of this step is to estimate the correlation between the forecast and the actual outcome. The correlation can be expressed as a co-efficient between 0 (no correlation) and 1 (perfect correlation). This can either be done on the basis of historical precedent (the accuracy of past similar forecasts) or through a subjective comparison with similar forecasting situations. For example, the studio executive might have the sense that the sales forecast would be more accurate than, say, the ability of a sports commentator to predict the score in next year's FA Cup Final but

not as accurate as a meteorologist's prediction of the temperature the day after tomorrow. By thinking carefully about the correlations between predictions and outcomes for these different types of domains, the executive should be able to estimate where the predictability of sales forecasts for films lies on an overall scale of predictability.

5. *Correct the intuitive estimate*: as noted, the estimate made in Step 3 is likely to be biased, and probably optimistically so (predictions will deviate too far – in an upward direction – from the average outcome of films in the reference class), so in Step 5 the aim is to adjust the estimate back towards the average by using the analysis of predictability conducted in Step 4. The less predictable the executive believes the environment to be, the less reliable the initial forecast and the more the forecast needs to be regressed towards the mean for the reference class. In the film example, the mean grossing of films in the reference class is $30 million; if the executive estimated $75 million worth of ticket sales, but a correlation coefficient between forecast and outcome of only 0.55, then the regressed estimate of sales would be calculated in the following way:

$$\$30m + [0.55(\$75m - \$30m)] = \$54.75m$$

The reduction from an estimate of $75 million to just over $50 million illustrates how the adjustment for an optimistic bias in Step 3 can be substantial – especially when the executive is not confident in the reliability of the prediction (i.e. in highly uncertain environments) (Lovallo & Kahneman, 2003). The studio executive example illustrates the applicability of the outside view in the organizational context, but it is relatively simple to see how the procedures could be applied to many of the judgment and decision-making tasks we face (see Lagnado & Sloman, 2004b). One important caveat to the general applicability of the approach is the difficulty in selecting the appropriate reference class. As we discussed in Chapter 5, generating the correct reference class is not a trivial problem (recall the example of introducing the traffic congestion charge in London), but if we can generate an appropriate class, then following the five steps advocated by Lovallo & Kahneman (2003) should serve to improve our forecasts and judgments in a range of different areas.

Consider the opposite

Another individual technique for improving decision making which is closely related to the 'outside view' is to 'consider the opposite' (Larrick, 2004; Mussweiler, Strack & Pfeiffer, 2000). As Larrick (2004) notes, this strategy simply amounts to asking oneself, 'What are some of the reasons that my initial judgment might be wrong?' It is effective because it counters the general tendency to rely on narrow and shallow hypothesis generation and evidence accumulation (e.g. Heath, Larrick & Klayman, 1998; Klayman, 1995; McKenzie, 2004).

An experimental example of the 'consider the opposite' principle in action comes from a study on judgmental anchoring by Mussweiler and colleagues (Mussweiler et al., 2000). Anchoring – the process by which numeric estimates are assimilated to a previously considered standard of comparison (e.g. Tversky & Kahneman, 1974, and see Chapter 9) – is one of the most robust judgment heuristics. Mussweiler et al. (2000) demonstrated that the magnitude of the anchoring effect could be reduced simply by asking people to list anchor-inconsistent arguments. Mussweiler et al. presented 60 car experts with an actual car and an anchor estimate of its value. The anchor was either set to be high (5000 German Marks) or low (2800 German Marks). The expert was first asked to state whether he thought the anchor was too high or too low, and then to provide his own estimate. (This is the standard procedure in anchoring experiments.)

The novel manipulation was that before providing an estimate, half of the experts were asked to consider possible reasons for why the anchor value might be inappropriate, whilst the other half made their own estimate directly after the comparative judgment. The results indicated a clear effect of this manipulation: when the experts were instructed to generate anchor-inconsistent arguments the effect of anchoring was much weaker. For example, experts given the high anchor and not asked to generate arguments provided a mean estimate of 3563 German Marks, whereas those asked to consider the arguments provided an estimate of only 3130 German Marks.

Mussweiler et al. (2000) suggest that considering the opposite mitigates anchoring because it 'debiases the informational basis for the judgment' (p. 1146). In other words using a technique that overcomes the tendency to only consider a narrow sample of evidence can greatly improve judgment. The general strategy of considering the opposite has also proved to be effective in reducing hindsight bias and over-confidence (Arkes, 1991; Soll & Klayman, 2004). Notably, it also forms the basis for what Herzog and Hertwig (2009) describe as harnessing the 'wisdom of the crowd in one mind'. Recall from the previous chapter the advantages that can be found from pooling individual estimates and then averaging. Herzog and Hertwig document how similar effects can arise when a person interrogates himself as to why an initial estimate of a quantity (e.g. how many seats are there in the Sydney Opera House?) might be wrong, then generates an alternative estimate and takes the average of the two.

CULTURAL TECHNIQUES FOR IMPROVING DECISION MAKING

We have seen throughout this book that there are myriad ways in which individual decision making can divert from the straight and narrow road. Although some of these errors and diversions may be more apparent than real (i.e. products of the artificial experimental situations – see Gigerenzer, 1996;

Hogarth, 1981), many are ubiquitous even in real-world situations (the anchoring effect described above is a good example).

However, we have also emphasized how, in many situations, the opportunity to learn and be exposed to useful feedback on our performance can reduce or eliminate some of these errors. Given that these shortcomings in individual decision making can be alleviated, are there any practices that a culture or institution can encourage to provide opportunities for learning and to counter the defective individual tendencies? Heath et al. (1998) suggest a number of practices that they argue can be used by institutions to 'effectively repair the cognitive shortcomings of individuals' (p. 1). In this section we will review briefly some of these practices.

Heath et al. note that when faced with a problem, decision makers often generate too few hypotheses and tend only to search for information confirming their initial diagnosis (e.g. Klayman, 1995; Wason, 1960; see McKenzie, 2004, for a detailed discussion). To combat this tendency in individuals the Toyota Company introduced the 'Five Whys' technique, encouraging employees to analyse problems in depth rather than superficially. For example, an employee faced with a broken machine might ask him or herself the following types of question (Imai, 1986): Q1: Why did the machine stop? A1: Because the fuse blew due to an overload. Q2: Why was there an overload? A2: Because the bearing lubrication was inadequate. Q3: Why was the lubrication inadequate? A3: Because the lubrication pump malfunctioned, etc. By asking a series of questions the employee is more likely to discover the root cause of the problem (in this case grime in the lubrication pump) rather than stopping the search for information when the first plausible hypothesis was generated (the blown fuse).

Although not noted by Heath et al., it is clear that the Five Whys technique resonates strongly with Kahneman and Lovallo's (1993) recommendation to take the 'outside view' and Mussweiler et al.'s (2000) suggestion to 'consider the opposite'. In asking the first question, the employee might invoke a detail that is specific to the problem at hand, but by delving deeper, the subsequent whys are likely to lead the employee to think about the problem in a broader situational context and thus to come up with a better solution.

A further problem with information search and evaluation that Heath et al. discuss is the tendency for individuals' samples of information to be biased by information that is readily available in memory. Tversky and Kahneman (1973) and many other researchers since (see Schwarz & Vaughn, 2002, for a more recent summary) have shown that information that is available is also perceived to be more frequent, probable and causally important. There is now some debate over whether availability effects are due to a bias in the cognitive process or bias in the external sample of information (see Fiedler, 2000; Fiedler & Juslin, 2006, and the discussion in Chapter 6), but regardless of the basis of the biasing effects, they are problematic if they result in erroneous judgments. Heath et al. (1998) describe a technique used by Motorola to overcome the effects of availability. Motorola had come to realize that a division developing equipment for cellular phones was devoting all its time and energy to their large clients while neglecting the large number of smaller customers. Presumably, larger clients were more salient and came to mind more easily and thus their needs were at the fore when new products were being developed. To overcome this 'availability bias' Motorola developed a Feature Prioritization Process in which they surveyed *all* their customers – not just the larger 'more available' ones – several times a year and then weighted the inputs based on customer volume and priority. By employing such a technique the company ensured that all relevant information was considered in the product-evaluation process.

The final 'cognitive repair' that we will consider is closely related to the mechanisms underlying some of the emotional effects that were reviewed in Chapter 15. Recall that many researchers have found evidence that information formats that support vivid imagery, or decision options that have high emotional content (and are thus vividly imagined) tend to have a disproportionately strong influence on decision makers (e.g. Rottenstreich & Hsee, 2001; Slovic et al., 2000). Heath et al. (1998) describe a technique used by Microsoft which capitalizes on this tendency for vivid information to be weighted more heavily than pallid information. According to Cusumano and Selby (1995), software developers at Microsoft were reluctant to believe the statistics obtained by the usability group on the ease of using particular programs and features. The developers often dismissed the statistics as being based on a non-representative sample of 'stupid' people who should just 'look in the manual' if they didn't understand something.

In an attempt to repair this tendency to ignore statistical information, Microsoft made the information more vivid by forcing developers to watch customers learning to use the new products. A 'usability lab' was set up with a one-way mirror allowing software developers to receive real-time and extremely vivid feedback about how people actually used new programs. The use of the lab led to much greater empathy between developers and customers. Heath et al. (1998) observe that this cognitive repair is interesting because it uses one kind of bias (the tendency to over-weight vivid information) to counteract another (the tendency to under-weight statistical information). Experimental data consistent with the over-weighting/under-weighting effect of vivid/statistical evidence was reported by Borgida and Nisbett (1977).

In summarizing their review of cognitive repairs, Heath et al. (1998) conclude that the most successful ones are likely to be those which are relatively simple, domain specific and emergent (bottom up) rather than imposed (top down). Simplicity and domain specificity are encouraged for the straightforward reason that a strategy which is easy to memorize and implement, and for which the applications (domains) are easy to recognize, is more likely to be put into practice than a complex procedure with non-obvious applicability. The emergent property of repairs is emphasized because of the need for decision makers to have a sense of ownership and input into generating solutions. A strategy imposed by management may be viewed with scepticism, but if a particular team has identified a bias or deficiency and developed their own repair, it is likely to be viewed in a much more positive light. As we will see in the next section, the lack of transparency and human input has been one of the major sources of resistance to many of the standard 'tools' for improving decision making (cf. Yates, Veinott & Patalano, 2003).

TOOLS FOR IMPROVING DECISION MAKING

The esteemed decision theorist Ward Edwards told the following story of how he helped a student to decide between two university courses (a problem that is probably pertinent to many readers). The student was trying to decide between two advanced courses (one in international relations and one in political science) that were being offered at the same time, thus preventing her from doing both. Both courses satisfied the student's degree requirements. In order to help her decide, Edwards (Edwards & Fasolo, 2001) used a decision-analytic technique called Multi-Attribute Utility Measurement (often called MAU for short, Keeney & Raiffa, 1976; Pidgeon & Gregory, 2004; Raiffa, 1968; von Winterfeldt & Edwards, 1986). The core assumption of MAU is that the value ascribed to the outcome of most decisions has multiple attributes. The technique employed by MAU allows for the aggregation of the value-laden attributes. This aggregated value can then act as input for a standard subjective utility maximizing framework for choosing between alternatives (see Chapter 8). The particular rule for aggregation depends on the interactions amongst attributes, but we need not concern ourselves too much with the details.

How does this apply to the student's 'choice-of-course' dilemma? Edwards began by eliciting attributes for the two course options from the student. Attributes included whether the student felt that she would learn something, the amount of work involved and feelings about the interpersonal interactions with the professor and other students. The next step was to assign weights (degree of importance) to the attributes. Again, the exact method used is not important, but part of the process involved a method called SMARTER (Edwards & Barron, 1994) in which rank orders of the weights are elicited and then the ranks are used as the basis for approximating the actual weights. The final step of elicitation required the student to score each of the two courses on a 0–100 scale for each attribute. For example, the student rated inter-national relations as 42 but political science as 80 on the 'interpersonal interactions' attribute, reflecting her stated dislike for the professor teaching the former course.

Edwards was now ready to compute the MAU for each course. This was done simply by multiplying the weight of each attribute by its score and summing across all the attributes. The result was clear cut – the MAU for international relations was 37.72 but for political science it was 54.57. Edwards made the obvious recommendation – according to this analysis if the student wanted to maximize her subjective expected utility she should choose political science. The student said she intended to choose the course; history does not relate whether she actually did.

To many of us the MAU procedure might seem rather complicated, time consuming and opaque (how exactly are the weights derived? How do we decide what attributes to consider?). Perhaps pre-empting these kinds of criticisms, Edwards (Edwards & Fasolo, 2001) justifies the use of the MAU tool by saying that the student showed a clear understanding of the methodology (even endorsing the 'rank order centroid weights' as being representative of her own values) and that the whole procedure, including explanation time, took less than three hours to complete. Moreover, the MAU tool is widely applicable and could be used in many of the situations we have discussed throughout this book, such as buying a car, choosing an apartment to rent, deciding where to invest our money, even the decision to marry. In all of these situations options can be defined (e.g. cars, financial institutions, people), attributes elicited (e.g. engine type, account type, sense of humour) and weighted for importance, and scores assigned to each attribute – just like in the student's course example. The MAU method provides a clear and principled way to make good, rational, decisions.

Nevertheless, the time needed to implement such a process is often more than we can afford even for important decisions (e.g. Gigerenzer et al., 1999). Are there any automated procedures that employ the same rational principles as decision-analytic techniques but take the 'hard yards' out of the process? As Larrick (2004) points out, perhaps the ultimate standard of rationality might be the decision to use superior tools.

The generic label for automated procedures for aiding decision processes is Decision Support Systems (DSS). Yates et al. (2003) define such a system as 'a computer based system, typically interactive, that is intended to support people's normal decision making activities' (p. 39). These systems are not intended to replace the decision maker, nor indeed to make a decision exclusively, but rather to aid in the decision-making process. Yates et al. (2003) describe such systems as having three main components: a data component which can provide substantial amounts of information at the touch of a button; a model component that can perform operations on retrieved data that are often far more complicated than a decision maker alone could perform; and a dialogue component which allows interaction with the system (for instance through a search engine).

Although we might associate DSS with major industry or government bodies (e.g. road and transport authorities, finance groups), now that searching for information and indeed purchasing products online is so prevalent, we often find ourselves interacting with such systems (Edwards & Fasolo, 2001; Yates et al., 2003). Given that consumer websites now commonly display information about a vast range of products, a person wishing to buy a new product – say a digital camera – might first access some online resource to discover what is available (cf. Fasolo et al., 2005, discussed in Chapter 3). Yates et al. (2003) suggest that the information contained in these sites can be considered the output from the data component of the consumer's 'shopping decision-support system'. The dialogue component could be thought of as comprising the consumer's computer, the software used to navigate the web and the site's facilities for displaying information in different orders and categories (e.g. listed by price, by number of megapixels, etc.). The model component is then represented by any functions that a consumer might use to decide on a favoured model. For example, overall ratings might be computed by summing weighted averages of the different attributes (in much the same way as Edwards did for his student). By engaging with the shopping DSS in this way the consumer can compare any number of given products and choose whichever one achieves the highest rating.

Edwards and Fasolo (2001) provide an excellent summary of the advantages and disadvantages of various web-based DSSs, comparing, for example, compensatory sites (those that focus on alternatives) with non-compensatory sites (those that focus on attributes). (Recall our discussion of information combination strategies of these types in Chapter 3.) Edwards and Fasolo note that decision makers on the web tend to prefer non-compensatory sites because these are more time-efficient than compensatory ones. This time efficiency is due largely to the fact that non-compensatory sites eliminate ('winnow out') options more quickly than compensatory sites. Although time efficient, there is an associated risk of 'winnowing out winners' – that is, eliminating an option early on in the process, which had it remained in the choice set, would have been the eventual winner (see the apartment-renting example in Chapter 3).

The conclusion seems to be that compensatory sites should be used to make decisions, but due to time pressure decision makers often opt for the less effective non-compensatory sites. The simple lesson is that when using web-based DSSs you should take time, and only eliminate an option if you are absolutely sure that it could never be included in your choice set (e.g. if you knew you'd never pay more than $500 for a camera). Despite some of the limitations with web-based DSSs, Edwards and Fasolo (2001) draw an upbeat conclusion, stating that 'decision tools will be as important in the 21st Century as spreadsheets were in the 20th' (p. 581).

Yates et al. (2003) are similarly optimistic about decision-support systems. They suggest that one of the reasons why these systems have been relatively successful and proved far more popular than some other basic decision-aiding tools (such as traditional decision analysis, social judgment theory, and debiasing techniques) is that they place a clear emphasis on improving outcomes. Many of the other techniques (decision analysis, for example) are more concerned about the normativity of a decision process or the statistical properties of multiple repeated instances rather than one-shot decisions (e.g. social judgment analysis).

In Yates et al.'s analysis of the reasons decision makers give for a decision being 'good' or 'bad' (see Chapter 2), a key finding was the role played by the experienced outcome. Eighty-nine per cent of bad decisions were described as bad because they resulted in bad outcomes; 95.4% of good decisions were described as good because they yielded good outcomes. DSSs are probably successful because they retain the decision maker as an integral part of the decision process (cf. Heath et al., 1998) while emphasizing improving outcomes. This is done principally by providing information that the decision maker may not otherwise have been aware of (e.g. the models and specifications of the cameras on the market), and by assisting in the process of winnowing out undesired options.

CHOICE ARCHITECTURE: THE ULTIMATE TOOL?

Decision Support Systems are very explicit tools designed to help us improve our decision making, but are there other, more subtle ways in which we can be encouraged to make better choices? Richard Thaler and Cass Sunstein in their highly influential book *Nudge* (2008) make the case that many of our decisions are influenced by the 'choice architecture' in which we find ourselves. The way that options are presented on a screen, or the way that food is arranged in a canteen can all 'nudge' us towards making particular choices. Take the example of organ donation (Johnson & Goldstein, 2003). In some countries, like Austria, the default is to be enrolled as an organ donor – there is a presumed consent that you are willing to donate your organs in the event of your death. In other countries, like Germany, you have to make an active decision to become a donor. Johnson and Goldstein found that this setting of the default had a profound effect on the rates of organ donation. For example, although Austria and Germany are similar countries in terms of socio-economic status and geographic location, only 12% of Germans were donors (in 2003) compared to 99.98% of Austrians.

Johnson and Goldstein explain this huge difference in terms of the choice architecture: when being a donor is the 'no-action' default, almost everyone consents, but when one needs to take action, because the choice architecture is not conducive, consent rates are much lower. The effect of defaults might not only be driven by the extra effort of opting in – factors like implied endorsement and social norms ('if that option is already selected, perhaps that is what I *should* do') and the sense of loss from giving up a chosen option might also contribute (Camilleri & Larrick, in press; McKenzie, Liersch & Finkelstein, 2006).

Defaults are but one aspect of choice architecture. Camilleri and Larrick (in press) discuss information restructuring and information feedback as other tools at the choice architect's disposal. The former refers simply to the way in which choice attributes and alternatives can be presented in order to highlight particular aspects of the choice environment, the latter to the idea that tools can present real-time feedback to users to guide choices and behaviour. Camilleri and Larrick identify several situations from the environmental domain – such as describing the fuel efficiency of vehicles, and tools for monitoring energy use – that take advantage of psychological insights.

Indeed, interest in nudges, choice architectures and the psychology of decision making that underlies them is burgeoning. In the UK and Australia, Behavioural Insights Teams have been set up by national and state governments with the remit to build on psychological knowledge to develop policy interventions (e.g. John et al., 2011). Much of this knowledge is derived from the topics we have covered in this book and it is exciting to see such widespread applications of these ideas. There are some significant success stories, with simple changes in framing leading to fines being paid more punctually, and increases in organ-donation rates. There have also been improvements in pension-saving behaviour resulting from interventions similar to those discussed in Chapter 1 (e.g. the save more tomorrow programme: Thaler & Benartzi, 2004). Whether this level of interest will be sustained remains to be seen. Some argue that the idea of a 'benevolent' choice architect designing environments to encourage particular choices has Orwellian overtones that encroach on our freedom (*The Economist*, February, 2014). However, the potential for real impacts in several domains – health, financial, environmental – suggests that the 'science of nudging' will be a growth industry in years to come.

SUMMARY

We can improve our decisions through a variety of simple cognitive mechanisms such as adopting an outside view, considering the opposite or challenging ourselves to discover the root cause of a problem. Additional support can be found in standard decision-theoretic techniques such as multi-attribute analysis, or the more user-friendly decision-support systems that many of us now use in our interactions with the Internet. Recognizing when it is appropriate to rely on our own thinking or to turn over our decision making to a superior tool might be one important standard of rationality. Recent applications of psychological insights are leading us to be nudged into various choices, and the potential for choice architects to improve our health, wealth and happiness (cf. Johnson et al., 2012; Thaler & Sunstein, 2008) is beginning to be realized.

This exploration of the techniques on offer to improve our decision making brings us almost to the end of our examination of the psychology of decision making. In the final chapter we summarize some of the key findings we have encountered and highlight why it so important to examine the learning environment in order to properly understand the judgments and decisions that we make.

Suggested further reading

- Johnson, E. J. et al. (2012). Beyond nudges: Tools of a choice architecture. *Marketing Letters, 23*, 487–504. A discussion paper authored by several leading researchers, which examines the potential of choice architectures.
- Larrick, R. P. (2004). Debiasing. In D. J. Koehler & N. Harvey (Eds), *The Blackwell handbook of judgment and decision making* (pp. 316–337). Malden, MA: Blackwell. A wide-ranging discussion of techniques for avoiding cognitive biases.
- Thaler, R. H., & Sunstein, C. R. (2008). *Nudge: Improving decisions about health, wealth, and happiness.* New Haven, CT: Yale University Press. An accessible account that describes how to 'nudge' people in a variety of domains. Written by the two pioneers of the approach.

18 Learning to make good decisions

When, how and why (not)?

The central theme of this book is that the best way to understand how and why decisions are made is in the context of the learning that precedes them and the feedback that follows them. Fostering this understanding requires careful examination of the mechanisms of learning and the structure of the environments in which those decisions are made. In this final chapter we summarize some of the things we have learned in our review of the field in an attempt to clarify when, how and why we can (or sometimes cannot) learn to make good decisions.

In order to answer these questions let us briefly revisit the two frameworks for assessing the quality of decisions that we introduced in Chapter 5: coherence and correspondence. Recall that the constraint of coherence serves to maintain the internal consistency of our probability judgments, whereas the requirement of correspondence (when available) serves to calibrate these judgments to the external world. The emphasis placed on these two criteria differs across areas of research, but in both traditions we have seen that the opportunity to learn and/or the provision of well-structured environments often leads to more accurate judgments and decisions. What are some examples?

WHEN DOES DECISION MAKING IMPROVE?

We have encountered several examples of situations in which judgments and decisions improve as a result of experience. Perhaps the clearest and simplest one is the demonstration that people can learn to probability maximize in a two-alternative forced-choice task. Recall that when faced with the choice between an option that pays out on 70% of trials and one that pays out on 30% of trials, the rational strategy is *always* to choose the 70% option. The research reviewed in Chapter 12 highlighted that although initially people tend to violate the rational strategy, and instead respond in a way that *matches the probability* of payouts, given enough trials, incentives and feedback, the majority of people learn to maximize. When we consider more complex problems with multiple cues, similar patterns of improvement emerge. Recall from Chapter 3 that participants who had to first learn – or *discover* – which of the cues in a given array were predictive took many hundreds of trials and days of trial-and-error experimentation before mastering the task. Experiments in which the relevant cues are identified for participants are not so onerous in terms of time, but again, as highlighted in Chapters 3 and 12, even when relationships between several cues and an outcome need to be learned, the provision of trial-by-trial experience and corrective feedback pushes people towards maximizing and/or more accurate predictions.

Studies examining more complex, dynamic control tasks (discussed in Chapter 4) also emphasize the importance of opportunities to interact with and learn from both feedback and feedforward. The latter refers to the information a participant can glean from the instructions, the framing of the task and expectations derived (presumably) from real-world experience in similar situations. Feedback and feedforward then combine to reduce the psychological uncertainty that people experience when interacting with these systems; crucially this uncertainty-reduction can only occur if the appropriate conditions for learning are provided, such as sufficient time, trials, feedback and opportunities to experiment.

The forecasting competition discussed in Chapter 16 is another illustration of how regular feedback can improve calibration. Recall that this tournament ran for several months and forecasters were asked a diverse range of questions about various geo-political events. Cue discovery, methods for integrating information, the process of updating estimates and how to use feedback were all left to the participants – there were no explicit instructions – and yet across the duration of the competition calibration significantly improved. This improvement is heartening and suggests that even outside the confines of tightly controlled experiments, when systematic, unambiguous feedback is provided over repeated occasions judgments can get better (see the discussion of calibration in Chapter 6 for further examples).

Learning in decision problems can lead to improvements by making them more closely *cohere* with rational axioms (e.g. probability maximizing) and by increasing correspondence with the external world (e.g. geo-political forecasting). However, the studies reviewed in Chapter 10 (decisions from experience) demonstrated that learning does not always *improve* decisions per se: it sometimes simply changes preferences for particular options. For example, one of the most striking findings from that literature is that rare events, which appear to loom large when presented in descriptions of gambles, receive much less attention when they are learned about via trial-by-trial experience. In some situations this under-weighting of the rare event leads to more coherent choices. For example, people given a choice between a gamble offering an 80% chance of $40 and a 20% chance of nothing (EV = $32) or $30 for sure (EV = $30) tend to choose the higher EV option when learning from experience, but show the opposite preference when the gambles are described. In other situations, however, experience can lead to preference for a lower EV option: in experience-based choice people prefer a gamble offering a 10%

chance of a loss of \$32, else nothing (EV = –\$3.2) to a sure loss of \$3 (EV = –\$3), but take the sure loss when the problem is described.

The explanation for the reversal in both cases is the same: the low-probability event – a 20% chance of getting nothing in the first example, and 10% chance of losing \$32 in the second – is under-weighted. This leads to preferences that are either 'more' (case 1) or 'less' (case 2) rational when appraised via coherence standards. These findings highlight how the context and the mechanisms underpinning learning interact to determine how we choose.

It is also important to emphasize that we don't always need hundreds of trials to see improvements in judgment. Sometimes immediate improvements in decision accuracy can be achieved via appropriate interventions. Take, for example, a classic error of correspondence, the anchoring bias. In the preceding chapter we discussed how anchoring can be overcome by forcing oneself to consider alternative answers – akin to giving oneself a multiple-trial estimation experiment. But there are other ways in which anchoring effects can be reduced. Countering many previous reports to the contrary, Simmons, LeBoeuf and Nelson (2010) found that they could achieve immediate attenuation of anchoring with financial incentives for accuracy. A very different example is Krynski and Tenenbaum's (2007) approach to countering a classic error of coherence – base-rate neglect (see Chapter 6, and the next section). They found that providing participants with additional information about the causal structure of the problem, namely an alternative cause of a false positive test, produced significant improvements in judgment accuracy.

HOW AND WHY DOES DECISION MAKING IMPROVE?

The examples discussed above emphasize that the opportunity to learn, the regular provision of feedback and the structure of the environment are important for determining when improvements in judgment and decision making are likely to occur. But how and why are those improvements conferred? In some situations years of experience appear to result in little advantage in predictive accuracy over simple statistical rules (see the seminal work of Meehl discussed in Chapters 2 and 3). The answer lies in the interaction between the opportunities to learn and the regularity or predictability of the environment in which decisions are made.

Several authors have discussed these ideas about how learning and the environment interact; here we will briefly review two recent and prominent treatments and highlight how they inform and complement our own perspective. Hogarth (e.g. Hogarth, 2001; Hogarth & Soyer, 2011) distinguishes between *kind* and *wicked* learning environments and also between *transparent* and *nontransparent* descriptions of decision problems. The kindness/wickedness of an environment is determined by the accuracy and completeness of the feedback one receives. If the feedback is complete and accurate it can help people reach unbiased estimates of the nature of the environment in which they are operating. If it is incomplete, missing or systematically biased, then an accurate representation cannot be acquired.

Recall the example of a doctor attempting to ascertain the relation between juvenile delinquency and abnormal electroencephalographic (EEG) recordings discussed in Chapter 3. The doctor finds herself in a potentially wicked environment because she observes a systematically biased sample of juveniles *with* delinquency making it difficult to assess the co-variance of abnormal EEG and bad behaviour.

Transparency refers to the ease with which the structure of a problem can be gleaned from a description. Hogarth and Soyer (2011) argue that a problem in which the probability of a single event affects an outcome is relatively transparent, whereas when a probability needs to be inferred from the conjunction of several events, then the problem becomes more opaque. By crossing these two dimensions one can develop a taxonomy of tasks or situations that range from the least amenable for accurate judgment, a nontransparent task in a wicked learning environment, to the most amenable, transparency in description and a kind environment.

They demonstrate that combining an opaque description with the opportunity to interact in a kind environment can lead to significant improvements in judgment relative to just providing a description. A good example is the kind of base-rate neglect problems that we considered in Chapters 5 and 6. Recall that people given statistics relating to the population prevalence of a disease (base rate), the sensitivity of a test and the false positive rate often find it very difficult to work out the probability that someone has a disease, given that they test positive (i.e. the posterior probability). Hogarth and Soyer show that if this descriptive information is augmented with an opportunity to sample outcomes from the posterior probability distribution, then judgments improve dramatically. In their experiments this sampling took the form of a simulator offering trial-by-trial experience of 'meeting different people' from the population who had a positive test result and either did or did not actually have the disease. Experiencing these sequentially simulated outcomes presumably highlighted the relative rarity of the disease − even in individuals who tested positive − thereby helping people overcome the lack of transparency inherent in the purely described version of the problem.

Kahneman and Klein (2009) also discuss many of the issues related to how experience improves judgment. Their discussion is intriguing because it pits two research traditions, which have taken very different views to assessing judgment, against each other, but concludes by finding a good deal of common ground. The heuristics and biases tradition (pioneered by Tversky and Kahneman − see Chapter 6) is often associated with the idea that experts can be very over-confident in their judgments and susceptible to errors. On the face of it, this seems at odds with the general contention that experience improves judgments and decisions. In contrast, naturalistic decision making

(NDM; associated with Klein – see Chapter 13) treats the expert as the fount of accurate knowledge and the basis for theories about how decisions are and should be made.

How can these views be reconciled? The answer echoes the sentiment we have emphasized throughout the book. Kahneman and Klein (2009) write: 'evaluating the likely quality of an intuitive judgment requires an assessment of the predictability of the environment in which the judgment is made and of the individual's opportunity to learn the regularities of that environment' (p. 515). In other words, when an individual has no opportunity to learn or the environment is so unpredictable that no regularities can be extracted (or both), then judgments are likely to be very poor. However, when an environment has some predictable structure and there is an opportunity to learn, judgments will be better and will improve with further experience. The divergence of opinion on the usefulness of expert judgment thus arises from focusing on different types of experts in very different environments. The NDM work grew out of the study of chess masters (see Chapter 13): highly skilled experts working in a very clearly controlled environment with explicit rules, cues, patterns and feedback. The heuristics and biases approach was inspired in part by the work of Meehl (see Chapters 2 and 3), who examined clinicians working in unstructured environments often with scarce and biased feedback.

Such conclusions about differences in the quality of expert judgment are borne out by studies that have compared expertise across professions. Shanteau (1992) categorized livestock judges, chess masters, test pilots and soil judges (among others) as exhibiting expertise in their professional judgments. In contrast, clinical psychologists, stockbrokers, intelligence analysts and personnel selectors (among others) were found to be poor judges. The reason for the difference again comes back to predictability, feedback and experience in the different professional environments. Livestock, it turns out, are more predictable than the stock market.

The overall picture that emerges from examining how and why decisions improve echoes our conclusions from earlier chapters (e.g. Chapters 7 and 13) in which we argued that expertise emerges via the same kind of core learning processes that we see in laboratory-based experimental tasks. Most of those tasks are highly structured and predictable and thus the improvements we see in simple and multiple-cue probability learning, the Iowa Gambling Task or decisions from experience are to be expected because participants are acquiring expertise in those particular tasks. When we consider a range of tasks, or broader domains, experience confers further advantages such as deeper insight, the ability to impart knowledge to others, and speed of acquisition and execution, but arguably the basic learning processes and the features of the environment that facilitate their operation remain the same.

CONCLUDING REMARKS

At the beginning of this book we argued that our learning-focused perspective on the psychology of decision making aims to reclaim the original reason for emphasizing the errors, pitfalls and biases that can befall us as we navigate our uncertain world. This original reason was that errors are informative because *we learn from them*. We learn from them both in a literal sense (once you get the bat-and-ball problem wrong once, you are unlikely to do so again; see Chapter 14) and also in a scholarly sense because, just like visual illusions, they tell us something about how the system that produces these errors typically works. The important point is that these errors should be viewed as quirks or anomalies that arise from a system which is in general extremely accurate in its functioning (Tversky & Kahneman, 1974). Our principal contention is that the system is accurate because we have remarkably finely tuned learning mechanisms that allow us to adapt to our ever-changing environment.

Other researchers have made similar arguments about the need to redress the balance, and emphasize the positive qualities of our decision-making abilities (e.g. Edwards, 1983; Gigerenzer et al., 1999; Hogarth, 1981). However, often this idea is lost behind a barrage of messages telling us how our decisions are routinely affected by cognitive biases and other factors that we are unaware of, that we should rely on our unconscious to decide, that too much choice will paralyse us, that our decisions should be left in the hands of benevolent choice architects (see Chapter 17), and so on.

Our hope is that having read this book you will be armed with the knowledge that will help you evaluate these claims and be more confident in your ability to make good decisions. Our conclusion that decision accuracy is most likely to improve when one has the opportunity to learn (and develop expertise) in well-structured 'kind' environments might not be as provocative and eye-catching as some other perspectives, but it is grounded solidly in the empirical evidence, as we have endeavoured to illustrate. We conclude with some words from one of the forefathers of the field, Ward Edwards (1983): 'if you need to perform a difficult intellectual task, both tools and expertise are likely to be very helpful – which seems hardly surprising, if a bit unglamorous' (p. 218). We agree wholeheartedly.

References

Adelman, L. (1981). The influence of formal, substantive, and contextual task properties on the relative effectiveness of feedback in multi-cue probability tasks. *Organizational Behavior and Human Performance, 27,* 423–442.

Agnoli, F., & Krantz, D. H. (1989). Suppressing natural heuristics by formal instruction: The case of the conjunction fallacy. *Cognitive Psychology, 21,* 515–550.

Aitken, C., Roberts, P., & Jackson, G. (2014). *Fundamentals of probability and statistical evidence in criminal proceedings.* London: Royal Statistical Society.

Aldag, R. J., & Fuller, S. R. (1993). Beyond fiasco: A reappraisal of the groupthink phenomenon and a new model of group decision processes. *Psychological Bulletin, 113,* 533–552.

Allais, M. (1953). La psychologie de l'homme rationnel devant le risque: Critique des postulats et axiomes de l'école Américaine. *Econometrica, 21,* 503–546.

Almy, B., & Krueger, J. I. (2013). Game interrupted: The rationality of considering the future. *Judgment and Decision Making, 8,* 521–526.

Alter, A. L., & Oppenheimer, D. M. (2006). Predicting short-term stock fluctuations by using processing fluency. *Proceedings of the National Academy of Sciences, 103,* 9369–9372.

Anderson, J. R. (1991). The adaptive nature of human categorization. *Psychological Review, 98,* 409–429.

Ariely, D., & Carmon, Z. (2003). Summary assessment of experiences: The whole is different from the sum of its parts. In G. Loewenstein, D. Read, & R. Baumeister (Eds), *Time and decision: Economic and psychological perspectives on intertemporal choice* (pp. 323–349). New York: Russell Sage Foundation.

Ariely, D., Kahneman, D., & Loewenstein, G. (2000). Joint comment on 'When does duration matter in judgment and decision making?' (Ariely & Loewenstein, 2000). *Journal of Experimental Psychology: General, 129,* 524–529.

Ariely, D., & Loewenstein, G. (2000). When does duration matter in judgment and decision making? *Journal of Experimental Psychology: General, 129,* 508–523.

Ariely, D., Loewenstein, G., & Prelec, D. (2003). 'Coherent arbitrariness': Stable demand curves without stable preferences. *Quarterly Journal of Economics, 118,* 73–105.

Ariely, D., & Norton, M. I. (2011). From thinking too little to thinking too much: A continuum of decision making. *Wiley Interdisciplinary Reviews: Cognitive Science, 2,* 39–46.

Ariely, D., & Wertenbroch, K. (2002). Procrastination, deadlines, and performance: Self-control by precommitment. *Psychological Science, 13,* 219–224.

Arkes, H. R. (1981). Impediments to accurate clinical judgment and possible ways to minimize their impact. *Journal of Consulting and Clinical Psychology, 49,* 323–330.

Arkes, H. R. (1991). Costs and benefits of judgment errors: Implications for debiasing. *Psychological Bulletin, 110,* 486–498.

Arkes, H. R., & Ayton, P. (1999). The sunk cost and Concorde effects: Are humans less rational than lower animals? *Psychological Bulletin, 125,* 591–600.

Arntz, A., van Eck, M., & Heijmans, M. (1990). Predictions of dental pain: The fear of any expected evil, is worse than the evil itself. *Behavior Research and Therapy, 28,* 29–41.

Arrow, K. J. (1958). Utilities, attitudes, choices: A review note. *Econometrica, 26,* 1–23.

Ashby, F. G., & Ell, S. W. (2002). Single versus multiple systems of learning and memory. In J. Wixted & H. Pashler (Eds), *Stevens' handbook of experimental psychology* (3rd edn, Vol. 4: *Methodology in experimental psychology,* pp. 655–691). New York: Wiley.

Ayton, P., & Fishcer, I. (2004). The hot hand fallacy and the gambler's fallacy: Two faces of subjective randomness? *Memory & Cognition, 32,* 1369–1378.

Ayton, P., Önkal, D., & McReynolds, L. (2011). Effects of ignorance and information on judgments and decisions. *Judgment and Decision Making, 6,* 381–391.

Balzer, W. K., Doherty, M. E., & O'Connor, R. (1989). Effects of cognitive feedback on performance. *Psychological Bulletin, 106,* 410–433.

Bar-Hillel, M., & Neter, E. (1993). How alike is it versus how likely is it: A disjunction fallacy in probability judgments. *Journal of Personality and Social Psychology, 65,* 1119–1131.

Baron, J. (2000). *Thinking and deciding.* Cambridge, UK: Cambridge University Press. (3rd edn).

Baron, J. (2008). *Thinking and deciding.* Cambridge, UK: Cambridge University Press. (4th edn).

Baron, J., Mellers, B. A., Tetlock, P. E., Stone, E., & Ungar, L. H. (2014). Two reasons to make aggregated probability forecasts more extreme. *Decision Analysis, 11,* 133–145.

Barron, G., & Erev, I. (2003). Small feedback-based decisions and their limited correspondence to description-based decisions. *Journal of Behavioral Decision Making, 16,* 215–233.

Barron, G., Leider, S., & Stack, J. (2008). The effect of safe experience on a warning's impact: Sex, drugs, and rock-n-roll. *Organizational Behavior and Human Decision Processes, 106,* 125–142.

Batchelor, R. A. (2004). The pros and cons of technical analysis: an academic perspective. *The Technical Analyst, 1,* 13–18.

Baxt, W. G. (1990). Use of an artificial neural network for data analysis in clinical decision-making: The diagnosis of acute coronary occlusion. *Neural Computation, 2,* 480–489.

Bechara, A. (2005). Decision making, impulse control and loss of willpower to resist drugs: A neurocognitive perspective. *Nature Neuroscience, 8,* 1458–1463.

Bechara, A., Damasio, H., & Damasio, A. R. (2000) Emotion, decision making and the orbitofrontal cortex. *Cerebral Cortex, 10,* 295–307.

Bechara A., Damasio, A., Damasio, H., & Anderson, S. (1994). Insensitivity to future consequences following damage to human prefrontal cortex. *Cognition, 50,* 7–15.

Bechara, A., Damasio, H., Tranel, D., & Damasio, A. (1997). Deciding advantageously before knowing the advantageous strategy. *Science, 275,* 1293–1295

Benartzi, S., & Thaler, R. H. (2001). Naïve diversification strategies in defined contribution savings plans. *American Economic Review, 91,* 78–98.

Benartzi, S., & Thaler, R. H. (2002). How much is investor autonomy worth? *The Journal of Finance, 152,* 1593–1616.

Berger, C. E. H., Buckleton J., Champod C., Evett I., & Jackson, G. (2011) Evidence evaluation: A response to the court of appeal judgement in R v T. *Science and Justice, 51*, 43–49.

Bergert, F. B., & Nosofsky, R. M. (2007). A response time approach to comparing generalized rational and take-the-best models of decision making. *Journal of Experimental Psychology: Learning, Memory, and Cognition, 33*, 999–1019.

Bernoulli, D. (1738/1954). Exposition of a new theory on the measurement of risk. *Econometrica, 22*, 23–36.

Berry, D. C., & Broadbent, D. E. (1984). On the relationship between task performance and associated verbalizable knowledge. *Quarterly Journal of Experimental Psychology, 36*, 209–231.

Berry, D. C., & Broadbent, D. E. (1988). Interactive tasks and the implicit–explicit distinction. *British Journal of Psychology, 79*, 251–272.

Biederman, I. & Shiffrar, M. M. (1987). Sexing day-old chicks: A case study and expert systems analysis of a difficult perceptual-learning task. *Journal of Experimental Psychology: Learning, Memory, and Cognition, 13*, 640–645.

Bitterman, M. E., Tyler, D. W., & Elam, C. B. (1955). Simultaneous and successive discrimination under identical stimulating conditions. *American Journal of Psychology, 68*, 237–248.

Björkman, M. (1972). Feedforward and feedback as determiners of knowledge and policy: Notes on a neglected issue. *Scandinavian Journal of Psychology, 13*, 152–158.

Bonner, C., & Newell, B. R. (2010). In conflict with ourselves? An investigation of heuristic and analytic processes in decision making. *Memory & Cognition, 38*, 186–196.

Borges, B., Goldstein, D. G., Ortmann, A., & Gigerenzer, G. (1999). Can ignorance beat the stock market? In G. Gigerenzer, P. M. Todd, & The ABC Research Group (Eds), *Simple heuristics that make us smart* (pp. 59–72). New York: Oxford University Press.

Borgida, E., & Nisbett, R. (1977). The differential impact of abstract versus concrete information on decisions. *Journal of Applied Social Psychology, 7*, 258–271

Bornstein, B. H., Emler, A. C., & Chapman, G. B. (1999). Rationality in medical treatment decisions: Is there a sunk-cost effect? *Social Science & Medicine, 49*, 215–222.

Bower, G. H. (1994). A turning point in mathematical learning theory. *Psychological Review, 101*, 290–300.

Bramley, N. R., Lagnado, D. A., & Speekenbrink, M. (in press). Conservative forgetful scholars: How people learn causal structure through sequences of interventions. *Journal of Experimental Psychology: Learning, Memory, and Cognition.*

Brehmer, B. (1979). Preliminaries to a psychology of inference. *Scandinavian Journal of Psychology, 20*, 193–210.

Brehmer, B. (1980). In one word: Not from experience. *Acta Psychologica, 45*, 223–241.

Brehmer, B. (1999). Reasonable decision making in complex environments. In P. Juslin, & H. Montgomery (Eds), *Judgment and decision making: New-Brunswikian and process-tracing approaches* (pp. 9–21). Hillsdale, NJ: Erlbaum.

Brehmer, B., & Allard, R. (1991). Dynamic decision making: The effects of task complexity and feedback delay. In J. Rasmussen, B. Brehmer, & J. Leplat (Eds), *Distributed decision making: Cognitive models for cooperative work* (pp. 319–334). Brisbane: Wiley.

Brenner, L., Griffin, D., & Koehler, D. (2005). Modeling patterns of probability calibration with Random Support Theory: Diagnosing case-based judgment. *Organizational Behavior and Human Decision Processes, 97*, 64–81.

Brenner, L. A., Koehler, D. J., & Rottenstreich, Y. (2002). Remarks on support theory: Recent advances and future directions. In T. Gilovich, D. Griffin, & D. Kahneman (Eds), *Heuristics and biases* (pp. 489–509). New York: Cambridge University Press.

Brier, G. W. (1950). Verification of forecasts expressed in terms of probability. *Monthly Weather Review, 78*, 1–3.

Broadbent, D. E., & Aston, B. (1978). Human control of a simulated economic system. *Ergonomics, 21*, 1035–1043.

Broadbent, D. E., Fitzgerald, P., & Broadbent, M. H. P. (1986). Implicit and explicit knowledge in the control of complex systems. *British Journal of Psychology, 77*, 33–50.

Bröder, A. (2000). Assessing the empirical validity of the 'Take-the-Best' heuristic as a model of human probabilistic inference. *Journal of Experimental Psychology: Learning, Memory, and Cognition, 26*, 1332–1346.

Bröder, A. (2003). Decision making with the adaptive toolbox: Influence of environmental structure, personality, intelligence, and working memory load. *Journal of Experimental Psychology: Learning, Memory, and Cognition, 29*, 611–625.

Bröder, A., & Eichler, A. (2006). The use of recognition information and additional cues in inferences from memory. *Acta Psychologica, 121*, 275–284.

Bröder, A., & Schiffer, S. (2003). 'Take-the-best' versus simultaneous feature matching: Probabilistic inferences from memory and the effects of representation format. *Journal of Experimental Psychology: General, 132*, 277–293.

Brooks, L. R., Norman, G. R., & Allen, S. W. (1991). The role of specific similarity in a medical diagnostic task. *Journal of Experimental Psychology: General, 120*, 278–287.

Brown, N. R., & Tan, S. (2011). Magnitude comparison revisited: An alternative approach to binary choice under uncertainty. *Psychonomic Bulletin & Review, 18*, 392–398.

Brunswik, E. (1952). *The conceptual framework of psychology.* Chicago: University of Chicago Press.

Brunswik, E. (1956). *Perception and the representative design of psychological experiments.* Berkeley, CA: University of California Press.

Buehler, R., Griffin, D., & Ross, M. (1994). Exploring the 'planning fallacy': Why people underestimate their task completion times. *Journal of Personality and Social Psychology, 67*, 366–381.

Buehler, R., Griffin, D., & Ross, M. (2002). Inside the planning fallacy: The causes and consequences of optimistic time predictions. In T. D. Gilovich, D. W. Griffin, & D. Kahneman (Eds), *Heuristics and biases* (pp. 250–270). New York: Cambridge University Press.

Burns, B. D., & Vollmeyer, R. (2002). Goal specificity effects on hypothesis testing in problem solving. *Quarterly Journal of Experimental Psychology: Human Experimental Psychology, 55(A)*, 241–261.

Busemeyer, J. R., & Johnson, J. G. (2004). Computational models of decision making. In D. Koehler & N. Harvey (Eds), *The Blackwell handbook of judgment and decision making* (pp. 133–154). Malden, MA: Blackwell.

Bush, R. R., & Mosteller, F. (1955). *Stochastic models for learning.* New York: Wiley.

Calderwood, R., Klein, G. A., & Crandall, B. W. (1988). Time pressure, skill, and move quality in chess. *American Journal of Psychology, 101*, 481–493.

Camerer, C. (2000). Prospect Theory in the wild: Evidence from the field. In D. Kahneman & A. Tversky (Eds), *Choices, values, and frames* (pp. 288–300). Cambridge, UK: Cambridge University Press.

Camilleri, A. R., & Larrick, R. P. (in press). Choice architecture. In R. A. Scott & S. M. Kosslen (Eds), *Emerging trends in the social and behavioral sciences*. Hoboken, NJ: Wiley.

Camilleri, A. R., & Newell, B. R. (2011a). When and why rare events are underweighted: A direct comparison of the sampling, partial feedback, full feedback and description choice paradigms. *Psychonomic Bulletin & Review, 18*, 377–384.

Camilleri, A. R., & Newell, B. R. (2011b). Description- and experience-based choice: Does equivalent information equal equivalent choice? *Acta Psychologica, 136*, 276–284.

Camilleri, A. R., & Newell, B. R. (2013). The long and short of it: Closing the description–experience 'gap' by taking the long run view. *Cognition, 126*, 54–71.

Casscells, W., Schoenberger, A., & Grayboys, T. (1978). Interpretation by physicians of clinical laboratory results. *New England Journal of Medicine, 299*, 999–1001.

Castellan, N. J. (1973). Multiple-cue probability learning with irrelevant cues. *Organizational Behavior and Human Performance, 9*, 16–29.

Castellan, N. J. (1974). The effect of different types of feedback in multiple-cue probability learning. *Organizational Behavior and Human Performance, 11*, 44–64.

Castellan, N. J., & Edgell, S. E. (1973). An hypothesis generation model for judgment in nonmetric multiple-cue probability learning. *Journal of Mathematical Psychology, 10*, 204–222.

Castellan, N. J., & Swaine, M. (1977). Long term feedback and differential feedback effects in nonmetric multiple-cue probability learning. *Behavioral Sciences, 22*, 116–128.

Ceci, S. J., & Liker, J. K. (1986). A day at the races: A study of IQ, expertise, and cognitive complexity. *Journal of Experimental Psychology: General, 115*, 255–266.

Chapman, G. B. (1991). Trial order affects cue interaction in contingency judgment. *Journal of Experimental Psychology: Learning, Memory, and Cognition, 17*, 837–854.

Chapman, G. B. (1996). Temporal discounting and utility for health and money. *Journal of Experimental Psychology: Learning, Memory, and Cognition, 22*, 771–791.

Chapman, G. B. (2003). Time discounting of health outcomes. In G. Loewenstein, D. Read, & R. Baumeister (Eds), *Time and decision: Economic and psychological perspectives on intertemporal choice* (pp. 395–417). New York: Russell Sage Foundation.

Chapman, G. B., & Winquist, J. R. (1998). The magnitude effect: Temporal discount rates and restaurant tips. *Psychonomic Bulletin & Review, 5*, 119–123.

Chater, N. (2003). How much can we learn from double dissociations? *Cortex, 39*, 167–169.

Chater, N., Oaksford, M., Nakisa, R., & Redington, M. (2003). Fast, frugal and rational: How rational norms explain behavior. *Organizational Behavior and Human Decision Processes, 90*, 63–80.

Christensen, C., Heckerling, P., Mackesyamiti, M. E., Bernstein, L. M., & Elstein, A. S. (1995). Pervasiveness of framing effects among physicians and medical students. *Journal of Behavioral Decision Making, 8*, 169–180.

Chu, Y.-P., & Chu, R.-L. (1990). The subsidence of preference reversals in simplified and market-like experimental settings: A note. *American Economic Review, 80*, 902–911.

Cobos, P. L., Almaraz, J., & Garcia-Madruga, J. A. (2003). An associative framework for probability judgment: An application to biases. *Journal of Experimental Psychology: Learning, Memory, and Cognition, 29*, 80–94.

Cohen, J. D., McClure, S. M., & Yu, A. J. (2007). Should I stay or should I go? How the human brain manages the trade-off between exploitation and exploration. *Philosophical Transactions of the Royal Society B: Biological Sciences, 362*, 933–942.

Connolly, T., & Gilani, N. (1982). Information search in judgment tasks: A regression model and some preliminary findings. *Organizational Behavior and Human Decision Processes, 30*, 330–350.

Connolly, T., & Serre, P. (1984). Information search in judgment tasks: The effects of unequal cue validity and cost. *Organizational Behavior and Human Performance, 34*, 387–401.

Connolly, T., & Thorn, B. K. (1987). Predecisional information acquisition: Effects of task variables on suboptimal search strategies. *Organizational Behavior and Human Decision Processes, 39*, 397–416.

Connolly, T., & Wholey, D. R. (1988). Information mispurchase in judgment tasks: A task-driven causal mechanism. *Organizational Behavior and Human Decision Processes, 42*, 75–87.

Conway, M. (1990). On bias in autobiographical recall: Retrospective adjustments following disconfirmed expectations. *Journal of Social Psychology, 130*, 183–189.

Cooksey, R. W. (1996). *Judgment analysis: Theory, methods, and applications.* San Diego, CA: Academic Press.

Cooksey, R. W. (2001). Pursuing an integrated decision science: Does 'naturalistic decision making' help or hinder? *Journal of Behavioural Decision Making, 14*, 361–362.

Cosmides, L., & Tooby, J. (1996). Are humans good intuitive statisticians after all? Rethinking some conclusions from the literature on judgment under uncertainty. *Cognition, 58*, 1–73.

Cox, J. C., & Grether, D. M. (1996). The preference reversal phenomenon: Response mode, markets and incentives. *Economic Theory, 7*, 381–405.

Crupi, V., Fitelson, B., & Tentori, K. (2008). Probability, confirmation, and the conjunction fallacy. *Thinking and Reasoning, 14*, 182–199.

Cusumano, M. A., & Selby, R. W. (1995). *Microsoft secrets.* New York: Free Press.

Czerlinski, J., Gigerenzer, G., & Goldstein, D. G. (1999). How good are simple heuristics? In G. Gigerenzer, P. M. Todd, & The ABC Research Group (Eds), *Simple heuristics that make us smart* (pp. 97–118). New York: Oxford University Press.

Damasio, A. R. (1996). The somatic marker hypothesis and the possible functions of the prefrontal cortex. *Philosophical Transactions of the Royal Society of London (Biol) 351*, 1413–1420.

Damasio, A. R. (2000). *The feeling of what happens: Body and Emotion in the making of consciousness.* FL, USA: Harcourt.

Dawes, R. M. (1979). The robust beauty of improper linear models in decision making. *American Psychologist, 34*, 571–582.

Dawes, R. M. (2001). *Everyday irrationality: How pseudoscientists, lunatics, and the rest of us fail to think rationally.* Boulder, CO: Westview Press.

Dawes, R. M., & Corrigan, B. (1974). Linear models in decision making. *Psychological Bulletin, 81*, 95–106.

Dawes, R. M., Faust, D., & Meehl, P. E. (1989). Clinical versus actuarial judgment. *Science, 243*, 1668–1674.

Dawid, A. P. (2002). Bayes's theorem and weighing evidence by juries. In R. Swinburne (Ed.), Bayes's Theorem. *Proceedings of the British Academy, 113*, 71–90.

Dawson, M. E., & Reardon, P. (1973) Construct validity of recall and recognition postconditioning measures of awareness. *Journal of Experimental Psychology, 98*, 308–315.

De Neys, W. (2006). Dual processing in reasoning: Two systems but one reasoner. *Psychological Science, 17*, 428–433.

De Neys, W., & Glumicic, T. (2008). Conflict monitoring in dual process theories of reasoning. *Cognition, 106,* 1248–1299.

De Neys, W., Vartanian, O., & Goel, V. (2008). Smarter than we think: When our brains detect that we are biased. *Psychological Science, 19,* 483–489.

Deane, D. H., Hammond, K. R., & Summers, D. A. (1972). Acquisition and application of knowledge in complex inference tasks. *Journal of Experimental Psychology, 92,* 20–26.

deGroot, A. D. (1965). *Thought and choice in chess.* The Hague: Mouton Publishers.

Denes-Raj, V., & Epstein, S. (1994). Conflict between intuitive and rational processing: When people behave against their better judgment. *Journal of Personality and Social Psychology, 66,* 819–829.

Denrell, J., & March, J. G. (2001). Adaptation as information restriction: The hot stove effect. *Organization Science, 12,* 523–538.

Desvousges, W. H., Johnson, F. R., Dunford, R. W., Boyle, K. J., Hudson, S. P., & Wilson, K. N. (1992). Measuring nonuse damages using contingent valuation: An experimental evaluation of accuracy. *Research Triangle Institute Monograph,* 92–1. North Carolina: Research Triangle.

Dhami, M., & Ayton, P. (2001). Bailing and jailing the fast and frugal way. *Journal of Behavioral Decision Making, 14,* 141–168.

Dhami, M. K., & Harries, C. (2001). Fast and frugal versus regression models of human judgement. *Thinking and Reasoning, 7,* 5–27.

Dickinson, A. (1980). *Contemporary animal learning theory.* Cambridge, UK: Cambridge University Press.

Dijksterhuis, A. (2004). Think different: The merits of unconscious thought in preference development and decision making. *Journal of Personality and Social Psychology, 87,* 586–598.

Dijksterhuis, A., Bos, M. W., Nordgren, L. F., & van Baaren, R. B. (2006). On making the right choice: The deliberation-without-attention effect. *Science, 311,* 1005–1007.

Dijksterhuis, A., van Knippenberg, A., Holland, R. W., & Veling, H. (2014). Newell and Shanks' approach to psychology is a dead end. *Behavioral and Brain Sciences, 37,* 25–26.

Doherty, M. E. (2003). Optimists, pessimists, and realists. In S. Schneider & J. Shanteau (Eds), *Emerging perspectives on judgment and decision research* (pp. 643–678). Cambridge, UK: Cambridge University Press.

Dougherty, M. R. P., Franco-Watkins, A. M., & Thomas, R. (2008). Psychological plausibility of the theory of probabilistic mental models and the fast and frugal heuristics. *Psychological Review, 115,* 199–211.

Dougherty, M. R. P., Gettys, C. F., & Ogden, E. E. (1999). Minerva-DM: A memory processes model for judgments of likelihood. *Psychological Review, 106,* 180–209.

Dowie, J. (1976). On the efficiency and equity of better markets. *Economica, 43,* 139–150.

Dudycha, A. L., Dumoff, M. G., & Dudycha, L. W. (1973). Choice behavior in dynamic environments. *Organizational Behavior and Human Decision Processes, 9,* 328–338.

Dunn, B. D., Dalgleish, T., & Lawrence, A. D. (2006). The somatic marker hypothesis: A critical evaluation. *Neuroscience & Biobehavioral Reviews, 30,* 239–271.

Dunn, J. C., & Kirsner, K. (1988). Discovering functionally independent mental processes: The principle of reversed association. *Psychological Review, 95,* 91–101.

Edgell, S. E., & Morrissey, J. M. (1992). Separable and unitary stimuli in nonmetric multiple cue probability learning. *Organizational Behavior and Human Decision Processes, 51,* 118–132.

Edwards, A., Elwyn, G., Covey, J., Mathews, E., & Pill R. (2001). Presenting risk information – a review of the effects of framing' and other manipulations on patient outcomes. *Journal of Health Communication, 6,* 61–82.

Edwards, W. (1961). Probability learning in 1000 trials. *Journal of Experimental Psychology*, 62, 385–394.

Edwards, W. (1965). Optimal strategies for seeking information: Models for statistics, choice reaction-times, and human information-processing. *Journal of Mathematical Psychology*, 2, 312–329.

Edwards, W. (1968). Conservatism in human information processing. In B. Kleinmuntz (Ed.), *Formal representation of human judgment* (pp. 17–52). New York: Wiley.

Edwards, W. (1983). Human cognitive capabilities, representativeness, and ground rules for research. Reproduced in Weiss, J. W., & Weiss, D. J. (Eds) (2009). *A science of decision making: The legacy of Ward Edwards* (pp. 212–218) Oxford: Oxford University Press.

Edwards, W., & Barron, F. H. (1994). SMARTS and SMARTER: Improved simple methods for multiattribute utility measurement. *Organizational Behavior and Human Decision Processes*, 60, 306–325.

Edwards, W., & Fasolo, B. (2001). Decision technology. *Annual Review of Psychology*, 52, 581–606.

Einhorn, H. J. (1972). Expert measurement and mechanical combination. *Organizational Behavior and Human Performance*, 7, 86–106.

Einhorn, H. J., & Hogarth, R. M. (1975). Unit weighting schemes for decision making. *Organizational Behavior and Human Performance*, 13, 171–192.

Einhorn, H. J., & Hogarth, R. M. (1978). Confidence in judgment: Persistence of the illusion of validity. *Psychological Review*, 85, 395–416.

Einhorn, H. J., & Hogarth, R. M. (1981). Behavioral decision theory: Processes of judgment and choice. *Annual Review of Psychology*, 32, 53–88.

Ellsberg, D. (1961). Risk, ambiguity and the Savage axioms. *Quarterly Journal of Economics*, 75, 643–679.

Enkvist, T., Newell, B. R., Juslin, P., & Olsson, H. (2006). On the role of causal intervention in multiple cue judgment: Positive and negative effects on learning. *Journal of Experimental Psychology: Learning, Memory, and Cognition*, 32, 163–179.

Erev, I., Ert, E., Roth, A. E., Haruvy, E. E., Herzog, S., Hau, R., . . . & Lebiere, C. (2010). A choice prediction competition, for choices from experience and from description. *Journal of Behavioral Decision Making*, 23, 15–47.

Erev, I., & Haruvy, E. (in press). Learning and the economics of small decisions. In J. H. Kagel & A. E. Roth (Eds), *The Handbook of Experimental Economics* (Vol. 2). Princeton: Princeton University Press.

Ericsson, K. A. (1996). The acquisition of expert performance: An introduction to some of the issues. In K. A. Ericsson (Ed.), *The road to excellence: The acquisition of expert performance in the arts and sciences, sports and games* (pp. 1–50). Mahwah, NJ: Erlbaum.

Ericsson, K. A., & Simon, H. A. (1980). Verbal reports as data. *Psychological Review*, 87, 215–251.

Ericsson, K. A., & Simon, H. A. (1984). *Protocol analysis: Verbal reports as data*. Cambridge, MA: Bradford Books/MIT Press.

Evans, J. St B. T. (2007). On the resolution of conflict in dual-process theories of reasoning. *Thinking & Reasoning*, 13, 321–329.

Evans, J. St B. T. (2008). Dual-processing accounts of reasoning, judgement and social cognition. *Annual Review of Psychology*, 59, 255–278.

Evans, J. St B. T. (2014). The presumption of consciousness. *Behavioral and Brain Sciences*, 37, 26.

Evans, J. St B. T., Clibbens, J., Cattani, A., Harris, A., & Dennis, I. (2003). Explicit and implicit processes in multicue judgment. *Memory & Cognition*, 31, 608–618.

Evans, J. St B. T., Handley, S. H., Perham, N., Over, D. E., & Thompson, V. A. (2000). Frequency versus probability formats in statistical word problems. *Cognition*, 77, 197–213.

Evans, J. St B. T., & Stanovich, K. E. (2013a). Dual-process theories of higher cognition: Advancing the debate. *Perspectives on Psychological Science*, 8, 223–241.

Evans, J. St B. T., & Stanovich, K. E. (2013b). Theory and metatheory in the study of dual processing: Reply to comments. *Perspectives on Psychological Science*, 8, 263–271.

Fasolo, B., McClelland, G. H., & Lange, K. A. (2005). The effect of site design and interattribute correlations on interactive web-based decisions. In C. P. Haugtvedt, K. Machleit, & R. Yalch (Eds), *Online consumer psychology: understanding and influencing behavior in the virtual world* (pp. 325–344). Hillsdale, NJ: Lawrence Erlbaum Associates.

Fenton, N., Berger, D., Lagnado, D., Neil, M., & Hsu, A. (2014). When 'neutral' evidence still has probative value. *Science & Justice*, 54, 274–287.

Fenton, N., & Neil, M. (2012). *Risk assessment and decision analysis with Bayesian networks*. Boca Raton, FL: CRC Press.

Fenton, N., Neil, M., & Lagnado, D. A. (2013). A general structure for legal arguments about evidence using Bayesian networks. *Cognitive Science*, 37, 61–102.

Festinger, L. (1957). *A theory of cognitive dissonance*. Stanford, CA: Stanford University Press.

Fiedler, K. (1988). The dependence of the conjunction fallacy on subtle linguistic factors. *Psychological Research*, 50, 123–129.

Fiedler, K. (2000). Beware of samples! A cognitive-ecological sampling approach to judgment biases. *Psychological Review*, 107, 659–676.

Fiedler, K., & Juslin, P. (2006). Taking the interface between mind and environment seriously. In K. Fiedler & P. Juslin (Eds), *Information sampling and adaptive cognition* (pp. 3–29). Cambridge, UK: Cambridge University Press.

Figner, B., & Murphy, R. O. (2011). Using skin conductance in judgment and decision making research. In M. Schulte-Mecklenbeck, A. Kuehberger, & R. Ranyard (Eds), *A handbook of process tracing methods for decision research* (pp. 163–184). New York: Psychology Press.

Figner, B., & Weber, E. U. (2011). Who takes risks when and why? Determinants of risk taking. *Current Directions in Psychological Science*, 20, 211–216.

Finetti, B. de (1937). Foresight: Its logical laws, its subjective sources. Translated in H. E. Kyburg & H. E. Smokler (Eds) (1980), *Studies in subjective probability* (pp. 53–118). New York: Wiley.

Finucane, M. L., Alhakami, A., Slovic, P., & Johnson, S. M. (2000). The affect heuristic in judgments of risks and benefits. *Journal of Behavioral Decision Making*, 13, 1–17.

Finucane, M. L., Peters, E., & Slovic, P. (2003). Judgment and decision making: The dance of affect and reason. In S. L. Schneider & J. Shanteau (Eds), *Emerging perspectives on judgment and decision research* (pp. 327–364). Cambridge, UK: Cambridge University Press.

Fiorina, M. P. (1971). A note on probability matching and rational choice. *Behavioral Science*, 16, 158–166.

Fischhoff, B. (2002). Heuristics and biases in application. In T. D. Gilovich, D. W. Griffin, & D. Kahneman (Eds), *Heuristics and biases* (pp. 730–748). New York: Cambridge University Press.

Fischhoff, B., Slovic, P., & Lichtenstein, S. (1978). Fault trees: Sensitivity of estimated failure probabilities to problem representation. *Journal of Experimental Psychology: Human Perception and Performance*, 4, 330–334.

Fishburn, P. C. (1974). Lexicographic orders, utilities and decision rules. *Management Science, 20*, 1442–1471.

Fitelson, B. (1999). The plurality of Bayesian measures of confirmation and the problem of measure sensitivity. *Philosophy of Science, 66*, 362–378.

Fletcher, P. C., Anderson, J. M., Shanks, D. R., Honey, R., Carpenter, T. A., Donovan, T., et al. (2001). Responses of human frontal cortex to surprising events are predicted by formal associative learning theory. *Nature Neuroscience, 4*, 1043–1048.

Fox, C. R. (1999). Strength of evidence, judged probability, and choice under uncertainty. *Cognitive Psychology, 38*, 167–189.

Fox, C. R., & Hadar, L. (2006) 'Decisions from experience' = sampling error + prospect theory: Reconsidering Hertwig, Barron, Weber & Erev (2004). *Judgment and Decision Making, 1*, 159–161.

Fox, C. R., Rogers, B. A., & Tversky, A. (1996). Options traders exhibit subadditive decision weights. *Journal of Risk and Uncertainty, 13*, 5–17.

Fox, C. R., & See, K. E. (2003). Belief and preference in decision under uncertainty. In D. Hardman & L. Macchi (Eds), *Thinking: Psychological perspectives on reasoning, judgment and decision making* (pp. 273–314). New York: Wiley.

Fox, C. R., & Tversky, A. (1995). Ambiguity aversion and comparative ignorance. *Quarterly Journal of Economics, 110*, 585–603.

Fox, C. R., & Tversky, A. (1998). A belief-based account of decision under uncertainty. *Management Science, 44*, 879–895.

Frederick, S. (2005). Cognitive reflection and decision making. *Journal of Economic Perspectives, 19*, 24–42.

Frederick, S., Loewenstein, G., & O'Donoghue, T. (2003). Time discounting and time preference: A critical review. In G. Loewenstein, D. Read, & R. Baumeister (Eds), *Time and decision: Economic and psychological perspectives on intertemporal choice* (pp. 13–86). New York: Russell Sage Foundation.

Frensch, P. A., & Funke, J. (1995). *Complex problem solving: The European perspective.* Hillsdale, NJ: Lawrence Erlbaum Associates.

Friedman, D. (1998). Monty Hall's three doors: Construction and deconstruction of a choice anomaly. *American Economic Review, 88*, 933–946.

Friedman, D., & Massaro, D. W. (1998). Understanding variability in binary and continuous choice. *Psychonomic Bulletin & Review, 5*, 370–389.

Friedman, D., Massaro, D. W., Kitzis, S. N., & Cohen, M. M. (1995). A comparison of learning models. *Journal of Mathematical Psychology, 39*, 164–178.

Fuller, S., & Aldag, R. (1998). Organizational Tonypandy: Lessons from a quarter century of the Groupthink phenomenon. *Organizational Behavior and Human Decision Processes, 73*, 163–184.

Galotti, K. M. (1995). Memories of a 'decision-map': Recall of a real-life decision. *Applied Cognitive Psychology, 9*, 307–319.

Gettys, C. F., Michel, C., Steiger, J. H., Kelly, C. W., & Peterson, C. R. (1973). Multiple-stage probabilistic information processing. *Organizational Behavior and Human Performance, 10*, 374–387.

Gigerenzer, G. (1994). Why the distinction between single-event probabilities and frequencies is relevant for psychology (and vice versa). In G. Wright & P. Ayton (Eds), *Subjective probability* (pp. 129–161). New York: Wiley.

Gigerenzer, G. (1996). On narrow norms and vague heuristics: A reply to Tversky and Kahneman. *Psychological Review, 103*, 592–596.

Gigerenzer, G. (2002). *Calculated risks: How to know when numbers deceive you.* New York: Simon & Schuster.

Gigerenzer, G. (2007) *Gut feelings: The intelligence of the unconscious.* New York: Viking Press.

Gigerenzer, G. (2014). How I got started: Teaching physicians and judges risk literacy. *Applied Cognitive Psychology, 28,* 612–614.

Gigerenzer, G., & Goldstein, D. G. (1996). Reasoning the fast and frugal way: Models of bounded rationality. *Psychological Review, 103,* 650–669.

Gigerenzer, G., & Goldstein, D. G. (1999). Betting on one good reason: The take-the-best heuristic. In G. Gigerenzer, P. M. Todd, & The ABC Research Group (Eds), *Simple heuristics that make us smart* (pp. 75–96). New York: Oxford University Press.

Gigerenzer, G., Hertwig, R., & Pachur, T. (2011). *Heuristics: The foundations of adaptive behavior.* New York: Oxford University Press.

Gigerenzer, G., & Hoffrage, U. (1995). How to improve Bayesian reasoning without instruction: Frequency formats. *Psychological Review, 102,* 684–704.

Gigerenzer, G., Hoffrage, U., & Kleinbölting, H. (1991). Probabilistic mental models: A Brunswikian theory of confidence. *Psychological Review, 98,* 506–528.

Gigerenzer, G., & Selten, R. (2001) Rethinking rationality. In G. Gigerenzer & R. Selten (Eds), *Bounded rationality: The adaptive toolbox* (pp. 1–12). Cambridge, MA: MIT Press.

Gigerenzer, G., Todd, P. M., & The ABC Research Group (1999). *Simple heuristics that make us smart.* New York: Oxford University Press.

Gigone, D., & Hastie, R. (1997). Proper analysis of the accuracy of group judgments. *Psychological Bulletin, 121,* 149–167.

Gilovich, T., Griffin, D., & Kahneman, D. (Eds) (2002). *Heuristics and biases.* New York: Cambridge University Press.

Girotto, V., & Gonzalez, M. (2001). Solving probabilistic and statistical problems: A matter of information structure and question form. *Cognition, 78,* 247–276.

Gladwell, M. (2005). *Blink: The power of thinking without thinking.* London: Penguin Books.

Glöckner A., & Engel C. (2013) Can we trust intuitive jurors? Standards of proof and the probative value of evidence in coherence based reasoning. *Journal of Empirical Legal Studies, 10,* 230–252.

Gluck, M. A., & Bower, G. H. (1988). From conditioning to category learning: An adaptive network model. *Journal of Experimental Psychology: General, 117,* 227–247.

Gluck, M. A., Shohamy, D., & Myers, C. (2002). How do people solve the 'weather prediction' task? Individual variability in strategies for probabilistic category learning. *Learning & Memory, 9,* 408–418.

Goldberg, L. R. (1968). Simple models or simple processes? Some research on clinical judgments. *American Psychologist, 23,* 483–496.

Goldstein, D. G., & Gigerenzer, G. (2002). Models of ecological rationality: The recognition heuristic. *Psychological Review, 109,* 75–90.

Goldstein, D., Gigerenzer, G., Hogarth, R., Kacelnik, A., Kareev, Y., Klein, G., Martignon, L., Payne, J., & Schlag, K. (2001). Why and when do simple heuristics work? In G. Gigerenzer & R. Selten (Eds), *Bounded rationality: The adaptive toolbox* (pp. 173–190). Cambridge, MA: MIT Press.

Goldstein, W. M., & Hogarth, R. M. (1997). Judgment and decision research: Some historical context. In W. M. Goldstein & R. M. Hogarth (Eds), *Research on judgment and decision making: Currents, connections, and controversies* (pp. 3–68). Cambridge, UK: Cambridge University Press.

Gonzalez, C. (2005). Decision support for real-time, dynamic decision making tasks. *Organizational Behavior and Human Decision Processes, 96,* 142–154.

Gonzalez, C., & Dutt, V. (2011). Instance-based learning: Integrating sampling and repeated decisions from experience. *Psychological Review, 118,* 523–551.

Gonzalez, C., Lerch, F. J., & Lebiere, C. (2003). Instance-based learning in dynamic decision making. *Cognitive Science, 27,* 591–635.

Goodie, A. S., & Fantino, E. (1999). What does and does not alleviate base-rate neglect under direct experience. *Journal of Behavioral Decision Making, 12,* 307–335.

Goodman, J. (1992). Jurors' comprehension and assessment of probabilistic evidence. *American Journal of Trial Advocacy, 16,* 361–389.

Goodman-Delahunty, J., & Newell, B. R. (2004). One in how many trillion? *Australasian Science, 25,* 14–17.

Goodnow, J. J. (1955). Determinants of choice-distribution in two-choice situations. *American Journal of Psychology, 68,* 106–116.

Gould, S. (1992). *Bully for brontosaurus: Further reflections in natural history.* London: Penguin Books.

Griffin, D., & Brenner, L. (2004). Probability judgment calibration. In N. Harvey & D. Koehler (Eds), *Blackwell handbook of judgment and decision making* (pp. 177–199). Chichester: Blackwell.

Griffiths, T. L., & Tenenbaum, J. B. (2009). Theory-based causal induction. *Psychological Review, 116,* 661–716.

Grove, W. M., & Meehl, P. E. (1996). Comparative efficiency of informal (subjective, impressionistic) and formal (mechanical, algorithmic) prediction procedures: The clinical/statistical controversy. *Psychology, Public Policy, and Law, 2,* 293–323.

Grove, W., Zald, D., Lebow, B., Snitz, B., & Nelson, C. (2000). Clinical versus mechanical prediction: A meta-analysis. *Psychological Assessment, 12,* 19–30.

Güney, S., & Newell, B. R. (in press). Overcoming ambiguity aversion through experience. *Journal of Behavioral Decision Making.*

Gureckis, T. M., James, T. W., & Nosofsky, R. M. (2011). Reevaluating dissociations between implicit and explicit category learning: An event-related fMRI study. *Journal of Cognitive Neuroscience, 23,* 1697–1709.

Hacking, I. (1975). *The emergence of probability: A philosophical study of early ideas about probability, induction and statistical inference.* Cambridge, UK: Cambridge University Press.

Hadar, L., & Fox, C. R. (2009). Information asymmetry in decision from description versus decision from experience. *Judgment and Decision Making, 4,* 317–325.

Haidt, J. (2001). The emotional dog and its rational tail: A social intuitionist approach to moral judgment. *Psychological Review, 108,* 814–834.

Hammond, J. S., Keeney, R. L., & Raiffa, H. (1999). *Smart choices: A practical guide to making better decisions.* Boston, MA: Harvard Business School Press.

Hammond, K. R. (1955). Probabilistic functioning and the clinical method. *Psychological Review, 62,* 255–262.

Hammond, K. R. (1971). Computer graphics as an aid to learning. *Science, 172,* 901–908.

Hammond, K. R. (1996). *Human judgment and social policy: Irreducible uncertainty, inevitable error, unavoidable injustice.* New York: Oxford University Press.

Hammond, K. R., & Adelman, L. (1976). Science, values, and human judgment. *Science, 194,* 389–396.

Hammond, K. R., & Boyle, P. J. R. (1971). Quasi-rationality, quarrels and new conceptions of feedback. *Bulletin of the British Psychological Society, 24,* 103–113.

Hammond, K. R., & Stewart, T. R. (Eds) (2001). *The essential Brunswik: Beginnings, explications, applications.* Oxford: Oxford University Press.

Hardisty, D. J., & Weber, E. U. (2009). Discounting future green: Money versus the environment. *Journal of Experimental Psychology: General, 138*, 329–340.

Harley, E. M., Carlsen, K. A., & Loftus, G. R. (2004). The 'saw-it-all-along' effect: Demonstrations of visual hindsight bias. *Journal of Experimental Psychology: Learning, Memory, and Cognition, 30*, 960–968.

Harries, C., Evans, J. S. B. T., & Dennis, I. (2000). Measuring doctors' self-insight into their treatment decisions. *Applied Cognitive Psychology, 14*, 455–477.

Harries, C., & Harvey, N. (2000). Taking advice, using information and knowing what you are doing. *Acta Psychologica, 104*, 399–416.

Harsanyi, J. C. (1977). *Rational behavior and bargaining equilibrium in games and social situations.* Cambridge, UK: Cambridge University Press

Harvey, N. (1997). Confidence in judgment. *Trends in Cognitive Sciences, 1*, 78–82.

Harvey, N., & Fischer, I. (2005). Development of experience-based judgment and decision making: The role of outcome feedback. In T. Betsch & S. Haberstroh (Eds), *The routines of decision making* (pp. 119–137). Mahwah, NJ: Erlbaum.

Hasher, L., & Zacks, R. T. (1979). Automatic and effortful processes in memory. *Journal of Experimental Psychology: General, 108*, 356–388.

Hasher, L., & Zacks, R. T. (1984). Automatic processing of fundamental information. *American Psychologist, 39*, 1327–1388.

Hastie, R. (1993). *Inside the juror: The psychology of juror decision making.* Cambridge and New York: Cambridge University Press.

Hastie, R., & Dawes, R. M. (2001). *Rational choice in an uncertain world.* Thousand Oaks, CA: Sage.

Hastie, R., & Kameda, T. (2005). The robust beauty of majority rules in group decisions. *Psychological Review, 112*, 494–508.

Hau, R., Pleskac, T. J., & Hertwig, R. (2010). Decisions from experience and statistical probabilities: Why they trigger different choices than a priori probabilities. *Journal of Behavioral Decision Making, 23*, 48–68.

Hau, R., Pleskac, T. J., Kiefer, J., & Hertwig, R. (2008). The description–experience gap in risky choice: The role of sample size and experienced probabilities. *Journal of Behavioral Decision Making, 21*, 1–26.

Hawkins, G. E., Camilleri, A. R., Heathcote, A., Newell, B. R., & Brown, S. D. (2014). Modeling probability knowledge and choice in decisions from experience. In P. Bello, M. Guarini, M. McShane, & B. Scassellati (Eds), *Proceedings of the 36th annual conference of the Cognitive Science Society* (pp. 595–600). Austin, TX: Cognitive Science Society.

Hawkins, S. A., & Hastie, R. (1990). Hindsight: Biased judgments of past events after the outcomes are known. *Psychological Bulletin, 107*, 311–327.

Hayes, B. K., Hawkins, G., Newell, B. R., Pasqualino, M., & Rehder, B. (2014). The role of causal models in multiple judgments under uncertainty. *Cognition, 133*, 611–620.

Hayes, B. K., & Newell, B. R. (2009). Induction with uncertain categories: When do people consider the alternative categories? *Memory & Cognition, 37*, 730–743.

Hayes, N. A., & Broadbent, D. E. (1988). Two modes of learning for interactive tasks. *Cognition, 28*, 249–276.

Heath, C., Larrick, R. P., & Klayman, J. (1998). Cognitive repairs: How organizational practices can compensate for individual shortcomings. In B. M. Staw & L. L. Cummings (Eds), *Research in Organizational Behavior, 20*, 1–37. Greenwich: JAI Press.

Heath, C., & Tversky, A. (1991). Preference and belief: Ambiguity and competence in choice under uncertainty. *Journal of Risk and Uncertainty, 4*, 5–28.

Henry, R. A. (1993). Group judgment accuracy: Reliability and validity of post discussion confidence judgments. *Organizational Behavior and Human Decision Processes, 56*, 11–27.

Henson, R. (2006). Forward inference using functional neuroimaging: dissociations versus associations. *Trends in Cognitive Science, 10,* 64–69.

Hertwig, R. (in press). Decisions from experience. In G. Keren & G. Wu (Eds), *Blackwell handbook of decision making.* Oxford: Blackwell.

Hertwig, R., Barron, G., Weber, E., & Erev, I. (2004). Decisions from experience and the effect of rare events. *Psychological Science, 15,* 534–539.

Hertwig, R., & Erev, I. (2009). The description–experience gap in risky choice. *Trends in Cognitive Science, 13,* 517–523.

Hertwig, R., Fanselow, C., & Hoffrage, U. (2003). How knowledge and heuristics affect our reconstruction of the past. *Memory, 11,* 357–377.

Hertwig, R., & Gigerenzer, G. (1999). The 'conjunction fallacy' revisited: How intelligent inferences look like reasoning errors. *Journal of Behavioral Decision Making, 12,* 275–305.

Hertwig, R., & Pleskac, T. J. (2010). Decisions from experience: Why small samples? *Cognition, 115,* 225–237.

Hertwig, R., & Todd, P. M. (2004). More is not always better: The benefits of cognitive limits. In D. Hardman & L. Macchi (Eds), *Thinking: Psychological perspectives on reasoning, judgment and decision making* (pp. 213–231). Chichester: Wiley.

Herzog, S. M., & Hertwig, R. (2009). The wisdom of many in one mind: Improving individual judgments with dialectical bootstrapping. *Psychological Science, 20,* 231–237.

Heyes, C. M. (2003). Four routes of cognitive evolution. *Psychological Review, 110,* 713–727.

Hilbig, B. E., Erdfelder, E., & Pohl, R. F. (2010). One-reason decision making unveiled: A measurement model of the recognition heuristic. *Journal of Experimental Psychology: Learning, Memory, and Cognition, 36,* 123–134.

Hilbig, B. E., & Pohl, R. F. (2009). Ignorance versus evidence-based decision making: A decision time analysis of the recognition heuristic. *Journal of Experimental Psychology: Learning, Memory, and Cognition, 35,* 1296–1305.

Hill, G. W. (1982) Group versus individual performance: Are $N + 1$ heads better than one? *Psychological Bulletin, 91,* 517–539.

Hills, T. T., & Hertwig, R. (2010). Information search in decisions from experience: Do our patterns of sampling foreshadow our decisions? *Psychological Science, 21,* 1787–1792.

Hills, T. T., & Hertwig, R. (2012). Two distinct exploratory behaviors in decisions from experience: Comment on Gonzalez and Dutt (2011). *Psychological Review, 119,* 888–892.

Hilton, D. J. (2003). Psychology and the financial markets. In I. Brocas & J. D. Carillo (Eds), *The Psychology of economic decisions. Volume I: Rationality and well being* (pp. 273–297). Oxford: Oxford University Press.

Hilton, D. J., & Slugoski, B. R. (1986). Knowledge-based causal attribution: The abnormal conditions focus model. *Psychological Review, 93,* 75–88.

Hintzman, D. L. (1988). Judgments of frequency and recognition memory in a multiple-trace memory model. *Psychological Review, 95,* 528–551.

Hoffman, R. R., Crandell, B., & Shadbolt, N. (1998). Use of critical decision method to elicit expert knowledge: A case study in the methodology of expert task analysis. *Human Factors, 40,* 254–276.

Hogarth, R. M. (1978). A note on aggregating opinions. *Organizational Behavior and Human Decision Processes, 21,* 40–46.

Hogarth, R. M. (1981). Beyond discrete biases: Functional and dysfunctional aspects of judgement heuristics. *Psychological Bulletin, 90,* 197–217.

Hogarth, R. M. (2001). *Educating intuition*. Chicago: The University of Chicago Press.

Hogarth, R. M. (2010) Intuition: A challenge for psychological research on decision making. *Psychological Inquiry, 21*, 338–353.

Hogarth, R. M., & Einhorn, H. J. (1990). Venture theory: A model of decision weights. *Management Science, 36*, 780–783.

Hogarth, R. M., & Karelaia, N. (2005). Ignoring information in binary choice with continuous variables: When is less 'more'? *Journal of Mathematical Psychology, 49*, 115–124.

Hogarth, R. M., & Soyer, E. (2011). Sequentially simulated outcomes: Kind experience versus nontransparent description. *Journal of Experimental Psychology: General, 140*, 434–463.

Holyoak, K. J., & Cheng, P. W. (2011). Causal learning and inference as a rational process: The new synthesis. *Annual Review of Psychology, 62*, 135–163.

Houghton, G. (Ed.) (2005). *Connectionist models in cognitive psychology*. Hove, East Sussex: Psychology Press.

Hsee, C. K. (1996). The evaluability hypothesis: An explanation for preference-reversal between joint and separate evaluations of alternatives. *Organizational Behavior and Human Decision Processes, 67*, 247–257.

Hume, D. (1748). *An enquiry concerning human understanding*. Oxford: Clarendon.

Humphreys, L. G. (1939). Acquisition and extinction of verbal expectations in a situation analogous to conditioning. *Journal of Experimental Psychology, 25*, 294–301.

Hux, J. E., & Naylor, C. D. (1995). Communicating the benefits of chronic preventative therapy: Does the format of efficacy data determine patients' acceptance of treatment? *Medical Decision Making, 15*, 152–157.

Imai, M. (1986). *Kaizen: The key to Japan's competitive success*. New York: McGraw-Hill Education.

Iyengar, S. S., & Lepper, M. R. (2000). When choice is demotivating: Can one desire too much of a good thing? *Journal of Personality and Social Psychology, 79*, 995–1006.

Jacoby, L. L., & Dallas, M. (1981). On the relationship between autobiographical memory and perceptual learning. *Journal of Experimental Psychology: General, 110*, 306–340.

Janis, I. (1972). *Victims of groupthink*. Boston, MA: Houghton Mifflin.

Janis, I., & Mann, L. (1977). *Decision making: A psychological analysis of conflict, choice and commitment*. New York: The Free Press.

Jeffrey, R. (1965). *The logic of decision*. New York: McGraw-Hill.

John, P., Cotterill, S., Moseley, A., Richardson L., Smith, G., Stoker, G., & Wales, C. (2011). *Nudge, nudge, think, think: Experimenting with ways to change civic behaviour*. London: Bloomsbury Academic Publishing.

Johnson, E. J., & Goldstein, D. G. (2003). Do defaults save lives? *Science, 302*, 1338–1339.

Johnson, E. J., Shu, S. B., Dellaert, B. G., Fox, C., Goldstein, D. G., Häubl, G., . . . & Weber, E. U. (2012). Beyond nudges: Tools of a choice architecture. *Marketing Letters, 23*, 487–504.

Jones–Lee, M. W., Loomes, G., & Phillips, P. R. (1995). Valuing the prevention of non–fatal road injuries: Contingent valuation vs. standard gambles. *Oxford Economic Papers, 47*, 676–695.

Juslin, P., Jones, S., Olsson, H., & Winman, A. (2003). Cue abstraction and exemplar memory in categorization. *Journal of Experimental Psychology: Learning, Memory, and Cognition, 29*, 924–941.

Juslin, P., Karlsson, L., & Olsson, H. (2008). Information integration in multiple cue judgment: A division of labor hypothesis. *Cognition, 106*, 259–298.

Juslin, P., & Montgomery, H. (1999). Introduction and historical remarks. In P. Juslin & H. Montgomery (Eds), *Judgment and decision making: New-Brunswikian and process-tracing approaches* (pp. 1–6). Hillsdale, NJ: Erlbaum.

Juslin, P., Nilsson, H., & Winman, A. (2009). Probability theory, not the very guide of life. *Psychological Review, 116*, 856–874.

Juslin, P., Olsson, H., & Olsson, A.-C. (2003). Exemplar effects in categorization and multiple-cue judgment. *Journal of Experimental Psychology: General, 132*, 133–156.

Juslin, P., & Persson, M. (2002). PROBabilities from EXemplars (PROBEX): A 'lazy' algorithm for probabilistic inference from generic knowledge. *Cognitive Science, 95*, 1–4.

Juslin, P., Winman, A., & Olsson, H. (2000). Naive empiricism and dogmatism in confidence research: A critical examination of the hard–easy effect. *Psychological Review, 107*, 384–396.

Kahneman, D. (2003). A perspective on judgment and choice: Mapping bounded rationality. *American Psychologist, 58*, 697–720.

Kahneman, D. (2011). *Thinking, fast and slow.* New York: Allen Lane.

Kahneman, D., & Frederick, S. (2002). Representativeness revisited: Attribute substitution in intuitive judgment. In T. D. Gilovich, D. W. Griffin, & D. Kahneman (Eds), *Heuristics and biases* (pp. 49–81). New York: Cambridge University Press.

Kahneman, D., Fredrickson, B. L., Schreiber, C. A., & Redelmeier, D. A. (1993). When more pain is preferred to less: Adding a better end. *Psychological Science, 4*, 401–405.

Kahneman, D., & Klein, G. A. (2009) Conditions for intuitive expertise: A failure to disagree. *American Psychologist, 64*, 515–526.

Kahneman, D., Knetsch, J. L., & Thaler, R. H. (1990). Experimental tests of the endowment effect and the Coase Theorem. *Journal of Political Economy, 98*, 1325–1348.

Kahneman, D., & Lovallo, D. (1993). Timid choices and bold forecasts: A cognitive perspective on risk and risk taking. *Management Science, 39*, 17–31.

Kahneman, D., Ritov, I., & Schkade, D. (1999). Economic preferences or attitude expressions? An analysis of dollar responses to public issues. *Journal of Risk and Uncertainty, 19*, 220–242.

Kahneman, D., Slovic, P., & Tversky, A. (Eds) (1982). *Judgment under uncertainty: Heuristics and biases.* Cambridge, UK: Cambridge University Press.

Kahneman, D., & Snell, J. (1992). Predicting a changing taste: Do people know what they will like? *Journal of Behavioral Decision Making, 5*, 187–200.

Kahneman, D., & Tversky, A. (1979a). Prospect theory: An analysis of decision under risk. *Econometrica, 47*, 263–291.

Kahneman, D., & Tversky, A. (1979b). Intuitive predictions: Biases and corrective procedures. *TIMS Studies in Management Science, 12*, 313–327.

Kahneman, D., & Tversky, A. (1982a). The simulation heuristic. In D. Kahneman, P. Slovic, & A. Tversky (Eds), *Judgment under uncertainty: Heuristics and biases* (pp. 201–208). Cambridge, UK: Cambridge University Press.

Kahneman, D., & Tversky, A. (1982b). Variants of uncertainty. In D. Kahneman, P. Slovic, & A. Tversky (Eds), *Judgment under uncertainty: Heuristics and biases.* (pp. 509–520). Cambridge, UK: Cambridge University Press.

Kahneman, D., & Tversky, A. (1984). Choices, values, and frames. *American Psychologist, 39*, 341–350.

Kahneman, D. & Tversky, A. (1996). On the reality of cognitive illusions. *Psychological Review, 103*, 582-591

Kahneman, D., & Tversky, A. (2000). *Choices, values, and frames.* Cambridge, UK: Cambridge University Press.

Kahneman, D., & Varey, C. A. (1990). Propensities and counterfactuals: The loser that almost won. *Journal of Personality and Social Psychology, 59*, 1101–1110.

Kaplan, R. J., & Newman, J. R. (1966). Studies in probabilistic information processing. *IEEE Transactions on Human Factors in Electronics, HFE-7*, 49–63.

Karelaia, N., & Hogarth, R. M. (2008). Determinants of linear judgment: A meta–analysis of lens model studies. *Psychological Bulletin, 134*, 404–426.

Katsikopoulos, K. V., & Martignon, L. (2006). Naive heuristics for paired comparisons: Some results on their relative accuracy. *Journal of Mathematical Psychology, 50*, 488–494.

Katsikopoulos, K. V., Schooler, L. J., & Hertwig, R. (2010). The robust beauty of ordinary information. *Psychological Review, 117*, 1259–1266.

Keeney, R. L., & Raiffa, H. (1976). *Decisions with multiple objectives: Preferences and value trade-offs.* New York: Wiley.

Keller, L. R. (1985). The effects of problem representation on the sure-thing and substitution principles. *Management Science, 31*, 738–751.

Kelley, C. M., & Jacoby, L. L. (2000). Recollection and familiarity: Process-dissociation. In E. Tulving & F. I. M. Craik (Eds), *The Oxford handbook of memory* (pp. 215–228). New York: Oxford University Press.

Kelley, H., & Friedman, D. (2002). Learning to forecast price. *Economic Inquiry, 40*, 556–573.

Keren, G. (1987). Facing uncertainty in the game of bridge: A calibration study. *Organizational Behavior and Human Decision Processes, 39*, 98–114.

Keren, G. (2013). A tale of two systems: A scientific advance or a theoretical stone soup? Commentary on Evans & Stanovich (2013). *Perspectives on Psychological Science, 8*, 257–262.

Keren, G., & Schul, Y. (2009). Two is not always better than one: A critical evaluation of two-system theories. *Perspectives on Psychological Science, 4*, 533–550.

Kerr, N. L., MacCoun, R., & Kramer, G. P. (1996). Bias in judgment: Comparing individuals and groups. *Psychological Review, 103*, 687–719.

Kerr, N. L., & Tindale, R. S. (2004). Group performance and decision making. *Annual Review of Psychology, 55*, 623–655.

Kitzis, S. N., Kelley, H., Berg, E., Massaro, D. W., & Friedman, D. (1998). Broadening the tests of learning models. *Journal of Mathematical Psychology, 42*, 327–355.

Klayman, J. (1984). Learning from feedback in probabilistic environments. *Acta Psychologica, 56*, 81–92.

Klayman, J. (1988a). Cue discovery in probabilistic environments: Uncertainty and experimentation. *Journal of Experimental Psychology: Learning, Memory, and Cognition, 14*, 317–330.

Klayman, J. (1988b). On the how and why (not) of learning from outcomes. In B. Brehmer & C. R. B. Joyce (Eds), *Human judgment: The SJT view* (pp. 115–160). North Holland: Elsevier.

Klayman, J. (1995). Varieties of confirmation bias. *The Psychology of Learning and Motivation, 32*, 385–418.

Klayman, J. (2001). Ambivalence in (not about) naturalistic decision making. *Journal of Behavioral Decision Making, 14*, 372–373.

Klayman, J., & Ha, Y.-W. (1987). Confirmation, disconfirmation, and information in hypothesis testing. *Psychological Review, 94*, 211–228.

Klayman, J., Soll, J. B., Juslin, P., & Winman, A. (2006). Subjective confidence and the sampling of knowledge. In K. Fiedler & P. Juslin (Eds), *Information sampling and adaptive cognition* (pp. 153–182). Cambridge, UK: Cambridge University Press.

Klein, G. A. (1993). A recognition-primed decision (RPD) model of rapid decision making. In G. A. Klein, J. Orasanu, R. Calderwood, & C. E. Zsambok (Eds), *Decision making in action: Models and methods* (pp. 138–147). Norwood, CT: Ablex.

Klein, G. A. (1998). *Sources of power: How people make decisions.* Cambridge, MA: MIT Press.

Klein, G. A. (2009). *Streetlights and shadows: Searching for the keys to adaptive decision making.* Cambridge, MA: MIT Press.

Klein, G. A., Wolf, S., Militello, L., & Zsambok, C. E. (1995). Characteristics of skilled option generation in chess. *Organization Behavior and Human Decision Processes, 62,* 63–69.

Knight, F. H. (1921). *Risk, uncertainty and profit.* New York: Hart, Schaffner and Marx.

Knowlton, B. J., Mangels, J. A., & Squire, L. R. (1996). A neostriatal habit learning system in humans. *Science, 273,* 1399–1402.

Koehler, D. J., & James, G. (2014). Probability matching, fast and slow. *The Psychology of Learning and Motivation, 61,* 103–132.

Koehler, J. J. (1993). Error and exaggeration in the presentation of DNA evidence. *Jurimetrics Journal, 34,* 21–39.

Koehler, J. J. (1996). The base rate fallacy reconsidered: Descriptive, normative, and methodological challenges. *Behavioral and Brain Sciences, 19,* 1–53.

Koehler, J. J., Chia, A., & Lindsey, S. (1995). The random match probability in DNA evidence: Irrelevant and prejudicial? *Jurimetrics Journal, 35,* 201–209.

Koehler, J. J., & Macchi, L. (2004). Thinking about low probability events. *Psychological Science, 15,* 540–545.

Koehler, J. J., & Macchi, L. (2009). Comments on 'Getting scarred and winning lotteries: Effects of exemplar cuing and statistical format on imagining low-probability events' by Newell, Mitchell, and Hayes (2008). *Journal of Behavioral Decision Making, 22,* 523–527.

Konstantinidis, E., & Shanks, D. R. (2014). Don't bet on it! Wagering as a measure of awareness in decision making under uncertainty. *Journal of Experimental Psychology: General, 143,* 2111–2134.

Koriat, A., Lichtenstein, S., & Fischhoff, B. (1980). Reasons for confidence. *Journal of Experimental Psychology: Human Learning and Memory, 6,* 107–118.

Kruglanski, A. W. (2013). Only one? The default interventionist perspective as a unimodel – Commentary on Evans & Stanovich (2013). *Perspectives on Psychological Science, 8,* 242–247.

Kruglanski, A. W., & Gigerenzer, G. (2011). Intuitive and deliberative judgements are based on common principles. *Psychological Review, 118,* 97–109.

Kruschke, J. K. (1992). ALCOVE: An exemplar-based connectionist model of category learning. *Psychological Review, 99,* 22–44.

Kruschke, J. K. (1996). Base rates in category learning. *Journal of Experimental Psychology: Learning, Memory, and Cognition, 22,* 3–26.

Krynski, T. R., & Tenenbaum, J. B. (2007). The role of causality in judgment under uncertainty. *Journal of Experimental Psychology: General, 136,* 430–450.

Kugler, T., Kausel, E. E., & Kocher, M. G. (2012). Are groups more rational than individuals? A review of interactive decision making in groups. *Wiley Interdisciplinary Reviews: Cognitive Science, 3,* 471–482.

Kunda, Z. (1990). The case for motivated reasoning. *Psychological Bulletin, 108,* 480–498.

Lagnado, D. A. (2011). Thinking about evidence. In P. Dawid, W. Twining, & M. Vasaliki (Eds), *Evidence, inference and enquiry* (pp. 183–224). Oxford: Oxford University Press/British Academy.

Lagnado, D. A., Fenton, N., & Neil, M. (2013). Legal idioms: A framework for evidential reasoning. *Argument and Computation, 4,* 46–63.

Lagnado, D. A., & Harvey, N. (2008). The impact of discredited evidence. *Psychonomic Bulletin and Review, 15,* 1166–1173.

Lagnado, D. A., Moss, T., & Shanks, D. R. (2006). Grouping choices. *Unpublished manuscript.* University College London.

Lagnado, D. A., Newell, B. R., Kahan, S., & Shanks, D. R. (2006). Insight and strategy in multiple cue learning. *Journal of Experimental Psychology: General, 135,* 162–183.

Lagnado, D. A., & Shanks, D. R. (2002). Probability judgment in hierarchical learning: A conflict between predictiveness and coherence. *Cognition, 83,* 81–112.

Lagnado, D. A., & Shanks, D. R. (2003). The influence of hierarchy on probability judgment. *Cognition, 89,* 157–178.

Lagnado D. A., & Sloman, S. A. (2004a). The advantage of timely intervention. *Journal of Experimental Psychology: Learning, Memory, and Cognition, 30,* 856–876.

Lagnado, D., & Sloman, S. A. (2004b). Inside and outside probability judgment. In D. J. Koehler & N. Harvey (Eds), *The Blackwell handbook of judgment and decision making* (pp. 157–176). Malden, MA: Blackwell.

Lagnado, D. A., & Sloman, S. A. (2006). Time as a guide to cause. *Journal of Experimental Psychology: Learning, Memory, and Cognition, 32,* 451–460.

Lagnado, D. A., Waldmann, M. R., Hagmayer, Y., & Sloman, S. A. (2007). Beyond covariation: Cues to causal structure. In A. Gopnik & L. Schultz (Eds), *Causal learning: Psychology, philosophy, and computation.* (pp. 154–172). Oxford: Oxford University Press.

Lan, C. H., & Harvey, N. (2006). *Ellsberg's paradoxes: Problems for rank-dependent utility explanations.* Paper presented at 12th International Conference on the Foundations and Applications of Utility, Risk and Decision Theory. LUISS, Rome.

Laplace, P. S. (1812). *Analytical theory of probability.* Paris: Courcier.

Larrick, R. P. (2004). Debiasing. In D. J. Koehler & N. Harvey (Eds), *The Blackwell handbook of judgment and decision making* (pp. 316–337). Malden, MA: Blackwell.

Laughlin, P. R. (1999). Collective induction: Twelve postulates. *Organizational Behavior and Human Decision Processes, 80,* 50–69.

Laughlin, P. R., VanderStoep, S. W., & Hollingshead, A. B. (1991). Collective versus individual induction: Recognition of truth, rejection of error, and collective information processing. *Journal of Personality and Social Psychology, 61,* 50–67.

Lee, D. (2013). Decision making: From neuroscience to psychiatry. *Neuron, 78,* 233–248.

Lee, M. D., & Cummins, T. D. R. (2004). Evidence accumulation in decision making: Unifying 'take the best' and 'rational' models. *Psychonomic Bulletin & Review, 11,* 343–352.

Lee, M. D., & Newell, B. R. (2011). Using hierarchical Bayesian methods to examine the tools of decision making. *Judgment and Decision Making, 6,* 832–842.

Lee, M. D., Newell, B. R., & Vandekerckhove, J. (2014). Modeling the adaptation of search termination in human decision making. *Decision, 4,* 223-251.

Lee, M. D., Zhang, S., & Shi, J. (2011). The wisdom of the crowd playing the Price is Right. *Memory & Cognition, 39,* 914–923.

Lee, Y. (1995). Effects of learning contexts on implicit and explicit learning. *Memory & Cognition, 23,* 723–734.

Lehrer, J. (2009) *The decisive moment: How the brain makes up its mind.* Melbourne: Text Publishing.

Lejarraga, T., Hertwig, R., & Gonzalez, C. (2012). How choice ecology influences search in decisions from experience. *Cognition, 124,* 334–342.

Levine, L. J., Lench, H. C., Kaplan, R. L., & Safer, M. A. (2012). Accuracy and artifact: Reexamining the intensity bias in affective forecasting. *Journal of Personality and Social Psychology*, *103*, 584–605.

Levy, I., Snell, J., Nelson, A. J., Rustichini, A., & Glimcher, P. W. (2010). Neural representation of subjective value under risk and ambiguity. *Journal of Neurophysiology*, *103*, 1036–1047.

Li, S. Y. W., Rakow, T., & Newell, B. R. (2009). Personal experience in doctor and patient decision making: From psychology to medicine. *Journal of Evaluation in Clinical Practice*, *15*, 993–995.

Li, Y., & Epley, N. (2009). When the best appears to be saved for last: Serial position effects on choice. *Journal of Behavioral Decision Making*, *22*, 378–389.

Lichtenstein, S., & Fischhoff, B. (1977). Do those who know more also know more about how much they know? *Organizational Behavior and Human Performance*, *20*, 159–183.

Lichtenstein, S., Fischhoff, B., & Phillips, L. D. (1982). Calibration of probabilities: The state of the art to 1980. In D. Kahneman, P. Slovic, & A. Tversky (Eds), *Judgment under uncertainty: Heuristics and biases* (pp. 306–334). Cambridge, UK: Cambridge University Press.

Lichtenstein, S., & Slovic, P. (1971). Reversals of preference between bids and choices in gambling decisions. *Journal of Experimental Psychology*, *89*, 46–55.

Lichtenstein, S., & Slovic, P. (1973). Response-induced reversals of preference in gambling: An extended replication in Las Vegas. *Journal of Experimental Psychology*, *101*, 16–20.

Lichtenstein, S., Slovic, P., Fischoff, B., Layman, M., & Coombs, B. (1978). Judged frequency of lethal events. *Journal of Experimental Psychology: Human Learning and Memory*, *4*, 551–578.

Lieberman, M. D. (2009). What zombies can't do: A social cognitive neuroscience approach to the irreducibility of reflective consciousness. In J. St B. T. Evans & K. Frankish (Eds), *In two minds: Dual processes and beyond* (pp. 293–316). Oxford: Oxford University Press.

Lindell, M. K., & Stewart, T. R. (1974). The effects of redundancy in multiple cue probability learning. *American Psychologist*, *87*, 393–398.

Lindley, D. V. (1985). *Making decisions* (2nd edn). London: Wiley.

Lindsey, S., Hertwig, R., & Gigerenzer, G. (2003). Communicating statistical evidence. *Jurimetrics Journal*, *43*, 147–163.

Lipshitz, R., Klein, G., Orasanu, J., & Salas, E. (2001). Taking stock of naturalistic decision making. *Journal of Behavioral Decision Making*, *14*, 331–352.

List, J. A. (2002). Preference reversals of a different kind: The 'more is less' phenomenon. *American Economic Review*, *92*, 1636–1643.

Loewenstein, G. (1987) Anticipation and the valuation of delayed consumption. *The Economic Journal*, *97*, 666–684.

Loewenstein, G. (1988). Frames of mind in intertemporal choice. *Management Science*, *34*, 200–214.

Loewenstein, G. (1996). Out of control: Visceral influences on behavior. *Organizational Behavior and Human Decision Processes*, *65*, 272–292.

Loewenstein, G., & Angner, E. (2003). Predicting and indulging changing preferences. In G. Loewenstein, D. Read, & R. Baumeister (Eds), *Time and decision: Economic and psychological perspectives on intertemporal choice* (pp. 351–391). New York: Russell Sage Foundation.

Loewenstein, G., Read, D., & Baumeister, R. (Eds) (2003). *Time and decision: Economic and psychological perspectives on intertemporal choice.* New York: Russell Sage Foundation.

Loewenstein, G., Weber, E., Hsee, C., & Welch, N. (2001). Risk as feelings. *Psychological Bulletin, 127,* 267–286.

Loomes, G., Starmer, C., & Sugden, R. (1992). Are preferences monotonic? Testing some implications of regret theory. *Economica, 59,* 17–33.

Loomes, G., & Sugden, R. (1982). Regret theory: An alternative theory of rational choice under uncertainty. *Economic Journal, 92,* 805–824.

Lorge I., & Solomon, H. (1958). Two models of group behavior in the solution of Eureka–type problems. *Psychometrika, 29,* 139–148.

Louie, T. A. (1999). Decision makers' hindsight bias after receiving favorable and unfavorable feedback. *Journal of Applied Psychology, 84,* 29–41.

Lovallo, D., & Kahneman, D. (2003). Delusions of success. *Harvard Business Review, 81,* 57–63.

Løvborg, L., & Brehmer, B. (1991). *NEWFIRE: A flexible system for running simulated fire-fighting experiments.* Risö National Laboratory, Roskilde, Denmark.

Lovibond, P. F., & Shanks, D. R. (2002). The role of awareness in Pavlovian conditioning: Empirical evidence and theoretical implications. *Journal of Experimental Psychology: Animal Behavior Processes, 28,* 3–26.

Luce, R. D., & Raiffa, H. (1957). *Games and decisions.* New York: Wiley.

Lynch, M., & McNally, R. (2003). Science, common sense and DNA evidence: A legal controversy about the public understanding of science. *Public Understanding of Science, 12,* 83–103.

MacCrimmon, K. R., & Larsson, S. (1979). Utility theory: Axioms versus 'paradoxes'. In M. Allais & O. Hagen (Eds), *Expected utility and the Allais paradox* (pp. 333–409). Dordrecht: D. Reidel Publishing Company.

Maddox, W. T., & Ashby, F. G. (2004). Dissociating explicit and procedural-learning based systems of perceptual category learning. *Behavioural Processes, 66,* 309–332.

Maia, T. V., & McClelland, J. L. (2004). A reexamination of the evidence for the somatic marker hypothesis: What participants really know in the Iowa gambling task. *Proceedings of the National Academy of Sciences, 101,* 16075–16080.

Maier, N., & Solem, A. (1952). The contribution of a discussion leader to the quality of group thinking: The effective use of minority opinion. *Human Relations, 5,* 277–288.

Malenka, D. J., Baron, J. A., Johansen, S., Wahrenberger, J. W., & Ross, J. M. (1993). The framing effect of relative and absolute risk. *Journal of General Internal Medicine, 8,* 543–548.

Mann, T., & Ward, A. (2004). To eat or not to eat: Implications of the attentional myopia model for restrained eaters. *Journal of Abnormal Psychology, 113,* 90–98.

Mantonakis, A., Rodero, P., Lesschaeve, I., & Hastie, R. (2009). Order in choice: Effects of serial position on preferences. *Psychological Science, 20,* 1309–1312.

March, J. G. (1991). Exploration and exploitation in organizational learning. *Organization Science, 2,* 71–87.

March, J. G., & Shapira, Z. (1987). Managerial perspectives on risk and risk taking. *Management Science, 33,* 1404–1418.

Markowitz, H. (1952). The utility of wealth. *Journal of Political Economy, 60,* 151–158.

Marr, D. (1982). *Vision.* San Francisco, CA: H. Freeman and Co.

Marschak, J. (1954). Towards an economic theory of organization and information. In R. M. Thrall, C. H. Coombs, & R. L. Davis (Eds), *Decision processes* (pp. 187–220). New York: Wiley.

Martignon, L., & Hoffrage, U. (1999). Why does one-reason decision making work? A case study in ecological rationality. In G. Gigerenzer, P. M. Todd, & The ABC Research Group (Eds), *Simple heuristics that make us smart* (pp. 119–140). New York: Oxford University Press.

Martignon, L., & Hoffrage, U. (2002). Fast, frugal and fit: Lexicographic heuristics for paired comparison. *Theory and Decision, 52*, 29–71.

Martire, K. A., Kemp, R. I., & Newell, B. R. (2013). The psychology of interpreting expert evaluative opinions. *Australian Journal of Forensic Sciences, 45*, 305–314.

Martire, K. A., Kemp R. I., Watkins I., Sayle, M., & Newell, B. R. (2013). The expression and interpretation of uncertain forensic science evidence: Verbal equivalence, evidence strength and the weak evidence effect. *Law & Human Behavior, 37*, 197–207.

Mathieu, M. T., & Gosling, S. D. (2012). The accuracy or inaccuracy of affective forecasts depends on how accuracy is indexed: A meta-analysis of past studies. *Psychological Science, 23*, 161–162.

Maule, J., & Villejoubert, G. (2007). What lies beneath: Reframing framing effects. *Thinking & Reasoning, 13*, 25–44.

McClelland, J. L. (1998). Connectionist models and Bayesian inference. In M. Oaksford & N. Chater (Eds), *Rational models of cognition* (pp. 21–53). Oxford: Oxford University Press.

McClelland, J. L., & Rumelhart, D. E. (1986). *Parallel distributed processing: Explorations in the microstructure of cognition. Vol. 2: Psychological and biological models*. Cambridge, MA: MIT Press.

McClure, S. M., Laibson, D. I., Loewenstein, G., & Cohen, J. D. (2004). Separate neural systems value immediate and delayed monetary rewards. *Science, 306*, 503–507.

McKenzie, C. R. M. (2004). Framing effects in inference tasks – and why they are normatively defensible. *Memory and Cognition, 32*, 874–885.

McKenzie, C. R. M., Liersch, M. J., & Finkelstein, S. R. (2006). Recommendations implicit in policy defaults. *Psychological Science, 17*, 414–420.

McMahon, K., Sparrow, B., Chatman, L., & Riddle, T. (2011). Driven to distraction: The impact of distracter type on unconscious decision making. *Social Cognition, 29*, 683–698.

McMillan, T. M., & Rachman, S. J. (1988). Fearlessness and courage in paratroopers undergoing training. *Personality and Individual Differences, 9*, 373–378.

McNeil, B. J., Pauker, S. G., Sox, H. C., & Tversky, A. (1982). On the elicitation of preferences for alternative therapies. *New England Journal of Medicine, 306*, 1259–1262.

Medin, D. L., & Edelson, S. M. (1988). Problem structure and the use of base–rate information from experience. *Journal of Experimental Psychology: General, 117*, 68–85.

Medin, D. L., & Schaffer, M. M. (1978). Context theory of classification learning. *Psychological Review, 85*, 207–238.

Meehl, P. E. (1954). *Clinical versus statistical prediction*. Minneapolis: University of Minnesota Press.

Mellers, B. A., Ungar, L., Baron, J., Ramos, J., Gurcay, B., Fincher, K., Scott, S. E., Moore, D., Atanasov, P., Swift, S. A., Murray, T., Stone, E., & Tetlock, P. E. (2014). Psychological strategies for winning geopolitical forecasting tournaments. *Psychological Science, 25*, 1106–1115.

Melrose, K. L., Brown, G. D. A., & Wood, A. M. (2013). Am I abnormal? Relative rank and social norm effects in judgments of anxiety and depression symptom severity. *Journal of Behavioral Decision Making, 26*, 174–184.

Muchinsky, P. M., & Dudycha, A. L. (1975). Human inference behavior in abstract and meaningful environments. *Organizational Behavior and Human Performance, 13*, 377–391.

Murphy, A. H., & Winkler, R. L. (1974). Subjective probability forecasting experiments in meteorology: Some preliminary results. *Bulletin of the American Meteorological Society, 55,* 1206–1216.

Murphy, A. H., & Winkler, R. L. (1977). Reliability of subjective probability forecasts of precipitation and temperature. *Applied Statistics, 26,* 41–47.

Murphy, G. L., & Ross, B. H. (1994). Predictions from uncertain categorizations. *Cognitive Psychology, 27,* 148–193.

Mussweiler, T., Strack, F., & Pfeiffer, T. (2000). Overcoming the inevitable anchoring effect: Considering the opposite compensates for selective accessibility. *Personality and Social Psychology Bulletin, 26,* 1142–1150.

Myers, J. L., & Cruse, D. (1968). Two-choice discrimination learning as a function of stimulus and event probabilities. *Journal of Experimental Psychology, 77,* 453–459.

Neimark, E. D., & Shuford, E. H. (1959). Comparison of predictions and estimates in a probability learning situation. *Journal of Experimental Psychology, 57,* 294–298.

Newell, B. R. (2005). Re-visions of rationality? *Trends in Cognitive Sciences, 9,* 11–15.

Newell, B. R. (2015). Wait! Just let me NOT think about that for a minute: What role do implicit processes play in higher level cognition? *Current Directions in Psychological Science, 24,* 65–70.

Newell, B. R., & Dunn, J. C. (2008). Dimensions in data: Testing psychological models using state-trace analysis. *Trends in Cognitive Sciences, 12,* 285–290.

Newell, B. R., Dunn, J. C., & Kalish, M. (2011). Systems of category learning: Fact or fantasy? *The Psychology of Learning & Motivation, 54,* 167–215.

Newell, B. R., & Fernandez, D. (2006). On the binary quality of recognition and the inconsequentiality of further knowledge: Two critical tests of the recognition heuristic. *Journal of Behavioral Decision Making, 19,* 333–346.

Newell, B. R., Koehler, D. J., James, G., Rakow, T., & van Ravenzwaaij, D. (2013). Probability matching in risky choice: The interplay of feedback and strategy availability. *Memory & Cognition, 41,* 329–338.

Newell, B. R., & Lagnado, D. (2003). Think-tanks, or think *tanks? The Psychologist, 16,* 176.

Newell, B. R., & Lee, M. D. (2011). The right tool for the job? Comparing an evidence accumulation and a naïve strategy selection model of decision making. *Journal of Behavioral Decision Making, 24,* 456–481.

Newell, B. R., Mitchell. C. J., & Hayes, B. K. (2008). Getting scarred and winning lotteries: Effects of exemplar cuing and statistical format on imagining low-probability events. *Journal of Behavioral Decision Making, 21,* 317–335.

Newell, B. R., & Rakow, T. (2007). The role of experience in decisions from description. *Psychonomic Bulletin & Review, 14,* 1133–1139.

Newell, B. R., & Rakow, T. (2011) Revising beliefs about the merits of unconscious thought: Evidence in favor of the null hypothesis. *Social Cognition, 29,* 711–726.

Newell, B. R., Rakow, T., Weston, N. J., & Shanks, D. R. (2004). Search strategies in decision making: The success of success. *Journal of Behavioral Decision Making, 17,* 117–137.

Newell, B. R., & Shanks, D. R. (2003). Take the best or look at the rest? Factors influencing 'one-reason' decision-making. *Journal of Experimental Psychology: Learning, Memory, and Cognition, 29,* 53–65.

Newell, B. R., & Shanks, D. R. (2004). On the role of recognition in decision making. *Journal of Experimental Psychology: Learning, Memory, and Cognition, 30,* 923–935.

Newell, B. R., & Shanks, D. R. (2014). Unconscious influences on decision making: A critical review. *Behavioral and Brain Sciences, 37,* 1–63.

Newell, B. R., Weston, N. J., & Shanks, D. R. (2003). Empirical tests of a fast and frugal heuristic: Not everyone 'takes-the-best'. *Organizational Behavior and Human Decision Processes, 91*, 82–96.

Newell, B. R., Weston, N. J., Tunney, R. J., & Shanks, D. R. (2009). The effectiveness of feedback in multiple-cue probability learning. *The Quarterly Journal of Experimental Psychology, 62*, 890–908.

Newell, B. R., Wong, K. Y., Cheung, J. C., & Rakow, T. (2009) Think, blink or sleep on it? The impact of modes of thought on complex decision making. *Quarterly Journal of Experimental Psychology, 62*, 707–732.

Nieuwenstein, M., & van Rijn, H. (2012) The unconscious thought advantage: Further replication failures from a search for confirmatory evidence. *Judgment and Decision Making, 7*, 779–798.

Nisbett, R. E., & Wilson, T. D. (1977) Telling more than we can know: Verbal reports on mental processes. *Psychological Review, 84*, 231–259.

Norman, G., Eva, K., Brooks, L., & Hamstra, S. (2006). Expertise in medicine and surgery. In K. A. Ericsson, N. Charness, P. Feltovich, & R. Hoffman (Eds), *The Cambridge handbook of expertise and expert performance* (pp. 339–353). Cambridge, UK: Cambridge University Press.

Nosofsky, R. M. (1986). Attention, similarity, and the identification–categorization relationship. *Journal of Experimental Psychology: General, 115*, 39–57.

Nosofsky, R. M., & Johansen, M. K. (2000). Exemplar-based accounts of 'multiple-system' phenomena in perceptual categorization. *Psychonomic Bulletin & Review, 7*, 375–402.

Nosofsky, R. M., & Kruschke, J. K. (1992). Investigations of an exemplar-based connectionist model of category learning. In D. L. Medin (Ed.), *The psychology of learning and motivation* (Vol. 28, pp. 207–250). San Diego: Academic Press.

Nosofsky, R. M., Kruschke, J. K., & McKinley, S. C. (1992). Combining exemplar-based category representations and connectionist learning rules. *Journal of Experimental Psychology: Learning, Memory, and Cognition, 18*, 211–233.

Nunes, A., & Kirlik, A. (2005). An empirical study of calibration in air traffic control expert judgment. *Proceedings of the 49th annual meeting of the Human Factors and Ergonomics Society* (pp. 422–426). Santa Monica, CA: HFES.

Olds, J., & Milner, P. (1954). Positive reinforcement produced by electrical stimulation of the septal area and other regions of the rat brain. *Journal of Comparative and Physiological Psychology, 47*, 419–427.

Olsson, A. C., Enkvist, T., & Juslin, P. (2006). Go with the flow: How to master a nonlinear multiple-cue judgment task. *Journal of Experimental Psychology: Learning, Memory, and Cognition, 32*, 1371–1384.

Oppenheimer, D. M. (2003). Not so fast (and not so frugal!): Rethinking the recognition heuristic. *Cognition, 90*, B1–B9.

Orasanu, J., & Connolly, T. (1993). The reinvention of decision making. In G. A. Klein, J. Orasanu, R. Calderwood, & C. E. Zsambok (Eds), *Decision making in action: Models and methods* (pp. 3–20). Norwood, CT: Ablex.

Ortmann, A., Gigerenzer, G., Borges, B., & Goldstein, D. (2008). The recognition heuristic: A fast and frugal way to investment choice? In C. R. Plott & V. L. Smith (Eds), *Handbooks of experimental economics results, Vol. 1* (pp. 993–1003). Amsterdam: North Holland/Elsevier Press.

Osman, M. (2004). An evaluation of dual-process theories of reasoning. *Psychonomic Bulletin & Review, 11*, 988–1010.

Osman, M. (2010). Controlling uncertainty: A review of human behavior in complex dynamic environments. *Psychological Bulletin, 136*, 65–86.

Osman, M. (2013). A case study: Dual-process theories of higher cognition – Commentary on Evans & Stanovich (2013). *Perspectives on Psychological Science, 8,* 248–252.

Pachur, T., Hertwig, R., & Wolkewitz, R. (2014). The affect gap in risky choice: Affect-rich outcomes attenuate attention to probability information. *Decision, 1,* 64–78.

Parducci, A. (1965). Category judgment: A range–frequency model. *Psychological Review, 72,* 407–418.

Parducci, A. (1995). *Happiness, pleasure, and judgment: The context theory and its applications.* Mahwah, NJ: Erlbaum.

Pascal, B. (1670). *Pensees.* (A. J. Krailsheimer, Intro. & Trans. In Penguin Classics series. Harmondsworth: Penguin Books, 1995.)

Payne, J. W. (1976). Task complexity and contingent processing in decision making: An information search and protocol analysis. *Organizational Behavior and Human Performance, 16,* 366–387.

Payne, J. W., Bettman, J. R., & Johnson, E. J. (1993). *The adaptive decision maker.* New York: Cambridge University Press.

Payne, J., Bettman, J. R., & Luce, M. (1998). Behavioral decision research: An overview. In M. Birnbaum (Ed.), *Measurement, judgment and decision making* (pp. 303–359). San Diego, CA: Academic Press.

Payne, J. W., Samper, A., Bettman, J. R., & Luce, M. F. (2008). Boundary conditions on unconscious thought in complex decision making. *Psychological Science, 19,* 1118–1123.

Pearl, J. (1988). *Probabilistic reasoning in intelligent systems: Networks of plausible inference.* San Mateo, CA: Morgan Kaufman Publishers.

Pearl, J. (2000). *Causality: Models, reasoning, and inference.* Cambridge, UK: Cambridge University Press.

Pennington, N., & Hastie, R. (1986) Evidence evaluation in complex decision making. *Journal of Personality and Social Psychology, 51,* 242–258.

Pennington, N., & Hastie, R. (1992) Explaining the evidence: Tests of the Story Model for juror decision making. *Journal of Personality and Social Psychology, 62,* 189–206.

Peters, E., Västfjäll, D., Gärling T., & Slovic, P. (2006). Affect and decision making: A 'hot' topic. *Journal of Behavioral Decision Making, 19,* 79–85.

Peterson, C. R., Hammond, K. R., & Summers, D. A. (1965). Optimal responding in multiple-cue probability learning. *Journal of Experimental Psychology, 70,* 270–276.

Peterson, C. R., & Ulehla, Z. J. (1965). Sequential patterns and maximizing. *Journal of Experimental Psychology, 69,* 1–4.

Pidgeon, N. F., & Gregory, R. (2004). Judgment, decision making and public policy. In D. Koehler & N. Harvey (Eds), *Blackwell handbook of judgment and decision making* (pp. 604–623). Oxford: Blackwell.

Pieters, R., Baumgartner, H., & Bagozzi, R. P. (2006) Biased memory for prior decision making: Evidence from a longitudinal field study. *Organizational Behavior and Human Decision Processes, 99,* 34–48.

Pleskac, T. J. (2007). A signal detection analysis of the recognition heuristic. *Psychonomic Bulletin & Review, 14,* 379–391.

Plous, S. (1993). *The psychology of judgment and decision making.* New York: McGraw Hill.

Poldrack, R. A. (2006). Can cognitive processes be inferred from neuroimaging data? *Trends in Cognitive Sciences, 10,* 59–63.

Pruitt, D. G. (1961). Informational requirements in decision making. *American Journal of Psychology, 74,* 433–439.

Pruitt, J. S., Cannon-Bowers, J. A., & Salas, E. (1997). In search of naturalistic decisions. In R. Flin, E. Salas, M. Strub, & L. Martin (Eds), *Decision making under stress: Emerging themes and applications* (pp. 29–42). Aldershot: Ashgate.

Purchase, I., & Slovic, P. (1999). Quantitative risk assessment breeds fear. *Human and Ecological Risk Assessment, 5*, 445–453.

Rachlin, H. (2000). *The science of self-control*. Cambridge, MA: Harvard University Press.

Raiffa, H. (1968). *Decision analysis*. Reading, MA: Addison-Wesley.

Rakow, T., Demes, K. A., & Newell, B. R. (2008). Biased samples not mode of presentation: Re-examining the apparent underweighting of rare events in experience-based choice. *Organizational Behavior and Human Decision Processes, 106*, 168–179.

Rakow, T., & Miler, K. (2009). Doomed to repeat the successes of the past: History is best forgotten for repeated choices with non-stationary payoffs. *Memory and Cognition, 37*, 985–1000.

Rakow, T., & Newell, B. R. (2010). Degrees of uncertainty: An overview and framework for future research on experience-based choice. *Journal of Behavioral Decision Making, 23*, 1–14.

Rakow, T., Newell, B. R., Fayers, K., & Hersby, M. (2005). Evaluating three criteria for establishing cue-search hierarchies in inferential judgment. *Journal of Experimental Psychology: Learning, Memory, and Cognition, 31*, 1088–1104.

Rakow, T., Newell, B. R., & Zougkou, K. (2010). The role of working memory in information acquisition and decision making: Lessons from the binary prediction task. *Quarterly Journal of Experimental Psychology, 63*, 1335–1360.

Ramsey, F. P. (1931). *The foundations of mathematics and other logical essays*. London: Routledge and Kegan Paul.

Read, D., & Loewenstein, G., (1995). Diversification bias: Explaining the discrepancy between combined and separate choices. *Journal of Experimental Psychology: Applied, 1*, 34–49.

Read, D., & van Leeuwen, B. (1998). Predicting hunger: The effects of appetite and delay on choice. *Organizational Behavior and Human Decision Processes, 76*, 189–205.

Reber, P. J., Knowlton, B. J., & Squire, L. R. (1996). Dissociable properties of memory systems: Differences in the flexibility of declarative and nondeclarative knowledge. *Behavioral Neuroscience, 110*, 861–871.

Redelmeier, D. A., Katz, J., & Kahneman, D. (2003). Memories of colonoscopy: A randomized trial. *Pain, 104*, 187–194.

Redelmeier, D., Koehler, D., Liberman, V., & Tversky, A. (1995). Probability judgment in medicine: Discounting unspecified possibilities. *Medical Decision Making, 15*, 227–230.

Redelmeier, D. A., & Shafir, E. (1995). Medical decision making in situations that offer multiple alternatives. *Journal of the American Medical Association, 273*, 302–305.

Reilly, B. A., & Doherty, M. E. (1989). A note on the assessment of self-insight in judgment research. *Organizational Behavior and Human Decision Processes, 44*, 123–131.

Reilly, B. A., & Doherty, M. E. (1992). The assessment of self-insight in judgment policies. *Organizational Behavior and Human Decision Processes, 53*, 285–309.

Reiskamp, J., & Hoffrage, U. (1999). When do people use simple heuristics and how can we tell? In G. Gigerenzer, P. M. Todd, & The ABC Research Group (Eds), *Simple heuristics that make us smart* (pp. 141–167). Oxford: Oxford University Press.

Reiskamp, J., & Otto, P. (2006). SSL: A theory of how people learn to select strategies. *Journal of Experimental Psychology: General, 135*, 207–236.

Rescorla, R. A., & Wagner, A. R. (1972). A theory of Pavlovian conditioning: Variations in the effectiveness of reinforcement and nonreinforcement. In A. H. Black & W. F. Prokasy (Eds), *Classical conditioning II: Current theory and research* (pp. 64–99). New York: Appleton-Century-Crofts.

Rettinger, D. A., & Hastie, R. (2001). Content effects on decision making. *Organizational Behavior and Human Decision Processes, 85,* 336–359.

Rettinger, D. A., & Hastie, R. (2003). Comprehension and decision making. In S. L. Schneider & J. Shanteau (Eds), *Emerging perspectives on judgment and decision research* (pp. 165–200). Cambridge, UK: Cambridge University Press.

Rey, A., Goldstein, R. M., & Perruchet, P. (2009). Does unconscious thought improve complex decision making? *Psychological Research, 73,* 372–379.

Richter, T., & Späth, P. (2006). Recognition is used as one cue among others in judgment and decision making. *Journal of Experimental Psychology: Learning, Memory, and Cognition, 32,* 150–162.

Rogers, T., & McClelland. J. (2004). *Semantic cognition: A parallel distributed processing approach.* Cambridge, MA: MIT Press.

Rolison, J. J., Evans, J. St B. T., Walsh, C. R., & Dennis, I. (2011). The role of working memory capacity in multiple-cue probability learning. *Quarterly Journal of Experimental Psychology, 64,* 1494–1514.

Ross, M. (1989). Relation of implicit theories to the construction of personal histories. *Psychological Review, 96,* 341–357.

Ross, M., & Buehler, R. (2001). Identity through time: Constructing personal pasts and futures. In A. Tesser & N. Schwarz (Eds), *Blackwell handbook in social psychology, Vol 1: Intra-individual processes* (pp. 518–544). Oxford: Blackwell.

Rottenstreich, Y., & Hsee, C. K. (2001). Money, kisses, and electric shocks: On the affective psychology of risk. *Psychological Science, 12,* 185–190.

Rottenstreich, Y., & Tversky, A. (1997). Unpacking, repacking, and anchoring: Advances in support theory. *Psychological Review, 104,* 406–415.

Rottman, B. M., & Hastie, R. (2014). Reasoning about causal relationships: Inferences on causal networks. *Psychological Bulletin, 140,* 109–139.

Rumelhart, D. E., & McClelland, J. L. (1986). *Parallel distributed processing: Explorations in the microstructure of cognition. Vol. 1: Foundations.* Cambridge, MA: MIT Press.

Samuelson, W., & Zeckhauser, R. J. (1988). Status quo bias in decision making. *Journal of Risk and Uncertainty, 1,* 7–59.

Sanderson, P. M. (1989). Verbalizable knowledge and skilled task performance: Association, dissociation, and mental models. *Journal of Experimental Psychology: Learning, Memory, and Cognition, 15,* 729–747.

Savage, L. J. (1951). The theory of statistical decision. *Journal of the American Statistical Association, 46,* 55–67.

Savage, L. J. (1954). *The foundations of statistics.* New York: Wiley.

Sawyer, J. (1966). Measurement and prediction: Clinical and statistical. *Psychological Bulletin, 66,* 178–200.

Scheibehenne, B., Greifeneder, R., & Todd, P. M. (2010). Can there ever be too many options? A meta-analytic review of choice overload. *Journal of Consumer Research, 37,* 409–425.

Scheibehenne, B., Rieskamp, J., & Wagenmakers, E. J. (2013). Testing adaptive toolbox models: A Bayesian hierarchical approach. *Psychological Review, 120,* 39–64.

Schmitt, N., & Dudycha A. (1975). A reevaluation of the effect of cue redundancy in multiple-cue probability learning. *Journal of Experimental Psychology: Human Learning and Memory, 1,* 307–315.

Scholten, M., & Read, D. (2010). The psychology of intertemporal tradeoffs. *Psychological Review, 117*, 925–944.

Schultz, W., & Dickinson, A. (2000). Neuronal coding of prediction errors. *Annual Review of Neuroscience, 23*, 473–500.

Schwartz, B. (2000). Self-determination: The tyranny of freedom. *American Psychologist, 55*, 79.

Schwarz, N., & Vaughn, L. A. (2002). The availability heuristic revisited: Ease of recall and content of recall as distinct sources of information. In T. Gilovich, D. Griffin, & D. Kahneman (Eds), *Heuristics and biases* (pp. 103–119). Cambridge, UK: Cambridge University Press.

Schweickart, O., & Brown, N. R. (2014). Magnitude comparison extended: How lack of knowledge informs comparative judgments under uncertainty. *Journal of Experimental Psychology: General, 143*, 273–294.

Sedikides, C., Ariely, D., & Olsen, N. (1999). Contextual and procedural determinants of partner selection: Of asymmetric dominance and prominence. *Social Cognition, 17*, 118–139.

Sedlmeier, P. (1999). *Improving statistical reasoning: Theoretical models and practical implications.* Mahwah, NJ: Lawrence Erlbaum Associates.

Sedlmeier, P., & Betsch, T. (Eds) (2002). *Etc.: Frequency processing and cognition.* Oxford: Oxford University Press.

Shafir, S., Reich, T., Tsur, E., Erev, I., & Lotem, A. (2008). Perceptual accuracy and conflicting effects of certainty on risk-taking behaviour. *Nature, 453*, 917–920.

Shanks, D. R. (1990). Connectionism and the learning of probabilistic concepts. *Quarterly Journal of Experimental Psychology, 42A*, 209–237.

Shanks, D. R. (1991). A connectionist account of base-rate biases in categorization. *Connection Science, 3*, 143–162.

Shanks, D. R. (1992). Connectionist accounts of the inverse base-rate effect in categorization. *Connection Science, 4*, 3–18.

Shanks, D. R., & St John, M. F. (1994) Characteristics of dissociable human learning systems. *Behavioral and Brain Sciences, 17*, 367–447.

Shanks, D. R., Tunney, R. J., & McCarthy, J. D. (2002). A re-examination of probability matching and rational choice. *Journal of Behavioral Decision Making, 15*, 233–250.

Shanteau, J. (1992). Competence in experts: The role of task characteristics. *Organizational Behavior and Human Decision Processes, 53*, 252–266.

Sides, A., Osherson, D., Bonini, N., & Viale, R. (2002). On the reality of the conjunction fallacy. *Memory & Cognition, 30*, 191–198.

Simmons, J. P., LeBoeuf, R. A., & Nelson, L. D. (2010). The effect of accuracy motivation on anchoring and adjustment: Do people adjust from provided anchors? *Journal of Personality and Social Psychology, 99*, 917–932.

Simon, D., & Holyoak, K. J. (2002). Structural dynamics of cognition: From consistency theories to constraint satisfaction. *Personality and Social Psychology Review, 6*, 283–294.

Simon, D., Snow, C., & Read, S. J. (2004). The redux of cognitive consistency theories: Evidence judgments by constraint satisfaction. *Journal of Personality and Social Psychology, 86*, 814–837.

Simon, H. A. (1955). A behavioral model of rational choice. *Quarterly Journal of Economics, 69*, 99–118.

Simon, H. A. (1956). Rational choice and the structure of environments. *Psychological Review, 63*, 129–138.

Simon, H. A. (1990). Invariants of human behavior. *Annual Review of Psychology, 41,* 1–19.

Simon, H. A. (1992). What is an explanation of behavior? *Psychological Science, 3,* 150–161.

Simonson, I. (1990). The effect of purchase quantity and timing on variety seeking behavior. *Journal of Marketing Research, 27,* 150–162.

Skolbekken, J. A. (1998). Communicating the risk reduction achieved by cholesterol reducing drugs. *British Medical Journal, 316,* 1956–1958.

Sloman, S. A. (1996). The empirical case for two systems of reasoning. *Psychological Bulletin, 119,* 3–22.

Sloman, S. A. (2005). *Causal models.* New York: Oxford University Press.

Sloman, S. A., & Lagnado, D. A. (2004). Causal invariance in reasoning and learning. In B. Ross (Ed.), *The psychology of learning and motivation* (Vol. 44, pp. 287–325). San Diego: Elsevier Science.

Sloman, S. A., & Lagnado, D. A. (2005). Do we 'do'? *Cognitive Science, 29,* 5–39.

Sloman, S. A., & Lagnado, D. A. (2015). Causality in thought. *Annual Review of Psychology, 66,* 223–247.

Sloman, S. A., & Over, D. E. (2003). Probability judgment: From the inside and out. In D. E. Over (Ed.), *Evolution and the psychology of thinking: The debate* (pp. 145–169). Hove: Psychology Press.

Sloman, S. A., Over, D., Slovak, L., & Stibel, J. M. (2003). Frequency illusions and other fallacies. *Organizational Behavior and Human Decision Processes, 91,* 296–309.

Sloman, S. A., Rottenstreich, Y., Wisniewski, E., Hadjichristidis, C., & Fox, C. R. (2004). Typical versus atypical unpacking and superadditive probability judgment. *Journal of Experimental Psychology: Learning, Memory, and Cognition, 30,* 573–582.

Slovic, P. (1974). Hypothesis testing in the learning of positive and negative linear functions. *Organizational Behavior and Human Performance, 11,* 368–376.

Slovic, P. (2010). *The feeling of risk: New perspectives on risk perception.* London: Earthscan.

Slovic, P., Fischhoff, B., & Lichtenstein, S. (1980). Facts and fears: Understanding perceived risk. In R. Schwing & W. A. Albers, Jr. (Eds), *Societal risk assessment: How safe is safe enough?* (pp. 181–214). New York: Plenum Press.

Slovic, P., & Lichtenstein, S. (1971). Comparison of Bayesian and regression approaches to the study of information processing in judgment. *Organizational Behavior and Human Performance, 6,* 649–744.

Slovic, P., Monahan, J., & MacGregor, D. M. (2000). Violence risk assessment and risk communication: The effects of using actual cases, providing instructions, and employing probability vs. frequency formats. *Law and Human Behavior, 24,* 271–296.

Slovic, P., & Tversky, A. (1974). Who accepts Savage's axiom? *Behavioral Science, 19,* 368–373.

Smith, E. R., & Miller, F. D. (1978). Limits on perception of cognitive processes: A reply to Nisbett and Wilson. *Psychological Review, 85,* 355–362.

Sniezek, J. (1986). The role of variable labels in cue probability learning tasks. *Organizational Behavior and Human Decision Processes, 38,* 141–161.

Sniezek, J. A. (1989). An examination of group process in judgmental forecasting. *International Journal of Forecasting, 5,* 171–178.

Sniezek, J. A., & Henry, R. A. (1989). Accuracy and confidence in group judgment. *Organizational Behavior and Human Decision Processes, 43,* 1–28.

Sniezek, J. A., & Henry, R. A. (1990). Revision, weighting, and commitment in consensus group judgment. *Organizational Behavior and Human Decision Processes, 45,* 66–84.

Soll, J. B., & Klayman, J. (2004). Overconfidence in interval estimates. *Journal of Experimental Psychology: Learning, Memory, and Cognition, 30,* 299–314.

Söllner, A., Bröder, A., Glöckner, A., & Betsch, T. (2014). Single-process versus multiple-strategy models of decision making: Evidence from an information intrusion paradigm. *Acta Psychologica, 146,* 84–96.

Speekenbrink, M., Channon, S., & Shanks, D. R. (2008). Learning strategies in amnesia. *Neuroscience and Biobehavioral Reviews, 32,* 292–310.

Speekenbrink, M., & Shanks, D. R. (2010). Learning in a changing environment. *Journal of Experimental Psychology: General, 139,* 266–298.

Stanovich, K. E., & West, R. F. (2000). Individual differences in reasoning: Implications for the rationality debate. *Behavioral and Brain Sciences, 23,* 645–726.

Starmer, C. (2000). Developments in non-expected utility theory: The hunt for a descriptive theory of choice under risk. *Journal of Economic Literature, 38,* 332–382.

Starmer, C., & Sugden, R. (1993). Testing for juxtaposition and event-splitting effects. *Journal of Risk and Uncertainty, 6,* 235–254.

Starmer, C., & Sugden, R. (1998). Testing alternative explanations of cyclical choices. *Economica, 65,* 347–361.

Steiger, J. H., & Gettys, C. F. (1972). Best-guess errors in multistage inference. *Journal of Experimental Psychology, 92,* 1–7.

Stewart, N. (2009). Decision by sampling: The role of the decision environment in risky choice. *Quarterly Journal of Experimental Psychology, 62,* 1041–1062.

Stewart, N., Chater, N., & Brown, G. D. A. (2006). Decision by sampling. *Cognitive Psychology, 53,* 1–26.

Stewart, N., Reimers, S., & Harris, A. J. L. (in press). On the origin of utility, weighting, and discounting functions: How they get their shapes and how to change their shapes. *Management Science.*

Steyvers, M., Tenenbaum, J., Wagenmakers, E. J., & Blum, B. (2003). Inferring causal networks from observations and interventions. *Cognitive Science, 27,* 453–489.

Stigler, G. J. (1961). The economics of information. *The Journal of Political Economy, 69,* 213–225.

Stone, E. R., Sieck, W. R., Bull, B. E., Yates, J. F., Parks, S. C., & Rush, C. J. (2003). Foreground:background salience: Explaining the effect of graphical displays on risk avoidance. *Organizational Behavior and Human Decision Processes, 90,* 19–36.

Stone, E. R., Yates, J. F., & Parker, A. M. (1997). Effects of numerical and graphical displays on professed risk taking behaviour. *Journal of Experimental Psychology: Applied, 3,* 243–256.

Stone, G. O. (1986). An analysis of the delta rule and the learning of statistical associations. In D. E. Rumelhart, J. L. McClelland, & The PDP Research Group (Eds), *Parallel distributed processing: Explorations in the microstructure of cognition. Vol. 1: Foundations* (pp. 444–459). Cambridge, MA: MIT Press.

Strack, F., & Mussweiler, T. (1997). Explaining the enigmatic anchoring effect: Mechanisms of selective accessibility. *Journal of Personality and Social Psychology, 73,* 437–446.

Surber, C. F. (1985) Measuring the importance of information in judgment: Individual differences in weighting ability and effort. *Organizational Behavior and Human Decision Processes, 35,* 156–178.

Surowiecki, J. (2005). *The wisdom of crowds: Why the many are smarter than the few.* London: Abacus.

Taroni, F., Aitken, C., Garbolino, P., & Biedermann, A. (2006). *Bayesian networks and probabilistic inference in forensic science.* Chichester: Wiley.

Tenenbaum, J. B., Kemp, C., Griffiths, T. L., & Goodman, N. D. (2011). How to grow a mind: Statistics, structure, and abstraction. *Science, 331*, 1279–1285.

Tentori, K., Crupi, V., Bonini, N., & Osherson, D. (2007). Comparison of confirmation measures. *Cognition, 103*, 107–119.

Tentori, K., Crupi, V., & Russo, S. (2013). On the determinants of the conjunction fallacy: Probability *vs.* inductive confirmation. *Journal of Experimental Psychology: General, 142*, 235–255.

Tetlock, P. E., Mellers, B. A., Rohrbaugh, N., & Chen, E. (2014). Forecasting tournaments: Tools for increasing transparency and improving the quality of debate. *Current Directions in Psychological Science, 23*, 290–295.

Thagard, P. (2002). *Coherence in thought and action.* Cambridge, MA: MIT Press.

Thaler, R. (1980). Towards a positive theory of consumer choice. *Journal of Economic Behavior and Organization, 1*, 39–60.

Thaler, R., & Benartzi, S. (2004). Save more tomorrow: Using behavioral economics to increase employee saving. *Journal of Political Economy, 112*, 164–187.

Thaler, R. H., & Sunstein, C. R. (2008). *Nudge: Improving decisions about health, wealth, and happiness.* New Haven, CT: Yale University Press.

The Economist. (February 7, 2014). The market for paternalism: Nudge unit leaves kludge unit. http://www.economist.com/blogs/freeexchange/2014/02/market-paternalism.

Thompson, V. A. (2013). Why it matters: The implications of autonomous processes for dual-process theories – Commentary on Evans & Stanovich (2013). *Perspectives on Psychological Science, 8*, 253–256.

Thompson, V. A. (2014) What intuitions are . . . and are not. *The Psychology of Learning & Motivation, 60*, 35–75.

Thompson, W. C. (2013). Forensic DNA evidence: The myth of infallibility. In S. Krimsky & J. Gruber (Eds), *Genetic explanations: Sense and nonsense* (pp. 227–255). Cambridge, MA: Harvard University Press.

Thompson, W. C., & Schumann, E. L. (1987). Interpretation of statistical evidence in criminal trials: The prosecutor's fallacy and the defense attorney's fallacy. *Law and Human Behavior, 11*, 167–187.

Thompson, W. C., Taroni F., & Aitken C. G. G. (2003). How the probability of a false positive affects the value of DNA evidence. *Journal of Forensic Science, 48*, 47–54.

Todd, P. M., & Hammond, K. R. (1965). Differential effects of feedback in two multiple-cue probability learning tasks. *Behavioral Science, 10*, 429–435.

Todd, P. M., Hills, T. T., & Robbins, T. W. (Eds) (2012). *Cognitive search: Evolution, algorithms, and the brain.* Cambridge, MA: MIT Press.

Toplak, M. E., West, R. F., & Stanovich, K. E. (2011). The cognitive reflection test as a predictor of performance on heuristics-and-biases tasks. *Memory & Cognition, 39*, 1275–1289.

Tucker, L. R (1964). A suggested alternative formulation in the developments by Hursch, Hammond, and Hursch, and by Hammond, Hursch, and Todd. *Psychological Review, 71*, 528–530.

Turner, M., & Pratkanis, A. (1998). Twenty-five years of groupthink theory and research: Lessons from the evaluation of a theory. *Organizational Behavior and Human Decision Processes, 73*, 105–115.

Tversky, A. (1972). Elimination by aspects: A theory of choice. *Psychological Review, 79*, 281–299.

Tversky, A., & Edwards, W. (1966). Information versus reward in binary choices. *Journal of Experimental Psychology, 71*, 680–683.

Tversky, A., & Fox C. R. (1995). Weighing risk and uncertainty. *Psychological Review*, *102*, 269–283.

Tversky, A., & Kahneman, D. (1973). Availability: A heuristic for judging frequency and probability. *Cognitive Psychology*, *5*, 207–232.

Tversky, A., & Kahneman, D. (1974). Judgment under uncertainty: Heuristics and biases. *Science*, *185*, 1124–1131.

Tversky, A., & Kahneman, D. (1981). The framing of decisions and the psychology of choice. *Science*, *211*, 453–458.

Tversky, A., & Kahneman, D. (1983). Extensional versus intuitive reasoning: The conjunction fallacy in probability judgment. *Psychological Review*, *90*, 293–315.

Tversky, A., & Kahneman, D. (1992). Advances in prospect theory: Cumulative representation of uncertainty. *Journal of Risk and Uncertainty*, *5*, 297–323.

Tversky, A., & Koehler, D. J. (1994). Support theory: A nonextensional representation of subjective probability. *Psychological Review*, *101*, 547–567.

Tversky, A., Sattath, S., & Slovic, P. (1988). Contingent weighting in judgment and choice. *Psychological Review*, *95*, 371–384.

Ubel, P. A. (2002). Is information always a good thing? Helping patients make 'good' decisions. *Medical Care*, *40*, 39–44.

Ungemach, C., Chater, N., & Stewart, N. (2009). Are probabilities overweighted or underweighted when rare outcomes are experienced (rarely)? *Psychological Science*, *20*, 473–479.

Usher, M., & McClelland, J. L. (2001). On the time course of perceptual choice: The leaky competing accumulator model. *Psychological Review*, *108*, 550–592.

Usher, M., Russo, Z., Weyers, M., Brauner, R., & Zakay, D. (2011). The impact of the mode of thought in complex decisions: Intuitive decisions are better. *Frontiers in Psychology*, *2*, 1–13.

van Ravenzwaaij, D., Moore, C. P., Lee, M. D., & Newell, B. R. (2014). A hierarchical Bayesian modeling approach to searching and stopping in multi-attribute judgment. *Cognitive Science*, *38*, 1384–1405.

Varey, C., & Kahneman, D. (1992). Experiences extended across time: Evaluation of moments and episodes. *Journal of Behavioral Decision Making*, *5*, 169–185.

Vartanian, O., & Mandel, D. R. (Eds) (2011). *Neuroscience of decision making*. New York: Psychology Press.

Villejoubert, G., & Mandel, D. R. (2002). The inverse fallacy: An account of deviations from Bayes's Theorem and the additivity principle. *Memory & Cognition*, *30*, 171–178.

Vlaev, I., Chater, N., Stewart, N., & Brown, G. D. A. (2011) Does the brain calculate value? *Trends in Cognitive Science*, *15*, 546–554.

von Neumann, J., & Morgenstern, O. (1947) *Theory of games and economic behavior* (2nd edn). Princeton: Princeton University Press.

von Winterfeldt, D., & Edwards, W. (1986) *Decision analysis and behavioral research*. Cambridge, UK: Cambridge University Press.

Vulkan, N. (2000). An economist's perspective on probability matching. *Journal of Economic Surveys*, *14*, 101–118.

Waldmann, M. R., & Hagmayer, Y. (2005). Seeing versus doing: Two modes of accessing causal knowledge. *Journal of Experimental Psychology: Learning, Memory, and Cognition*, *31*, 216–227.

Ward, A., & Mann, T. (2000). Don't mind if I do: Disinhibited eating under cognitive load. *Journal of Personality and Social Psychology*, *78*, 753–763.

Wason, P. C. (1960). On the failure to eliminate hypotheses in a conceptual task. *Quarterly Journal of Experimental Psychology*, *12*, 129–140.

Watkinson, P., Wood, A. M., Lloyd, D., & Brown, G. D. A. (2013). Pain ratings reflect cognitive context: A range frequency model of pain. *Pain, 154,* 743–749.

Weber, E. U., Blais, A.-R., & Betz, N. (2002). A domain-specific risk-attitude scale: Measuring risk perceptions and risk behaviors. *Journal of Behavioral Decision Making, 15,* 263–290.

Weber, E. U., Johnson, E. J., Milch, K. F., Chang, H., Brodscholl, J. C., & Goldstein, D. G. (2007). Asymmetric discounting in intertemporal choice: A query-theory account. *Psychological Science, 18,* 516–523.

Wedell, D. H., & Böckenholt, U. (1990). Moderation of preference reversals in the long run. *Journal of Experimental Psychology: Human Perception and Performance, 16,* 429–438.

Weiss, D. J., & Shanteau, J. (2003). Empirical assessment of expertise. *Human Factors, 45,* 104–116.

Weiss, J. W., & Weiss, D. J. (Eds) (2009). *A science of decision making: The legacy of Ward Edwards.* Oxford: Oxford University Press.

Werner, P. D., Rose, T. L., & Yesavage, J. A. (1983). Reliability, accuracy, and decision-making strategy in clinical predictions of imminent dangerousness. *Journal of Consulting and Clinical Psychology, 51,* 815–825.

White, C. M., & Koehler, D. J. (2007). Choice strategies in multiple-cue probability learning. *Journal of Experimental Psychology: Learning, Memory, and Cognition, 33,* 757–768.

Wicklund, R. A., & Brehm, J. W. (1976). *Perspective on cognitive dissonance.* Hillsdale, NJ: Erlbaum.

Widrow, B., & Hoff, M. E. (1960). Adaptive switching circuits. *1960 IRE WESCON Convention Record, Pt. 4,* 96–104.

Wilson, T. D. (2002). *Strangers to ourselves: Discovering the adaptive unconscious.* Cambridge, MA: Belknap Press.

Wilson, T. D., & Gilbert, D. T. (2013). The impact bias is alive and well. *Journal of Personality and Social Psychology, 105,* 740–748.

Wilson, T. D., & Schooler, J. W. (1991) Thinking too much: Introspection can reduce the quality of preferences and decisions. *Journal of Personality and Social Psychology, 60,* 181–192.

Wilson, T. D., Wheatley, T. P., Meyers, J. M., Gilbert, D. T., & Axsom, D. (2000). Focalism: A source of durability bias in affective forecasting. *Journal of Personality and Social Psychology, 78,* 821–836.

Wirtz, D., Kruger, J., Scollon, C. N., & Diener, E. (2003). What to do on spring break? The role of predicted, on-line, and remembered experience in future choice. *Psychological Science, 14,* 520–524.

Wolford, G., Newman, S. E., Miller, M. B., & Wig, G. S. (2004). Searching for patterns in random sequences. *Canadian Journal of Experimental Psychology, 58,* 221–228.

Wu, G., & Gonzalez, R. (1996). Curvature of the probability weighting function. *Management Science, 42,* 1676–1690.

Yamagishi, K. (1997). When a 12.86% mortality is more dangerous than 24.14%: Implications for risk communication. *Applied Cognitive Psychology, 11,* 495–506.

Yates, J. F. (1990). *Judgment and decision making.* Englewood Cliffs, NJ: Prentice-Hall.

Yates, J. F., Veinott, E. S., & Patalano, A. L. (2003). Hard decisions, bad decisions: On decision quality and decision aiding. In S. L. Schneider & J. Shanteau (Eds), *Emerging perspectives on judgment and decision research* (pp. 13–63). New York: Cambridge University Press.

Yechiam, E., & Busemeyer, J. R. (2005). Comparison of basic assumptions embedded in learning models for experience-based decision making. *Psychonomic Bulletin & Review, 12,* 387–402.

Yechiam, E., & Busemeyer, J. R. (2006). The effect of foregone payoffs on underweighting small probability events. *Journal of Behavioral Decision Making*, *19*, 1–16.

Yechiam, E., Erev, I., & Barron, G. (2006). The effect of experience on using a safety device. *Safety Science*, *44*, 515–522.

Yechiam, E., Rakow, T., & Newell, B. R. (2015). Super-underweighting of rare events with repeated descriptive summaries. *Journal of Behavioural Decision Making*, *28*, 67–75.

Zajonc, R. (1980). Feeling and thinking: Preferences need no inferences. *American Psychologist*, *35*, 151–175.

Zauberman, G., Kim, B. K., Malkoc, S. A., & Bettman, J. R. (2009). Discounting time and time discounting: Subjective time perception and intertemporal preferences. *Journal of Marketing Research*, *46*, 543–556.

Zsambok, C. E. (1997). Naturalistic decision making: where are we now? In C. E. Zsambok & G. A. Klein (Eds). *Naturalistic decision making* (pp. 3–16). Mahwah, NJ: Erlbaum.

Index

Tables are indicated by *italics*. Figures are indicated by **bold**.